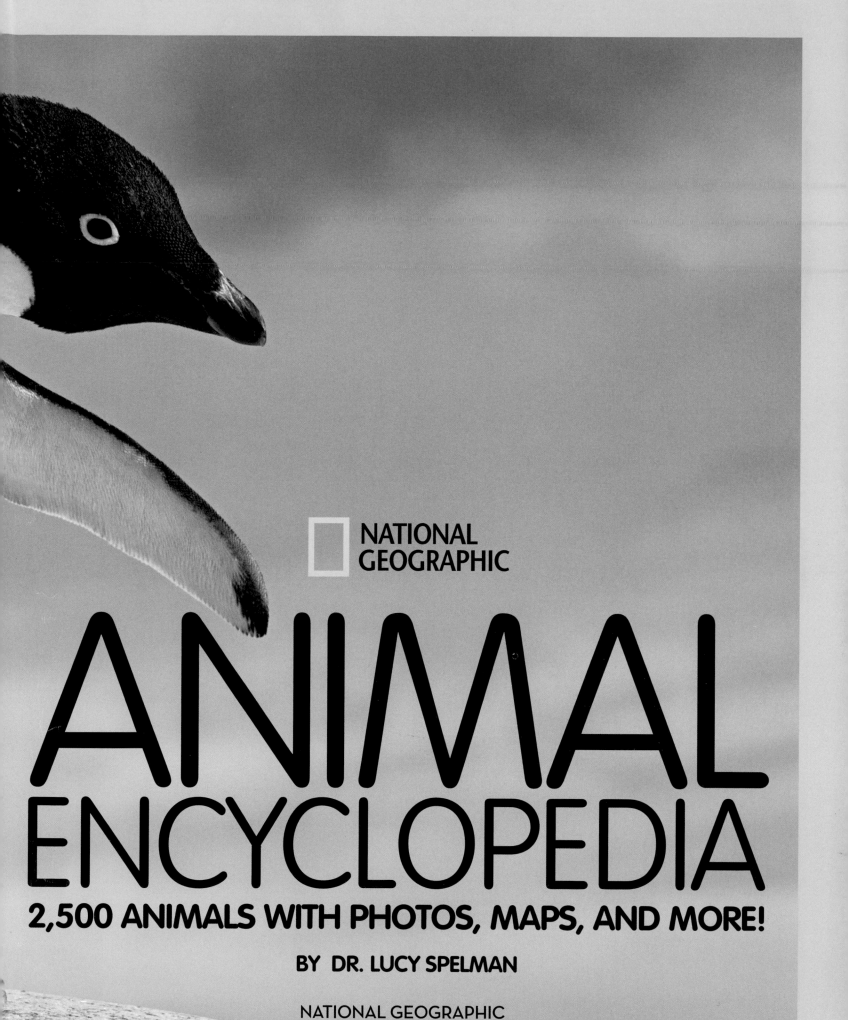

NATIONAL GEOGRAPHIC

ANIMAL ENCYCLOPEDIA

2,500 ANIMALS WITH PHOTOS, MAPS, AND MORE!

BY DR. LUCY SPELMAN

NATIONAL GEOGRAPHIC

WASHINGTON, D.C.

TARPON AND SILVERSIDES

RED-EYED TREE FROG

EASTERN FOX SQUIRREL

AFRICAN ELEPHANT

POLAR BEAR

WESTERN MEADOWLARK

LEOPARD

MEERKATS

SPINNER DOLPHINS

MANDRILL

BLACK-TAILED JACKRABBIT

SEA OTTER

GREEN SEA TURTLE

GREEN ANOLE

ARCTIC FOX

GIANT PANDA

AFRICAN LION

SOUTHERN STINGRAY

RIVER OTTER

AMERICAN BLACK BEAR

GALÁPAGOS SEA LION

MUSKOX

ORCA

ORANGE-EYED TREE FROG

COMMON CHAMELEON

MUGGER CROCODILE

EAST AFRICAN LAND SNAIL

AMERICAN BEAVER

GOLDEN EAGLE

RED ANT

HUNTSMAN SPIDER

GENTOO PENGUIN

RED STINK BUG

AMERICAN CROCODILE

ROSEATE SPOONBILLS

CONTENTS

BIRDS

MAMMALS

REPTILES

AMPHIBIANS

FISH

INVERTEBRATES

# HOW TO USE THIS BOOK

The *National Geographic Animal Encyclopedia* is divided into eight parts. The first chapter introduces you to the world of animals through features such as animal life cycles and babies, senses and communication, homes and habitats, adaptations and camouflage, endangered species, and animal conservation.

The second through seventh chapters present the major animal groups: Mammals, Birds, Reptiles, Amphibians, Fish, and Invertebrates. Each chapter begins with an opener followed by a gallery spread. Since it is impossible to include every animal on Earth in one volume, these galleries are designed to portray as much animal diversity as is possible on two pages. Following the gallery is the "What Is" spread, which introduces the groups of animals within each section. This spread is followed by grouping spreads, which introduce specific species along with key facts about them, including their common and scientific names, endangered status, habitat, range, diet, and a short text block about each species. In addition, illustrated diagrams convey information about animal life cycles, sonar, size comparisons, and much more.

Throughout these chapters you will find seventeen "From the Field" reports and six "From the Lens" images. The reports present accounts from National Geographic explorers, grantees, and photographers in the field. Each "From the Lens" provides a visual break, featuring a stunning National Geographic animal photograph. Concluding each chapter are animal records. These pages are full of animal superlatives from the tallest and biggest, to the smallest and smelliest animals.

The eighth section in this book is a listing of more than 1,000 additional animals. Like the gallery spreads, this list serves as a tool to give you a sense of the vast diversity and size of the animal kingdom. Here you will find common and scientific names and size, diet, range, and habitat information about animals in each of the six animal groups (mammals, birds, reptiles, amphibians, fish, and invertebrates).

HOW THE ANIMAL KINGDOM IS ORGANIZED

The kingdom Animalia includes one phylum, Chordata, for animals with a backbone (vertebrates) and eight for those without one (invertebrates). There are eight classes of vertebrates: mammals, birds, reptiles, amphibians, and four classes of fish. The eight invertebrate phyla are Arthropoda (insects, arachnids, centipedes and millipedes, and horseshoe crabs), Mollusca (squid, octopus, cuttlefish, and snails), Cnidaria (corals, jellyfish, and hydras), Annelida (earthworms, leeches, and polychaetes), Platyhelminthes (flukes and tapeworms), Nematoda (roundworms), Echinoderms (starfish, sea urchins, and sea cucumbers), and Porifera (sponges).

SIZE ABBREVIATIONS

cm: centimeters
in: inches
km: kilometers
m: meters
oz: ounces

ft: feet
kg: kilograms
lb: pounds
mm: millimeters

ENDANGERED STATUS BOX

Throughout this book you will notice solid-colored circles accompanying animal photographs as well as the list of animals in the back of the book. These colors represent different conservation statuses. Below is a key identifying each status, along with its definition. These statuses are based on information from the International Union for the Conservation of Nature (IUCN) Red List of Threatened Species 2012.

- **ALERT** Animal species at serious risk of dying out. Some may even be extinct in the wild, and exist only in places like zoos.
- **IN TROUBLE** Animal species likely to become endangered without conservation action.
- **STABLE** Animal species whose populations are decreasing, but slowly.
- **UNDER STUDY** Animal species that have experienced a decline in numbers and are being evaluated. They are at risk of falling into either the "In Trouble" or the "Alert" categories.
- **NOT LISTED** Animal species that have not yet been listed. This category includes most fish and invertebrates.
- **DOMESTICATED** Animal species domesticated for food, clothing, sport, and companionship. Their numbers are plentiful.

RANGE MAPS

You will find two kinds of range maps in this book. The range maps that appear with the "From the Field" reports illustrate the range of the featured species. The range maps that appear on the "Records" spreads illustrate ranges for all of the record-holding animals presented on those pages.

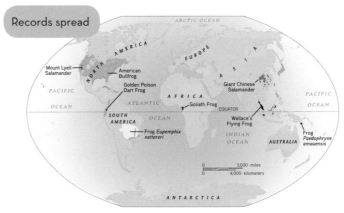
Records spread

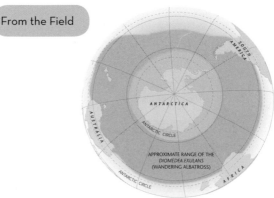
From the Field

Bold headings highlight the chapter names.

Color-coded tabs appear on every page to tell you which section you are in and help you navigate the book.

Opening text introduces you to each animal chapter and describes the general characteristics of the animals you will read about in the chapter.

Diagrams depict the unique physical features and anatomy of the animals in the chapter.

Colorful boxes provide fun animal facts.

Classification boxes explain the way in which animals in each section are grouped.

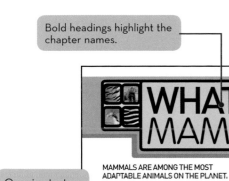

Bold headings highlight animal groups.

Color-coded tabs appear on every page to tell you which section you are in and help you navigate the book.

Opening text introduces you to the species on the page and provides an overview of the species on the page or spread.

Illustrated diagrams portray information such as animal life cycles and special features.

Habitat icons represent the type of environment each animal lives in. Descriptions are detailed on page 18.

Fact boxes provide common and scientific names and key facts for each featured species.

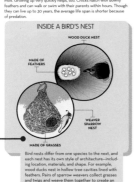

The animal kingdom is an amazing, diverse group of living organisms. It includes microscopic mites, gigantic whales, migrating butterflies, marching penguins, 100-year-old tortoises, regenerating worms, air-breathing fish, mouth-brooding frogs, and bamboo-eating bears.

To keep track of biodiversity, scientists use a classification system. Organisms with similar features, or traits, are grouped together. The largest group is a kingdom. The smallest is a species. In between are phylum, class, order, family, and genus. The phrase "kids prefer cheese over fried green spinach" is one way to remember how it all works. Examples of traits used to classify animals are body structure, life cycle, and social behavior.

So what does a fly have in common with a chimpanzee? How is a human like a gecko? Like all members of the kingdom Animalia—1.3 million species and counting—they share the following traits. They are multicellular, they must find their own food, they develop into adult forms, and they are capable of movement.

Genetic studies also are used to classify animals. Related species share a common ancestor and more of the same genes. They usually look alike, but not always. The genome is full of surprises.

NAMING OF SPECIES

Remembering the different subcategories can be difficult. To make things easier, scientists use only the last two—genus and species—when referring to a specific animal. For example, a common housecat's genus is *Felis* and its species is *catus*. So scientists refer to it as *Felis catus*. This is the cat's binomial nomenclature, or scientific name.

Why can't scientists just use a common name when referring to an animal? That can get complicated. Some animals have many common names. For example, a "panther" in one region may be called a "cougar" in another; this can cause people to believe that the same cat is two different animals. Because the scientific name is always the same, it eliminates confusion.

When coming up with a genus and species name for an animal, scientists have a few rules they must follow. The name must be Greek or Latin. Or it can be a "Latinized" version of a word such as a place or a person's name. Some scientists have a sense of humor when naming organisms. In 1993, arachnologist Norman I. Platnick named a spider *Calponia harrisonfordi* in honor of Harrison Ford, the actor who portrayed Han Solo in the *Star Wars* movies.

COLD-BLOODED VS. WARM-BLOODED

All organisms within the animal kingdom are either cold-blooded or warm-blooded. Warm-blooded animals, such as mammals and birds, have a body temperature that remains constant even when the temperature of their environment varies. In mammals, body temperature is controlled by the hypothalamus in the brain. If the body becomes too warm, the hypothalamus signals the sweat glands to cool it by releasing sweat. If body temperature begins to drop, the hypothalamus signals that the body should shiver to warm itself.

In birds, special air sacs that extend from the lungs help the body perform heating and cooling functions. In addition, birds have feathers to help trap heat, and animals have hair.

In cold-blooded animals, which include reptiles, amphibians, fish, insects, and arthropods, body temperature rises and falls with the temperature of their environment. To keep body temperature constant, these animals have developed a variety of behaviors. For example, a crocodile may bask in the sun to keep itself warm, and move to a shady area to cool off.

HOW ANIMALS ARE CLASSIFIED

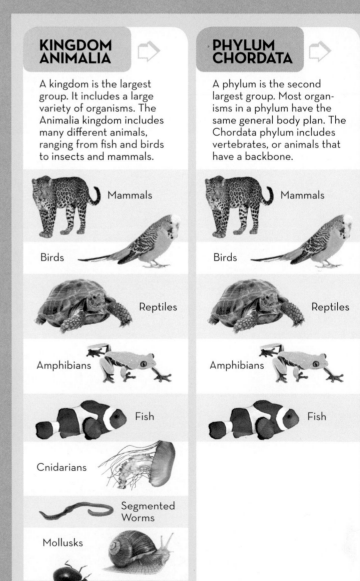

KINGDOM ANIMALIA

A kingdom is the largest group. It includes a large variety of organisms. The Animalia kingdom includes many different animals, ranging from fish and birds to insects and mammals.

- Mammals
- Birds
- Reptiles
- Amphibians
- Fish
- Cnidarians
- Segmented Worms
- Mollusks
- Arthropods

PHYLUM CHORDATA

A phylum is the second largest group. Most organisms in a phylum have the same general body plan. The Chordata phylum includes vertebrates, or animals that have a backbone.

- Mammals
- Birds
- Reptiles
- Amphibians
- Fish

VERTEBRATE OR INVERTEBRATE

All organisms in the animal kingdom are either vertebrates or invertebrates. But which is which?

YELLOW TANG FISH

MACAWS

RED-EYED TREE FROG

ARCTIC FOXES

SEA TURTLE

Vertebrates are animals with a backbone. They are grouped into a single phylum (Chordata) with five classes: fish, amphibians, reptiles, birds, and mammals.

RED AND SILVER DEWDROP SPIDER

BROWN GARDEN SNAIL

EARTHWORMS

Invertebrates are animals that do not have a backbone. Many invertebrates have an exoskeleton, a hard skeleton on the outside of the body, to protect the delicate organs inside. Invertebrates include earthworms (annelids), insects and spiders (arthropods), jellyfish (cnidarians), and snails (mollusks).

CLASS MAMMALIA ⇨

A class shares more traits than those in a phylum. Animals in the class Mammalia are warm-blooded mammals that have a backbone, fur, or hair, and can nurse their young with milk.

red panda

platypus

kangaroo

white-tailed deer

beaver

bat

tree shrew

leopard

human

ORDER PRIMATE ⇨

An order consists of organisms that share even more common traits than those of a class. Primate is a group of mammals that includes humans, apes, monkeys, and lemurs.

ring-tailed lemur

potto

black howler monkey

olive baboon

tarsier

white-handed gibbon

chimpanzee

FAMILY HOMINIDAE ⇨

A family is a smaller grouping of organisms. The Hominidae family includes the great apes as well as humans.

human

chimpanzee

bonobo

western lowland gorilla

eastern mountain gorilla

Sumatran orangutan

Bornean orangutan

GENUS PAN ⇨

A genus is a group of different organisms that are closely related but cannot produce offspring together. The genus *Pan* includes the chimpanzee and the bonobo.

chimpanzee

bonobo

SPECIES PAN TROGLODYTES

A species is the smallest and most closely related group of organisms. Members of a species can produce offspring with one another. *Pan troglodytes* is the chimpanzee species.

chimpanzee

Every animal starts out life as an egg produced by a female. Most eggs that develop into adult animals have been fertilized with sperm produced by a male. There are exceptions, though. Worker honeybees, for example, lay eggs that are never fertilized; they develop into male bees called drones. The fertilized eggs of vertebrate animals develop into embryos. In mammals—except for the platypus—these grow inside the female's body, developing organs and limbs over time until she gives birth to live young. This is also the case for some fish and reptiles. But for most, and for all birds and amphibians, their eggs develop inside eggs laid by the female.

After an animal is born, it must learn to survive in the wild. Some learn by imitating their parents, whereas others must fend for themselves. The animal grows until it reaches maturity. At this point, it is ready to mate—producing an offspring of its own and enabling another life cycle to begin.

LIVE BIRTH

SHORT-BEAKED SADDLEBACK DOLPHIN ○ ◠
DELPHINUS DELPHIS
Like most mammals, short-beaked saddleback dolphins give birth to live young. The female gestates, or carries her calf, for 10 to 12 months. At the end of that period, the calf is born underwater. The young dolphin feeds on its mother's milk for six months, at which point it can eat solid food, such as fish and mollusks.

EGG

MACARONI PENGUIN ○ ◠
EUDYPTES CHRYSOLOPHUS
Macaroni penguins lay eggs to reproduce. The female bird deposits two eggs inside a nest—usually a small depression in the ground lined with pebbles or grass. Then the female and her mate take turns keeping the clutch warm. One penguin spends 8 to 12 days incubating the eggs while the other goes in search of food. This continues until the eggs hatch (up to 37 days).

GROWING UP
WESTERN GORILLA ●
GORILLA BERINGEI

Western gorillas weigh only four pounds (2 kg) at birth and spend about four years sharing a nest with their mother. A lot happens during that time. When the apes are two months old, they begin to crawl. At six months, they learn to walk, but often hitch a ride on their mother's back to travel. The next three years are spent play-fighting and imitating older members of their troop.

Did you know? A group of ducklings is called a brood.

METAMORPHOSIS
MONARCH BUTTERFLY ● ● ●
DANAUS PLEXIPPUS

During its life cycle, the monarch butterfly undergoes a complete change, called a metamorphosis, in four stages. A butterfly begins life as an egg. After four days, a caterpillar, or larva, hatches. For two weeks, it feasts on its eggshell and milkweed plants. Then it becomes a pupa by forming a protective shell called a chrysalis. Two weeks later, a butterfly emerges.

CARING FOR YOUNG
MALLARD (DUCK) ● ● ●
ANAS PLATYRHYNCHOS

A mallard mother is very protective of her young. Shortly after her ducklings have hatched, she leads them to a water source, keeping a watchful eye along the way. If a predator, such as a red fox, is lurking nearby, the mother bird will pretend to be injured to distract the fox from her brood.

15

SENSES AND COMMUNICATION

All animals have five senses: sight, hearing, touch, taste, and smell. They use them to find food, shelter, and each other, as well as to navigate, communicate, avoid predators, and attract a mate.

Depending on their lifestyle and evolutionary history, some animals have more developed senses than others. Eagles, for instance, have excellent vision and, like other birds, humans, and some rain forest primates, they can see in color. Dogs and their relatives have an incredible sense of smell. Naked mole rats and other burrowing animals live mostly by feel, using their extra-sensitive whiskers and hairs to find their way in the dark. For aquatic animals like fish, dolphins, and whales, hearing is by far the most important sense. For one thing, sounds travel farther underwater than through air. For another, there is very little light in the deep ocean. Taste is used by all animals to test their food for chemicals, such as toxins that may be harmful.

Some species have a sixth—or even a seventh—sense. For example, sharks find their prey by picking up electrical signals, and snakes can detect heat.

The senses are part of the nervous system. Animals collect sensory information using different types of specialized cells, called sensory receptors. Examples are photoreceptors (light), mechanoreceptors (pressure), thermoreceptors (heat), and chemoreceptors (chemicals)—better known as tastebuds in humans!

SOUND
BELUGA WHALE ○○○
DELPHINAPTERUS LEUCAS
Beluga whales use clicks, whistles, and clangs to communicate with members of their pod. They also use sound—in the form of echolocation—to find food. While hunting, the whale emits sounds that travel underwater until they encounter an object. The sounds then bounce back to the whale, revealing the location of its target.

SIGHT ○○
WEDGE-TAILED EAGLE ●◐
AQUILA AUDAX
The wedge-tailed eagle can see twice as far as a human. Its eyes are packed with sensory cells called rods and cones that allow it to see with great clarity. In addition, eagle eyes can see five colors. (Humans can only see three.) This ability allows them to easily pick out prey that may be camouflaged.

TASTE
SUMATRAN ORANGUTAN
DERMOCHELYS ●○
CORIACEA
Like all mammals, orangutans have taste buds on their tongues. Most animals rely on these receptors to determine what they can—and cannot—eat. Typically, bitter, unripe fruits can be toxic, so most animals stay away from them. But orangutans eat them. They also eat soil rich in minerals that apparently help neutralize the toxins.

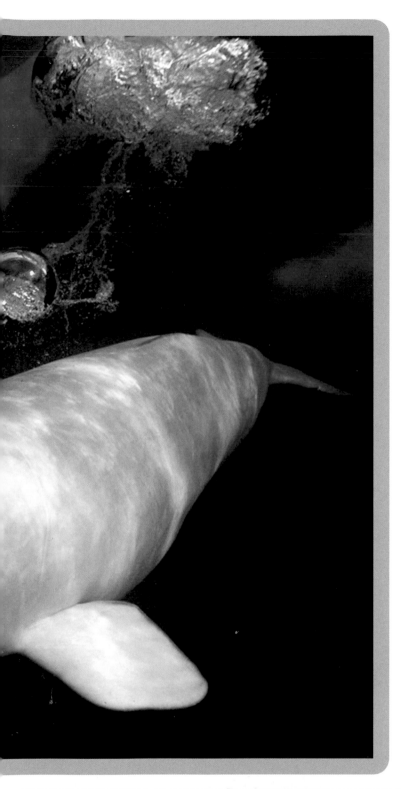

ELEPHANT
COMMUNICATION

Elephants use a variety of sounds to communicate. They trumpet at the sight of a predator to warn the herd. They rumble to greet each other. They also make long-distance contact calls. These travel by seismic, or ground, vibrations. They are so low in frequency that humans cannot hear them. But the elephants can, as long as they are listening. To listen for a contact call, elephants rest their trunks on the ground and hold one leg up. This position helps the sound wave travel through the elephant's feet, up its body, and into its ears. Elephants are not the only animals that use seismic communication. Others include spiders, scorpions, kangaroo rats, and golden moles.

SMELL
BLOODHOUND
CANIS LUPUS FAMILIARIS

All dogs have keen sniffing abilities, but the bloodhound's sense of smell is among the strongest. It has about 230 million olfactory receptors, or scent cells, inside its nose. That's 40 times as many as humans! The large number of receptors increases the dog's ability to pick up odors. In addition, bloodhounds can remember scents for several days.

TOUCH
CATFISH
(CHANNEL CATFISH)
ICTALURUS PUNCTATUS

Catfish are named for the whisker-like organs that extend from each side of their mouths. These organs—called barbels—help the fish feel for prey in the murky water at the bottom of a lake. Some species—like the channel catfish—have up to four pairs of barbels.

HOMES AND HABITATS

All animals and plants need a place to live. Most choose— or are born into— particular habitats. Habitats are places in nature that provide food, protection from predators and unfavorable weather, and a home in which to raise young.

Habitats are characterized most often by climate and location. They can range from warm, moist areas near the Equator— such as the Amazon rain forest—to cold polar areas such as the Arctic.

The animals and plants that live in a particular habitat have adaptations that allow them to survive there. For example, spider monkeys—which live in the trees of some tropical forests—have flexible tails that allow them to grasp and balance along branches. And a cactus that grows in the desert has spines that help collect and retain moisture.

Some animals build homes in their habitat. Beavers use wood and mud to construct lodges; some toads dig burrows. Other animals don't have to do such work. They find their homes in natural places such as caves and trees.

To the right, you'll find sets of icons that represent different habitats around the world, as well as descriptions for each one. These icons appear throughout the book. Refer to this page whenever you see a habitat icon as you read.

HABITATS

GRASSLAND/OPEN AREAS/ SHRUBLAND	Flat, open areas covered with wild grasses and few trees. Some grasslands—called tropical savannahs—are warm all year, while others—called temperate savannahs—experience hot summers and cold winters.	
DESERT/DRY/DRY AND ROCKY	A large area of land that receives less than ten inches (25 cm) of precipitation each year. Some deserts, like the Sahara, are hot all year, while others, like the Gobi, are cool.	
TROPICAL FOREST/ RAIN FOREST	Habitats near Earth's Equator that receive at least 160 inches (406 cm) of rainfall each year.	
TEMPERATE FOREST/ WOODLAND	Forests that experience four seasons, and are characterized by tall trees with broad leaves.	
CONIFEROUS FOREST/ WOODLAND	Forests with pine-producing trees, such as fir and pine, that experience long, cold winters and short, moist summers.	
MOUNTAINS/HIGHLANDS/ SLOPES/TEMPERATE AND TROPICAL	Masses of rock pushed upward. Climate in these rocky regions becomes cooler as the elevation increases.	
POLAR REGIONS/ARCTIC/ TUNDRA AND ANTARCTIC	Vast, treeless regions where temperatures can dip below 32°F (0°C) for ten months a year. These regions are characterized by permafrost, a layer of soil that is frozen all year.	
FRESHWATER/FLOWING/ RIVERS AND STREAMS/ LAKES/RIVERS AND WETLANDS	Bodies of water flowing continuously in one direction. These areas may vary in oxygen content, level of dissolved nutrients, and clarity.	
FRESHWATER/STILL/ WETLANDS/BOGS/ SWAMPS/PONDS/LAKES	Bodies of standing water that are home to many aquatic plants and have very low salt concentration.	
OCEANS/INSHORE AREAS AND OPEN SEA	Bodies of water that cover 75 percent of Earth's surface. The presence of sunlight in this habitat is great near the surface, but decreases with depth.	
COASTAL AREAS INCLUDES MANGROVE SWAMPS	Areas along the shoreline that are characterized by saltwater, and may be subject to strong winds and waves.	
CORAL REEFS	Rainbow-colored structures that line the ocean floor. Coral reefs are made of limestone that is deposited by animals called polyps.	
URBAN AREAS/CITIES/ INDOOR PARKS/GARDENS	Areas in which the food supply and environmental conditions are largely controlled or influenced by humans.	
OUTDOOR/FARMLAND/ RURAL AREAS	Land where agricultural products such as food and livestock are raised. These places have less human development and are more open than urban areas.	

HOMES

HIVE
A container in which a colony of honeybees lives and produces honey. Hives are often built by people to collect the bees' honey.

INSECT GALL
A swelling of a plant tissue caused by some insects, parasites, and mites. Gall-making animals may use the gall as shelter and a food source.

NEST
A structure made by some birds, insects, or small mammals to lay eggs and live in. Nests are often made of sticks, leaves, fur, and other found objects.

LODGE
A dome of sticks and mud built in a body of water. A lodge has underwater entrances that lead to a plant-lined living area above water level.

BURROW
A hole or tunnel dug in the ground by an animal that lives or hides in it.

HOLE
A cavity or hollow place in a solid object such as a tree. Some animals, such as woodpeckers, peck holes in trees, and then roost inside them.

DEN
A lair in which some female animals give birth to and care for their young.

SHELL
A hard bone covering that protects some animals' bodies. Some animals—such as turtles—grow their own shell, while others—like the hermit crab—find one and move into it.

WEB
A net of silky threads spun by some spiders to trap prey. Webs can vary in shape, ranging from spiral to tube-shaped.

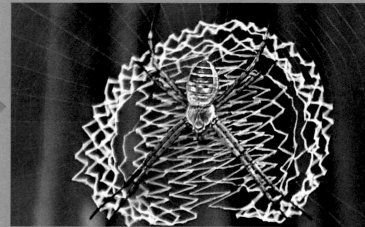

TERMITE MOUND
A tall mound built by termites using saliva and soil. A termite mound contains hundreds of air tunnels to help cool the structure when the weather is hot.

CAVE
A large natural hole in a hillside or cliff, or underground. Caves provide a cool, dark shelter for animals that have little or no vision—such as eyeless shrimp and some bats.

HOLLOW
A cavity or space within an object that is often the result of natural forces. Animals such as raccoons and some owls may use tree hollows for shelter.

TREE TRUNK
Many birds, insects, and other animals seek protection from predators and weather inside tree trunks. They may peck holes inside tree trunks, or move into existing tree hollows.

TREES
Trees provide a safe place for animals that want to avoid predators on the ground. Trees are often homes to animals whose bodies are adapted for climbing and balancing on branches.

AQUATIC PLANTS
Some plants—such as duckweed and water lilies—thrive in aquatic environments. These plants can provide shade and are a protective shelter for some frogs and fish.

MIGRATIONS

any animals move from one area to another on a regular basis, a behavior known as migration. Animals migrate in search of food, water, shelter, or a mate, usually in response to changing seasons. When and where they go depends on the species. The albatross, for example, flies around the world—every year. Elephants walk from one watering hole to the next. Wood frogs hop from dry land to shallow ponds and back again. What keeps them on track? Genetics play a role, as do environmental cues such as certain smells, changes in air or water temperature, water currents, the position of the sun and stars, and the Earth's geomagnetic field. In some cases, we do not yet understand how migrating animals find their way. But one thing is clear: They are programmed to move!

WOOD
FROG
RANA SYLVATICA
Wood frogs range in size from two to three inches (5 to 8 cm). They live in swamps, ravines, and wooded areas, where they feed on ground-dwelling creatures. These include insects, spiders, and earthworms. When it's time to breed, the frogs migrate about a half-mile (1 km) to seasonal wetlands, or vernal pools.

ARCTIC OCEAN

NORTH AMERICA

The wood frog range is shown here in dark blue.

PACIFIC

OCEAN

ATLANTIC

Migration routes shown are some of the longer examples for the particular species.

SOUTH
AMERICA

OCEA

0 ——————— 3,000 miles
0 ——————— 4,000 kilometers

AFRICAN
ELEPHANT
LOXODONTA AFRICANA
Elephants migrate in search of water, following the same routes every year. As each elephant travels, it consumes up to 300 pounds (136 kg) of roots, grasses, fruit, and bark daily. The large meal is necessary to sustain its large frame, which measures 16 to 26 feet (5 to 8 m) long.

ANTARCTI

ARCTIC
TERN
STERNA PARADISAEA
Arctic terns are only 13 to 15 inches (33 to 39 cm) long. But don't let their small size fool you. These sea birds are capable of great migrations. Each year, the birds fly 25,000 miles (44,000 km) from their summer breeding grounds in the Arctic to summer in Antarctica and back. Along the way, they may stop to feed on small fish and crustaceans.

RED
CRAB
GECARCOIDEA NATALIS
The red crab, which measures three to five inches (5 to 8 cm), is found only on Australia's Christmas Island. Most of the year, it lives on the rain forest floor, feeding on leaves, fruits, seedlings, and flowers. But during the rainy season, it migrates up to one mile (1.6 km) to the sea to breed. Millions of crabs take part in this migration, crossing roads and stopping traffic along the way.

EUROPE

A S I A

PACIFIC OCEAN

The African elephant range is shown here in gold.

AFRICA

EQUATOR

INDIAN OCEAN

The red crab range is shown here in the teal circle.

AUSTRALIA

LEATHERBACK
TURTLE
DERMOCHELYS CORIACEA
The leatherback is the world's largest turtle. It measures six to eight feet (2 m) long! During breeding season, these giant reptiles migrate to the same region where they hatched to lay their eggs. After the eggs hatch, the young turtles head to the sea, perhaps guided by geomagnetic forces, the frequency of the waves, or both. They survive on a diet of jellyfish and salps.

BLUE
SHARK
PRIONACE GLAUCA
These sharks migrate to find cooler water. They prefer water temperatures in the range of 45 to 61°F (7 to 16°C). Blue sharks grow 6 to 13 feet (2 to 4 m) and eat a diet of bony fish and squid.

ADAPTATIONS
FOR SURVIVAL

ife in the wild has many challenges. Animals must find enough food to survive, endure the climate of their environment, and protect themselves from predators. Fortunately, animals have adaptations —body parts or behaviors—that help them meet these challenges.

TEETH
Carnivores, like the jaguar, have sharp teeth to tear into meat. The teeth also are used as a weapon if the animal is attacked.

TOUGH SKIN, SCALES, SHELLS
A tough exterior can protect an animal from bites and cuts. The three-banded armadillo has a body shield of bony plates that it curls into when under attack.

CLAWS
Sharp claws can be used as weapons. The brown bear has sharp claws on each paw, which it uses to climb, forage for food, and slash enemies when provoked.

HOOVES
Some animals, like goats, have hooves at the tips of their toes. Thanks to these tough hooves, goats can navigate difficult and rocky terrain.

TAILS
When a predator grabs a three-leaf gecko's tail, it breaks off! This tail shedding ability surprises the predator and allows the lizard to escape.

HORNS AND ANTLERS
Horns are made of keratin, like fingernails. Antlers are made of bone covered in skin that is shed just before the breeding season. Horns and antlers are both useful for headbutting.

SPITTING
The fulmar is a type of seabird that can spit oil from its stomach onto its enemies. The oil can damage its attackers' feathers or fur.

ADAPTATIONS FOR PROTECTION
To avoid being eaten, many animals have body parts that they use as weapons, such as claws and horns. Others find ways to confuse or hide from their predators.

CAMOUFLAGE
An animal's ability to disguise its appearance, often by using its coloring or body shape to blend in with its surroundings.

STINGING
Sharp organs called stingers can be used to pierce the skin of attackers and deliver venom. Bee stingers release venom for several minutes after the stinger has entered its target.

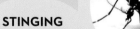

ODOR
A foul odor can ward off some predators. Skunks let loose a terrible-smelling spray that can linger for weeks.

TUSKS
Tusks are long, pointy teeth that grow from an animal's head. Elephants use their tusks for digging, marking trees, and even fighting.

TONGUES
Snakes flick their tongues to smell their surroundings. This helps them know when danger is nearby.

POISON
The strawberry poison dart frog has glands in its skin that are packed with poison. The poison isn't made inside the frog's body. It comes from formicine ants that the frog eats.

WEBBED FEET

Many water animals, such as ducks and some frogs, have a thin membrane, or web, between their toes. This allows them to paddle through water and walk on muddy surfaces.

WHISKERS

Whiskers can help an animal navigate at night. A tiger's whiskers have sensory nerves at the base. This helps the tiger detect movement. (It also helps the tiger determine where to bite its prey.)

ADAPTATIONS FOR LIFE IN UNIQUE HABITATS

Over time, animals adapt to the environments in which they live. These adaptations, which include traits like fur and wings, allow them not only to survive, but also to reproduce, even in extreme temperatures, on remote islands, and underwater.

BEAKS

All birds use their beaks to feed. A toucan uses its long, colorful beak to reach fruits on high branches. The beak is also serrated like a knife, to tear apart the bird's meal.

GILLS

All fish need oxygen to breathe underwater. Organs called gills absorb oxygen from the water and then send it to the fish's bloodstream.

SCALES

Reptiles have scales that cover their skin. A crocodile's tough scales protect it against rocky surroundings, whereas desert-dwelling lizards and snakes have scales to help keep in moisture. A snake's scales also help reduce friction as it moves.

WINGS

Wings allow many birds to cover large distances while searching for food. Birds may use their wings to fly through the air or glide from tree to tree.

FEATHERS

A bird's feathers vary depending on the habitat. Some desert birds, such as the sand grouse, have barbs on their feathers that help retain water. Meanwhile, seabirds, like the pelican, have water-repellent feathers.

FUR

Arctic animals, like the polar bear, have fur to help keep warm. A polar bear's fur consists of an undercoat, which traps body heat against the skin, as well as a thick coat of water-repellent guard hairs on top.

MORE ON CAMOUFLAGE

COLORS Many animals have coats, feathers, or skin that naturally match their environment. A prairie dog's reddish brown coat matches its earthy surroundings.

PATTERNS Patterns can also help an animal match its environment. A peacock flounder can change its pattern to match the pebbly ocean floor.

BLENDING If animals can't rely on their skin color and patterns to match their environment, they may use objects to blend in. A dresser crab places pieces of coral and sponge on its body to conceal itself from predators.

MIMICRY Some animals can mimic, or copy, another organism's appearance or behavior. The walking stick is an insect that mimics a stick.

SPOTS False eyespots can make an animal look like a larger and scarier animal. The two large spots behind a hawk moth caterpillar's head make it look like a snake.

STRIPES Stripes can create an optical illusion. When zebras stand in a herd, it's hard to tell where one zebra ends and another begins. This makes the herd look like one giant animal.

SKIN Special skin cells that contain pigment allow some animals—like the octopus—to change the color of their skin to match the environment.

FUR Some animals have fur that changes color seasonally to match their surroundings. The arctic fox's coat changes from white in the cold, snowy winter to brown or gray in the spring and summer to match the rock-covered terrain.

FEATHERS Some birds, such as the Willow Ptarmigan, molt their white winter feathers to make way for brown feathers in the spring and summer.

ENDANGERED

Many animal species are at risk of becoming extinct, or dying out. Although natural causes can be a factor, humans are largely responsible. Activities such as logging, farming, and construction have destroyed many animal habitats, and illegal hunting has only added to the problem.

A group called the International Union for the Conservation of Nature (IUCN) surveys different animal populations to determine if they are at risk. Use the IUCN status symbols below to determine each species' status.

AMERICAN BALD EAGLE

HALIAEETUS LEUCOCEPHALUS
The bald eagle was once at risk of becoming extinct. Hunting and a deadly pesticide called DDT were responsible. DDT, which had been used to control mosquitoes, leaked into streams and lakes, where it infected fish. Eagles that ate the fish had problems reproducing. Eventually, the government banned DDT, and the bald eagle population rebounded.

ARCTIC OCEAN

NORTH AMERICA

ATLANTIC

PACIFIC

OCEAN

OCEAN

SOUTH

AMERICA

| 0 | | 3,000 miles |

| 0 | | 4,000 kilometers |

ANTARCTIC

GIANT PANDA

AILUROPODA MELANOLEUCA
Less than 1,600 giant pandas remain in the wild. All of them live in China's bamboo forests. Farming and logging, as well as road and railroad construction, have reduced the panda's habitat—as well as its primary food source: bamboo.

24

SHARK
SPHYRNA LEWINI

Hundreds of young hammer-heads have been known to migrate together in schools. Unfortunately, this behavior has made the sharks an easy target for fishermen, who catch the fish for their meat, oil, and skin.

CALIFORNIA TIGER
SALAMANDER
AMBYSTOMA CALIFORNIENSE

The grassland habitat of the California tiger salamander once spanned 27,000 square miles (70,000 sq km) through California. In recent years, however, farming, grazing animals, and road construction all have reduced the area to fragments, thus threatening the existence of the salamander.

AP KEY
PROXIMATE RANGES OF SELECTED ENDANGERED ANIMALS

- Giant Panda
- American Bald Eagle
- Scalloped Hammerhead Shark
- Central Asian Tortoise
- Karner Blue Butterfly
- California Tiger Salamander

EUROPE

ASIA

PACIFIC

OCEAN

AFRICA

EQUATOR

INDIAN

OCEAN

AUSTRALIA

CENTRAL
ASIAN
TORTOISE
TESTUDO HORSFIELDII

Decreasing numbers of this tortoise can be found in parts of the central Asian countries from Iran to China, from Kazakhstan to Pakistan. Many Asian tortoises have been taken from the wild and sold as pets, and others have been hunted for food. Habitat destruction from farming and war has taken a toll as well.

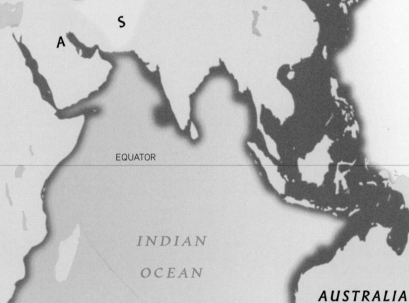

KARNER BLUE
BUTTERFLY
LYCAEIDES MELISSA SAMUELIS

As a caterpillar, the Karner blue butterfly feeds on wild lupine plants. Lately, the plant's habitat has been reduced by construction and encroaching forests, which hinder the growth of the flower. Without its main food source, the butterfly population has been decreasing.

CONSERVATION

According to the IUCN, more than 19,000 animal and plant species are at risk of becoming extinct, many due to the actions of humans. Contributing factors include illegal trade and hunting, overfishing, habitat destruction, invasive species, emerging diseases, and climate change.

Although extinction is a normal process, the historical rate based on the fossil record was 10 to 100 species per year—for all species everywhere. The current rate is at least 1,000 times higher.

In response, scientists are working together with research and conservation organizations, communities, and governments to gather the information needed to protect animals at risk. Their methods include monitoring population size, protecting ecosystems, and captive breeding.

On this map are animal species whose future depends on whether we take steps to conserve them, or not.

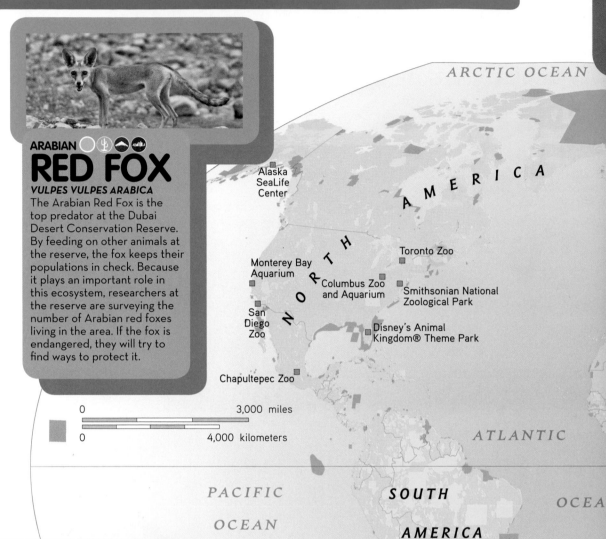

ARABIAN RED FOX
VULPES VULPES ARABICA

The Arabian Red Fox is the top predator at the Dubai Desert Conservation Reserve. By feeding on other animals at the reserve, the fox keeps their populations in check. Because it plays an important role in this ecosystem, researchers at the reserve are surveying the number of Arabian red foxes living in the area. If the fox is endangered, they will try to find ways to protect it.

ARCTIC OCEAN

NORTH AMERICA

Alaska SeaLife Center

Monterey Bay Aquarium

Toronto Zoo

Columbus Zoo and Aquarium

Smithsonian National Zoological Park

San Diego Zoo

Disney's Animal Kingdom® Theme Park

Chapultepec Zoo

| 0 | 3,000 miles |
| 0 | 4,000 kilometers |

ATLANTIC

PACIFIC OCEAN

SOUTH AMERICA

OCEA

São Paulo Zoo

HAWAIIAN CROW
CORVUS HAWAIIENSIS

This crow is extinct in the wild. Conservationists on the Hawaiian island of Maui, U.S.A., however, have preserved a small number of them by breeding the species in captivity. Today, there are approximately 31 of the crows in captivity.

ANTARCTI

ATLANTIC BLUEFIN
TUNA ●●●
THUNNUS THYNNUS
The Atlantic bluefin tuna measures 6.5 feet (2 m) long and weighs a whopping 550 pounds (250 kg). Unfortunately, its hefty size does little to protect it against the countless fishermen who raid the ocean for these giant fish. Laws have been passed to curb overfishing, and conservationists are working to protect the species' spawning grounds—particularly the Gulf of Mexico and the Mediterranean Sea.

ARCHEY'S
FROG ●●●
LEIOPELMA ARCHEYI
A combination of disease and habitat change in the forested alpine areas of New Zealand have led to a sharp decline in the Archey's frog population. A study completed in 2002 showed frog numbers decrease by 88 percent in an area called Tapu Ridge alone. In an effort to preserve these frogs, conservationists are breeding captive species.

ological Society
London

Berlin
Zoological
Garden
Prague Zoo

EUROPE

Barcelona Zoo

ASIA

AFRICA

Ueno
Zoological
Gardens

PACIFIC

OCEAN

Dubai Desert
Conservation Reserve

EQUATOR   Singapore Zoo

INDIAN   OCEAN

MAP KEY
- ■ Aquarium/Park/Zoo
- ■ Marine conservation area
- ■ Land conservation area

AUSTRALIA
Australia Zoo

National Zoological
Gardens of South Africa

Auckland Zoo

SALTWATER
CROCODILE ●
CROCODYLUS POROSUS
Saltwater crocodiles are not endangered. However, some experts believe that the increasing demand for crocodile goods, such a shoes and handbags, will eventually cause this reptile population to dip. Scientists are currently keeping tabs on the population by tagging the crocs with electronic devices, and then monitoring their behavior.

RED-BARBED
ANT ●●
FORMICA RUFIBARBIS
Although the red-barbed ant thrives in some parts of Europe, it is endangered in Great Britain. A loss of habitat and the spread of the slave making ant—a species that steals the young of red-barbed ants and kills any ant that tries to stop it—are largely responsible for the decline. To help preserve the ant, researchers are breeding the ants and releasing them into the wild.

All mammals have hair at some point in their lives. (Even dolphins are born with a few hairs on their snout!) But the most striking coat of hair—or fur—may belong to the giant panda. Its black-and-white woolly coat helps keep this mammal warm in the cool bamboo forests of central China, where it lives.

MAMMALS

POLAR BEAR

RED PANDA

AFRICAN LIONS

QUARTER HORSE

RED-NECKED WALLABY

SOUTHERN ELEPHANT SEAL

SIBERIAN TIGER

VIRGINIA OPOSSUM

AFRICAN ELEPHANTS

30

CHIMPANZEES

GOLDEN RETRIEVER

CHEETAH

BACTRIAN CAMEL

BOTTLENOSE DOLPHIN

GRAY WOLF

KOALA

31

WHAT IS A MAMMAL?

MAMMALS ARE AMONG THE MOST ADAPTABLE ANIMALS ON THE PLANET.

They are found on every continent and in every ocean, and range in size from tiny bumblebee bats to enormous blue whales. One reason for their success is the way they move. Mammals as a group use every possible form of locomotion. Terrestrial species walk, run, jump, climb, hop, swing, dig, and burrow. Aquatic ones swim, shuffle, and dive. A few even fly.

Diet and behavior vary, too. Many carnivores, for example, are top predators that live generally solitary lives. These include jaguars, tigers, and polar bears. By contrast, lions, otters, wolves, and dolphins live in family groups. Even more social are some of the herbivores, especially hoofed animals like deer and zebra. By living in large groups, they gain both protection against becoming another animal's meal and more opportunities to breed. Among omnivores, primates are known for their high intelligence, and rodents for their high numbers.

Mammal bones, especially skulls, are used for identification, and to work out the evolutionary history of each species. The jaws of a house cat are more lion- than wolf-like, for example. The teeth of horses and zebras look alike. The ear bones of mammals were once the jaws of prehistoric reptiles. And so on.

Despite these differences, all mammals share four traits that are shown in the diagram below: hair, mammary glands, a hinged jaw, and three tiny middle ear bones. Most have specialized teeth and moveable external ears.

MAMMAL TRAITS

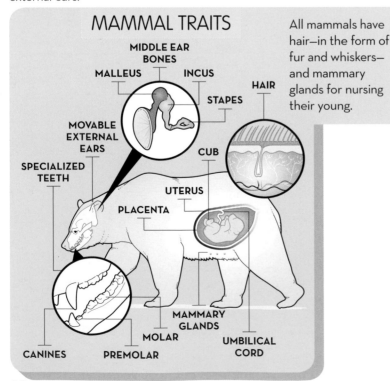

All mammals have hair—in the form of fur and whiskers—and mammary glands for nursing their young.

MIDDLE EAR BONES
MALLEUS
INCUS
STAPES
HAIR
MOVABLE EXTERNAL EARS
SPECIALIZED TEETH
CUB
UTERUS
PLACENTA
CANINES
PREMOLAR
MOLAR
MAMMARY GLANDS
UMBILICAL CORD

CLASSIFICATION OF MAMMALS

1 Mammals are organized into 28 orders, but this classification scheme is not set in stone. It changes as fossils are discovered and DNA studies shed new light on the relatedness of species.

2 Mammals are divided into three big groups based on how the embryo develops.

3 Monotremes such as the platypus are the egg-laying mammals.

4 Marsupials such as kangaroos have a short gestation period and give birth to live young that crawl immediately into a pouch.

5 Placental mammals have a long gestation made possible by a placenta and give birth to live young.

6 Twenty-five percent of all mammals are members of the order Chiroptera (bats).

7 Forty percent of all mammals are members of the order Rodentia (rodents).

8 Five percent of all mammals are members of the order Soricomorpha (shrewlike small mammals).

9 Some of the more familiar mammals are in the order Carnivora such as cats, dogs, and bears.

Did you know? Blue whales are the largest animals on Earth.

When this gentle giant, a humpback whale, surfaces to breathe, the water it sprays from its blowhole can soar as high as 30 feet (9 m) into the air.

MONOTREMES AND MARSUPIALS

The egg-laying mammals, or monotremes, are strange-looking relics of the past. Though they were once common, there are only two species groups remaining: the platypus and the echidna. The marsupials, or mammals with pouches, are a more familiar group. They include a number of appealing species, such as kangaroos and koalas.

Similar to other (placental) mammals, monotremes and marsupials produce milk and nurse their young, have hair, and hear as a result of the vibration of three middle-ear bones. But they are really quite different in a number of other ways! They have several unique anatomical features, for example. One is the cloaca, a common opening for their reproductive, intestinal, and urinary tracts. Birds and reptiles have something similar.

Their reproductive strategies also differ. Monotremes lay eggs and produce milk for their young but lack nipples. Marsupials give birth to live young known as joeys and have multiple nipples located within their pouches. Some joeys remain in the pouch for as long as one year, or until the next baby is born.

Another difference is where they are found. Monotremes live only in Australia, Tasmania, and New Guinea and are represented by only five species. Most of the 334 species of marsupials also are found in Australia and New Guinea. They were once much more widespread, however. Fossils of extinct marsupials show they once lived alongside placental mammals in the Americas, for example. Today, only one survives in North America, the Virginia opossum; 19 in Central America; and 79 in South America.

Life spans for monotremes and marsupials range up to 50 years.

COMMON BRUSHTAIL POSSUM
TRICHOSURUS VULPECULA

RANGE: Australia, Tasmania, New Zealand

SIZE: 3.3 to 9.9 lb (1.5 to 4.5 kg)

DIET: Leaves, flowers, shrubs

In most parts of the world, small animals that live in trees, have long tails, and eat leaves are monkeys—placental mammals. In Australia they are marsupials. The solitary and nocturnal brushtail possum is one example.

LIFE IN A POUCH

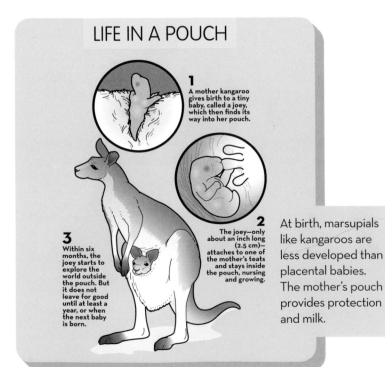

1 A mother kangaroo gives birth to a tiny baby, called a joey, which then finds its way into her pouch.

2 The joey—only about an inch long (2.5 cm)—attaches to one of the mother's teats and stays inside the pouch, nursing and growing.

3 Within six months, the joey starts to explore the world outside the pouch. But it does not leave for good until at least a year, or when the next baby is born.

At birth, marsupials like kangaroos are less developed than placental babies. The mother's pouch provides protection and milk.

VIRGINIA OPOSSUM
DIDELPHIS VIRGINIANA

RANGE: Central America and Mexico to Ontario, Canada

SIZE: 0.7 to 14 lb (0.3 to 6.4 kg)

DIET: Insects and carrion

Though its lifespan is short (1.5 years), the opossum is a highly successful marsupial. Diet is one reason. This species eats anything, including garbage. It is also excellent at playing dead when threatened by a hungry hawk or coyote.

KOALA ⚪⚪⬤
PHASCOLARCTOS CINEREUS

RANGE: Eastern Australia

SIZE: 11.2 to 26 lb (5.1 to 11.8 kg)

DIET: Leaves and shoots of eucalyptus trees

After eating a pound of eucalyptus leaves each night, koalas spend their days resting and digesting. Sometimes, they climb down to the ground to change trees or eat soil, which helps with digestion. They never drink.

Did you know?
Echidnas use their backward-pointing rear feet to remove soil.

SHORT-BEAKED ECHIDNA ⚪⚪⬤⬤
TACHYGLOSSUS ACULEATUS

RANGE: Australia, New Guinea, Tasmania

SIZE: 4.4 to 15.4 lb (2.0 to 7.0 kg)

DIET: Termites, ants, other small invertebrates

Echidnas are diggers. They are also spiny anteaters. Like the platypus, they use their sensitive snouts to find food using electrolocation. The egg-laying monotremes are the only mammals with this sixth sense.

DUCK-BILLED PLATYPUS ⬤⬤⬤
ORNITHORHYNCHUS ANATINUS

RANGE: Eastern Australia, Tasmania

SIZE: 1.8 to 5.6 lb (0.8 to 2.5 kg)

DIET: Aquatic insects, larvae, fish

This unusual animal spends most of its time in water. The platypus has a super-sensitive nose shaped like a bill, which it uses to hunt for insects and small fish. It finds its food by feel and by detecting electrical signals.

TASMANIAN DEVIL ⬤⚪⬤⬤
SARCOPHILUS HARRISII

RANGE: Tasmania

SIZE: 8.8 to 26 lb (4.0 to 11.8 kg)

DIET: Dead animals and small mammals

One look at the teeth of a Tasmanian devil and it is clear that this marsupial is a carnivore. It will eat anything ranging in size from a possum to a wallaby. Its large head and neck give it a very powerful bite.

WESTERN GRAY KANGAROO ⚪⚪⬤
MACROPUS FULIGINOSUS

RANGE: Southern Australia

SIZE: 60 to 120 lb (27 to 54 kg)

DIET: Grasses, forbs, leaves, tree bark, shrubs

The kangaroo's long, furry muzzle hides its massive molar teeth, suited for chewing plants. Imagine its face with larger eyes and more delicate ears. This herbivore is the marsupial equivalent of deer and antelope, species not found in Australia.

MAMMALS

35

TREE KANGAROO

Matschie's tree kangaroos *(Dendrolagus matschiei)* are among the rarest animals on Earth. They lead secret lives in Papua New Guinea's ancient cloud forests, spending most of their time hidden in a maze of moss-covered tree branches nearly 100 feet (30 m) above ground. I had studied tree kangaroos in captivity for nearly a decade and wanted to investigate them in the wild. Many people warned that I may never find one—that it was impossible to track them—but I wanted to learn their secrets to help save them from extinction.

At the time, area villagers tracked tree kangaroos with hunting dogs, so I flew to Papua New Guinea and for three weeks met with local landowners and the best local tree kangaroo hunter. I expressed my desire to study wild tree kangaroos, and they led me through the forest to look for one. On the very last day of the trip, one of the hunting dogs barked wildly. His eyes fixed on a red-and-brown tree kangaroo 40 feet (12 m) above our heads! It gazed down at us and tears welled in my eyes—I had finally seen a wild Matschie's tree kangaroo. Since then, local landowners and hunters have guided our team into the forest year after year to study them. Seven *years* passed before we saw another tree 'roo, but a couple of years later we *caught* one and attached a special collar that allows us to monitor its movements, and thanks to the hunters who help us track the tree kangaroos, we recently captured the first images of their secret lives in the canopy—including a female caring for a tiny joey in her pouch!

APPROXIMATE RANGE OF THE
DENDROLAGUS MATSCHIEI
(MATSCHIE'S TREE KANGAROO)

0   200 miles

0   200 kilometers

A S I A

New Guinea

A U S T R A L I A

OBSERVATION
TIPS

1 Wear comfortable hiking boots on your trip of a lifetime to Papua New Guinea. You'll be trekking over steep hills and rugged peaks to look for tree 'roos.

2 Tree kangaroos blend into moss-covered branches—use binoculars to spot their dangling tails.

3 To track Matschie's tree kangaroos, look for nibbled leaves, scratched trees, and even poop!

4 Heads up! Matschie's tree kangaroos can safely leap 60 or more feet (18 m) from a tree branch to the ground.

Lisa Dabek is founder and director of the Tree Kangaroo Conservation Program at Woodland Park Zoo in Seattle, Washington, U.S.A. She began studying Matschie's tree kangaroos in 1987 and continues to work with local landowners in Papua New Guinea to study them and conserve their natural habitat.

Matschie's tree kangaroos give birth to a single baby, called a joey. The naked, lima bean–size newborn crawls up its mother's belly into her pouch to nurse on milk and continue to develop. After about ten months, the joey permanently leaves its mother's pouch—though it still pushes its head inside to drink milk for another four months! The joey follows its mother closely, learning to navigate the maze of tree branches and how to find food before setting off to live on its own.

Rodents are not as ordinary as their name sounds. They are an extraordinarily successful group of placental mammals, for one thing. About 40 percent of all mammals—more than 2,000 species—are rodents! They are found everywhere except Antarctica and a few islands.

Rodents also have very interesting front teeth: Their incisors are self-sharpening. The front surface of these long, curved teeth is hard, made of enamel. The back surface is soft, made of dentine. When a rodent chews, the harder tooth surfaces sharpen the softer ones, like a chisel. As a result, the animals in this group are capable of gnawing through and eating just about anything—from wood to wire.

Rodents are divided into mouse-like (this page), squirrel-like, and cavy-like (page 40), based upon the way their jaws work. The mouse-like rodents include mice, rats, and voles, as well as gerbils, hamsters, jerboas, lemmings, and muskrats. The animals in this group have two well-developed jaw muscles that allow them to chew and gnaw in all directions.

Life spans for rodents are one to three years.

BROWN RAT
RATTUS NORVEGICUS

RANGE: Worldwide, except polar regions

SIZE: 5 to 18 oz (140 to 500 g)

DIET: Anything they can find

Before ships carried rats as stowaways around the world, this species was native to northern China. Brown rats have a keen sense of smell and are highly social. They live in packs and are known for their intelligent behavior.

BARBARY STRIPED GRASS MOUSE
LEMNISCOMYS BARBARUS

RANGE: North and central Africa

SIZE: 0.8 to 1.4 oz (24 to 40 g)

DIET: Grass stems, leaves, roots, fruit, crops, seeds

Some rodents breed year-round, but striped mice reproduce only during the rainy season, when food and water are readily available. Females give birth to two to ten pups every 28 days for four months in a row!

HARVEST MOUSE
MICROMYS MINUTUS

RANGE: Europe and Asia

SIZE: 0.14 to 0.23 oz (4 to 7.5 g)

DIET: Seeds and small insects

This tiny mouse is a climber. It uses its prehensile tail and strong, flexible toes to hold on to the narrowest of plant stems while feeding on seeds, berries, and insects. Harvest mice also build their nests high above the ground.

Did you know? The harvest mouse feeds for 30 minutes every three hours.

FAT-TAILED GERBIL
PACHYUROMYS DUPRASI

RANGE: North Africa

SIZE: 0.8 to 1.75 oz (20 to 50 g)

DIET: Insects, leaves, seeds

Gerbils are native to the Sahara, where they spend the daytime in burrows. At night, they search for insects when temperatures are cooler. Some live in colonies, whereas others live as solitary animals.

GOLDEN HAMSTER
MESOCRICETUS AURATUS

RANGE: Syria and Turkey

SIZE: 3.5 to 4.4 oz (100 to 125 g)

DIET: Nuts, seeds, insects such as ants

Golden hamsters are territorial and show aggression toward their own species by chattering their teeth. These rodents are a food source for many animals, including foxes, snakes, and birds of prey such as eagles.

HOUSE MOUSE
MUS MUSCULUS

RANGE: Worldwide, except polar regions

SIZE: 0.5 to 1 oz (10 to 35 g)

DIET: Anything they can find

Rodents—especially house mice and rats—have a bad reputation. They damage tons of crops and stored goods each year. They also carry diseases. Yet they are important in the food web, both as seed dispersers and as prey.

YELLOW-NECKED FIELD MOUSE
APODEMUS FLAVICOLLIS

RANGE: North America, as far west as the Rocky Mountains

SIZE: 1.2 to 2.3 oz (34.0 to 65.2 g)

DIET: Grass, herbs, seeds, grains, bark, tubers

Field mice also are known as meadow voles. This species digs burrows, where it stores food and where females give birth to their young. In the process, field mice can damage the roots of fruit trees, garden plants, and crops.

MUSKRAT
ONDATRA ZIBETHICUS

RANGE: North America, Europe, north and east Asia

SIZE: 1.25 to 4.5 lb (.6 to 2.0 kg)

DIET: Aquatic and land vegetation

This species is related to the common vole. Instead of burrowing underground, however, muskrats dig into the banks of swamps and marshy areas. Like beavers, they have a flat tail that functions as a rudder.

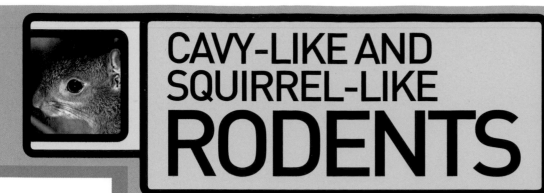

CAVY-LIKE AND SQUIRREL-LIKE RODENTS

BRAZILIAN PORCUPINE
COENDOU PREHENSILIS

RANGE: Trinidad and the forests of northern South America

SIZE: 2 to 11 lb (0.9 to 5.0 kg)

DIET: Leaves, stems, fruit, blossoms, roots, trees, bark

Worldwide, there are 29 species of porcupines. Those found in the Americas, like the Brazilian porcupine, are good climbers. Those found in Asia, Europe, and Africa spend most of their time on the ground. All release their quills when threatened.

Squirrel-like rodents (opposite page) range from all types of squirrels (tree, ground, and flying) to prairie dogs, marmots, beavers, chipmunks, and kangaroo rats. When these animals take a bite out of something, their jaws move forward. Like all rodents, they can gnaw through anything. The result, in the case of the beaver, can be disruptive. Beaver dams often cause widespread flooding, especially in urban areas.

Hibernation is another interesting feature of this group. Ground squirrels and marmots hibernate for several months during the winter, when food supplies are short. They become inactive, living off their fat stores. To conserve energy, their body temperature drops to equal that of the environment. Their heart and respiratory rates drop, too. But they are not asleep. All hibernating animals sporadically become active and warm up, usually every 10 to 15 days. Some squirrels and beavers can live more than 20 years.

The cavy-like rodents (this page) have chewing muscles that attach to both the lower and upper jaws, giving them a very strong bite. The animals in this group have large heads relative to their bodies, and vary greatly in size. The smallest is the mouse-size naked mole rat. The largest is the pig-size capybara, the world's largest rodent. The most respected—for its painful quills—is the porcupine. Many cavy-like rodents, such as the guinea pig and chinchilla, have been domesticated for food and clothing, and as pets. Life spans in this group also vary. Naked mole rats and porcupines can live as long as 20 years.

NAKED MOLE RAT
HETEROCEPHALUS GLABER

RANGE: Kenya, Somalia, Ethiopia

SIZE: 1.2 oz (35 g)

DIET: Roots, bulbs, tubers, other underground plant parts

Naked mole rats live in dark, warm burrows. They find their food by smell and their way by feel, using their sensitive whiskers. They live in large colonies with a single breeding female, or queen, and dozens of workers.

CAPYBARA
HYDROCHOERUS HYDROCHAERIS

RANGE: Tropical areas of South America

SIZE: 77 to 145 lb (34.9 to 65.8 kg)

DIET: Grasses and aquatic plants

Despite their large size, or maybe because of it, capybaras are one of the green anaconda's favorite foods. For protection, these semi-aquatic herbivores live in groups of 10 to 20. Young stay with their mothers for up to a year.

NAKED MOLE RAT BURROW

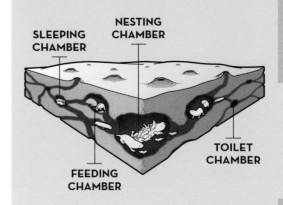

SLEEPING CHAMBER

NESTING CHAMBER

FEEDING CHAMBER

TOILET CHAMBER

Naked mole rats live in underground burrows with separate feeding, sleeping, nesting, and toilet chambers.

SQUIRREL-LIKE RODENT

WOODCHUCK
MARMOTA MONAX

RANGE: Canada and eastern and central United States

SIZE: 4.4 to 13.1 lb (2 to 5 kg)

DIET: Roots, bulbs, tubers, seeds

The woodchuck is the most common species of marmot found in North America. In some places, it is also known as the groundhog or whistle pig. Woodchucks hibernate, and breed shortly after waking in the spring.

SQUIRREL-LIKE RODENT

KANGAROO RAT
DIPODOMYS ORDII

RANGE: Western North America

SIZE: 2 to 3.4 oz (56.7 to 96.4 g)

DIET: Seeds; some grasshoppers and moths

Kangaroo rats are solitary, nocturnal animals that hop and build burrows in sandy soil. To protect their homes and avoid the heat of the day, they kick sand over the entrance, covering the hole from the inside.

SQUIRREL-LIKE RODENT

SILKY POCKET MOUSE
PEROGNATHUS FLAVUS

RANGE: Western and southwestern United States, northern Mexico

SIZE: 0.2 to 0.3 oz (5.7 to 8.5 g)

DIET: Seeds, some green vegetation, some insects

There are several species of pocket mice. This one prefers sandy soils, though it also is found in rocky habitats. The silky pocket mouse is named for its unusually soft fur.

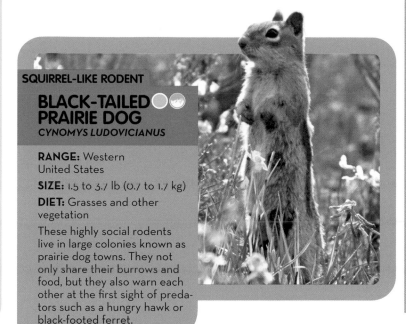

SQUIRREL-LIKE RODENT

BLACK-TAILED PRAIRIE DOG
CYNOMYS LUDOVICIANUS

RANGE: Western United States

SIZE: 1.5 to 3.7 lb (0.7 to 1.7 kg)

DIET: Grasses and other vegetation

These highly social rodents live in large colonies known as prairie dog towns. They not only share their burrows and food, but they also warn each other at the first sight of predators such as a hungry hawk or black-footed ferret.

SQUIRREL-LIKE RODENT

AMERICAN BEAVER
CASTOR CANADENSIS

RANGE: North America, except deserts and northern Canada

SIZE: 29 to 70 lb (13 to 32 kg)

DIET: Tree bark, especially willow, maple, poplar, beech, birch, alder, aspen

Beavers are mostly aquatic rodents, with huge incisors for cutting through wood—their primary food. Young are born fully furred with their eyes open and can swim within 24 hours. They spend up to two years with their parents.

SQUIRREL-LIKE RODENT

EASTERN GRAY SQUIRREL
SCIURUS CAROLINENSIS

RANGE: Eastern to midwestern United States

SIZE: 0.7 to 1.6 lb (0.3 to 0.7 kg)

DIET: Nuts, buds, flowers of trees

There are more than 100 species of tree squirrels, and each plays a role in plant dispersal. As winter approaches, the eastern gray squirrel buries more food than it will recover. The buried seeds and nuts germinate the following spring.

41

BATS

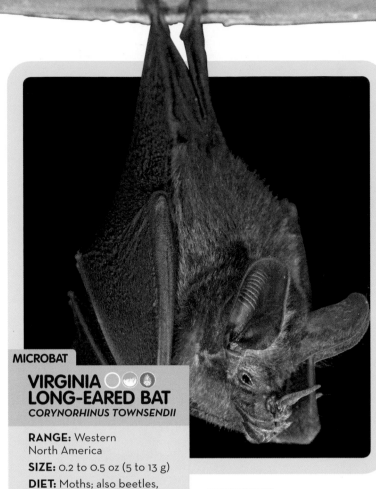

Like birds, bats have wings and can fly. The difference is that instead of flying by flapping feathered arms, bats hold out their elbows and flap their webbed, outstretched hands. The bat wing is a special double layer of skin that stretches from one finger to another and attaches to the side of the bat's body, like a fan.

Because they fly, bats are one of the most successful groups of animals on Earth. Twenty percent of all mammals are bats—about 925 species. They are also beneficial. Bats eat massive amounts of insects. They also help pollinate a variety of plants. There are two main groups of bats: microbats and megabats.

Bats are among the longest-living mammals, with average life spans of 10 to 25 years and a longevity record of 33 years. This is unusual, since small animals rarely live as long as large ones. Some experts think this is because bats have such an efficient metabolism that there is less wear and tear on their tissues over time. This type of age-related damage is known as oxidation. Hibernation also limits this damage because it essentially serves as a rest period.

MICROBAT

VIRGINIA LONG-EARED BAT
CORYNORHINUS TOWNSENDII

RANGE: Western North America

SIZE: 0.2 to 0.5 oz (5 to 13 g)

DIET: Moths; also beetles, flies, other small insects

The ridges on the inside of this bat's ears and the flap of skin over its nose help focus sounds. They also help the bat detect very soft sounds, like insect wings flapping. All of these features are important in echolocation.

MICROBAT

VAMPIRE BAT
DESMODUS ROTUNDUS

RANGE: From Mexico to Argentina and Chile

SIZE: 0.5 to 1.7 oz (15 to 50 g)

DIET: Blood of other vertebrates

Many people fear bats because of their behavior: They are nocturnal, secretive animals that rest by hanging upside down by their feet. Another reason? The vampire bat. Although it prefers cattle blood, it will feed on humans.

MICROBAT

MEXICAN FREE-TAILED BAT
TADARIDA BRASILIENSIS

RANGE: Most of North, Central, and South America

SIZE: 0.25 to 0.4 oz (7 to 12 g)

DIET: Moths, beetles, dragonflies, flies, true bugs, wasps, bees, ants

Millions of free-tailed bats migrate from Mexico to Texas each year to breed. They are following migrating moths and will fly as high as 10,000 feet (3,048 m) to catch them. The moths are a problem because they feed on crops like corn. The bats limit the damage by eating 1,000 tons a night!

MEGABAT

GEOFFREY'S ROUSETTE FRUIT BAT
ROUSETTUS AMPLEXICAUDATUS

RANGE: Southeast Asia, from Myanmar to Papua New Guinea

SIZE: 2.8 to 6 oz (80 to 170 g)

DIET: Fruit

This species is unusual among fruit bats because it uses echolocation as well as sight to find its food. The Geoffrey's Rousette fruit bat is also known for its roosting behavior: Thousands live together in caves.

MICROBAT
GREAT FRUIT-EATING BAT
ARTIBEUS LITERATUS

RANGE: Central and South America

SIZE: 2.3 oz (65 g)

DIET: Fruit

The great fruit bat has especially sharp canines used to cut into its food: mostly unripe figs, which have very tough skin. It also uses the claw at the end of its first digit—the equivalent of a thumb—to hold onto the fig.

MICROBAT
CHESTNUT SHORT-TAILED BAT
CAROLLIA CASTANEA

RANGE: Honduras to northern South America

SIZE: 0.5 oz (14 g)

DIET: Fruit of the piper plant

This species is one of many in the group known as leaf-nosed bats. Although it is capable of using echolocation, the chestnut short-tailed bat eats fruit, rather than insects, and plays an important role in seed dispersal in tropical forests.

MAMMALS

MEGABAT
WAHLBERG'S EPAULETTED FRUIT BAT
EPOMOPHORUS WAHLBERGI

RANGE: Sub-Saharan Africa

SIZE: 1.9 to 4.4 oz (54 to 125 g)

DIET: Fruit, especially guava, figs

Guava is one of the favorite foods of Wahlberg's epauletted fruit bat. This species is common in southern Africa, where it feeds on both wild and farmed fruits. It finds its food by detecting the smell of ripening fruit.

MEGABAT
INDIAN FLYING FOX
PTEROPUS GIGANTEUS

RANGE: Tropical parts of Central Asia

SIZE: 1.3 to 3.5 lb (0.6 to 1.6 kg)

DIET: Fruit, including guava, mango, and fig

The Indian flying fox is a fruit bat that roosts in trees during the day. Like most bats, they are very social: Hundreds may be found in a single tree. If they get too hot in the sun, they fan themselves with their wings.

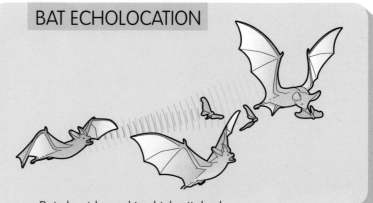

MEGABAT
STRAW-COLORED FRUIT BAT
EIDOLON HELVUM

RANGE: Sub-Saharan Africa, including Madagascar

SIZE: 8.1 to 12.3 oz (230 to 349 g)

DIET: Variety of fruit

The straw-colored fruit bat has long, narrow wings that it uses to fly long distances—roosts may be as far as 120 miles apart. This species flies straighter and at higher altitudes than other fruit bats. When it feeds, it swallows the juice of fruit and spits out the fiber.

BAT ECHOLOCATION

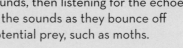

Bats hunt by making high-pitched sounds, then listening for the echoes of the sounds as they bounce off potential prey, such as moths.

43

RABBITS
AND RELATIVES

There are two ways to avoid becoming another animal's meal: fight or flight. Rabbits and their relatives—hares and pikas—take the second approach. These animals are capable of running or hopping with great speed and agility, turning on a dime, and finding places to hide. Two other features give them an edge: acute hearing and excellent vision.

The animals in this group have another form of defense: They reproduce quickly and in very high numbers. Eastern cottontail rabbits, for example, can breed every two months. In the course of one year, they can have up to six litters and produce as many as 72 babies. Females also start breeding at a young age: three months. As always in nature, though, there is a trade-off.

Many baby bunnies do not survive to adulthood, becoming food for predators, such as foxes, wolves, and hawks. As a result, the recorded life spans for some of the animals in this group range from one to three years. Species like the European hare live longer, up to 15 years.

SNOWSHOE HARE
LEPUS AMERICANUS

RANGE: Northern United States and Canada

SIZE: 3.2 to 3.4 lb (1.45 to 1.54 kg)

DIET: Green plants, grasses, twigs, shoots, buds

Snowshoe hares have reddish brown to gray fur in summer and white fur in winter. This change in coat color—known as seasonal molt—gives them better camouflage. It takes about 2.5 months. In between, they are white and brown.

AMERICAN PIKA
OCHOTONA PRINCEPS

RANGE: Mountains of western North America

SIZE: 4.3 to 6.2 oz (121.9 to 175 g)

DIET: Shrubs, plants, grasses

All pikas live in cold climates, but they do not hibernate. Instead, they prepare for winter by gathering greens and grasses and stashing them near their burrows. The pile soon turns into hay, which the pika uses for bedding and food.

EASTERN COTTONTAIL RABBIT
SYLVILAGUS FLORIDANUS

RANGE: Southern Manitoba and Quebec, Canada; northeast United States to the Great Plains, to central and northwestern South America

SIZE: 1.7 to 3.4 lb (0.8 to 1.5 kg)

DIET: Green vegetation, bark, twigs

Rabbits are born fully furred, with their eyes closed. The mother visits the nest to nurse them for only a few minutes a day. She begins to wean them by ten days, and they are on their own by three to four weeks of age.

ARCTIC HARE
LEPUS ARCTICUS

RANGE: Greenland, Arctic islands in Canada

SIZE: 6.6 to 11 lb (3.0 to 5.0 kg)

DIET: Grasses, herbs, shrubs, roots, twigs

With their compact bodies and powerful rear legs, arctic hares are capable of running 30 miles an hour (48 km/h) to escape a predator. These are nocturnal animals that feed on the twigs and roots of willow and other trees.

ALPINE PIKA
OCHOTONA ALPINA

RANGE: China, Kazakhstan, Mongolia, Russia

SIZE: 2.5 to 10.6 oz (70 to 300 g)

DIET: Plants

The alpine pika, like its relatives, gathers bits of plants before winter to make a hay pile. It is not the only animal that benefits from this special stash of food, however. When the snow is deep, Siberian deer and reindeer will eat the pika's hay.

SHREWS AND SMALL INSECTIVORES

Shrews, tree shrews, elephant shrews, moles, golden moles, tenrecs, and hedgehogs are insect-eaters, though not exclusively. They prefer to eat worms and bug larvae, but also will eat plants, seeds, and small animals like lizards and fish.

The animals in this group are generally shy and nocturnal. Instead of relying on their vision, which is poor, they use their mobile snouts and excellent sense of smell to find their food. Some, like the hedgehog and moles, also have good hearing.

These characteristics also describe the first mammals, primitive species that evolved more than 200 million years ago. The smallest of today's insectivores, shrews and moles, are living examples of yesterday's early mammals. Their opportunistic diet, small size, and secretive behavior helped them survive 66 million years ago when other species, including the dinosaurs, went extinct.

Life spans range from two to six years.

GOLDEN-RUMPED ELEPHANT SHREW
RHYNCHOCYON CHRYSOPYGUS

RANGE: Forested areas of coastal Kenya in Africa

SIZE: 1.1 to 1.2 lb (0.50 to 0.54 kg)

DIET: Worms, spiders, insects

Elephant shrews use their long, flexible noses to look under leaves for insects. This species also mates for life and is found in pairs. At night, they sleep in a ground nest made by digging out a hollow and lining it with leaves.

LESSER TENREC
ECHINOPS TELFAIRI

RANGE: Madagascar

SIZE: 6.4 oz (181.4 g)

DIET: Insects and other invertebrates

Like hedgehogs, tenrecs use their spines for defense by rolling up into a ball. But if the predator persists, they will unroll and attack. They can also vibrate their spines to make a rasping sound.

EUROPEAN HEDGEHOG
ERINACEUS EUROPAEUS

RANGE: Europe and Central Asia

SIZE: 1.8 to 2.6 lb (0.8 to 1.2 kg)

DIET: Insects, berries, bird eggs, frogs

Except for the fur on its face and underbelly, this kind of hedgehog is covered in spines—about 5,000 of them. Each is ¾ to 1 inch (2 to 2.5 cm) long with a white tip, and brown and black stripes. When threatened, the hedgehog curls into a ball and stiffens its spines.

STAR-NOSED MOLE
CONDYLURA CRISTATA

RANGE: Eastern North America

SIZE: 1.2 to 2.6 oz (34 to 74 g)

DIET: Aquatic crustaceans, small fish, water insects

This semi-aquatic mole has a nose made up of 22 very sensitive, and always active, tentacles. It uses its nose to move dirt and catch prey, such as worms, leeches, and fly larvae, and uses its paddle-like feet to swim.

MADRAS TREE SHREW
ANATHANA ELLIOTI

RANGE: India

SIZE: 4.8 oz (136 g)

DIET: Insects, fruit, leaves

At first glance, tree shrews look like squirrels, with their long bodies and bushy tails. They even use their feet to hold on to their food. Their diet is different, though. Tree shrews don't eat nuts.

ANTEATERS, ARMADILLOS, AND SLOTHS

Anteaters, aardvarks, armadillos, pangolins, and sloths share several features. All have powerful front legs with long claws used for digging or hanging on to tree branches, and reduced or absent teeth.

The two largest animals in this group, anteaters (South America) and aardvarks (Africa), are interesting because although they prey on tiny insects, neither is a small animal. The giant anteater weighs as much as 80 pounds and the aardvark almost twice as much at 140 pounds. Both are known as "antbears" in the countries where they live.

The explanation is their hunting strategy. Instead of looking for one insect at a time, anteaters and aardvarks learn the location of ant and termite nests, or mounds. Because these are social insects, each nest contains hundreds of thousands of them. Antbears move from one nest to another, digging a hole in each and eating what they can without getting stung too badly. The worker ants or termites repair the damage, and the nest is still there for the next visit.

Life spans for the animals in this group range from 10 to 25 years.

GIANT ANTEATER
MYRMECOPHAGA TRIDACTYLA

RANGE: Central and South America, from Belize to Argentina

SIZE: 40 to 86 lb (18 to 39 kg)

DIET: Ants, termites, grubs

Inside its 1.5-foot (0.5-m)-long snout, the giant anteater has a 2-foot (0.6-m)-long tongue—and no teeth! It also has glands that produce sticky saliva. To feed, it flicks its tongue 150 times a minute, grabbing its food.

LARGE HAIRY ARMADILLO
CHAETOPHRACTUS VILLOSUS

RANGE: Paraguay, Bolivia, central Argentina

SIZE: About 4.4 lb (2 kg)

DIET: Insects, other invertebrates, small rodents, lizards, plants, carrion

Armadillos have armor-like skin to protect themselves when threatened. This protective layer is made up of flat bones, or scutes, covered by keratin, the same material that makes up hair and nails.

HOFFMAN'S TWO-TOED SLOTH
CHOLOEPUS HOFFMANNI

RANGE: Central and South America

SIZE: 8.8 to 17.7 lb (4 to 8 kg)

DIET: Leaves, twigs, fruit

The sloth's curved toes help it hang on to tree branches without wasting energy. All species of sloths are similar: They eat leaves, buds, and twigs; move very slowly; and climb to the ground weekly to defecate. They rarely drink water.

Did you know? Only the three-banded armadillo can roll up into a hard ball.

COLLARED ANTEATER
TAMANDUA TETRADACTYLA

RANGE: South America

SIZE: 9.9 lb (4.5 kg)

DIET: Ants and termites

This species has two other names: lesser anteater, or southern tamandua. It spends its time in the trees feeding on ants. Though much smaller than its giant cousin, the tamandua also has a very long tongue—up to 1.3 feet (0.4 m)!

PALE-THROATED THREE-TOED SLOTH
BRADYPUS TRIDACTYLUS

RANGE: Central and South America

SIZE: 4.9 to 12.1 lb (2.2 to 5.5 kg)

DIET: Twigs, buds, leaves

Because they live in the rain forest and rarely move, sloths often grow algae on their fur. The relationship is an example of commensalism, which means the algae have a place to live, and the sloth is better camouflaged. The algae may even be nutritious.

SOUTHERN TWO-TOED SLOTH
CHOLOEPUS DIDACTYLUS

RANGE: Central and South America

SIZE: 8.8 to 17.6 lb (4 to 8 kg)

DIET: Leaves, twigs, fruit

Because of their diet, sloths have a slow metabolism and cannot maintain a high body temperature. So, like reptiles, they move into the sun when they need to get warm. Their digestion is the slowest of any herbivorous mammal: up to 2.5 days.

INDIAN PANGOLIN
MANIS CRASSICAUDATA

RANGE: Eastern Pakistan; India, Bangladesh, Sri Lanka

SIZE: 11 to 77 lb (5 to 35 kg)

DIET: Mainly termites, ants, ant eggs

Pangolins are covered in armor-like scales made of clumps of hair. Like anteaters, they have a very long tongue and no teeth. Like birds, they have a thick stomach wall that grinds up their food.

HOW DO ANTEATERS EAT?

All four species of anteaters have one thing in common: They are edentates, which means they lack teeth. How would you eat your food if you didn't have teeth? You would suck it up through a straw, of course. And that's about what they do. Giant anteaters creep up on a termite mound or anthill and rip it open with their sharp claws. They stick their tongues into the opening and create almost a vacuum with their throats, sucking up their prey. Their tongues are also sticky, which speeds up the process. An anteater may spend as little as one minute feasting on an anthill, flicking its tongue up to 150 times.

Smaller anteaters like the silky anteater and tamandua prefer to search trees for bugs to eat. Either way, that's some fancy feasting!

DOGS, WOLVES, AND RELATIVES

Smell is everything to a dog. All 34 species in the dog, or Canid (CAY-nid), family use their noses to find food, track one another's whereabouts, and identify competitors as well as potential predators.

A dog's nose is also important for temperature control. Wolves, coyotes, jackals, foxes, and wild and domestic dogs lack sweat glands. They cannot shed heat by perspiration. Instead, they open their mouths and pant through their noses.

Panting is more complicated than it looks. Cooler air is inhaled and warmer air is exhaled. But the process only works if the tongue and nasal passages are wet, and the outside temperature is lower than the animal's body temperature. This is why it is dangerous—and against the law in many countries—to leave a dog in a parked car in the sun.

Though dogs are more likely to pant than most carnivores, there are several other species that use their noses to keep cool. Polar bears are one example.

Dogs, wolves, and their relatives have a life span of 12 to 15 years.

AFRICAN WILD DOG
LYCAON PICTUS

RANGE: Africa

SIZE: 70 to 79 lb (18 to 36 kg)

DIET: Antelopes, impalas, zebras, wildebeest

This species, also called the painted hunting dog or ornate wolf, is the only member of the dog family with spotted fur. It hunts in packs and has the strongest bite relative to its body size of all living carnivores!

FENNEC FOX
VULPES ZERDA

RANGE: Sahara of North Africa

SIZE: 1.7 to 3.3 lb (0.8 to 1.5 kg)

DIET: Small rodents, birds, insects, lizards

The smallest Canid, this fox is highly specialized for life in the desert. Its huge ears help to get rid of heat as well as gather sound. Fennec foxes hunt by listening for rodents, reptiles, and insects moving under the sand.

COYOTE
CANIS LATRANS

RANGE: North and Central America

SIZE: 15 to 46 lb (6.8 to 20.9 kg)

DIET: Rodents, rabbits, snakes, insects, carrion, fruit, berries, grasses, fish, frogs, crustaceans

Coyotes are a very successful species, especially in places where there are no wolves. This is one reason they are now common in cities and urban areas. Another is diet: Coyotes prefer to eat rodents.

FOX FOOD WEB

Among mammals, the top predator in a food web is often a member of the order Carnivora, such as a fox. As shown here, rabbits, birds, and insects consume plants, whereas foxes consume all of these food sources.

DHOLE ● ◐ ◐
CUON ALPINUS

RANGE: South and Southeast Asia

SIZE: 37 to 46 lb (17 to 21 kg)

DIET: Wild pigs, hares, goats, sheep, berries, insects, lizards

Though also called the Asiatic wild dog, dholes are only distantly related to wolves. They have fewer molars; a shorter, thick nose; and longer, thin legs. Dholes can jump as high as 12 feet (3.7 m) and leap more than 20 feet (6.1 m).

BLACK-BACKED JACKAL ○ ◐ ◐ ◐
CANIS MESOMELAS

RANGE: Southern Africa; East Africa, including Kenya, Somalia, Ethiopia

SIZE: 11 to 23 lb (5 to 10 kg)

DIET: Insects, small mammals, carrion, reptiles, birds

Black-backed jackals live in small groups, usually a male and female pair with their young. Like other members of the dog family, they will sometimes gather together in small packs to hunt down larger prey, like antelopes.

RED WOLF ● ◐ ◐ ◐
CANIS RUFUS

RANGE: Southeastern United States

SIZE: 35 to 90 lb (16 to 41 kg)

DIET: Small mammals; some insects, berries

The red wolf is named for the red fur on its ears and back. It also has a long, bushy tail with a black tip and white fur on its lips. Genetic studies suggest this species is more closely related to the coyote than to other wolves.

DOMESTIC DOG ○ ◐ ◐
CANIS LUPUS SSP. FAMILIARIS

RANGE: Worldwide

SIZE: Less than 1 to 200 lb (less than 0.5 to 91 kg)

DIET: Mainly meats, grains, vegetables.

Since first domesticated in Asia about 15,000 years ago, dogs have been used to hunt, both for food and sport. Today, they are also companions, protectors, rescuers, herders, and healers. There are dozens of specific and mixed breeds.

CARNIVORES

The order Carnivora includes about 270 species of mammals divided into 18 families. The name of this group is a bit confusing, though, because not all are strict meat-eaters. Many are omnivores. All share a common ancestry, however. The fossil record shows that the first mammalian carnivores appeared about 65 million years ago. They were small, shrew-like animals that ate whatever they could find, including other small animals. Over time, they evolved into two types: the dog-like and the cat-like carnivores. The dog group is more flexible in its choice of food and includes coyotes, foxes, raccoons, bears, civets, and mongooses. The cat group became specialized at eating meat and includes all species of cats from margays to tigers. Whatever they eat, carnivores are predators. All are capable of preying on other animals—even the bamboo-eating giant panda! One way to tell the two carnivore groups apart is to look at their tracks. Though there are exceptions, the footprints of most dog-like carnivores have oval-shaped footpads and obvious toenail marks. Cat-like carnivores leave behind only the impressions of their round footpads. The reason: Cats have retractable claws, whereas dogs do not.

49

FROM THE FIELD:
JIM BRANDENBURG

ARCTIC WOLF

Most wolves are afraid of humans—if they sense a human's presence, they'll often slink into the forest to avoid confrontation. This is why the highlight of my career as a wildlife photographer was living with arctic wolves (*Canis lupus* ssp. *arctos*) on the treeless tundra of Canada's high Arctic—as long as I could keep up with them, the wolves had nowhere to hide. So I pitched my tent near their den and settled in for the next three years.

I followed the wolves—which are a subspecies of the gray wolf—day and night, and they tolerated my presence. I got to know their personalities and eventually named the seven adults: Buster was the alpha male; then there was Mom, Mid-Back, Shaggy, Lone Ranger, Left Shoulder, and Scruffy—a young male who often babysat the pack's six pups. The adults roamed the tundra, hunting Arctic hares and musk-oxen to bring back to the pups, while the pups played and harassed Scruffy—and I photographed all of it. Eventually, the assignment ended, and it was time for me to fly home. I had followed the pack tirelessly for a very long time, and on my last day I got a wonderful surprise—they followed *me*. Scruffy ran alongside my four-wheeler the entire seven miles (11 km) to the airstrip; and as I boarded the plane, the rest of the pack trotted up and lined the runway. They had come, it seemed, to say goodbye.

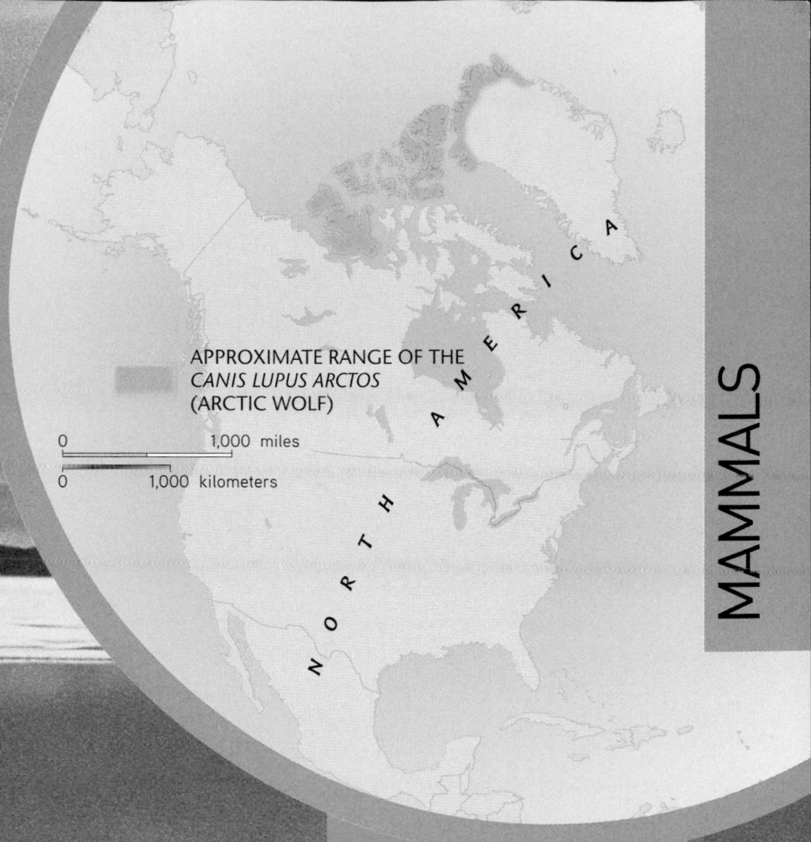

APPROXIMATE RANGE OF THE
CANIS LUPUS ARCTOS
(ARCTIC WOLF)

0   1,000 miles

0   1,000 kilometers

NORTH AMERICA

OBSERVATION **TIPS**

1 Summer is the best time to spot Arctic wolves—their white fur stands out against the brown and green tundra, and you can see them from miles away.

2 When it snows, you can track wolves by following their pawprints!

3 Arctic wolves may sleep for 12 or 16 hours after a hunt, but can take off at a moment's notice—so you have to be ready to go at all times!

4 Be quiet and still, and always respect a wolf's space. If it senses danger, it will often run away.

Jim Brandenburg is an internationally acclaimed wildlife photographer. He has photographed wolves for more than 40 years, including three unforgettable years in the Arctic.

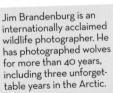

Arctic wolves live in family groups, called packs. The alpha female births four to six pups each year in her den, where they nurse on their mother's milk until they can chew solid food. It takes a team effort to feed growing wolf pups—when pack members return from a hunt, the pups "mob" them, licking the adults' mouths until they regurgitate meat for the pups to eat. The playful pups also practice howling, pin one another to the ground, and play tug-of-war with food scraps!

SKUNKS
AND STINK BADGERS

Skunks and stink badgers are nocturnal omnivores in the Mephitid (meh-FIT-id) family that live in dens or burrows. Most are distinctively colored white and black. These markings act to warn predators, which include coyotes, badgers, foxes, mountain lions, civets, eagles, and owls.

The sickening smell of a skunk is difficult to ignore. Though it may seem the skunk has sprayed its oil everywhere, these animals are very accurate, aiming right between the eyes of any potential predator.

First, the skunk arches its back and stomps its feet as a warning. Unless the attacker leaves, the skunk does a handstand, of sorts, by jumping up with its rear legs off the ground. At the same time, it squeezes the muscles on either side of its anal glands—located right beneath the tail—and squirts a noxious stream of fluid over its head a distance of up to ten feet (3 m).

Skunk life spans range from five to ten years.

What's black and white and strikes fear into the hearts of predators five times its size? A skunk. So why is something smaller than a housecat feared by so many? Its powerful scent, of course: a thick, pungent odor similar to rotten eggs that is enough to send anybody running in the other direction. But did you know that skunks themselves don't actually stink? What you're really smelling is a skunk's number one line of defense. Skunks can shoot an oily mist up to ten feet (3 m). The stinky substance comes from special glands located under their tails. The liquid is composed of compounds that contain sulfur, a naturally occurring chemical that is responsible for the icky stench.

HONEY BADGER ○●●●
MELLIVORA CAPENSIS

RANGE: Africa, Middle East, India

SIZE: 20 to 26 lb (9.1 to 11.8 kg)

DIET: Small reptiles, rodents, birds, insects, carrion, fruit, berries, roots, plants, eggs

The honey badger not only releases a terrible odor from its anal glands when threatened, but it also hisses and rattles its teeth. It is much bigger than either a skunk or stink badger and is a member of the otter family.

PALAWAN STINK BADGER ○●●●
MYDAUS MARCHEI

RANGE: Palawan and Busuanga Islands in the Philippines

SIZE: 5.5 lb (2.5 kg)

DIET: Worms and other soil insects

The Palawan stink badger, a member of the skunk family, is skunk-like when threatened—it smells nasty. It is also a digger. Unlike skunks, it has a much more specific diet—mostly worms—and a narrow range: two islands in the Philippines.

WESTERN SPOTTED SKUNK ○●●●
SPILOGALE GRACILIS

RANGE: Western United States

SIZE: 0.8 to 1.25 lb (0.4 to 0.6 kg)

DIET: Rodents, young rabbits, birds, eggs, insects, fruit

Spotted skunks are good climbers and diggers. As with other members of the skunk family, they rarely spray each other or around their dens. They don't like the smell, either.

STRIPED SKUNK ○○●
MEPHITIS MEPHITIS

RANGE: North America

SIZE: 2.5 to 9 lb (1.3 to 4.1 kg)

DIET: Mice, eggs, insects, berries, carrion

Skunk kits are born with their eyes closed and a thin layer of fur. They stay with their mother for up to one year. Mother skunks will readily spray to protect their young.

OTTERS, WEASELS, AND RELATIVES

O tters, weasels, and their relatives are in the Mustelid (MUS-tell-id) family. This is an extremely successful group of carnivores, with 56 species distributed worldwide. Most are small, with short ears and noses, elongated bodies, long tails, and soft, dense fur. All are expert hunters.

Otters, for example, are just one type of mustelid. There are four species of otters in Asia, one in Europe, two in Africa, two in North America, and four in South America, for a total of 13. Though most live in freshwater rivers, lakes, and wetlands, a few are found in the Pacific Ocean—the sea otter, and the smaller, lesser-known marine otter.

Similarly, there are 17 species of weasels, nine of badgers, and eight of martens, each found in different parts of the world.

Otters and their relatives were once hunted extensively for their fur—many to the point of near extinction. Despite regulations designed to protect them, many species remain at risk from pollution and habitat loss.

Life spans range from 10 to 20 years.

AMERICAN BADGER
TAXIDEA TAXUS

RANGE: Great Plains region of North America

SIZE: 8 to 26 lb (4 to 12 kg)

DIET: Small animals

Digging is what American badgers do best. They dig for their food—small animals that live underground, including pocket gophers, moles, marmots, prairie dogs, kangaroo rats, deer mice, wood rats, hibernating skunks, ground-nesting birds, and insects.

ASIAN SMALL-CLAWED OTTER
AONYX CINEREA

RANGE: Southeast Asia

SIZE: 5 to 11 lb (2.3 to 5.0 kg)

DIET: Clams, mussels, crabs

This is the smallest—and least aquatic—of the otter species. Asian small-clawed otters prefer shallow water and wetlands. They hunt by feel, using their finger-like toes to search in the mud for mollusks and crustaceans.

LEAST WEASEL
MUSTELA NIVALIS

RANGE: Europe, Asia, North America, North Africa

SIZE: 1.3 oz to 3 oz (36.9 to 85.0 g)

DIET: Small rodents, bird eggs, chicks, small reptiles, lizards

Among the carnivores, the least weasel is the smallest. Even so, it is capable of killing a rabbit up to ten times its size. This weasel is also food for other predators, such as foxes, snakes, and owls.

WOLVERINE
GULO GULO

RANGE: Scandinavia, Russia, Siberia, Canada, Alaska, western United States

SIZE: 19 to 66 lb (8.6 to 29.9 kg)

DIET: Reindeer, roe deer, wild sheep, elk or red deer, maral, moose; also berries

The scientific name for the wolverine comes from the word "glutton." This large mustelid is capable of killing and eating anything it can find in the snow. Wolverines have snowshoe-like footpads that help them run down reindeer and moose.

ERMINE
MUSTELA ERMINEA

RANGE: Circumpolar Northern Hemisphere

SIZE: 0.9 oz to 0.25 lb (25.5 g to 0.11 kg)

DIET: Rodents, rabbits, birds, eggs, fish, insects

The ermine has a narrow head and long body typical of its relatives. It, too, is an excellent hunter. The ermine listens for insects and sniffs out rodents. In winter its coat turns white, giving it the advantage of camouflage.

FROM THE FIELD:
NICOLE DUPLAIX

GIANT OTTER

Giant otters (*Pteronura brasiliensis*) are skittish around humans—and rightfully so. Once hunted to near extinction for their luxurious pelts, these river giants are picky about whom they let near. When I first went to Suriname to study giant otters, I paddled up and down dozens of rivers and creeks for months without glimpsing a single otter. I'd hear their screams or coos in the distance, but they were long gone when I paddled by—or so I thought. Eventually, they'd pop their heads out of the water to peer at me, and soon after, they warmed to the sound of my clanking metal canoe. I had been following one otter couple along a stretch of river for months, slowly building their trust. One day I paddled near their campsite as they slept on the riverbank. They raised their heads to check me out and lowered them back down to finish their siesta. I remained silent and still, hoping they would get up. Suddenly, with a snort and a splash, both otters dove into the river and disappeared. I was confused—I hadn't done anything to startle them. But a few minutes later, a fisherman floated by in a perfectly silent canoe—at least I thought it was silent. The otters heard him coming long before he drifted into sight. Once he paddled up the creek and around the bend, the pair popped out of the water and onto the bank again to play. That's when I knew they had fully accepted me into their world.

APPROXIMATE RANGE OF THE
PTERONURA BRASILIENSIS
(GIANT OTTER)

SOUTH

AMERICA

0   1,000 miles

0   1,000 kilometers

OBSERVATION
TIPS

1 Giant otters are active during the day and sleep at night—just like humans!

2 Sandy clearings and dens burrowed into riverbanks are signs you're in giant otter territory.

3 Giant otters live in groups and often snuggle together at their campsites and in their dens.

4 Be respectful and keep your distance. Let giant otters invite you into their world.

Nicole Duplaix is a biologist, photographer, and writer. She was the first biologist to study giant otters in the wild and has been instrumental in protecting their habitat to ensure their survival in the wild.

Giant otters live in tight-knit family groups. They dig dens and strip large areas of vegetation to create campsites along river banks, where they play and lounge. Otter cubs remain with their families for at least two years. The older cubs help keep an eye on the younger ones. While their family is gone fishing, though, curious cubs sneak out of their dens to play, oblivious to the ever-present threat of wandering caiman, anacondas, and jaguars.

CIVETS,
FOSSAS, AND RELATIVES

Civets, fossas, and their relatives in the Viverrid (vie-VER-rid) family resemble cats more than dogs. Most of these species have small heads and long tails, and are just as comfortable high up in the trees as on the ground. Their dietary preferences differ from those of cats, though. They eat insects and some fruit, in addition to rodents, birds, and eggs.

Civets in particular are believed to look—and act—like the earliest carnivores. They are nocturnal, secretive, and solitary omnivores. Based on the fossil record, the civet has changed very little in more than 20 million years!

Life spans are not well known; they are likely to range up to 25 years.

AFRICAN CIVET
CIVETTICTIS CIVETTA

RANGE: Southern and central Africa

SIZE: 24 to 33 lb (10.9 to 15.0 kg)

DIET: Rodents, insects, eggs, carrion, birds; also millipedes and some fruit

Civets have a distinctive masked face, striped fur around their necks, and spotted fur down their backs. Like many carnivores, they communicate by scent marking. The oil in their glands, diluted many times, has been used to make perfume.

BINTURONG
ARCTICTIS BINTURONG

RANGE: India, China, Cambodia, Vietnam, Burma, Thailand, Southeast Asia

SIZE: 20 to 50 lb (9.1 to 22.7 kg)

DIET: Fruit and other plant matter, insects, eggs, birds

The binturong, or Asian bearcat, is the only carnivore with a prehensile tail, which it uses to hang upside down in the trees. Though it eats a variety of foods, this animal prefers figs.

SMALL-SPOTTED GENET
GENETTA GENETTA

RANGE: North Africa, Europe

SIZE: 2.2 to 6.6 lb (1.0 to 3.0 kg)

DIET: Small mammals, birds, reptiles, insects

The genet is so agile it can squeeze through a hole the size of its head. Its tail is also incredibly long—up to one-and-a-half times its body length. Though mostly cat-like, it has a long nose like a dog.

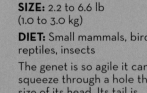
Did you know?
Sharp claws help fossas to climb down trees headfirst.

FOSSA
CRYPTOPROCTA FEROX

RANGE: Madagascar

SIZE: 12 to 26 lb (5.4 to 11.8 kg)

DIET: Mostly lemurs; also rodents, other small animals

Fossas and lemurs, their preferred food, are endemic to the island of Madagascar, meaning they are found only there. With its long tail and semi-retractable claws, this carnivore hunts by day and night, on the ground and in the trees.

MONGOOSES

Most species in the Herpestid (her-pes-tid) family are found in Africa. All are excellent hunters, but meat is not their only food. Many also eat insects, seeds, plants, and fruits. Mongooses are considered a more primitive form of carnivore, like the members of the civet family. The difference is they are more active during the day.

Most mongooses live in small groups. The meerkat, or slender-tailed mongoose, is unusual because of its highly social behavior.

Meerkats live in packs with up to 30 individuals and three family groups. Members of the pack serve a variety of important roles. One is the role of lookout, or sentinel. These meerkats sound an alarm call at the first sight or smell of a predator like an eagle or jackal. Packs also raise their young cooperatively. Older meerkats share food with young ones, and nonbreeding members act as aunts and uncles, helping to take care of young so nursing mothers can take the time to feed.

Most mongooses have life spans of ten years in the wild.

BANDED MONGOOSE
MUNGOS MUNGO

RANGE: Africa, south of the Sahara

SIZE: 2.1 to 3.3 lb (1.0 to 1.5 kg)

DIET: Insects, fruit, snakes, lizards, eggs, frogs

All mongooses have short legs and ears, slender bodies, and long claws for digging up insects and invertebrates. Banded mongooses are known to eat toxic animals, including frogs. They first roll them around in the dirt to remove the poisons.

RING-TAILED MONGOOSE
GALIDIA ELEGANS

RANGE: Madagascar

SIZE: 1.5 to 2 lb (0.7 to 0.9 kg)

DIET: Small animals, eggs, fruit

This mongoose is the most common carnivore on the island of Madagascar. It is also known for its exceptional climbing ability. Ring-tailed mongooses have large footpads for gripping and a bushy tail for balance.

EGYPTIAN MONGOOSE
HERPESTES ICHNEUMON

RANGE: Spain, Portugal, Israel, most of Africa

SIZE: 3.7 to 8.8 lb (1.7 to 4 kg)

DIET: Invertebrates, fish, small vertebrates, fruit, eggs

Eggs are a favorite food of the Egyptian mongoose. To eat one, the mongoose picks it up with its front feet and throws it against a hard surface, either straight down on the ground, or back between its hind legs, as if hiking a football.

DWARF MONGOOSE
HELOGALE PARVULA

RANGE: Ethiopia, Angola, southeastern region of Africa

SIZE: 0.6 lb (0.3 kg)

DIET: Mainly insects; also small vertebrates, eggs, fruit

Dwarf mongooses live in small groups in which only one pair breeds, and females are dominant over males. The breeding female is number one in the social hierarchy; her mate number two; and their youngest female offspring number three.

MEERKAT
SURICATA SURICATTA

RANGE: Southern Africa

SIZE: 1.5 to 1.8 lb (0.7 to 0.8 kg)

DIET: Mainly insects; also small vertebrates, eggs, plants

Female meerkats are capable of giving birth to as many as 12 cubs a year, or 3 cubs every 4 months. When the young leave the burrow at 3 weeks of age, the adults in the group surround them for protection.

RACCOONS,
RED PANDAS, AND RELATIVES

Raccoons, kinkajous, coatis, cacomistles, and olingos are members of the raccoon family. All are omnivores and most have banded tails, facial markings, or a bandit-like mask. Most are also smaller animals. The exception is the North American raccoon, which can weigh up to 23 pounds (11 kg). This species is also known for its dexterous front paws, which it uses like hands, and excellent sense of touch.

The raccoon family is most closely related to the bear family—both are descendants of the dog-like carnivore group. The same is true for the red panda. But exactly which family it belongs to is a point of debate. Some biologists place red pandas in the raccoon family, others place them in the bear family, and still others place them in their own family. Red pandas are also omnivores, though they prefer bamboo leaves and shoots.

Most raccoons and their relatives have short lives in the wild—from five to ten years.

RED PANDA
AILURUS FULGENS

RANGE: Himalaya in Asia

SIZE: 8 to 14 lb (3.6 to 6.4 kg)

DIET: Grasses, roots, fruit, acorns, berries, blossoms, bamboo leaves, small leaves of other plants, bird eggs

Bamboo is a major part of the red panda's diet. Like the giant panda, this relative of the raccoon has an extra wrist bone, which it uses to grasp the bamboo stalk while it fills its mouth with leaves.

NORTHERN RACCOON
PROCYON LOTOR

RANGE: North America and northern South America

SIZE: 4 to 23 lb (1.8 to 10.4 kg)

DIET: Frogs, fish, small land animals, birds, turtle eggs, fruit, corn, nuts, seeds

Raccoons use their front feet like hands. They pick up their food to eat, washing it first whenever possible. They feel for insects in tree trunks, eggs in nests, and crayfish in mud. They can even pry the lid off a garbage can.

Did you know? Kinkajous can turn their feet backward to run in any direction.

SOUTH AMERICAN COATIMUNDI
NASUA NASUA

RANGE: Colombia, Venezuela, Uruguay, northern Argentina

SIZE: 6.6 to 13.2 lb (3 to 6 kg)

DIET: Fruit, scorpions, centipedes, eggs, beetle larvae, termites, lizards, spiders, ants, small mammals, rodents, carrion

Coatis (kuh-WAH-teez) hunt with their long noses held close to the ground. They prefer insects to other food. Males are solitary, but females, their young, and juvenile males travel together in groups of up to 20.

KINKAJOU
POTUS FALVUS

RANGE: Mexico to Brazil

SIZE: 4.4 to 10 lb (2 to 4.6 kg)

DIET: Fruit, insects, nectar, flowers

Kinkajous are sometimes mistaken for monkeys, even though they are active only at night. They are small, furry animals with prehensile tails, and they pluck fruit from trees with their tiny hands. They even live in small groups and groom one another.

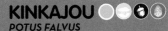

HYENAS AND AARDWOLVES

There are four species in the hyena family—three types of hyena and the aardwolf. Though these animals at first appear dog-like, they are more closely related to cats, civets, and mongooses. Mostly, they are strange-looking.

The front legs of a hyena are so long compared to the back ones that the animal looks like it is walking uphill. Hyenas also have very round faces because of their massive chewing muscles. Combined with big ears, they look almost friendly. On the contrary, these are aggressive animals, capable of killing live prey or scavenging dead carcasses. Weirdest of all, male and female hyenas are indistinguishable.

The aardwolf is a small version of a striped hyena, except it eats only termites. It cannot tear open a termite mound on its own, however. Instead, it either wanders around looking for termites, or it follows and scavenges after the aardvark, a totally unrelated species that can dig into termite mounds.

Life spans are up to 25 years.

AARDWOLF
PROTELES CRISTATA

RANGE: Africa

SIZE: 17 to 31 lb (7.7 to 14.1 kg)

DIET: Termites

Aardwolves eat only a particular type of termite—a species that nests in dried grass. As a result, both predator and prey are found only in certain areas. One aardwolf requires about 1.5 square miles (389 ha) of territory.

SPOTTED HYENA
CROCUTA CROCUTA

RANGE: Sub-Saharan Africa

SIZE: 100 to 175 lb (45.5 to 79.4 kg)

DIET: A variety of hoofed mammals, including wildebeest, zebras, gazelles, impalas; also porcupines, jackals, ostrich eggs, bat-eared foxes, termites

Spotted hyena cubs are born covered in black fur and with their eyes open. Newborns of the same sex are capable of fighting with one another—until one dies. Yet the cubs stay with their mother for up to three years.

STRIPED HYENA
HYAENA HYAENA

RANGE: North and eastern Africa, Middle East, Asia

SIZE: 55 to 99 lb (24.9 to 44.9 kg)

DIET: Carrion and human refuse; also fruit, insects, small animals such as hares, rodents, reptiles, birds

The striped hyena is tough enough to steal a fresh kill from a lion or cheetah. But it will not even try to defend its meal from a spotted hyena. Wherever they are found together, striped hyenas act submissively toward their larger relative.

Did you know? Aardwolves can consume up to 300,000 termites in one night.

BEARS

The fossil record for the Ursid (ER-sid), or bear, family is one of the most complete for all carnivores. It shows that the eight species alive today are the descendants of a 30-million-year-old bear-like animal that resembled a cross between a dog and a raccoon.

Much has changed since then! All modern bears are larger, stocky animals with nonretractable claws, shaggy fur, an excellent sense of smell, and short tails. They are solitary, except for mothers with cubs, and generally diurnal. During the time of year when food is scarce, most bears have an effective survival solution: sleep.

All bears are considered omnivores—and all love the taste of honey—yet each species has a preferred diet. Polar bears are carnivores, for example, preferring to eat seals. American black bears prefer berries and insect larvae whenever they are available. Giant pandas prefer bamboo, and sloth bears prefer ants and termites.

Bears are generally long-living, with life spans of up to 25 years in the wild and 50 in captivity.

BROWN BEAR
URSUS ARCTOS

RANGE: North America, Siberia, Europe

SIZE: 176 to 1,320 lb (79.8 to 603.3 kg)

DIET: Fruit, nuts, roots, seaweed, grasses, moss, bulbs, insects, fish, small vertebrates, carrion, mice, ground squirrels, marmots

Some brown bears eat more salmon than others. Those found along the coast of Alaska eat the most—and are the largest. Those found in the Rocky Mountains, also known as grizzly bears, are smaller, but not by much!

SLOTH BEAR
MELURSUS URSINUS

RANGE: India, Sri Lanka, Bangladesh, Nepal, Bhutan

SIZE: 121 to 308 lb (54.9 to 139.7 kg)

DIET: Insects; also leaves, honey, flowers, fruit

The name given to these bears is misleading. They are very fast runners—and eaters. A sloth bear can tear a hole in a termite mound, push its nose inside, and inhale a full meal in just a few seconds.

Did you know?
A sloth bear is the only bear that carries its babies on its back.

WINTER DORMANCY

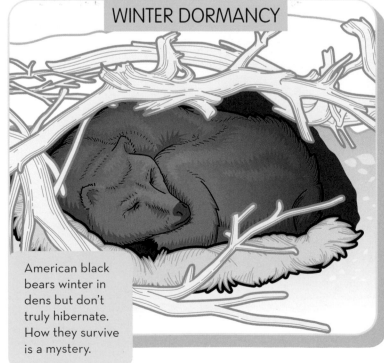

American black bears winter in dens but don't truly hibernate. How they survive is a mystery.

ASIATIC BLACK BEAR
URSUS THIBETANUS

RANGE: Asia

SIZE: 143 to 330 lb
(64.9 to 149.7 kg)

DIET: Mainly plant matter;
also fruit, nuts, insect larvae,
ants; may also prey on cattle,
sheep, goats

These bears are known for their
opportunistic eating habits.
Mostly they are vegetarians, but
they will also eat small animals
and carrion—typically left over
from a tiger's kill. They are the
main prey of the Siberian tiger.

POLAR BEAR
URSUS MARITIMUS

RANGE: Circumpolar: Alaska,
Greenland, Russia, Iceland

SIZE: 330 to 1,760 lb
(149.7 to 708.3 kg)

DIET: Seals, walruses, seabirds
and their eggs, small mammals,
fish

Female polar bears breed in
the spring and give birth in
the fall, but only if they have
not lost too much weight
over the summer. This species
normally builds up its fat stores
during winter by hunting ringed
seals from the pack ice. Global
warming threatens their
life cycle.

GIANT PANDA
AILUROPODA MELANOLEUCA

RANGE: Sichuan, China

SIZE: 176 to 275 lb
(79.8 to 124.7 kg)

DIET: Bamboo

Giant pandas eat only
bamboo. To survive on
such a high-fiber, low-
calorie diet, pandas spend
all day eating. They have
massive chewing muscles—
and an appealing round
face—as a result.

SUN BEAR
HELARCTOS MALAYANUS

RANGE: Nepal, China,
Myanmar, Malay Peninsula

SIZE: 59.4 to 143 lb
(26.9 to 64.9 kg)

DIET: Bees, termites, earthworms; also fruit

This is the smallest member
of the Ursid family. Sun
bears have long tongues to
pull termites and bees out
of their nests and honey
from hives. They also will
scavenge garbage and raid
crops like bananas.

LARGE CATS

The "large cats" are the lion, tiger, leopard, jaguar, clouded leopard, and snow leopard. Based on their skull and voice box anatomy, the first four are grouped together in the same genus, *Panthera,* and are known as the "roaring" or "great" cats.

Though there are just six species of large cats, there seem to be many more! This is because there are variations, or subspecies, of each. These include Asiatic and African lions; Bengal, Sumatran, and Siberian tigers; and nine subspecies of leopards found across Asia, Europe, and Africa.

Cats are not the only animals that exist as subspecies. Geographic variation is common in the animal kingdom. Each subspecies is given a three-part name. The first two parts identify the species (genus species). The third part is specific to the subspecies. For example, all leopards are *Panthera pardus (P.p.).* The subspecies in Kenya is called *P.p. pardus,* whereas the one in the Russian Far East, Korea, and northeast China is *P.p. orientalis.*

AFRICAN LION
PANTHERA LEO

RANGE: Sub-Saharan Africa

SIZE: 275 to 600 lb (124.7 to 272.2 kg)

DIET: Gazelles, antelopes, zebras, buffalos; also smaller animals, birds

Lions are by far the most social species of cat. They live in family groups, or prides. The females are related and will often nurse each other's cubs. Lions have two unique features: a tufted tail and, in the males, a mane.

JAGUAR
PANTHERA ONCA

RANGE: Warmer regions of North and South America

SIZE: 150 to 300 lb (68.0 to 136.1 kg)

DIET: Peccaries, tapirs, deer; also caimans, turtles, snakes, porcupines, capybaras, fish, large birds

Jaguars are excellent swimmers. They also depend on water to keep cool. Like leopards, they have a genetic color mutation known as melanism. The gene is dominant, which means black phase jaguars, or black panthers, are relatively common.

CLOUDED LEOPARD
NEOFELIS NEBULOSA

RANGE: South of Himalaya in Nepal, Bhutan, Myanmar, India, southern China, Taiwan

SIZE: 24 to 50 lb (11 to 23 kg)

DIET: Birds, fish, monkeys, deer, rodents

Clouded leopards are very secretive. They spend much of their time in trees, where they hunt monkeys and birds. They have the greatest size difference between sexes among cat species—males are twice the size of females.

SNOW LEOPARD
UNCIA UNCIA

RANGE: Parts of Nepal, Mongolia, Afghanistan, Pakistan, China

SIZE: 55 to 165 lb (24.9 to 74.8 kg)

DIET: Wild boar, wild sheep, mice, deer, hares, marmots, other small mammals; birds; sometimes domestic livestock

Snow leopards live in cold, mountainous areas, where they hunt blue sheep, ibex, rodents, and birds. To keep warm, they curl up underneath their long, furry tail. Unlike the other large cats, snow leopards have gray-green instead of yellow-gold eyes.

FELIDS

The 36 species in the cat, or Felid (FEE-lid), family are remarkably similar. All have excellent vision, hearing, and sense of smell. They are ambush hunters with sharp retractable claws, powerful jaws, and teeth specialized for grabbing and tearing meat.

Cats are strong, agile predators. They either hide and wait for their prey, or walk silently behind on padded feet, pouncing when the time is right. They are also obligate carnivores. The definition is not simply that they eat only meat. Cats must also eat skin and bones to get the nutrition they need.

Except for lions, cats are nocturnal, secretive, and solitary. They hunt at night and interact with each other only to defend territory or breed. Even so, cats communicate in plenty of other ways—through scent and scratch marks.

Not every species of cat is the same, of course. They differ in size and fur color. Whether or not they can roar depends on their anatomy. All can purr, but only lions, tigers, leopards, and jaguars can roar.

Cat life spans range from 15 to 25 years.

SIBERIAN TIGER
PANTHERA TIGRIS ALTAICA

RANGE: East Asia, in Russia, China, North Korea

SIZE: 200 to 710 lb (90.7 to 322.1 kg)

DIET: Hoofed animals

This tiger subspecies is the largest cat. Siberian tigers also have the longest canine teeth—up to four inches (10 cm)—and can eat up to 40 pounds (18 kg) of meat at one meal.

LEOPARD
PANTHERA PARDUS

RANGE: Africa, Europe, Asia

SIZE: 35 to 145 lb (16 to 66 kg)

DIET: Small antelopes, gazelles, deer, pigs, primates, domestic livestock; also birds, reptiles, rodents, arthropods, carrion

Asiatic and African leopards are similar, apart from their fur. In the rain forests of Asia, these cats are more likely to be melanistic, or black—a color mutation caused by a recessive gene that allows better camouflage. In the right light, their rosettes, or spots, are still visible.

BENGAL TIGER
PANTHERA TIGRIS TIGRIS

RANGE: Myanmar, Bangladesh, India, Nepal, Bhutan

SIZE: 200 to 570 lb (90.7 to 258.5 kg)

DIET: Hoofed animals

Bengal tigers socialize through scent markings and scratch marks. One male's territory may overlap that of one to seven females. These cats use their body weight to knock their prey to the ground before going for the neck.

AN ANIMAL'S FUR can serve multiple purposes. The tawny coat of the African lion *(Panthera leo)* helps this wild cat blend in with its background as it travels through a dry riverbed in Africa. Meanwhile, its majestic mane—common only to males—may intimidate enemies.

SMALL AND MEDIUM CATS

There are 30 species of small and medium cats.

The domestic cat is by far the most successful species in this group. Many of the others, especially the smallest cats, are threatened with extinction due to habitat loss. These are the rusty-spotted cat (India and Sri Lanka), the black-footed cat (Africa), the kod kod (Chile and Argentina), the oncilla (South America), and the flat-headed cat (Asia).

Cats the next size up include the African golden cat and marbled cat from Southeast Asia; the sand cat from northern Africa and southern Asia; and, from South America, the Andean cat, Geoffrey's cat, and sand margay.

The medium-size cats range in size from wild cats found in parts of Europe, Africa, and Asia to cheetahs (Africa) and mountain lions (North and South America). The diversity in this group includes five species found in the Americas (ocelots, jaguarundis, caracals, bobcats, and the Canada lynx), three in Asia (fishing cats, Asiatic golden cats, and marbled cats), two in Africa (African golden cats and servals), and two in Europe (the Spanish and Eurasian lynx). The largest of the medium cats are the cheetah and the mountain lion.

OCELOT
LEOPARDUS PARDALIS

RANGE: Southeastern United States to south-central South America

SIZE: 18 to 35 lb (8.2 to 15.9 kg)

DIET: Mostly small rodents, reptiles, medium-size mammals, birds, crustaceans, fish

These medium-size cats have two black stripes on their cheeks, a white spot on the backs of their ears, and a ringed tail. As with other striped and spotted cats, individual ocelots can be identified by their unique markings.

FISHING CAT
PRIONAILURUS VIVERRINUS

RANGE: India, Sri Lanka, Nepal, Bangladesh, Vietnam, Thailand, Java, Sumatra

SIZE: 13 to 26 lb (5.9 to 11.8 kg)

DIET: Mostly fish and shellfish

When hungry, these cats go fishing. If the water is shallow, they wade in. In deeper water, they swim or dive in after their prey. Fishing cats also hunt from the water's edge, using their sharp claws like fishhooks.

CANADA LYNX
LYNX CANADENSIS

RANGE: Canada, Alaska, northwestern United States

SIZE: 9.5 to 38 lb (4.3 to 17.2 kg)

DIET: Mainly snowshoe hares; also rodents, birds, fish

In areas where Canada lynx prefer snowshoe hares to any other prey the hare population gradually declines, followed by the lynx population. With fewer lynx around, the hare population increases again. This cycle repeats every nine to ten years.

SERVAL ◐◐◑
LEPTAILURUS SERVAL

RANGE: Mainly southern Africa

SIZE: 20 to 40 lb (9.1 to 18.1 kg)

DIET: Rats, mice, shrews, birds, insects, frogs, lizards

Servals listen for their next meal using their huge ears. As soon as this long-legged cat picks up the sound of a rodent rustling in the grass, it moves closer. Then it pounces—from up to 12 feet (3.7 m) away.

HERE KITTY, KITTY!

Although the origin of many animal species is a bit fuzzy, most scientists agree that today's domestic cat descended from a Middle Eastern wildcat, *Felis sylvestris*, which means "cat of the woods." Dogs were domesticated well before cats because humans were a society of hunters and tamed gray wolves (the ancestor of domestic dogs) to be their hunting companions. It wasn't until people began to settle down and live together in communities, farm the fields, and construct mills to store crops that cats became necessary. Wild cats began to wander into town, attracted by the mice and small prey lured by silos and mills chock full of grain. Humans liked this natural pest control and welcomed them. As time went on, people chose cats with more docile personalities to live on their farms, and as generations had kittens and grandkittens, the "wild" was eventually bred out completely.

MARGAY ◐◑
LEOPARDUS WIEDII

RANGE: Northern Mexico to Uruguay and northern Argentina

SIZE: 5.5 to 9 lb (2.5 to 4.1 kg)

DIET: Mammals, birds and their eggs, reptiles, amphibians, arthropods, fruit

Margays are close relatives of the ocelot. They look alike—though the margay is smaller—and they hunt the same prey and live in the same areas. What distinguishes them is their behavior. Margays are aboreal and diurnal. Ocelots are terrestrial and nocturnal.

BOBCAT ◯◐◑
LYNX RUFUS

RANGE: North America

SIZE: 8 to 33 lb (3.6 to 15.0 kg)

DIET: Mainly small mammals, such as rabbits and rodents; also small ungulates, large ground birds, reptiles

Throughout its range, the fur color and markings of the bobcat vary. For example, bobcats living in northern forests have darker coats than those living in southern deserts. Each distinct form is considered a subspecies.

CHEETAH ◯◐◑
ACINONYX JUBATUS

RANGE: Sub-Saharan Africa and northern Iran

SIZE: 34.0 to 160 lb (15.4 to 72.6 kg)

DIET: Hares, jackals, small antelopes, gazelles

The cheetah runs faster than any other animal for a variety of reasons. Its nose is one of them. Compared to other cats, cheetahs have wider nostrils and larger nasal passages. Both allow it to take in more oxygen with each running breath.

FROM THE FIELD:

BEVERLY AND DERECK JOUBERT

LEOPARD

Leopards *(Panthera pardus)* are silent and secretive animals—the ghosts of the forest. Their yellowish fur and black spots camouflage their bodies as they slink through the shadows and slither through the grass, eluding predators and surprising their prey. And they almost always avoid humans. That's why the highlight of our lives began the day we met a little leopard cub in the Okavango Delta, in Botswana. She was just eight days old when we spotted her, and we decided to spend the next four years watching her grow up.

Three months later, a horrible storm broke out while the cub's mother was off hunting. The sky turned black, rain pounded the ground, and lightning crackled all around us. Dereck and I huddled together in our jeep, but on the ground, the cub shivered with fear. It was her first storm. Suddenly, a bolt of lightning struck a nearby tree. There was a deafening crash, leaves showered us, and a pungent smell filled the air. We thought the cub would run away—but she came charging out of the thicket, straight toward us, and sat down next to Dereck's feet! After that, we called her Legadema, which means "light from the sky," or "lightning."

EUROPE

ASIA

AFRICA

The Jouberts' base camps

APPROXIMATE RANGE
OF THE *PANTHERA PARDUS*
(LEOPARD)

0   1,000 miles

0   1,000 kilometers

OBSERVATION
TIPS

1 Leopards are sneaky. You usually have to follow their paw prints to find them!

2 To see leopards behaving naturally, you have to watch for a long time—even at night, which is usually when they hunt.

3 Watch nature unfold from a respectable distance, and never interfere.

4 Stay alert! There are many other wild—and dangerous—animals in the area.

Beverly and Dereck Joubert have spent more than 25 years studying, filming, and photographing animals all over Africa, dedicating their lives to understanding and conserving Earth's magnificent places and creatures. This multi-award-winning team lives in the wild surrounded by the animals they love.

Leopard cubs have a lot to learn about living in the wild. They're easy targets for hungry predators, so they stay with their mothers for about two years while they figure out where the best hiding spots are, which trees are easiest to climb, and how to hunt. If a predator does approach, the cub can be carried to safety. But life in the forest isn't always serious—there's plenty of time to play, too!

69

SEALS, SEA LIONS, AND FURRED SEALS

There are three families of carnivores that spend most of their time in salt water. These are the eared seals, or otarids; the true seals, or phocids; and walruses. Together, these animals are often called pinnipeds (PIN-uh-pedz), which means "fin-footed" in Latin. All hunt a variety of marine prey, including fish, mollusks, and, in some cases, each other. They are also highly social during the breeding and calving seasons, when they gather in large, often noisy herds on beaches and rocky areas.

Seals, sea lions, and walruses have streamlined bodies for swimming, and large eyes so they can see their prey underwater. Their lungs are reinforced with cartilage to withstand the pressure changes when they dive. To save energy, their heart rate also goes down during a dive.

The eared seals have dog-like earflaps. These are the sea lions and their close relatives, the furred seals. In water, they swim with their front flippers. On land, they pull their rear flippers up and under their bodies and use them like feet. True seals, by comparison, do not have earflaps and cannot use their rear flippers for walking. They move like inch worms on dry land. True seals are also excellent divers and can hold their breath for up to two hours.

Life spans for seals, sea lions, furred seals, and walruses range from 15 to 30 years.

BROWN FUR SEAL
ARCTOCEPHALUS PUSILLUS

RANGE: Off coasts of Africa and Australia

SIZE: 79 to 792 lb (36 to 360 kg)

DIET: Mostly fish; also crustaceans, squid, octopus

Male pinnipeds often weigh hundreds of pounds more than females of the same species. The northern fur seal is one example. The female (shown here) weighs 80 to 220 pounds (36 to 110 kg). The male weighs 440 to 790 pounds (200 to 360 kg).

GALÁPAGOS SEA LION
ZALOPHUS WOLLEBAEKI

RANGE: Galápagos Islands

SIZE: 110.1 to 550.7 lb (50 to 250 kg)

DIET: Fish, octopus, crustaceans, squid

When not in the water hunting, sea lions "haul out" on dry land. Female sea lions often sunbathe together on the beach. The lead male patrols the beach to fight off competitors. When he can, he rests in the shade under a tree or rock cliff.

SOUTHERN ELEPHANT SEAL
MIROUNGA LEONINA

RANGE: Antarctica, Australia, Argentina, New Zealand, South Africa, South Sandwich and South Georgia Islands

SIZE: 661 to 8,811 lb (300 to 4,000 kg)

DIET: Sharks, fish, squid, shrimp, crabs

Male southern elephant seals are larger than any other carnivore. Females are much smaller. Both have short front flippers for steering and webbed back flippers for propelling forward.

Did you know? Mother and baby fur seals recognize each other by their calls.

BEARDED SEAL ◯◯
ERIGNATHUS BARBATUS

RANGE: Arctic Ocean

SIZE: 440 to 950 lb
(199.6 to 430.9 kg)

DIET: Crustaceans and
mollusks

Bearded seals prefer
shallow arctic waters with
plenty of fish—and floating
ice. This species has no
need for dry land. Instead,
it climbs onto a piece of
ice and drifts with it, migrating north in winter and south
in summer.

LEOPARD SEAL ◯◯
HYDRURGA LEPTONYX

RANGE: Antarctic coast
and islands, coasts of South
Africa and southern Australia,
Tasmania, New Zealand, Cook
Islands, South America

SIZE: 440 to 1,300 lb
(199.6 to 589.7 kg)

DIET: Krill; other seals,
especially fur and crabeater;
penguins; also squid, fish

Leopard seals are top predators in the Antarctic. About a
third of their diet is krill, which
they filter using special molars.
Other seals make up another
third. The rest is penguins,
fish, and squid.

NORTHERN ◯◯◯
ELEPHANT SEAL
MIROUNGA ANGUISTIROSTRIS

RANGE: Off coast of North
America, from Gulf of Alaska
to Baja California, Mexico

SIZE: 1,300 to 5,000 lb
(600 to 2,300 kg)

DIET: Squid, octopus, fish,
small sharks, skates

Male elephant seals have a
large nose called a proboscis.
By filling it with air, they can
make loud calls that establish
breeding rights. These seals can
dive as deep as a mile (1500 m)
and stay down for more than
an hour.

WALRUSES

The walrus is more like a seal than a sea lion except that it can
bend its back flippers forward. It is found only in arctic waters,
where it uses its whiskers and snout to find food.

The modified canine teeth of the walrus are used in fighting
with other males. Though this species can hold its breath, the
longest it can stay underwater is ten minutes. Walruses tend to stay
near the shoreline, as they are a favorite food of the killer whale.

Did you know?

Walruses use their large ivory tusks to haul
their huge bodies out of the water onto
the ice and to make breathing holes in the
ice. Males also use their tusks to fight.

WALRUS ◯◯◯
ODOBENUS ROSMARUS

RANGE: The Arctic

SIZE: 880 to 3,740 lb
(399.2 to 1,696.4 kg)

DIET: Bottom-living invertebrates, such as mollusks,
mussels, crustaceans; some
fish, seals

Walruses are the most social
marine carnivores. Thousands
often haul out together,
though males and females
only mix during the breeding
season. To attract females,
males do more than display
their tusks: They sing, click,
cluck, bellow, and whistle.

ELEPHANTS

Imagine a time when there were dozens of elephant-like animals roaming across Africa, each with stout legs, oversized upper lips, and special incisors made of ivory, known as tusks. This was the case in the Pleistocene period two million years ago. These giant, plant-eating animals belonged to a group known as the *Proboscids* (pro-BOS-skids), named after the Latin word for "trunk."

Today, only three species of elephants remain. They are now the largest land mammals, weighing up to 13,230 pounds (6,000 kg).

Both Asian and African elephants are highly social. Herds consist of females and their young led by the oldest female, or matriarch. Males, known as bulls, live alone or in bachelor groups, interacting with the herd only to breed. They are also highly intelligent. Elephants communicate by making sounds that range from low-frequency rumbles to high-pitched trumpet calls. When a member of the herd is injured or trapped, others will work together to help. Elephants also mourn their dead.

Elephants can live up to 70 years. Unfortunately, many populations in Africa and Asia are endangered from habitat loss and illegal hunting, or poaching, for their ivory tusks.

ASIAN ELEPHANT
ELEPHAS MAXIMUS

RANGE: India and Southeast Asia

SIZE: 6,600 to 11,000 lb (2,993.7 to 4,989.5 kg)

DIET: Grasses, leaves, shoots, fruit

Elephants are extremely agile. They place one foot in front of the other, leaving behind a remarkably narrow trail. In the forests where they live, Asian elephants easily climb up and down muddy, slippery slopes.

AFRICAN SAVANNA ELEPHANT
LOXODONTA AFRICANA

RANGE: Sub-Saharan Africa

SIZE: 7,900 to 13,200 lb (3,583.4 to 5,987.5 kg)

DIET: Leaves, shoots, twigs, roots, fruit

Savanna elephants are known for their incredibly large herds and for the great distances they travel in search of water. Crop damage often results, causing conflict with people. Fences made of active beehives help keep elephants away from crops.

AFRICAN FOREST ELEPHANT
LOXODONTA CYCLOTIS

RANGE: West and central Africa

SIZE: 6,000 to 13,200 lb (2,700 to 6000 kg)

DIET: Fruit, leaves, bark, twigs of rain forest trees

Forest elephants are smaller than savanna elephants. They have four toes on their front feet instead of five, and three on the back instead of four. They travel in small family groups of two to eight.

ELEPHANT GROWTH

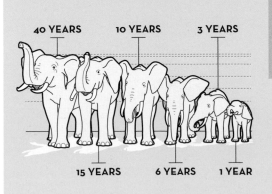

40 YEARS   10 YEARS   3 YEARS

15 YEARS   6 YEARS   1 YEAR

The oldest elephants in a herd are the largest. Breeding starts in the early teens. Births occur every three to five years.

SEA COWS

Dugongs and manatees are often called sea cows. They are large, slow-moving, vegetarian marine mammals. They have large, rounded noses, nostrils with flaps they can close while underwater, and fleshy lips for grazing on sea grasses and other plants. Like other aquatic mammals, they were once a terrestrial species. They must swim up to the water's surface to take a breath of air.

Before boats and ships were common in shallow areas, dugongs and manatees were seen only rarely. Sailors who spotted them thought they were mermaids, mythical half woman–half fish sea creatures. The name Sirenia is based on this myth. Siren is another name for mermaid.

Sea cows eat a lot—up to a quarter of their body weight in plant material each day. The gas produced by their digestive systems makes them very buoyant. To help them stay submerged, their bones, especially the ones in their flipper-like front limbs, are very dense.

Sadly, all four species are threatened by hunting and injury from boat propellers. The result is that there are fewer sea cows left on Earth compared to any other single group of mammal. They can live up to 70 years.

DUGONG ◯◯
DUGONG DUGON

RANGE: Warm coastal waters in the Indo-Pacific region

SIZE: 880 lb (399.2 kg)

DIET: Seaweed and sea grasses

Dugongs are marine sea cows once found along the coasts of at least 48 countries. They have a single pair of tusk-like incisors and a sharply angled snout. Based on their strange anatomy, dugongs are considered relatives of hyraxes, elephants, and hoofed animals.

WEST INDIAN MANATEE ◯◯◯
TRICHECHUS MANATUS

RANGE: Southeastern United States; Caribbean; east coast Central America; northern coast South America

SIZE: 440 to 3,300 lb (200 to 1,500 kg)

DIET: Water lettuce and water hyacinths

West Indian manatees reproduce very slowly. Females are at least seven years old before they have their first calf. Their gestation period is 12 to 14 months, and they usually have only one baby, though twins are possible.

COWS, SHEEP, AND GOATS

Cows, sheep, and goats are some of the best known hoofed animals. These species—and their relatives—are known as ruminants. All have an even number of toes and a series of four digestive chambers, the largest of which is known as the rumen.

Ruminants are experts at digesting plants that are very high in fiber, or cellulose. To start the process, they chew their food twice. A cow that is chewing its cud, for example, is breaking up its meal into tiny bits and mixing it with saliva. This process is called rumination.

Next, the food moves into the rumen, which is filled with partially digested plant material and millions of microbial organisms like protozoa and bacteria. These microbes eat the plant fiber and release energy—fat, glucose, and methane gas. This type of digestion is called fermentation.

From the rumen, the plant material passes into a much smaller chamber called the reticulum, where it is filtered. Larger pieces stay in the rumen to be re-chewed. Smaller pieces pass into the third chamber, the omasum, where water and other nutrients are absorbed. Only then does the food pass into the true stomach, or fourth chamber, called the abomasum. From there, digestion proceeds much the way it does in nonruminant mammals.

Many species of cows, sheep, and goats have been domesticated and bred on farms worldwide for their meat, milk, wool, and leather. Others are kept as pets. Their life spans range up to 30 years.

TAKIN ○ ⦿⦿
BUDORCAS TAXICOLOR

RANGE: Eastern Himalaya in Asia

SIZE: 330 to 880 lb (150 to 400 kg)

DIET: Leaves, grasses, herbs

Takin look as though they are part cow, part goat, and part antelope. They live high in the mountains during the summer, and in very large herds. During winter, they break into smaller groups and move down to the forested valleys.

AMERICAN BISON ○○
BISON BISON

RANGE: Protected areas of the western U.S. and Canada (before near extinction: range was North America, from Alaska to northern Mexico)

SIZE: 700 to 1,980 lb (317.5 to 898.1 kg)

DIET: Mostly grasses; also other vegetation such as sagebrush

There were once 60 million American bison. Their presence—they grazed in large herds—helped to maintain the prairie ecosystem. They were hunted to near extinction, however, by 1890; today, they are found only in protected areas.

HOOFED MAMMALS

The hoofed mammals are the most successful group of herbivores. There are 244 species found all over the world.

One reason for their success is their ability to digest cellulose, the fiber found in grass. Another is their ability to escape predators. Not only do they have excellent vision and an acute sense of smell, but they are also strong and fast runners. Most hoofed mammals also have either antlers or horns. These are used for defense as well as for breeding displays.

Depending on the species, hoofed mammals stand on one, two, three, or four elongated toe bones. In other words, they bear weight on their tiptoes! They have equally long tendons running down the backs of their legs that connect to the hoof. These give the animals a spring in their step and the power to run and kick.

The hoofed animals that stand on an even number of toes are divided into three groups: ruminants (cows, sheep, goats, deer, antelopes, giraffes), hippos and pigs, and camels and llamas.

The odd-toed hoofed mammals are divided into two groups: horses and relatives, and rhinos and tapirs.

BIGHORN SHEEP
OVIS CANADENSIS

RANGE: Rocky Mountains of North America from southern Canada to Colorado, U.S.A., deserts from Nevada, U.S.A., to Mexico

SIZE: 116.6 to 279.4 lb (52.9 to 126.7 kg)

DIET: Grasses, herbs, sedges, forbs

Bighorn sheep live only in drier deserts or mountainous areas. Their small hooves are adapted to fit the narrow ledges between rocks, but they are too blunt to claw through snow to find food.

DOMESTIC MOUFLON SHEEP
OVIS ARIES

RANGE: Worldwide

SIZE: 44 to 440 lb (20 to 200 kg)

DIET: Mainly grasses; also a wide variety of hays and oats

Mouflon sheep were first domesticated about 10,000 years ago in the Middle East and Central Asia. Since then, they have been bred for their meat, hide, milk, and wool. With more than 200 breeds, domestic sheep now outnumber all other species of sheep.

NUBIAN IBEX
CAPRA NUBIANA

RANGE: Northern Africa and Middle East

SIZE: 55 to 154 lb (24.9 to 69.9 kg)

DIET: Herbs, shrubs, tree foliage, buds, fruit, grasses

Nubian ibex have a special strategy for protecting their young from predators. They lead them into a nursery of sorts—a walled-in area, like a canyon. The mothers leave the nursery to graze, returning often to nurse their young.

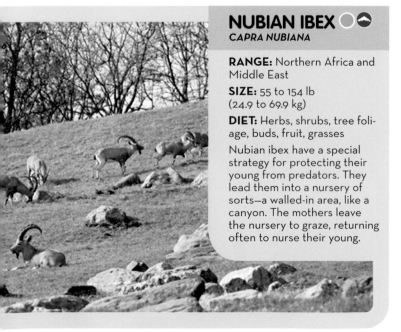

MOUNTAIN GOAT
OREAMNOS AMERICANUS

RANGE: Northern Rocky Mountains in North America

SIZE: 125 to 180 lb (57 to 82 kg)

DIET: Grasses, woody plants, mosses, lichens, herbs

Mountain goats have oval hooves with rubber-like soles that help them grip rocks. Each year, they migrate—vertically. At the end of winter, they shed their thick coats and climb up to 16,000 feet (4,877 m). By summer, they are back down at 3,200 feet (975 m).

DOMESTIC COW
BOS TAURUS

RANGE: Worldwide

SIZE: 300 to 3,000 lb (136.1 to 1,360.8 kg)

DIET: Grasses and stems

Cows were domesticated 10,000 years ago in India, the Middle East, and North Africa. Today there are more than 800 breeds. Cows are used for plowing and moving heavy loads, and as sources of meat, milk, cheese, glue, soap, leather, and fertilizer.

YAK
BOS GRUNNIENS

RANGE: Asia's Tibetan Plateau

SIZE: 660 to 2,200 lb (299.4 to 997.9 kg)

DIET: Low-lying grasses and grass-like plants

Wild yaks live at very high elevations, up to 17,700 feet (5,395 m). Domesticated yaks are smaller, but equally well adapted to the altitude. For thousands of years, yaks have been used as pack animals as well as sources of meat, milk, cheese, clothing, blankets, and tents.

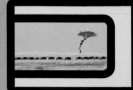

ANTELOPES AND PRONGHORNS

Most of the 91 species of antelopes are found in the grasslands of Africa. A few—such as the Saiga and Tibetan antelopes—live in Asia. The pronghorn is a closely related species found only in North America.

All are browsers, grazers, or both. This explains their diversity. There may be several species of antelopes in one area, but each specializes on a different part of the available plants. Gerenuks, for example, browse on tree leaves by standing on their hind legs. Thomson's gazelles graze on short, fine grasses. Wildebeest nip off the tips of larger, tough grasses.

Like all ruminants, antelopes have horns that are bony structures made of keratin that grow continuously. Some are straight; others are curved. A few species, like kudus and elands, have elaborate, spiraled horns.

Antelopes live in social groups that vary in size from a few individuals to hundreds. Every dry season in East Africa, several species of antelopes join together in huge herds, along with zebras, buffalos, and elephants, in search of water.

Life spans for antelopes and pronghorns range from 15 to 20 years.

PRONGHORN ○○○
ANTILOCAPRA AMERICANA

RANGE: Western North America

SIZE: 80 to 150 lb (36.3 to 68.0 kg)

DIET: Sage, forbs, grasses, cacti

Pronghorns are in a family all their own. Like African antelopes, they are flighty and fast. Like deer, they shed their prongs once a year. Unlike both, they cannot jump. As a result, pronghorns are afraid of fences.

THOMSON'S GAZELLE ○○
EUDORCAS THOMSONII

RANGE: Kenya and Tanzania

SIZE: 33 to 77 lb (15.0 to 34.9 kg)

DIET: Short grasses, foliage, twigs, seeds, leaves

Thomson's gazelles are mostly grazers. During the rainy season, when the grass is very tall, they are often found in mixed herds of zebras and wildebeest. They wait their turn to graze until the larger herbivores make the first cut.

GERENUK ○○
LITOCRANIUS WALLERI

RANGE: Somalia, eastern Ethiopia, Kenya, Tanzania

SIZE: 63 to 127 lb (29 to 58 kg)

DIET: Leaves, shoots, fruit, flowers, buds

Among the gazelle species, gerenuks (JER-a-nooks) have unusually long legs and necks. Their name means "giraffe-necked" in Somali. Gerenuks feed on whatever they can reach that other antelopes cannot.

BLUE WILDEBEEST ○○○○
CONNOCHAETES TAURINUS

RANGE: Eastern and southern Africa

SIZE: 260 to 600 lb (117.9 to 272.2 kg)

DIET: Grasses; rarely, leaves

Wildebeest live in small herds led by a territorial bull. Unlike many of their smaller relatives, they cannot survive without water. Wildebeest migrate up to 75 miles (121 km) from one home range to the other, depending on the time of year.

DEER
AND ELK

Deer and elk live mostly in wooded or forested areas and are found in Europe and the Americas, as well as Asia and Africa. Most of the male animals in this group have antlers—they grow a new set each year—instead of horns.

Antlers start out as living tissue covered in soft, furred skin, known as velvet. When they reach their final length and shape, they lose their blood supply, and the velvet falls off, leaving a dry, bone-like structure. Now the male is ready for rut, a type of breeding display also known as horning and adorning. After the breeding season, the antlers fall off, usually within a day or two of each other. The three-dimensional shape of the antlers is unique to each male and is the same each year, like a fingerprint.

Instead of antlers for displays and defense, some smaller deer use their teeth. Muntjacs, for example, have four razor-sharp canines.

Life spans for deer, elk, and their relatives range from 10 to 15 years.

CARIBOU
RANGIFER TARANDUS

RANGE: Circumpolar

SIZE: 120 to 700 lb (54.4 to 317.5 kg)

DIET: Grass, plants, lichens

Caribou, or reindeer, are unusual among deer because both males and females have antlers. Their calves also mature incredibly fast. New-borns nurse within minutes of birth, follow their mother within an hour, and can run full speed after one day.

ELK
CERVUS ELAPHUS

RANGE: North America and East Asia

SIZE: 145 to 1,100 lb (65.8 to 499.0 kg)

DIET: Grasses, sedges, forbs; also clover, dandelions, violets

Elk are one of the most vocal species in the deer family. During the mating season, males roar, or bellow, loudly and repeatedly to attract females and advertise their territory. This behavior is called bugling.

WHITE-TAILED DEER
ODOCOILEUS VIRGINIANUS

RANGE: North, Central, and South America, as far south as Bolivia

SIZE: 125 to 300 lb (56.7 to 136.1 kg)

DIET: Grasses, weeds, shrubs, twigs, fungi, nuts, lichens

Like many other herbivores, a female white-tailed deer protects her young by leaving it alone. The doe hides, or "tucks," her newborn on the forest floor or in tall grass. With its neck stretched out and white spots for camou-flage, the fawn blends right in.

MOOSE
ALCES ALCES

RANGE: Northern North America

SIZE: 590 to 1,320 lb (267.7 to 598.7 kg)

DIET: Stems, twigs, leaves, shoots

During winter, moose are found in forests where there is snow cover. Their large bodies retain heat, and they have no problem staying warm. During summer, they often are found standing in lakes or swamps to keep cool.

GIRAFFES AND OKAPIS

Giraffes and okapis are found only in Africa, and both are incredibly well camouflaged.

Giraffes blend right in among the bush and acacia trees. An entire herd can disappear into a thicket! Their blotchy brown spots blend in perfectly with the shadows created by the thorny branches. Okapis are difficult to see in the forest, where the sunlight creates shadows. Against the alternating light and dark of the forest, their striped legs and dark bodies are almost invisible. They also walk and run differently from most other hoofed animals. They pace, meaning they move the front and rear legs on the same side at the same time. This is their only gait, yet they are surprisingly agile.

Both are also very quiet. Giraffes and okapis communicate using sounds most animals—including humans—cannot hear. A giraffe, for example, will arch its neck to force air through its long windpipes. This action creates very low-frequency sounds, known as infrasound.

Life spans are up to 25 years.

RETICULATED GIRAFFE
G. C. RETICULATA

RANGE: Africa

SIZE: 2,600 to 4,250 lb (1,180 to 1,930 kg)

DIET: Leaves, flowers, seed pods, fruit; also soil

Giraffes exist as nine subspecies. Each has a different coat color and pattern. All have the same genus and species name, *Giraffa camelopardalis*, followed by the subspecies name, which is *reticulata* for the reticulated giraffe.

ANGOLAN GIRAFFE
G. C. ANGOLENSIS

RANGE: Africa

SIZE: 2,600 to 4,250 lb (1,180 to 1,930 kg)

DIET: Leaves, flowers, seed pods, fruit; also soil

All giraffes share several unique traits. One is a series of valves in the arteries and veins of their necks. These help to maintain a constant blood pressure in the giraffe's head, whether it is held high or lowered to eat or drink.

MASAI GIRAFFE
G. C. TIPPELSKIRCHI

RANGE: Africa

SIZE: 2,600 to 4,250 lb (1,180 to 1,930 kg)

DIET: Leaves, flowers, seed pods, fruit; also soil

Masai giraffes are the tallest of the subspecies, reaching 20 feet (6 m). Their coats have dark-brown patches with jagged edges surrounded by white. For comparison, Angolan giraffes have larger brown patches with fewer notches, and reticulated giraffes have large, light-brown patches separated by thin white lines.

OKAPI
OKAPIA JOHNSTONI

RANGE: Northeastern Democratic Republic of the Congo

SIZE: 440 to 660 lb (199.6 to 299.4 kg)

DIET: Leaves, buds, shoots

Okapis and giraffes are similar in many ways. Both have bluish black tongues—long enough to reach their ears—that they use for plucking leaves. Both also have a type of horn unique among mammals: It is made of bone covered by furred skin.

HIPPOS AND PIGS

Hippos and pigs and their relatives are grouped with one another, ruminants, and camels mostly because of their hooves. All stand on an even number of toes. The difference is that hippos, pigs, peccaries, and warthogs stand on four toes, rather than two.

They are different in many other ways, too. Hippos, for example, are semi-aquatic. They graze on land, only at night, and spend their days resting in the water, and digesting. Their closest relatives may be whales. Instead of a rumen, they have a compartmentalized stomach.

Pigs, warthogs, and peccaries, on the other hand, are omnivores. They also have special snouts: The very end is made up of cartilage and bone so they can use it like a bulldozer.

The most visible features shared by hippos and pigs are their tusk-like canines. These modified teeth are used for fighting as well as digging. If provoked, they can inflict severe wounds.

For example, hippos kill more people in Africa each year than any single disease, except malaria. Unfortunately, they are often surprised at night by people visiting the river to fetch water, bathe, or wash their clothes.

Life spans range from 15 to 20 years for pigs and relatives, and 55 to 60 years for hippos.

NILE HIPPOPOTAMUS
HIPPOPOTAMUS AMPHIBIUS

RANGE: Sub-Saharan Africa

SIZE: 1,400 to 8,000 lb (635 to 3,629 kg)

DIET: Short grasses and other plants; fallen fruit

With their eyes, ears, and nostrils just above the surface, hippos let their body sink under the water. This behavior is related to eating—hippos need to rest to digest all of the food they eat.

COLLARED PECCARY
PECARI TAJACU

RANGE: Southern United States, Central America, South America

SIZE: 33 to 60 lb (15 to 25 kg)

DIET: Roots, fungi, bulbs, nuts, fruit, eggs, carrion, small reptiles, fish

Collared peccaries are found in two very different habitats: rain forests and deserts. In both places, they eat a variety of plant roots and bulbs. In the desert, there is one plant they need: the prickly pear. Without it, they would die of thirst.

COMMON WARTHOG
PHACOCHOERUS AFRICANUS

RANGE: Africa

SIZE: 110 to 330 lb (50 to 150 kg)

DIET: Short grasses, roots, berries, bark of young trees; sometimes carrion

The "wart" in "warthog" refers to bumps made of cartilage-like tissue on the animal's face. There are warts above and below the eyes, as well as along the lower jaw. These warts also have long, white bristles, which give the warthog a beard.

WILD BOAR
SUS SCROFA

RANGE: Europe, Asia, North Africa; domesticated worldwide

SIZE: 110 to 770 lb (50 to 349 kg)

DIET: Tubers, bulbs, grains, nuts, fruit, fungi, other plant material; manure, insect larvae, eggs, small vertebrates, invertebrates

The wild boar is the ancestor of the domestic pig. There are now more than 100 breeds—each a different mix of coat color, size, tail length, and shape of the ears and snout. All are the same species, and all like the same thing: wallowing in mud.

CAMELS AND RELATIVES

Instead of hooves, camels and their relatives walk on two padded toes. All are grazers. They have a three-chambered stomach that includes a fermentation compartment for digesting plant fiber.

The animals in this group are extremely hardy. They are found in some of the harshest, driest habitats in the world—in Africa and Asia as well as the Americas. The Bactrian and dromedary camels are native to North Africa, Central Asia, and western Asia. The vicuña and guanaco are native to the high-altitude grasslands of the Andes, mountains in western South America.

All four camel species have been domesticated—kept and bred—for transportation as well as their milk, meat, and hair. There are more than 14 million domestic dromedaries in Africa and Asia, and another million running free in Australia, the descendants of animals brought there for transport. Wild dromedaries are extinct. There are far fewer domestic Bactrian camels: about 1.4 million, with only about 1,000 left in the wild. Domesticated guanacos are llamas. Domesticated vicuñas are alpacas.

Camel life spans range from 25 to 50 years.

DROMEDARY CAMEL ○○○⚲
CAMELUS DROMEDARIUS

RANGE: Originally found in South Asia and the Arabian Peninsula; since domestication, they are found in arid regions of the Middle East, India, Africa

SIZE: 660 to 1,518 lb (272.2 to 688.6 kg)

DIET: Leaves, plants, grasses

Dromedary camels have been extinct in the wild since the time of their domestication 2,000 years ago. They are excellent pack animals in hot, dry regions. To conserve water, they do not sweat until their body temperature reaches 106°F (41°C).

BACTRIAN CAMEL ●⚲
CAMELUS BACTRIANUS

RANGE: Asia north of Himalaya

SIZE: 990 to 1,100 lb (408.2 to 499.0 kg)

DIET: Leaves, roots, tubers, wood, bark, stems, seeds, grains, nuts, fruit

About 1,000 wild Bactrian camels remain in the Gobi, a desert in China and Mongolia, where they thrive despite extreme heat and cold. After a drought, these camels can drink up to a quarter of their body weight at one time.

GUANACO ○◔
LAMA GUANICOE

RANGE: Northern Peru to southern Chile

SIZE: 253 to 308 lb (115 to 140 kg)

DIET: Grasses and other plants

The guanaco (gwa-NAH-koh) rarely drinks water. Instead, it relies on the moisture in its plant diet, including the dew on cactus leaves. When threatened, the guanaco, like its relative the llama, makes a bleating sound. It also spits.

VICUÑA ○○
VICUGNA VICUGNA

RANGE: Andes in South America

SIZE: 77 to 143 lb (35 to 65 kg)

DIET: Grasses

Unlike other members of the camel family, the vicuña (vih-KOON-yuh) cannot go without water. It is also much smaller, has rodent-like incisors for grazing, and lives only at high elevations—up to 18,800 feet (5,750 m).

HORSES AND RELATIVES

H orses and their seven relatives are members of the Equid (EE-quid) family. The animals in this group differ from even-toed, hoofed mammals in several ways. For one thing, they bear weight on a single digit. They are odd-toed.

They also digest their food differently, fermenting it in a dilated portion of their large intestine rather than in a rumen. This process, known as hindgut fermentation, is not nearly as efficient as rumination. As a result, horses and zebras eat constantly. Other herbivores like rabbits use the same strategy—and face the same challenge. The need to graze puts the animals at risk of greater predation, which is one reason these animals are able to run so fast.

Equids are among the most graceful animals on Earth. The faster they gallop, the more amazing they are to watch. The horse, domesticated 6,000 years ago, is also one of the most important animals in human history, having been used for work, transportation, war, and pleasure.

Life spans range from 10 to 30 years for horses and their relatives.

HORSE
EQUUS FERUS CABALLUS

RANGE: Original species: steppe zone of Europe and Asia; domesticated 6,000 years ago and now worldwide

SIZE: 660 to 4,400 lb (300 to 2,000 kg)

DIET: Grasses, but often have domestic diets that include grains and hays

Domestic horses are currently considered a subspecies of the now-extinct wild horse (*Equus ferus*) that once lived in Europe and Asia. The other living subspecies is the only true wild horse: the very rare Przewalksi's horse. The animals called wild horses, such as mustangs and brumbies, are escaped domestic horses.

AFRICAN WILD ASS
EQUUS AFRICANUS

RANGE: Northern Africa, Arabian Peninsula; domesticated subspecies is the donkey, which is found worldwide

SIZE: 400 to 550 lb (181 to 250 kg)

DIET: Grasses and herbs

The donkey is the same species as the African, or Somali, wild ass. Like all Equids, they have long jaws lined with molars for chewing grass, large eyes with binocular vision, and large, sensitive ears.

KIANG
EQUUS KIANG

RANGE: Tibet, parts of China, Nepal, India

SIZE: 550 to 970 lb (250 to 440 kg)

DIET: Grasses and plants

The kiang is the largest species of wild ass. They are found at high elevations of up to 23,000 feet (7,010 m) and live in close-knit family groups led by an older female. Single males, called stallions, follow the herd and fight for breeding rights.

BURCHELL'S ZEBRA
EQUUS QUAGGA BURCHELLII

RANGE: Africa

SIZE: 385 to 847 lb (175 to 384 kg)

DIET: Primarily grasses; also herbs, leaves, twigs

There are three species of zebras: mountain, Grevy's, and plains. The most widespread is the plains zebra, which exists as several subspecies, including Burchell's, shown here. Plains zebras live in groups called harems that include one stallion and up to six females with foals.

RHINOS AND TAPIRS

R hinos and tapirs (TAY-peerz) are another type of odd-toed, hoofed mammal. Unlike horses, however, they walk on three digits and a footpad.

The other interesting thing about rhino and tapir feet is that they differ depending on where the animal lives. Species that live on firm grassland, like the black and white rhinos of Africa, have relatively short toes and a flat, firm footpad. Species that live in the tropics and swampy areas, like the greater one-horned rhino and Brazilian tapir, have longer toes and a soft footpad for better traction in mud.

Hair is another feature that varies among the species in this grouping. African rhinos have hairy ear tips and eyelashes. Asian rhinos have tufts of hair on their ears and tails. The Sumatran rhino has hair all over its body, an adaptation for life in the buggy tropics.

Like rhinos, tapirs have very little hair. Only the mountain species has a thick coat. The others have bristly manes, right in the location where a jaguar would take its first bite.

Life spans range up to 30 years for tapirs, and up to 50 for rhinos.

BRAZILIAN TAPIR
TAPIRUS TERRESTRIS

RANGE: South America

SIZE: 330 to 551 lb (150 to 250 kg)

DIET: Fruit, leaves, other plant material

Like all tapirs, the Brazilian tapir is mostly nocturnal, lives in dense forest near water, and has a mobile nose called a proboscis, which it uses to grasp its food. It is more vocal than its relatives, however, and makes a loud, piercing whistle when disturbed.

MALAYAN TAPIR
TAPIRUS INDICUS

RANGE: Swamps in Malaysia and Sumatra

SIZE: 500 to 800 lb (227 to 363 kg)

DIET: Aquatic vegetation, grasses, leaves, buds, fruit

The Malayan tapir looks different from its three South American relatives. The light-gray fur around its body helps to provide camouflage in the shadows of the rain forest. Also, it eats aquatic plants in addition to land vegetation.

BLACK RHINOCEROS
DICEROS BICORNIS

RANGE: Once found throughout sub-Saharan Africa; now only in Cameroon, Kenya, South Africa

SIZE: 1,760 to 3,080 lb (798 to 1,397 kg)

DIET: Leaves, buds, shoots of bushes and small trees

Compared to the white rhino, also found in Africa, the black rhino is smaller and usually has darker skin. Both have two horns. The way to identify the black rhino for certain is to look at its lips. Since black rhinos are browsers, they have a pointed, mobile upper lip for grabbing leaves, twigs, and other plants.

WHITE RHINOCEROS
CERATOTHERIUM SIMUM

RANGE: Once found in central, eastern, and southern Africa; now only in game reserves and parks

SIZE: 3,000 to 8,000 lb (1,361 to 3,629 kg)

DIET: Grasses

White rhinos are grazers. Also called the square-lipped rhino, they have a flat upper lip for cropping grasses. Though some white rhino populations are well protected, all rhinos, both in Asia and Africa, are threatened with extinction because of poaching for their horns.

JAVAN RHINOCEROS
RHINOCEROS SONDAICUS

RANGE: Once widespread in Indonesia, India, China; now fewer than 50 animals in two parks in Southeast Asia

SIZE: 1,980 to 3,080 lb (898 to 1,397 kg)

DIET: Leaves, young shoots, twigs, fruit

This species is also known as the lesser one-horned rhino. It looks very similar to its larger Asian relative and was once the most common rhino in Asia. Sadly, the Javan rhino has been killed for its horn and is one of the rarest animals on Earth.

GREATER ONE-HORNED RHINOCEROS
RHINOCEROS UNICORNIS

RANGE: Northern Pakistan, India, Bangladesh

SIZE: 3,300 to 4,400 lb (1,500 to 2,000 kg)

DIET: Grasses, weeds, twigs, fruit, leaves, branches, aquatic plants, farm crops

The greater one-horned, or Asian, rhino is a browser. Like the black rhino, it has a pointed upper lip that it uses to eat tall grasses. Its skin has thick folds and bumps on the surface that make it look like armor.

SUMATRAN RHINOCEROS
DICERORHINUS SUMATRENSIS

RANGE: Asia, from foothills of Himalaya in India and Bhutan to Thailand, Malaysia, Indonesia

SIZE: 1,760 to 4,400 lb (800 to 2,000 kg)

DIET: Plants, fruit, twigs

The Sumatran rhino is smaller than its relatives and has more hair—especially the calves. The only Asian rhino with two horns, it lives in forested areas near water or in swamps. It, too, is critically endangered because of poaching.

BAIRD'S TAPIR
TAPIRUS BAIRDI

RANGE: Mexico, Central America, Colombia

SIZE: 330 to 661 lb (150 to 300 kg)

DIET: Leaves, fruit, twigs, flowers, grasses

Baird's tapirs are the largest of the tapir species found in South America. To stay cool, they rest in the shade or in shallow pools of water. Despite their size, they are very fast—on land and in water.

DOLPHINS, PORPOISES, AND OTHER TOOTHED WHALES

Dolphins, porpoises, and whales are marine mammals belonging to the order Cetacea (ce-TAY-sha.) They are highly social and intelligent animals with relatively large brains and fish-like bodies. Though they live in water, all breathe air. Their nostrils are located on the top of their heads, just inside the blowhole. When a cetacean exhales, it blows both water and air out the hole, creating a spray. Based on the fossil record, their common ancestor was a land mammal related to the hippo.

The animals in this group are divided into two suborders, the toothed and baleen whales.

There are 73 species of toothed whales. They include dolphins, porpoises, orcas, sperm whales, and beaked whales. All have teeth, which they use to grab their prey, and a single blowhole. Most have a special sensory organ known as the "melon" located between their eyes. The melon is used to gather and focus sound waves.

Sounds travel farther in water than in air, and toothed whales rely on their hearing more than any other sense. They communicate using clicks, whistles, moans, calls, and songs. Many also echolocate, meaning they use sound to find each other, forage for food, and navigate.

Life spans for dolphins, porpoises, and other toothed whales range from 40 to 90 years.

BOTTLENOSE DOLPHIN
TURSIOPS TRUNCATUS

RANGE: Indian, Atlantic, and Pacific Oceans; Mediterranean Sea

SIZE: 572 to 1,100 lb (259 to 499 kg)

DIET: Fish, invertebrates, squid

In shallow water, bottlenose dolphins take several breaths per minute, compared to one breath every two minutes between dives in deeper water. Females breed once every three to six years beginning at the age of 20, and can reproduce past the age of 40.

HARBOR PORPOISE
PHOCOENA PHOCOENA

RANGE: All oceans in Northern Hemisphere

SIZE: 99 to 132 lb (45 to 60 kg)

DIET: Fish, squid, crustaceans

Compared to dolphins, porpoises are smaller and have a more rounded nose. They also reproduce faster and have shorter life spans. Female harbor porpoises, for example, give birth to one calf a year, starting at age five. They live eight to ten years.

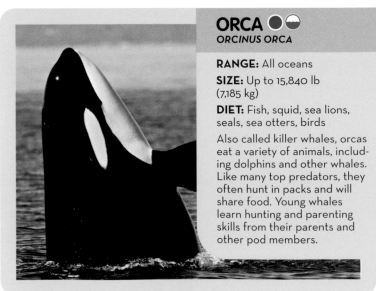

ORCA
ORCINUS ORCA

RANGE: All oceans

SIZE: Up to 15,840 lb (7,185 kg)

DIET: Fish, squid, sea lions, seals, sea otters, birds

Also called killer whales, orcas eat a variety of animals, including dolphins and other whales. Like many top predators, they often hunt in packs and will share food. Young whales learn hunting and parenting skills from their parents and other pod members.

BALEEN WHALES

The baleen whales include the blue whale, right whale, sperm whale, bowhead whale, fin whale, and gray whale. All have a two-part, V-shaped blowhole. They are filter feeders. Like toothed whales, they use sound to communicate.

Instead of a row of teeth like other mammals, these whales have a brush-like structure known as a baleen plate. The baleen is a bristly material that hangs down from a plate attached to the inner surface of the whale's upper jaw. Like hair and nails, baleen is made of keratin. It grows slowly over time as the ends wear out. To feed, the whale fills its lower jaw with water, closes its mouth, and pushes its tongue up against the baleen. This traps the whale's food—zooplankton like krill, copepods, and small fish—against the baleen. All it has to do next is squirt out the excess water and swallow. Filter feeding is incredibly efficient. Baleen whales can eat up to four tons of food a day.

Baleen whales prefer warmer waters and migrate to avoid cool water during winter. The record for the longest migration is for the humpback whale: 5,176 miles (8,330 km). The life spans range from 60 to 70 years, possibly as long as 100 or more for some individuals.

NORTHERN ATLANTIC RIGHT WHALE
EUBALAENA GLACIALIS

RANGE: North Atlantic Ocean

SIZE: 121,145 to 209,251 lb (55,000 to 95,000 kg)

DIET: Zooplankton—mainly krill and copepods

These whales were hunted to near extinction for their meat and oil. Though protected, their future remains uncertain. They live in shallow coastal waters, where they often are struck by ships, caught in fishing nets, and harmed by pollution—including underwater noise.

BOWHEAD WHALE
BALAENA MYSTICETUS

RANGE: Coastal polar waters of the Northern Hemisphere

SIZE: 165,000 to 220,000 lb (75,000 to 100,000 kg))

DIET: Zooplankton—krill and other crustaceans

The bowhead whale is named for the U-shape of its lower jaw. Its head is huge compared to its body, and its baleen plates are the largest of any whale species. For insulation, it has a two-foot (0.6-m)-thick layer of blubber!

SEI WHALE
BALAENOPTERA BOREALIS

RANGE: All oceans and seas, except polar and tropical waters

SIZE: 44,000 to 55,116 lb (20,000 to 25,000 kg)

DIET: Zooplankton—krill, other crustaceans, small fish

Sei whales are big—and fast. Most are 50 feet (15 m) long and can swim up to 31 miles an hour (50 km/h). They are not divers, however; they feed only at the surface, swimming on their sides with their mouths open through a swarm of zooplankton.

BLUE WHALE
BALAENOPTERA MUSCULUS

RANGE: All oceans

SIZE: Up to 418,502 lb (190,000 kg)

DIET: Zooplankton—mainly krill, and some copepods

Blue whales are the largest whales. They also eat more krill in a day than any other species: up to 40 million! They communicate using low-pitched calls, or songs. The male's song can travel thousands of miles in the deep ocean.

FROM THE FIELD:
FLIP NICKLIN

ORCA

Killer whales, or orcas (*Orcinus orca*), used to have a bad rap. People thought of them only as voracious killers, and the U.S. Navy once listed them as dangerous marine animals. But when we got to know them, we fell in love with them. And while people were still shifting their opinions, I was assigned to take underwater photos of these animals. Luckily, a couple researchers studying killer whales near Vancouver Island saw a softer side of the ocean giants and invited me to join them in the field.

They led me to a hidden cove where killer whales gathered to massage their bellies and rumps on the rocky bottom. This was my opportunity to take underwater photos—only, if I so much as dipped my foot into the water, the whales disappeared like ghosts! So we had to get creative. A narrow crack in the cove wall led down to the floor, and one afternoon I hid in the crevice and waited for the whales to appear. I heard their spouting blowholes, and my heart pounded as several large, black figures appeared in the murky water. I took a deep breath, sunk ten feet (3 m) to the bottom of the cove, and slowly crawled over the jagged rocks to the smooth rubbing area. In front of me, a 25-foot (7.6-m) killer whale wiggled its massive body back and forth over the pebbles! Several whales swam into the cove that day—gliding by me as if I were invisible—and I snapped the first-ever published images of this unique underwater behavior.

MAP KEY

APPROXIMATE RANGE OF THE
ORCINUS ORCA (ORCA)

ASIA

PACIFIC
OCEAN

INDIAN
OCEAN

NORTH
AMERICA

EUROPE

AUSTRALIA

ATLANTIC OCEAN

AFRICA

PACIFIC
OCEAN

SOUTH
AMERICA

ANTARCTICA

ANTARCTICA

Flip Nicklin is widely regarded as the world's leading cetacean photographer. He free-dives up to 90 feet (27 m), has logged more than 5,500 dives, and has photographed more than 30 species of whales and dolphins. Flip co-founded Whale Trust, a nonprofit that develops public education programs based solely on scientific research.

OBSERVATION TIPS

1 Look for killer whales with people who know the animals and their habits. You'll be more likely to find them.

2 Hang with the locals—killer whales sometimes follow fishing boats in hopes of nabbing a free meal.

3 When whale watching, look for patterns—killer whales typically surface more than once.

4 Killer whales travel in large pods, so usually if you see one, you'll see more.

Like humans, there are different types, or cultures, of killer whales—they have different behaviors and habits, and they live all over the world. Most killer whales travel in family groups, called pods, and females give birth to one calf every three to ten years. Other pod members help care for the calf, which nurses on its mother's milk until it can catch its own dinner. When it's time to play, killer whales leap out of the water or splash and roll around on the surface.

 # LEMURS AND RELATIVES

L emurs are found only on the island of Madagascar and the Comoros Islands. No other country has as many endemic primates as Madagascar. Biologists are still working out how to organize this group—there may be as many as 100 species. Because they more closely resemble ancestral forms, lemurs are considered primitive primates.

Lemurs are known for their incredible diversity. This group includes the smallest primate on Earth, the 0.9-oz (25-g) pygmy mouse lemur. Some, like the dwarf lemur, are small, shy, nocturnal, and arboreal. Others, like the ring-tailed lemur, are diurnal and more often seen on the ground. There are lemurs with thick fur (woolly lemurs) as well as colorful fur (red, black, brown, and white-and-black ruffed lemurs). Many have distinct vocalizations. The indri, for example, makes a sad, siren-like call.

Another unusual feature among the social lemurs is female dominance. Females decide the hierarchy within a group. The males are responsible only for territorial defense.

Life spans for ring-tailed lemurs and sifakas are 25 to 30 years. Smaller lemurs live shorter lives (10 to 15 years) because of predation.

COQUEREL'S SIFAKA
PROPITHECUS COQUERELI

RANGE: Northern Madagascar

SIZE: 8 to 9.4 lb (3.6 to 4.2 kg)

DIET: Leaves, seeds, flowers, fruit, bark

Sifakas are herbivores that prefer fresh leaves over anything else. As with other social lemurs, females are dominant over males. When the troop finds a choice patch of leaves, the females eat first.

RED RUFFED LEMUR
VARECIA RUBRA

RANGE: Northeastern Madagascar

SIZE: 7.5 to 7.7 lb (3.4 to 3.5 kg)

DIET: Mainly fruit, nectar, pollen; also leaves and seeds

Red ruffed lemurs are very vocal primates. They bark to stay together while feeding, and squawk to warn each other of danger. Their calls are essential to survival—Madagascar is also home to the fossa, a marsupial that feeds exclusively on lemurs.

VERRAUX'S SIFAKA
PROPITHECUS VERREAUXI

RANGE: Western and southwestern Madagascar

SIZE: 6.6 to 15.4 lb (3 to 7 kg)

DIET: Mainly leaves, seeds, flowers, fruit, bark

Sifakas (se-FA-kas) are known as leaping, or dancing, lemurs because of the way they move. In the trees, they leap from one branch to another without injury. On the ground, they hop sideways on two legs, holding their short arms up in the air.

RING-TAILED LEMUR
LEMUR CATTA

RANGE: Southern and southwestern Madagascar

SIZE: 5 to 7.7 lb (2.3 to 3.5 kg)

DIET: Fruit, leaves, bark, grass

Lemurs communicate using vocalizations, body language, and scent. Ring-tailed lemurs set up "stink battles." They rub secretions from their scent glands into their tails and wave them at the opposition.

GREATER DWARF LEMUR
CHEIROGALEUS MAJOR

RANGE: Eastern and northern Madagascar

SIZE: 0.4 to 1.3 lb (0.18 to 0.6 kg)

DIET: Fruit, flowers, nectar; also insects

These small lemurs are nocturnal. During the drier months, when food is scarce, they become inactive to save energy, living off fat stored in their tails. This behavior is called torpor.

POTTOS,
LORISES, AND GALAGOS

L ike the lemurs, the species in this grouping are considered primitive primates. Galagos and pottos are found in Africa. Lorises are found in Asia. All are small, arboreal primates with large, round eyes and dense fur. Galagos are known for their ability to leap—up to 39 feet (12 m)—from one branch to another. Lorises and pottos move deliberately from one branch to another and are excellent climbers. They can walk along the underside of a branch just as well as along the top.

Life spans for pottos, lorises, and galagos are up to 20 years.

POTTO
PERODICTICUS POTTO

RANGE: Equatorial Africa
SIZE: 1.3 to 3.5 lb (0.6 to 1.6 kg)
DIET: Mostly fruit; also insects, snails, plant gums

Though they eat mostly fruit, pottos also hunt for insects. They use their excellent sense of smell to find them and their human-like fingers to catch them. They tend to eat spiny or bad-smelling species like ants, beetles, caterpillars, millipedes, and spiders.

SLENDER LORIS
LORIS TARDIGRADUS

RANGE: Sri Lanka
SIZE: 4.5 to 8 oz (128 to 227 g)
DIET: Insects and small animals, especially lizards and geckos

The slender loris and its relatives communicate with each other through a variety of whistles, hums, growls, and screams. They also use body language, facial expressions, huddling, grooming, and urine and scent marking.

GREATER SLOW LORIS
NYCTICEBUS COUCANG

RANGE: Sumatra, Malaysia, Thailand, Singapore
SIZE: 2.2 to 4.4 lb (1 to 2 kg)
DIET: Fruit, insects, birds, leaves

This loris moves slowly along branches and prefers to eat fruit. Like other lorises, it has skin glands on its forearms that produce an oily substance used to mark territory. This secretion is also toxic.

SENEGAL GALAGO
GALAGO SENEGALENSIS

RANGE: Sub-Saharan Africa
SIZE: 3.3 to 10.6 oz (95 to 300 g)
DIET: Insects, birds, eggs, fruit, seeds, flowers, plant sap, tree gum

Galagos (guh-LAY-gohz) are known as bush babies because their alarm calls sound like human babies crying. These small primates hunt for grasshoppers, beetles, and other insects by listening with their large ears, which they can wrinkle and bend.

PRIMATES

All primates, animals in the order Primata, descend from species that once lived strictly in trees. Today, most live in or near forests, but many spend time on the ground, too.

A number of features shared by primates reflect their arboreal, or tree-living, history. All have binocular-style vision, and eyes that face forward and are protected by a bony rim, or orbit. They have opposable thumbs (except for colobus monkeys) and big toes, as well as very mobile upper arms—the result of a combination of a ball-and-socket shoulder joint with bones in the arms (radius and ulna) and legs (femur and tibia) that allow for rotation, and a clavicle, or collarbone. All primates have either a tail or the bones to support one. In humans, these bones are fused together and known as the coccyx, or tailbone; it is easily bruised! All primates communicate using gestures, body language, and vocalizations.

Primates are divided into two main groups: one that includes monkeys, apes, and tarsiers, sometimes called "higher primates," and a second that includes lemurs, galagos, lorises, and pottos, sometimes called "lower" or "prosimian" primates. In both groups, many species are at risk of extinction due to loss of their habitat.

MONKEYS

OLD WORLD MONKEYS

The easiest way to identify a monkey as Old World (Africa, Asia, Europe) or New World (Americas) is to look at the shape of its nose and the length of its tail.

Old World monkeys have a downward-turned nose with large nostrils and short, or absent, tails. The males also have very long and sharp upper canines, which they use to display. In addition, the primates in this group have hard pads where they sit down, and males are often two to three times the size of females.

Most species in this group, which include baboons, mandrills, and macaques, are omnivores and have large cheek pouches that they use to store food. A few, like the colobus monkey and langur, eat only leaves.

All Old World monkeys are highly social and live either in large multi-male troops, or in harems with many females and a single breeding male. Life spans range up to 40 years.

RHESUS MONKEY
MACACA MULATTA

RANGE: South, Central, and Southeast Asia

SIZE: 8.8 to 26.4 lb (4 to 12 kg)

DIET: Roots, herbs, fruit, insects, crops, small animals

This species has the widest geographic range (Asia) of any primate apart from humans. They are also highly social. Rhesus monkeys live in large groups of up to 200 and communicate with each other through body language, facial expressions, and calls.

OLIVE BABOON
PAPIO ANUBIS

RANGE: Equatorial Africa

SIZE: 30 to 55 lb (13 to 25 kg)

DIET: Grasses, pods, seeds, fruit, roots, leaves, buds, bark, flowers, insects, meat

Olive baboons live in troops of related females and unrelated males. This is because female babies never leave, but males do. Before they reach adult size, young male baboons will join a different troop, working their way up the dominance ladder to gain breeding rights.

ANGOLAN COLOBUS
COLOBUS ANGOLENSIS

RANGE: Central and East Africa

SIZE: 13 to 26 lb (6 to 12 kg)

DIET: Mainly leaves; also stems, bark, flowers, buds, shoots, fruit

Of all the African monkeys, the colobus is the most specialized for life in the trees. They eat mostly leaves, and lots of them—several pounds a day. Like cows, they have a complex stomach that allows them to digest plant fiber.

MANDRILL
MANDRILLUS SPHINX

RANGE: Parts of central West Africa

SIZE: Up to 118 lb (53.5 kg)

DIET: Fruit, nuts, leaves, insects; small invertebrates and vertebrates

Compared to the female, the colors on the face of the male mandrill are much brighter. They also have a larger yellow beard. Their hard pads, where they sit down, are purple. Females are attracted to the more brightly colored males.

NEW WORLD MONKEYS

New World monkeys have flat, upturned noses and long tails. All are strictly arboreal. They include marmosets and tamarins, capuchin and squirrel monkeys, owl monkeys, titi and saki monkeys, and the species best known for their prehensile tails—howler monkeys and spider monkeys.

There is no single social organization common to this group. Squirrel monkeys are often found in very large groups of 100 or more, often traveling with several dozen capuchins and a small family group of saki monkeys. Marmosets and tamarins live in small family groups in which the younger members help raise the offspring. Spider monkeys have a social system similar to chimpanzees in which groups of males and females mix, split, and mix again. Howler monkeys live in family groups and move slowly among the treetops. Their distinctive calls are used to advertise their location to avoid conflict with other families.

Life spans for New World monkeys range from 15 to 25 years.

GOLDEN LION TAMARIN
LEONTOPITHECUS ROSALIA

RANGE: Brazil

SIZE: 0.75 to 1.5 lb (0.3 to 0.7 kg)

DIET: Fruit, plant sap, insects, lizards, small birds, bird eggs

Like all tamarins and marmosets, this species is tiny, active, and athletic. Golden lion tamarins move easily through dense rain forest, running along small branches and jumping among tangled vines. To meet their energy needs, they eat a high-calorie diet.

COTTON-TOP TAMARIN
SAGUINUS OEDIPUS

RANGE: Northwest Colombia

SIZE: 9 to 13 oz (260 to 380 g)

DIET: Insects, fruit, sap; small reptiles and amphibians

Family life for this species is similar to that of other tamarins: The male raises the young with help from older offspring. What makes the cotton-top different is that twice a year the female gives birth to non-identical twins. The babies ride around on the back of their father and older siblings.

RED-HANDED HOWLER
ALOUATTA BELZEBUL

RANGE: Amazonian Brazil

SIZE: 10 to 17 lb (4.5 to 7.7 kg)

DIET: Leaves; sometimes tree bark or woody twigs; also fruit during rainy seasons

Howlers are the largest and loudest of the New World monkeys. They roar, bark, and grunt to keep track of one another and howl in unison—often before dawn. Their early morning chorus can be heard a mile (1.6 km) away.

BLACK HOWLER
ALOUATTA CARAYA

RANGE: Central South America

SIZE: 8.8 to 22 lb (4 to 10 kg)

DIET: Leaves; some fruit, buds, flowers

Howlers live in family groups of 5 to 20 monkeys. They move slowly through the treetops, eating leaves as they go, using their prehensile tails like a fifth arm to hold on to branches. They come down only during the dry season to drink water.

SOUTH AMERICAN SQUIRREL MONKEY
SAIMIRI SCIUREUS

RANGE: South America

SIZE: 1.5 to 2 lb (0.7 to 0.9 kg)

DIET: Fruit; also leaves, seeds; some insects

The white fur around the eyes of the squirrel monkey makes it look as though it is wearing a mask. These monkeys prefer to move along the narrowest of branches—no wider than an inch (2.5 cm)—using their long tails for balance.

APES AND TARSIERS

pes are large primates with an upright or semi-upright stance capable of bipedalism—walking on two legs. All have flat nails on their fingers and toes. The lesser apes, siamangs and gibbons, have perfected the action of swinging through trees and have exceptionally long arms.

The great apes, which include gorillas, chimpanzees, orangutans, and bonobos, have flattened forearms and large brain cases. They are also our closest relatives. Great apes share more than 98 percent of their DNA with humans. Their common ancestor lived 14 million years ago.

Tarsiers are a very primitive species related to apes and monkeys. Today, they are found only in Asia, but their fossils—as much as 40 million years old—are found in North America, Europe, and North Africa.

Primate brains differ from those of other mammals in terms of how they process information. This is especially true among the great apes. More nerve cells, for example, are devoted to processing sight compared to smell. The front part of the brain—the cerebral cortex—is also larger in highly social primate species. Intelligence, thinking, planning, and communicating are among the many functions of the cerebrum.

Life spans for apes are from 35 to 60 years.

WHITE-CHEEKED GIBBON
NOMASCUS LEUCOGENYS

RANGE: Southeast Asia

SIZE: 10 to 13 lb (4.5 to 6 kg)

DIET: Pulp of fruit; also leaves, flowers, insects

The adult females of this species are cream-colored, and the males are black. As babies, they all look like females. Then, at two years of age, their fur changes, and they all begin to look like males. Their final coat color does not appear until they approach breeding age at six or seven years old.

CHIMPANZEE
PAN TROGLODYTES

RANGE: Central Africa

SIZE: 50 to 175 lb (23 to 79 kg)

DIET: Plant material, including fruit, nuts, leaves, bark, shoots; also eggs and insects

Among the great apes, chimpanzees have the most in common with humans. For example, chimps communicate using a combination of facial expressions, gestures, and grunts. They use tools. In addition, they are capable of planning a hunt or organizing an attack against their rivals.

SUMATRAN ORANGUTAN
PONGO ABELII

RANGE: Sumatra

SIZE: 60 to 200 lb (27 to 91 kg)

DIET: Figs, leaves, flowers, bark, insects

Adult orangutans are solitary, except for females with their offspring. Juveniles stay with their mothers until they are nine or ten years old. They spend some of this time learning how to survive, and the rest of it playing.

WHITE-HANDED GIBBON
HYLOBATES LAR

RANGE: Southeast Asia

SIZE: 9.9 to 13.2 lb (4.5 to 6 kg)

DIET: Ripe leaves, buds, and fruit

White-handed gibbons live in small family groups made up of a male and female pair and their young. Like all gibbons, this species defends its territory by using loud calls. Males and females usually call out together.

PHILIPPINE TARSIER
TARSIUS SYRICHTA

RANGE: Rain forests of the Philippines

SIZE: 3 to 6 oz (85 to 170 g)

DIET: Insects, spiders, lizards, small vertebrates

Tarsiers are nocturnal insectivores with huge eyes and excellent vision, as well as acute hearing. They also are specialized leapers. They use their long tails for balance and their long fingers and toes to grab on to branches.

BONOBO
PAN PANISCUS

RANGE: Democratic Republic of the Congo, Congo Basin

SIZE: 59 to 134 lb (27 to 61 kg)

DIET: Mostly fruit; also nuts, stems, shoots, leaves, roots, tubers, flowers

Compared to the chimpanzee, bonobos have darker skin and longer hair. They are more likely to walk on two legs, and they are much less aggressive toward each other. Instead of fighting, bonobos groom and mate with each other.

BORNEAN ORANGUTAN
PONGO PYGMAEUS

RANGE: Borneo

SIZE: 60 to 200 lb (27 to 91 kg)

DIET: Mainly fruit; also leaves, seeds, young birds, eggs

Orangutans rarely leave the trees. Their legs are weak and short compared to their long, strong arms. They swing from one limb to the next, or use their huge hands to pull themselves along the length of the branches.

EASTERN MOUNTAIN GORILLA
GORILLA BERINGEI BERINGEI

RANGE: Virunga volcanoes, Rwanda; Uganda, Democratic Republic of the Congo, central Africa

SIZE: 130 to 400 lb (59 to 181 kg)

DIET: Roots, leaves, stems, vines, shrubs, bamboo

Compared to lowland gorillas, mountain gorillas have stockier bodies and shorter arms for climbing, longer fur for keeping warm, and larger jaws for crushing bamboo and other plants. Their behavior is different, too. Mountain gorilla groups often include several breeding males.

WE ARE FAMILY

The great apes, with their expressive eyes, playful attitudes, and intelligent behavior, seem like not-too-distant cousins of humans. As it turns out, that's exactly what they are. We belong to the same family, called Hominidae. Scientific research shows that humans and great apes are descended from a common ancestor, one that lived about 14 million years ago. And that we share 98 percent of our DNA. It's no wonder that great apes can learn, express emotion, and even reason like humans. So, does all this mean that in some prehistoric time your ancestor was a chimpanzee? Not exactly. Within the hominid family, humans, chimps, and bonobos are the most closely related. But the connection is still pretty distant. Our common ancestor was a chimp-like ape that lived six to eight million years ago.

SIAMANG
SYMPHALANGUS SYNDACTYLUS

RANGE: Sumatra and mountains of the Malay Peninsula

SIZE: 20 to 30 lb (9 to 14 kg)

DIET: Fruit, especially figs; also flowers, leaves, shoots, some insects, bird eggs

Siamangs mate for life and live in pairs. Both males and females have large throat sacs used to amplify their calls. They sing a duet to mark their territory, a song that starts with a series of hoots and ends in a whooping noise.

FROM THE FIELD:

EMMA STOKES

GORILLA

WESTERN LOWLAND

Western lowland gorillas *(Gorilla gorilla)* live in dense rain forests that are difficult to navigate. Your best bet at spotting one of these gorillas is in large, swampy clearings, called bais, where they gather to feast on floating plants. I camped next to a bai in the Republic of Congo's Nouabalé-Ndoki National Park for three years on an assignment for the Wildlife Conservation Society, and every day more than 100 gorillas waded into the clearing. I observed them through binoculars and telescopes from a wooden platform 25 feet (7.6 m) up in a tree. Although they could see me and the other researchers, the gorillas generally avoided us, except for one bold silverback we called Vincent.

Vincent had no family and was always alone—and he might have been roughed up a bit, because he had only one ear! But he was fearless toward us researchers. We often stumbled across him on the trail we hiked from our camp to the tree platform—he'd bark to signal his presence, and we'd veer off the path and walk around him to avoid confrontation. Then he got bolder—he climbed the tree next to our platform and peered over at us! A looming, 400-pound (181-kg) gorilla can be quite intimidating, but Vincent showed no signs of aggression, and we began to think that this lonely gorilla just wanted to be our friend!

APPROXIMATE RANGE OF THE
GORILLA GORILLA
(WESTERN LOWLAND GORILLA)

0   1,000 miles

0   1,000 kilometers

A F R I C A

OBSERVATION **TIPS**

1 A good pair of bin-oculars is essential for observing gorillas from a safe distance.

2 In the wet season, you can track gorillas by following their hand and foot imprints in the damp leaf litter.

3 If you hear a loud barking sound in the forest, it's likely a gorilla alerting you to its presence. Stop, locate the gorilla, and walk away. Remember, you are walking in the gorillas' home, so always be respectful.

4 Pack plenty of quick-drying clothes and river sandals, because you *will* get wet in the rain forest.

Emma Stokes is a wildlife biologist and conservationist. Through her work in the Republic of Congo, she discovered an unknown population of 125,000 lowland gorillas in an unexplored region of Nouabalé-Ndoki National Park.

Gorillas are a lot like humans—they live in family groups, and females typically have one baby at a time. Newborn gorillas depend completely on their mothers—they nurse on their mothers' milk and must be carried everywhere. After about three years, the infants munch on plants and fruit alongside the adults. Playful infants roll around on the ground and swing from branches, but they also can throw horrendous tantrums if they don't get their way!

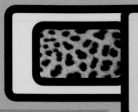

RECORDS

W hat mammal can paralyze a victim with its deadly venom? Which is so tiny it's lighter than a bumblebee bat? Want to find out? Then check out these mystifying record holders of the mammal world!

MOST RECORDS
→
BLUE WHALE
BALAENOPTERA MUSCULUS

If the animal kingdom held Olympic Games, the blue whale would swim away with the gold medal for the most gold medals. At 80 feet long (24 m) and weighing up to 240,000 pounds (108,860 kg), this massive mammal is not only the largest and heaviest animal on the planet, it boasts a few other titles, too:

Whoa, Baby! A newborn blue whale calf is the largest baby in the world: 26 feet long (7.9 m) and 4,000 to 6,000 pounds in weight (1,814 to 2,722 kg).

Loudest Blue whales communicate in deep hums and bellows that can reach 188 decibels—40 decibels louder than a jet engine.

Biggest Appetite Blue whales eat up to 11,000 pounds (5,000 kg) of krill each day, roughly the weight of an African elephant.

BIGGEST LAND ANIMAL
→
AFRICAN BUSH ELEPHANT
LOXODONTA AFRICANA

Blue whales may own the seas, but on land, elephants rule. Standing up to 13 feet (4 m) tall at the shoulder and weighing as much as 14,000 lb (6,350 kg), the African bush elephant is the largest land animal in the world. Fortunately, for other animals, these powerful pachyderms are vegetarians, eating up to 300 pounds (136 kg) of tree bark, fruit, leaves, and grasses each day.

SMALLEST MAMMAL
→
PYGMY SHREW
SOREX HOYI

Barely nudging the bumblebee bat out of the competition by one one-hundredth of an ounce (28 g), the American pygmy shrew is considered to be the world's smallest mammal. With a body length of 1.5 to 2 inches (3.8 to 5 cm) and weighing .07 ounces (2 g), these tiny predators must eat at least three times their body weight daily to stay alive.

FASTEST RUNNER
→
CHEETAH
ACINONYX JUBATUS

Now, here's a contest about which there's no debate. When it comes to fastest runner, the cheetah has this competition locked up. Able to go from 0 to 60 miles an hour (96 km/h) in just three seconds, these powerful cats are built for quick acceleration and short-distance sprinting. With physical features like a flexible spine, long legs, and a sturdy tail for balance, cheetahs win this race hands (or paws) down.

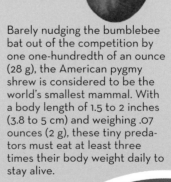

SLOWEST
SLOTH
BRADYPUS VARIEGATUS (PICTURED)

Just like a cheetah's built for speed, two- and three-toed sloths are built for, well, no speed. These mammals move a mere six to eight feet (1.8 to 2.4 m) per minute. Because sloths would be easy prey for any predator on the rain forest floor, they spend their entire lives hanging in trees, rarely ever moving to the ground.

LONGEST
TONGUE
GIANT
ANTEATER
MYRMECOPHAGA TRIDACTYLA

Boasting the longest and perhaps most useful tongue in the animal kingdom, the giant anteater's tongue can extend two feet (61 cm) beyond its mouth. Good thing, too. Measuring more than six feet (1.8 m) in length, these medium-size mammals slurp up about 30,000 ants per day to get their fill.

MOST POISONOUS
MAMMAL
PLATYPUS
ORNITHORHYNCHUS ANATINUS

When it comes to venom, there is no shortage of deadly toxins in the animal kingdom. One animal takes the cake among mammals, however. The male platypus, despite its innocent appearance, actually has a venom-producing gland in its rear leg, connected to a sharp, pointy spur on the inside of its ankle. Victims as large as dingos (wild dogs) will be dead in minutes if this paralyzing predator strikes.

TALLEST
GIRAFFE
GIRAFFA CAMELOPARDALIS

It may not be the largest animal on Earth, but standing a staggering 19 feet (5.8 m) tall, the giraffe is certainly the tallest. With a neck alone measuring more than 7 feet (2.1 m), these skyscrapers of the savanna use their height to great advantage—they can reach the leaves at the tops of trees that shorter herbivores can't.

MAP KEY

APPROXIMATE RANGES OF RECORD-SETTING MAMMALS

- Pygmy Shrew
- Cheetah
- Giant Anteater
- Two-toed Sloth
- African Elephant
- Platypus
- Giraffe
- Blue Whale

Want to know where these record-holding mammals live around the world? Take a look at this range map to find out.

The Blue Whale range covers almost all oceans.

Feathers are a defining characteristic of all birds. They can vary in size and shape, and they help with many functions, such as warmth, flight, and courtship. This snowy owl's feathers also serve as camouflage, helping to conceal it in its Arctic habitat.

BIRDS

KING PENGUINS

WILLOW PTARMIGAN

COMMON KINGFISHER

SCARLET MACAW

SOUTHERN WHITE-FACED OWL

MALLARD DUCKLING

RHODE ISLAND RED CHICKEN

YELLOW BITTERN

BARNACLE GEESE

RED-FOOTED BOOBY

BALD EAGLE

PILEATED WOODPECKER

SANDHILL CRANE

AMERICAN ROBINS

KEEL-BILLED TOUCAN

WHAT IS A BIRD?

BIRDS ARE VERTEBRATE ANIMALS ADAPTED FOR FLIGHT.

Many can also run, jump, swim, and dive. Some, like penguins, have lost the ability to fly but retained their wings. Birds are found worldwide and in all habitats. The largest is the nine-foot-tall ostrich. The smallest is the two-inch-long bee hummingbird.

Everything about the anatomy of a bird reflects its ability to fly. The wings, for example, are shaped to create lift. The leading edge is thicker than the back edge, and they are covered in feathers that narrow to a point. Airplane wings are modeled after bird wings.

The bones and muscles of the wing are also highly specialized. The main bone, the humerus, which is similar to the upper arm of a mammal, is hollow instead of solid. It also connects to the bird's air sac system, which, in turn, connects to its lungs. The powerful flight muscles of the shoulder attach to the keel, a special ridge of bone that runs down the center of the wide sternum, or breastbone. The tail feathers are used for steering.

Birds have a unique digestive system that allows them to eat when they can—usually on the fly—and digest later. They use their beaks to grab and swallow food. Even the way a bird reproduces is related to flight. Instead of carrying the extra weight of developing young inside their bodies, they lay eggs and incubate them in a nest.

The fossil record shows that birds evolved alongside the dinosaurs during the Jurassic period 160 million years ago. The best known fossil is *archaeopteryx*, which was about the size of a crow.

BIRD TRAITS

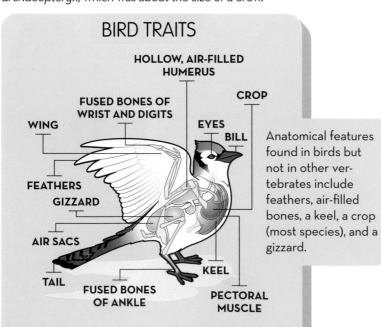

HOLLOW, AIR-FILLED HUMERUS

FUSED BONES OF WRIST AND DIGITS

CROP

WING

EYES

BILL

FEATHERS

GIZZARD

AIR SACS

TAIL

FUSED BONES OF ANKLE

KEEL

PECTORAL MUSCLE

Anatomical features found in birds but not in other vertebrates include feathers, air-filled bones, a keel, a crop (most species), and a gizzard.

CLASSIFICATION OF BIRDS

There are about 9,800 bird species organized into 28 orders. The largest is the order Passeriformes, known as the perching birds. Of the 28 orders, the most familiar groupings are:

1 PERCHING BIRDS (PASSERIFORMES)

2 DUCK, GEESE, AND SWANS (ANSERIFORMES)

3 CHICKENS AND RELATIVES (GALLIFORMES)

4 EAGLES, FALCONS, AND OWLS (FALCONIFORMES AND STRIGIFORMES)

5 PARROTS (PSITTACIFORMES)

6 PENGUINS (SPHENISCIFORMES)

Did you know? Birds are the only animals that have feathers.

Female robins weave nests made out of twigs, grass, feathers, and mud. Inside, soft grasses cushion delicate eggs. Males and females work together to raise their young.

EAGLES, FALCONS, HAWKS, AND OWLS

Eagles, falcons, hawks, and owls are top predators that hunt from the air. All are strong fliers with excellent vision, a hooked beak, powerful feet, and sharp nails known as talons. Because of their hunting style, they are known both as birds of prey and as raptors, from the Latin word *rapere*, which means "to take by force."

Eagles can spot their prey from a mile or more away. Owls, which also have excellent hearing and soft, quiet feathers, hunt at night. Buzzards and kestrels hover over their prey. Hawks are ambush hunters, like cats. Falcons dive or swoop through the air.

Many birds of prey have dietary preferences, too. Ospreys eat only live fish, honey buzzards eat wasps, peregrine falcons eat other birds, and secretary birds eat snakes. Vultures, condors, and kites prefer dead animals, known as carrion.

There is also quite a range in the size of birds in this group. The smallest, the falconet, is about the size of a sparrow. The largest is the condor, which has a ten-foot (3.2-m) wingspan. Life spans vary from 20 years for smaller species to 60 years for larger ones.

SAKER FALCON
FALCO CHERRUG

RANGE: Eastern Europe, Central Asia, parts of Africa

SIZE: 17 to 21 in (45 to 55 cm)

DIET: Mostly small mammals, ground birds, other birds

The saker falcon is a patient and persistent hunter. It will pursue prey as small as a lizard and as large as a gazelle. This species is considered the best for falconry, the practice of hunting using a trained bird of prey.

ANDEAN CONDOR
VULTUR GRYPHUS

RANGE: Western South America throughout the Andes

SIZE: 3.2 to 4.2 ft (1 to 1.2 m)

DIET: Carrion

Unlike other birds of prey, Andean condor males are larger than females and have a colorful face. They have fleshy red tissue at the base of their beak similar to a male rooster—the top piece is a comb, the bottom is a wattle.

AMERICAN BALD EAGLE
HALIAEETUS LEUCOCEPHALUS

RANGE: North America, including northern Mexico

SIZE: 2.3 to 3.1 ft (0.7 to 0.95 m)

DIET: Fish, reptiles, amphibians, mammals, carrion

Bald eagles are large, powerful, aggressive birds known for stealing food—even garbage—from others. They are named for their bright white feathers. In animals, "bald" means "an area marked with white."

LAPPET-FACED VULTURE
TORGOS TRACHELIOTOS

RANGE: Africa

SIZE: 31 to 45 in (78 to 115 cm)

DIET: Mostly carrion; also small reptiles, fish, birds, mammals

The lappet-faced vulture, like other condors and vultures, is bald for a reason: to keep clean. These birds splatter blood on their faces as they tear into their meals. Because of their habitat and behavior, they rarely take a bath.

RED-TAILED HAWK ⊙⊙
BUTEO JAMAICENSIS

RANGE: North and Central America

SIZE: 17.7 to 25.5 in (45 to 65 cm)

DIET: Rodents, reptiles, birds

Red-tailed hawks hunt from a carefully chosen perch, usually a tree branch, fence post, or telephone pole located along the edge of an open field. They dive with their legs stretched behind them and their wings open.

SNOWY OWL ● ◐◐
NYCTEA SCANDIACA

RANGE: Northern North America

SIZE: 20.5 to 28 in (52 to 71 cm)

DIET: Small mammals, birds, fish

Snowy owls are the heaviest owls found in North America not just because of their size, but also because of their heavy, thick, insulating feathers. These owls live mostly in the Arctic tundra. Only some populations fly south in winter.

GALÁPAGOS HAWK ⊙⊙●
BUTEO GALAPAGOENSIS

RANGE: Galápagos Islands

SIZE: 21.5 in (55 cm)

DIET: Lizards, rats, doves, centipedes, both land and marine iguanas, goats, boobies, grasshoppers, carrion

Galápagos hawks hunt together in groups of two or three either for live prey or for a carcass. The dominant hawk gets to eat first. These days, their diet includes several introduced species, such as chickens and rats.

Did you know? The California condor is the largest flying bird in North America.

BURROWING OWL ⊙⊙🌵
ATHENE CUNICULARIA

RANGE: North and South America

SIZE: 8.5 to 11 in (21.6 to 27.9 cm)

DIET: Insects, frogs, small mammals

These owls often will nest in holes in the ground dug by other animals, including prairie dogs and skunks. In addition to small mammals, the burrowing owl eats a wide variety of insects, including scorpions and dung beetles.

GREAT HORNED OWL ⊙⊙⊙
BUBO VIRGINIANUS

RANGE: North and South America

SIZE: 19.7 in (50 cm)

DIET: Mammals and birds

This owl is named for the feather tufts above its ears that look like horns. Its hooting call sounds like whoo, whoo-hoo, whoo, whoo. When a male hoots to establish his breeding territory, a female will often respond.

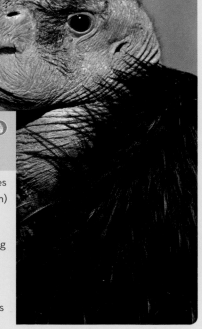

CALIFORNIA CONDOR ●⊙⊙⊙
GYMNOGYPS CALIFORNIANU

RANGE: Western United States

SIZE: 3.8 ft to 4.3 ft (1.1 to 1.3 m)

DIET: Carrion

The California condor can soar for miles without flapping its wings. It is nearly extinct because it scavenges on animals shot by hunters with lead bullets and on garbage. Plastic, lead, and other metals are toxic to these birds.

FROM THE FIELD:
ADRIAN SEYMOUR

HARPY EAGLE

One of the scariest assignments of my life was filming a harpy eaglet *(Harpia harpyja)* in the Imataca rain forest in Venezuela. Fully grown female harpies only weigh about 20 pounds (9 kg), but they have wingspans of up to 6.5 feet (2 m) and razor-sharp talons the size of grizzly bear claws. And they're fiercely protective of their chicks. During our 21 weeks of filming, the mother harpy launched several attacks on our crew—usually when we were dangling defenselessly from a rope 70 feet (21.3 m) off the ground. Stab vests and helmets were part of our daily uniform, but the worst attack came when I least expected it.

I was a good distance from the harpy nest and it was boiling hot, so I decided to leave my bulky vest on the ground. I made it safely into the canopy and was admiring a beautiful sunset when a massive jolt to my back knocked me breathless. The mother harpy had struck again—this time sinking her claws a half-inch (1 cm) deep into my skin. My shirt was ripped to shreds, and blood poured out of four puncture wounds. After that, each time I clipped onto the rope to climb into the canopy—even with my vest on—my heart raced with fear.

APPROXIMATE RANGE OF THE
HARPIA HARPYJA (HARPY EAGLE)

NORTH
AMERICA

ATLANTIC
OCEAN

0   1,000 miles
0   1,000 kilometers

PACIFIC
OCEAN

SOUTH
AMERICA

OBSERVATION
TIPS

1 Harpy nests are very difficult to find in the rain forest. Ask a local guide to help you pinpoint one.

2 To see a harpy chick in the rain forest, you have to climb a tree near its nest and use binoculars to scan the forest canopy.

3 Use a slingshot to launch climbing rope around tree branches 70 feet (21.3 m) above the ground.

4 Stab vests and helmets protect sensitive body parts from angry harpy mothers.

Adrian Seymour is a wildlife ecologist and filmmaker. He has spent nearly a decade living and working in the jungles of Asia and South America, where he combines scientific research and filmmaking to raise awareness of some of the world's most remote—and often endangered—animals.

Harpy eagles build huge nests—the size of a double bed!—high up in the treetops. Parents raise one chick at a time and take turns hunting for monkeys, sloths, and opossums, which they snatch from tree branches and rip into tiny bits to feed to the chick. After a few months, the chick begins hopping around the nest and jumping to nearby branches to test its wings and prepare for its first flight.

107

DUCKS, GEESE, AND SWANS

Ducks, geese, and swans have streamlined bodies and webbed feet for swimming, thick feathers for warmth, and short, powerful wings for flying. For the most part, they live in fresh water. Many migrate long distances between their summer breeding grounds to where they spend the winter.

Most are vegetarians. They have wide, flat beaks for feeding on aquatic plants or grazing on grass. The diving ducks are the exception. Mergansers, buffleheads, and eiders, for example, have narrow beaks for catching fish.

Preening is especially important for birds that live in the water. This behavior involves using the beak to spread an oily substance, secreted by a gland located above the base of the tail, throughout the feathers. The oil creates a waterproof surface, like a raincoat.

Taking too much time to preen can be risky, though. Ducks and their eggs, in particular, are the favorite food of foxes, snakes, owls, crows, and humans. It is for this reason that the birds in this group are often referred to as waterfowl. Escape is an option, except for the time of year when these birds lose their flight feathers, known as the annual molt. Growing up very quickly helps, too. Chicks hatch with downy feathers and can walk or swim with their parents within hours. Though they can live up to 30 years, the average life span is shorter because of predation.

INSIDE A BIRD'S NEST

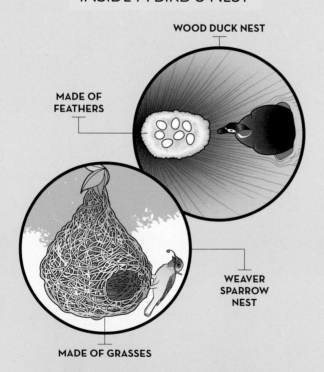

WOOD DUCK NEST

MADE OF FEATHERS

WEAVER SPARROW NEST

MADE OF GRASSES

Bird nests differ from one species to the next, and each nest has its own style of architecture—including location, materials, and shape. For example, wood ducks nest in hollow tree cavities lined with feathers. Pairs of sparrow weavers collect grasses and twigs and weave them together to create an apartment complex of hanging basket-like nests.

CHINESE GOOSE
ANSER CYGNOIDES

RANGE: Russia, Mongolia, China

SIZE: 2.7 to 3.1 ft (0.8 to 0.9 m)

DIET: Plants and flowering plants

Most domesticated geese are descendants of the Chinese, or swan, goose, the males of which have a knob at the base of their upper bill. This species is easily identified by its black bill and orange legs and feet.

CANADA GOOSE
BRANTA CANADENSIS

RANGE: North America

SIZE: 2.5 to 3.6 ft (0.76 to 1.1 m)

DIET: Grasses, flowering and aquatic plants, seeds, berries

Some populations of Canada geese fly south during winter to find food, whereas others have no need to migrate. Parks and golf courses, for example, provide plenty of grass. Geese also feed on crop grains like wheat and barley.

AMERICAN WOOD DUCK
AIX SPONSA

RANGE: East coast of North America to the Gulf of Mexico

SIZE: 1.5 to 1.7 ft (0.45 to 0.5 m)

DIET: Seeds, insects, arthropods; sometimes nuts and grain

Wood ducks are named because of where they like to nest: in tree holes in wooded swamps. Their short wings help them fly among the trees with ease. These ducks are omnivores, meaning they eat both plant and animal foods.

HOODED ○○🦆🦆
MERGANSER
LOPHODYTES CUCULLATUS

RANGE: North America

SIZE: 1.3 to 1.6 ft (0.4 to 0.5 m)

DIET: Aquatic insects and fish

Like wood ducks, hooded mergansers nest in wooded swamps and ponds. Their feeding habits are different, though: They are fish-eaters that dive for their food. During winter, they fly south only as far as needed to find ice-free ponds, lakes, and rivers.

SNOW ○○🦆
GOOSE
ANSER CAERULESCENS

RANGE: North America

SIZE: 2.3 ft (0.7 m)

DIET: Aquatic vegetation and wild rice

Snow geese migrate from the Gulf of Mexico in winter to the Arctic tundra in spring, and back again in the fall. Hundreds of thousands stop to rest along the way. From a distance, their huge flocks look like snow.

AUSTRALIAN ○○🐟
SHELDUCK ○○🦆
TADORNA TADORNOIDES

RANGE: Eastern Australia, Tasmania

SIZE: Up to 2.3 ft (0.7 m)

DIET: Green grass, insects, algae, mollusks

Ducks and geese make a wide range of sounds, in addition to the familiar *quack, quack* and *honk, honk*. The sounds are unique to each species. The Australian shelduck, for example, is known for being very noisy when it flies.

BLACK-NECKED ○○
SWAN
CYGNUS MELANCORYPHUS

RANGE: South coastal and inland lakes of South America

SIZE: 3.3 to 4 ft (1 to 1.2 m)

DIET: Aquatic vegetation

Both male and female black-necked swans have a distinctive upper bill. Where the beak meets the skin under the eyes, there is a bright red, two-lobed knob known either as a comb or caruncle (CAR-uncle). This species also has pink legs.

HARLEQUIN ○○🦆🦆
DUCK
HISTRIONICUS HISTRIONICUS

RANGE: Coastal parts of northeastern and northwestern North America, Greenland, Iceland, Russia

SIZE: 1.1 to 1.7 ft (0.33 to 0.5 m)

DIET: Aquatic insects and fish

These ducks find their food by dabbling, swimming, and diving. They also have dense feathers that make them very buoyant. This versatile duck spends the winter on rocky coasts by the ocean, and the breeding season near fresh water.

SMEW ○○🦆🦆
MERGELLUS ALBELLUS

RANGE: Northern taiga of Europe and Asia

SIZE: 1.25 to 1.4 ft (0.4 to 0.44 m)

DIET: Aquatic insects and fish

With their compact bodies and hooked upper bills, smew are expert divers and fishers. Like many ducks, the male and female have very different coloration. Males are white with distinctive black lines. Females are gray with a brown head crest.

GULLS, PUFFINS,
AND SANDPIPERS

All of the birds in this group feed in, or near, water. Some, like terns and puffins, live in marine environments. Others, like skimmers and oystercatchers, are freshwater species. All eat other animals, with one exception: the seed-snipe.

Each species has a different hunting strategy, however. Seagulls, for example, are opportunistic feeders. They eat everything from human garbage to fish, eggs, clams, small birds, and mammals. To feed, they use their strong beak to grab their prey and their hooked upper beak to tear it apart. Jacanas, by comparison, walk on floating plants—like the leaves of water lilies—and use their short, narrow beak to probe for insects and seeds. The American avocet, a long-legged bird, wades in shallow water and sweeps its long beak back and forth through the mud, picking up tiny bits of food.

Life spans range from 5 years for smaller species to 30 years for puffins, and up to 50 years for herring gulls.

RING-BILLED GULL
LARUS DELAWARENSIS

RANGE: North America

SIZE: 16.9 to 21.3 in (43 to 54 cm)

DIET: Fish, insects, small mammals, grain

Like all gulls, the ring-billed gull is a strong, acrobatic flier. This species is very common in urban and agricultural areas across North America because of its opportunistic diet. It also nests inland, near fresh water.

ATLANTIC PUFFIN
FRATERCULA ARCTICA

RANGE: North Atlantic

SIZE: 11.5 to 13.5 in (29.2 to 34.3 cm)

DIET: Fish, mollusks, crustaceans

Atlantic puffins use their short, wide wings for swimming underwater to catch fish, as well as for flying. They cannot take off without a running start. During the breeding season, the male's bill turns bright yellow, blue, and orange.

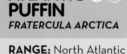

RUDDY TURNSTONE
ARENARIA INTERPRES

RANGE: Breeds in Arctic, migrates worldwide

SIZE: 6.3 in (16 cm)

DIET: Insects

This sandpiper relative is named for the way it feeds. It has a short, flat, wide bill that it uses to poke under rocks and sticks. Then it flips them over, looking for insects to eat.

BIRD-BRAINED

Birds have amazing adaptations that help them with their everyday chores. Some species, like the macaw, have strong beaks with which to crack open nuts. Others, like the toucan, have long beaks that allow them to pluck fruit from the end of a branch. But for some birds, adaptation just isn't enough; they make their own tools to help them survive. For example, crows on the island of New Caledonia have been seen using their beaks as scissors to create hooks out of twigs. They then stick the hooks down into a tree trunk to fish out whatever they cannot reach with their beaks. Even seagulls, generally considered a nuisance to beachgoers, have been observed using tools. And the lesser black-backed gull throws bread into the water to lure fish to the surface!

BLACK SKIMMER ⬤○○○
RYNCHOPS NIGER

RANGE: Atlantic coast and southern Pacific coast of North America, the Caribbean, and most of South America

SIZE: 15.7 to 19.7 in (40 to 50 cm)

DIET: Fish, insects, crustaceans

Skimmers fish by flying with their long, wide lower bills just under the water's surface. They are also a very social species and warn each other of predators. Their warning call sounds like a barking dog.

INCA TERN ○○○
LAROSTERNA INCA

RANGE: Chile and Peru

SIZE: 16 in (41 cm)

DIET: Small fish

Inca terns catch small fish using their spear-like beaks, either from the air in a plunge dive, or from the surface of the water while swimming. Like many sea birds, they live in large colonies. Their call sounds like a cat's meow.

COMMON GUILLEMOT ○○
URIA AALGE

RANGE: Coastlines and islands in the Northern Hemisphere

SIZE: 15 to 16.9 in (38 to 43 cm)

DIET: Fish and other marine vertebrates

This seabird is penguin-like. It dives to fish, has a white underside for camouflage in the water, stands up to walk, and nests in colonies. The male and female in a pair alternate duties incubating a single egg.

BIRDS

Did you know?

Atlantic puffins nest at the same place each year.

PHEASANT-TAILED JACANA ○○○
HYDROPHASIANUS CHIRURGUS

RANGE: India, Southeast Asia, Indonesia

SIZE: 5.5 to 9.8 in (14 to 25 cm); tail: 9.8 to 13.8 in (25 to 35 cm)

DIET: Insects, invertebrates, some vegetation

Jacanas live among floating leaves, such as water lilies. Using their huge feet, they walk, run, and hop from one leaf to another. Male jacanas build nests and raise the young, while females defend them.

SEMIPALMATED SANDPIPER ○○
CALIDRIS PUSILLA

RANGE: Central and eastern North America, northern South America

SIZE: 5.9 in (15 cm)

DIET: Insects

The term "palmated" means "webbed." This sandpiper has webbed toes, an adaptation for life near water. This small bird breeds in the open tundra during summer and migrates in large numbers to the coast of northern South America in winter.

SNOWY PLOVER ○○○
CHARADRIUS NIVOSUS

RANGE: Coasts of western United States to South America

SIZE: 5.9 to 6.7 in (15 to 17 cm)

DIET: Insects and other invertebrates

Snowy plovers breed only on sandy beaches and brackish inland lakes—places where there are a lot of people and housing developments. This tiny bird makes a small, shallow, difficult-to-see nest in the sand.

ALBATROSSES,
PELICANS, AND RELATIVES

Fish—both freshwater and marine—are central to the diets of many birds, especially those that rarely stray far from open waters. These include ocean birds that spend very little time on land, like albatrosses, petrels, shearwaters, boobies, tropicbirds, and some species of pelicans.

What and how these birds hunt is evident in the shape and size of their bodies, beaks, and feet. Pelicans are large birds with four webbed toes and a throat pouch. They scoop up their meals. Albatrosses are gull-like birds with very long wings. They fish on the fly, grabbing squid from just beneath the surface of the water with their hooked beaks. The giant petrel has a huge beak, which it uses to feed on seals, penguins, and whale carcasses. Gannets straighten their bodies like an arrow and plunge-dive into the water; if they catch a fish they swallow it instantly. They fish primarily for school fish like mackerel and herring, often following dolphins and bluefish feeding in the same area. Frigatebirds either skim the water for fish, or steal from others.

The larger seabirds have long life spans, up to 30 years for pelicans and 50 for the wandering albatross.

BULLER'S ALBATROSS
THALASSARCHE BULLERI

RANGE: Islands off New Zealand

SIZE: 2.6 ft (0.8 m)

DIET: Fish, squid, tunicates, crustaceans

This albatross, like others, has tube-shaped nostrils located on either side of its hooked bill and an excellent sense of smell. It also has glands that remove excess salt from its body.

BROWN PELICAN
PELECANUS OCCIDENTALIS

RANGE: Atlantic and Pacific coasts of the Americas, from central U.S. to Venezuela, including the Gulf Coast, parts of the Caribbean

SIZE: 3 to 4.5 ft (1 to 1.3 m)

DIET: Fish and marine invertebrates

Pelicans are large birds, but they weigh relatively little. The reason: pockets of air under the skin and in their bones. They feel crinkly. All that air makes it easier for them to fly, float, and surface after a dive.

NORTHERN GANNET
MORUS BASSANUS

RANGE: Atlantic coast of North America and northern Europe, including Quebec, Newfoundland, and Scotland

SIZE: 2.6 to 3.6 ft (0.8 to 1.1 m)

DIET: Mainly fish; some squid

Gannets nest along cliffs and ledges in large, dense colonies. The female lays just one egg, though if it is lost or damaged, she will lay another. Similar to penguins, the parents alternate incubating, protecting, and feeding the young.

SNOW PETREL
PAGODROMA NIVEA

RANGE: Antarctica

SIZE: 14 to 16 in (36 to 41 cm)

DIET: Mainly krill; also fish, mollusks, carrion

Snow petrels breed only in Antarctica and live as far south as the South Pole. About the size of a pigeon, their soft, white feathers help them withstand the extreme cold. These birds squirt a smelly oil to keep intruders from their nests.

MAGNIFICENT FRIGATEBIRD
FREGATA MAGNIFICENS

RANGE: Tropical coasts of the Americas, Cape Verde Islands, Galápagos Islands

SIZE: 2.9 to 3.7 ft (0.9 to 1.13 m)

DIET: Fish, squid, crabs

Frigatebirds spend most of their lives in flight, gliding on their long, wide wings. During the breeding season, the male inflates his bright red throat pouch, called a gular (GOO-lar) sac, and makes a drumming sound to attract females.

BLUE-FOOTED BOOBY
SULA NEBOUXII

RANGE: Pacific coast of the Americas from California, U.S.A., to Galápagos Islands

SIZE: 2.6 ft (0.8 m)

DIET: Fish

The male blue-footed booby does a dance with his colorful, oversized—and otherwise clumsy—feet to attract a female. Once bonded, the pair uses their feet for another purpose: to incubate their eggs and protect their chicks from the cold.

WHITE AMERICAN PELICAN
PELECANUS ERYTHRORHYNCHOS

RANGE: North America; winters along Atlantic and Pacific coasts, including Gulf Coast; breeds inland on lakes in northern Great Plains and western mountains

SIZE: 4 to 5.5 ft (1.2 to 1.6 m)

DIET: Fish

The pelican's lower bill is unique among birds. A soft, expandable throat pouch, instead of firm beak tissue, connects the two lower jawbones. This pouch, or gular (GOO-lar) sac, is used like a basket to scoop up fish.

WHITE-BREASTED CORMORANT
PHALACROCORAX CARGO SSP. LUCIDUS

RANGE: Sub-Saharan Africa

SIZE: 2.6 to 3.25 ft (0.8 to 1 m)

DIET: Fish and eels

Instead of oiling their feathers to repel water, cormorants allow them to get wet. This allows them to dive more easily. The trade-off: After a meal, the cormorant cannot fly again until it holds its wings out to dry.

NORTHERN FULMAR
FULMARUS GLACIALIS

RANGE: Northern oceans

SIZE: 15.4 to 19.7 in (39 to 50 cm)

DIET: Fish, squid, zooplankton

Northern fulmars live mostly in the open ocean, though they nest on rocky cliffs close to the shore. They are one of the longest-living species of birds, with recorded life spans in the wild of more than 50 years.

ANHINGA
ANHINGA ANHINGA

RANGE: North, Central, and South America, from southern U.S. to French Guiana; parts of the Caribbean

SIZE: 2.8 ft (0.9 m)

DIET: Fish

Anhingas are called snakebirds because they swim with their long neck and head just above water. They also are called water turkeys because they perch with tail feathers spread fan-like to dry.

WANDERING ALBATROSS

Catching one of the largest birds in the world requires crafty thinking—especially when the bird spends most of its time at sea. My first encounter with a wandering albatross (*Diomedea exulans*) was startling. I was on a ship sailing to Marion Island, near Antarctica, to attach scientific recording devices, called tags, to adult albatrosses. Out of nowhere, a huge shadow loomed overhead. I thought it was a jumbo jet, but it was a giant wandering albatross soaring above our boat!

When we landed at Marion Island, I quickly realized *everything* about these birds is gigantic—even their chicks! Imagine two fluffy pillows tied together with a beak poking out the top and two rubbery feet the size of human hands dangling from the bottom. I was told that the best way to catch an adult albatross is by hiding its chick, because once a parent returns from the sea with dinner, it stays put until Junior gets fed. So I wrapped my arms around the nearest chick and headed down a muddy slope. But the chick was so fluffy and big I could barely see where I was going, and when its down feathers tickled my nose, I slipped on the mud and tumbled to the ground. Then it kicked me in my face with its big feet! I finally got the chick down the hill, and when its parent returned to the nest, I walked right up to the giant bird, closed its beak with my hands, wrapped my arms around its massive wings, and heaved it off the ground so my colleague could attach the tag. Mission accomplished!

APPROXIMATE RANGE OF THE
DIOMEDEA EXULANS
(WANDERING ALBATROSS)

SOUTH AMERICA

ANTARCTICA

ANTARCTIC CIRCLE

AUSTRALIA

ANTARCTIC CIRCLE

AFRICA

OBSERVATION **TIPS**

1 Pack a windbreaker. Albatrosses need wind to fly, so they nest on remote islands with strong, gusting gales.

2 Beware of incoming albatrosses. They fly gracefully but usually make crash landings!

3 Approach an albatross from upwind to cut off its runway, so it can't fly away.

4 Give adult wandering albatrosses space—their wingspan is around 11 feet (3.4 m)! If an albatross feels threatened, it may snap its beak.

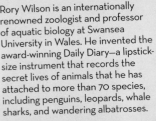

Rory Wilson is an internationally renowned zoologist and professor of aquatic biology at Swansea University in Wales. He invented the award-winning Daily Diary—a lipstick-size instrument that records the secret lives of animals that he has attached to more than 70 species, including penguins, leopards, whale sharks, and wandering albatrosses.

Albatrosses perform funny-looking song and dance routines to attract mates. They build nests out of mud and grass, and the female lays a single egg. Fluffy down feathers protect the chick from blustery winds while its parents are off fishing, sometimes for weeks at a time. When a parent returns, it squirts an amber-colored oil into the chick's mouth. After several months, the chick begins to lose its baby feathers, giving it a funny hairdo! It's finally ready to test its wings.

HERONS, FLAMINGOS, AND RELATIVES

Herons and their relatives—storks, egrets, ibises, and spoonbills—and the five species of flamingos are found in wetlands, waterways, and ponds.

These birds often are referred to as wading birds because of their hunting strategy. Most stand or walk in shallow water to feed. They have long legs and long necks so their beaks can reach the water.

Beak styles vary with diet. Herons, for example, are spear fishers. They have long, sharp beaks, which they use to pierce fish and frogs. Boat-billed herons catch similar prey, but they do so by scooping it out of the mud. Cattle egrets have short, sharp beaks for catching insects and other invertebrates disturbed by larger animals, like cows. Flamingos use an entirely different approach. They are filter-feeders. To make this work, though, they have to hold their head upside down with their beak underwater. Life spans for the birds in this group range up to 25 years.

GREAT BLUE HERON
ARDEA HERODIAS

RANGE: North and Central America, Caribbean, South America

SIZE: 3.2 to 4.5 ft (1 to 1.3 m)

DIET: Fish, frogs, invertebrates

For better aerodynamics in flight, the great blue heron curls its long neck into an S shape. These grayish-blue birds have rust-colored feathers on their thighs, green legs, and a black band above their eyes.

ROSEATE SPOONBILL
PLATALEA AJAJA

RANGE: Southern North America, Central America, Caribbean, northern South America

SIZE: 2.3 to 2.8 ft (0.7 to 0.9 m)

DIET: Fish

Instead of a pointed tip, the end of the roseate (ROW-zee-yate) spoonbill's beak is round and flat. The bird uses this spoon-like structure to catch minnows, other aquatic organisms, and plants by sweeping it from side to side in shallow water.

AMERICAN FLAMINGO
PHOENICOPTERUS RUBER

RANGE: Coastal South America, Caribbean, Galápagos Islands.

SIZE: 3.9 to 4.8 ft (1.2 to 1.4 m)

DIET: Bacteria, worms, crustaceans, insects, small fish

Turning its head upside down, a flamingo filters water through its beak for bits of food like brine shrimp and blue-green algae. These tiny plants and animals contain the chemicals that give the American flamingo its brilliant pink-red color.

WHITE IBIS
EUDOCIMUS ALBUS

RANGE: Southern North America, Central America, Caribbean, northern South America

SIZE: 1.8 to 2.2 ft (0.5 to 0.7 m)

DIET: Crustaceans and insects

White ibises are social birds. They fly, roost, nest, and feed together. They find crayfish, crabs, and insects by probing the water with their long beaks. Ibises usually wash the mud off their food before swallowing it whole.

SCARLET IBIS
EUDOCIMUS RUBER

RANGE: Northern South America

SIZE: 4.7 ft to 6.4 ft (1.4 to 2 m)

DIET: Crayfish, crabs, insects, frogs, mollusks, small snakes, fish

Scarlet ibises share their habitat with other wading birds, including spoonbills. The benefit to such a mix of species is safety in numbers. Individual birds are better able to hide from potential predators like jaguars and hawks.

MADAGASCAR CRESTED IBIS
LOPHOTIBIS CRISTATA

RANGE: Madagascar

SIZE: 20 in (50 cm)

DIET: Invertebrates, frogs, reptiles

Not all ibises live in wetlands. The Madagascar crested ibis is a forest bird that hunts for invertebrates, frogs, and reptiles on the forest floor. Breeding pairs build a large, platform-like nest high up in the tree canopy.

CHILEAN FLAMINGO
PHOENICOPTERUS CHILENSIS

RANGE: Parts of South America

SIZE: 2.6 to 4.8 ft (0.8 to 1.5 m)

DIET: Algae, aquatic plants and seeds

Flamingos are known for their copycat-style breeding displays. One male starts by making a specific motion, like opening his wings, or side-stepping. A second male copies him, then another, and so on—like a wave.

CATTLE EGRET
BUBULCUS IBIS

RANGE: Native to Africa and Asia; introduced in 19th century to South America; now in North and Central America

SIZE: 18.1 to 22 in (46 to 56 cm)

DIET: Insects, spiders, frogs

Cattle egrets are found in wet as well as dry grassland habitats. They are common in agricultural areas, where they often perch on the backs of cattle or follow tractors. Both stir up insects from the grass, which the egret catches.

Did you know?

Saddlebill storks are known to build large, flat nests 66 to 98 ft (20 to 30 m) high in trees.

SADDLEBILL STORK
EPHIPPIORHYNCHUS SENEGALENSIS

RANGE: Sub-Saharan Africa

SIZE: 4.9 ft (1.4 m)

DIET: Fish, frogs, crabs

Saddlebill storks are tall wetland birds. Their wingspan is eight to almost nine feet (2.4 to 2.7 m). Males and females look alike—both have a long, colorful, sharp bill for spearing their prey.

SHOEBILL STORK
BALAENICEPS REX

RANGE: East-central Africa

SIZE: 3.6 to 4.6 ft (1 to 1.4 m)

DIET: Fish, especially lungfish; water snakes, other reptiles

The shoebill stork has a strange way of catching food. It falls forward into the water, grabs the fish or reptile along with some vegetation in its bill, gets up, shakes the grasses out of its mouth, and decapitates its prey.

PAINTED STORK
MYCTERIA LEUCOCEPHALA

RANGE: Parts of Asia, including India, Sri Lanka, southern China

SIZE: 3 to 3.5 ft (1 to 1.1 m)

DIET: Fish, insects, crustaceans, reptiles

With their bill held open under the water, painted storks hunt for fish and other aquatic animals by feel. They walk slowly, stirring up the mud with their feet. When a fish moves, they snap it up.

LOONS AND GREBES

Some water birds are so streamlined for life in the water that they can barely stand up on dry land. This is the case with the diving birds—the loons and grebes.

Loons, for example, are compact birds with short legs set way back on their bodies close to the tail. The result is they have trouble balancing on two feet. Ducks, by comparison, run and walk easily. In the water, loons have the advantage. They can dive as deep as 250 feet (75 m) while hunting for fish or escaping predators.

In addition to their body shape, grebes are known for their in-the-water courtship rituals. A pair of male and female western grebes, for example, will begin with the "rush" dance. They flap their wings and run across the surface of the water, side by side. If all goes well, they continue with the "weed" dance, in which the pair dive and retrieve clumps of weeds for each other.

Life spans for loons and grebes range from 20 to 30 years.

RED-THROATED LOON
GAVIA STELLATA

RANGE: Northern Hemisphere

SIZE: 20.9 to 27.2 in (53 to 69 cm)

DIET: Marine and freshwater fish

Loons are fish-eaters that find their food by diving. They have good underwater vision and sharp beaks for catching their prey. They have no trouble taking off from the water, but only the red-throated loon can take off from land.

GREAT CRESTED GREBE
PODICEPS CRISTATUS

RANGE: Europe, Asia, Africa, Australia

SIZE: 18 to 20 in (46 to 51 cm)

DIET: Fish, crustaceans, insects, small frogs

Great crested grebes nest along the edges of lakes and carry their newly hatched chicks—which are striped—on their backs. The parents show their chicks how to fish by leaving them on the surface of the water while they dive.

COMMON LOON
GAVIA IMMER

RANGE: North America

SIZE: 27.5 to 35.4 in (70 to 90 cm)

DIET: Fish and other aquatic animals

Common loons are easily disturbed by people. They only nest on secluded ponds and lakes, where male and female pairs make flute-like calls, including one known as a wail.

AUSTRALASIAN GREBE
TACHYBAPTUS NOVAEHOLLANDIAE

RANGE: Australia, New Zealand, and nearby Pacific islands

SIZE: 9 to 10 in (25 to 27 cm)

DIET: Small fish and insects

Like many water birds, Australasian grebes are brightly colored during the breeding season. Males and females have a chestnut neck stripe and white face patch. These birds carry their striped chicks on their backs.

Did you know?

Unlike other birds, loons have solid bones that enable them to dive deep to catch food.

CRANES,
BUSTARDS, AND RELATIVES

Cranes are tall, long-legged, long-necked wetland birds. They live in pairs during the breeding season and in small family groups during the rest of the year—often in large flocks. Cranes are known for their courtship dances and songs. These include alternating calls between the male and female known as duets. Breeding pairs of sandhill cranes, for example, sound like trumpets playing.

Bustards are a related species of long-legged ground bird found only in Africa. These birds also dance and make loud calls during the breeding season. The male kori bustard, for example, spreads its wide tail feathers in a fan, inflates its neck, and makes a loud booming sound.

The many relatives of cranes and bustards include a variety of omnivorous birds with long legs and noisy courtship dances. Examples are trumpeters, sun bitterns, seriemas, rails, coots, and crakes.

Life spans for this group range up to 25 years.

GRAY CROWNED CRANE
BALEARICA REGULORUM

RANGE: Sub-Saharan Africa

SIZE: 39 to 43 in (100 to 110 cm)

DIET: Insects and other invertebrates; small reptiles and mammals; grass seeds

When the gray crowned crane makes its breeding call, it fills the bright red gular sac under its throat with air and makes a loud honking sound. The male and female look similar, but the male is larger.

SANDHILL CRANE
GRUS CANADENSIS

RANGE: North America

SIZE: 23 in (120 cm)

DIET: Grains, seeds, insects

During its winter migration, the sandhill crane flies south from Canada and the northern United States to New Mexico and Florida, U.S.A. Along the way, these birds stop to rest in huge numbers—up to 40,000—along the Platte River in Nebraska.

GRAY-WINGED TRUMPETER
PSOPHIA CREPITANS

RANGE: Amazon River basin and northeastern South America

SIZE: 17.2 to 21.2 in (43 to 53 cm)

DIET: Vegetation, including fruit; also insects, snakes

The thick black feathers on the trumpeter's head and neck look like velvet. These birds are named for their trumpet-like alarm calls. They also make a drumming sound while feeding, usually in groups, along the forest floor.

KORI BUSTARD
ARDEOTIS KORI

RANGE: Sub-Saharan Africa

SIZE: 41 to 50 in (105 to 128 cm)

DIET: Lizards and other small reptiles, insects, mammals, birds, vegetation, carrion

Kori bustards walk slowly through the grass, taking huge steps, looking mostly for lizards. They take dust baths to stay clean. Bustards weigh up to 42 pounds (19 kg), making them one of the heaviest flying birds.

CHICKENS,
TURKEYS, AND RELATIVES

There are nearly 300 relatives of chickens and turkeys. These include partridges, pheasants, quail, chachalacas (chock-a-LOCK-as), and curassows. All are potential prey for a host of predators, including humans.

In addition to being the favorite food of many, the birds in this group share two additional features.

First, the males have conspicuous colors, and their breeding displays often include crowing or clucking. Red jungle fowl, the wild ancestor of the domestic chicken, is one example. The common peafowl, or peacock, is another.

Second, these are ground-dwelling birds. They have short legs for digging up roots and short beaks for pecking seeds and insects. When startled or threatened, they head for the cover of bushes or the safety of a high tree limb. They lack stamina, however, and many are poor fliers. Domesticated species have lost the ability to fly entirely.

Life spans are generally short (two to seven years) because of the high risk of being eaten.

RED JUNGLEFOWL
GALLUS GALLUS

RANGE: Asia

SIZE: 11 in (28 cm)

DIET: Vegetation, grain, worms.

Red jungle fowl are tropical pheasants first domesticated in Asia thousands of years ago. They were bred with gray junglefowl to produce domestic chickens. Compared to females, the males are much larger, with red combs and colorful wattles.

RUFFED GROUSE
BONASA UMBELLUS

RANGE: Northern North America

SIZE: 15.7 to 19.7 in (40 to 60 cm)

DIET: Insects, leaves, twigs, acorns

The ruffed grouse is named for the way the male puffs out his neck feathers and fans his tail while defending his territory or trying to attract a mate. He also beats his wings against his sides to create a drumming sound.

Did you know? Red jungle fowl are not able to taste anything sweet.

CRESTED GUINEAFOWL
GUTTERA PUCHERANI

RANGE: Sub-Saharan Africa

SIZE: 19.7 in (50 cm)

DIET: Insects, seeds, roots

The crested guineafowl is named for the soft, curly, black feathers on its head. The male also has colorful bare skin around his eyes and neck. During the breeding season, he repeatedly brings food to the female.

PEACOCK FEATHER DISPLAY

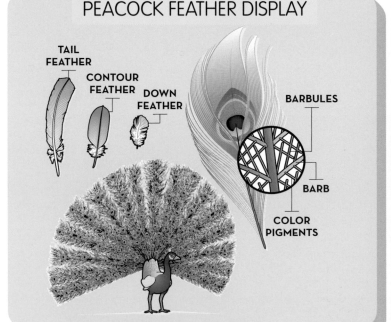

TAIL FEATHER
CONTOUR FEATHER
DOWN FEATHER
BARBULES
BARB
COLOR PIGMENTS

As in all birds, the brightly colored feathers of the male peacock result from a combination of color pigments and the way the barbules reflect light.

OCELLATED TURKEY
MELEAGRIS OCELLATA

RANGE: Yucatán Peninsula, Belize, Guatemala

SIZE: 35 in (89 cm)

DIET: Seeds, berries, insects

Compared to wild turkeys, this species is more colorful. Ocellated turkeys also have white tail spots like those found on peacocks. This pattern is called ocellated, for "ocelli," which means "spots."

GAMBEL'S QUAIL
CALLIPEPLA GAMBELII

RANGE: Southwest U.S.A.

SIZE: 9.8 in (25 cm)

DIET: Seeds, fruit, insects

Gambel's quails live in groups called coveys. The weather in the desert from one year to the next affects their populations. There are more quail during wetter years because there is more vegetation to eat.

WILD TURKEY
MELEAGRIS GALLOPAVO

RANGE: North America

SIZE: 36 to 39 in (91 to 99 cm)

DIET: Acorns, seeds, insects, fruit

In addition to a colorful comb and wattle, male wild turkeys have a snood—fleshy skin that hangs from the top of their bill. The domestic turkey is the same species, except it has been bred for meat and can no longer fly.

RING-NECK PHEASANT
PHASIANUS COLCHICUS

RANGE: Europe and Asia

SIZE: 16.7 to 21.1 in (42.5 to 53.6 cm)

DIET: Vegetation, seeds, insects, other small invertebrates

Ring-neck, or common, pheasants are ground birds that roost in trees. But they can also fly. When surprised, they launch themselves vertically into the air, a behavior known as flushing.

CRESTED WOOD PARTRIDGE
ROLLULUS ROULOUL

RANGE: Myanmar, Thailand, Malaysia, Sumatra, Borneo

SIZE: 26 in (66 cm)

DIET: Fruit, seeds, invertebrates

Like many of their relatives, crested wood partridges use their feet to find their food. They scratch and dig among the leaves looking for insects, seeds, and fruit. They often follow wild pigs, eating their half-eaten leftovers.

PIGEONS AND DOVES

The pigeons found in cities are far more common than their dove relatives. But there are more than 300 other species of pigeons and doves. Often, but not always, the smaller species are named doves and the larger ones pigeons. City pigeons, for example, are descendants of the wild rock dove, native to parts of Europe, Asia, and North Africa.

Pigeons and doves are strong fliers capable of traveling long distances. Most live in tropical forests and feed on a variety of seeds or fruits. Like all plant-eating birds, they are also prey for a number of other species. When threatened, they take off, flapping their wings loudly to surprise the potential predator.

Unfortunately, many doves and pigeons are endangered. Some have been hunted to near extinction, either for food or because they are considered pests that damage crops. Others are very susceptible to habitat destruction. The dodo bird and passenger pigeon, for example, are already extinct.

In the wild, doves and pigeons have relatively short life spans: three to five years.

MOURNING DOVE
ZENAIDA MACROURA

RANGE: North America to Panama

SIZE: 9.1 to 13.4 in (23 to 34 cm)

DIET: Seeds

Millions of mourning doves are hunted each year. Yet they still are extremely common. The reason: There is plenty of food for them in urban areas and on farms—they eat seeds off the ground. Telephone wires also make good perches.

VICTORIA CROWNED PIGEON
GOURA VICTORIA

RANGE: New Guinea and surrounding islands

SIZE: 29 in (74 cm)

DIET: Fruit and seeds

The Victoria crowned pigeon is the largest in the pigeon family. Sadly, it is in trouble due to a combination of hunting and logging. This brightly colored forest bird is easily spotted when disturbed, making it an easy target.

NAMAQUA DOVE
OENA CAPENSIS

RANGE: Sub-Saharan Africa, Madagascar, Arabian Peninsula, Turkey

SIZE: 8 in (22 cm)

DIET: Small seeds; grasses, sedges, weeds

The namaqua (nam-AH-kwa) dove is the smallest in the pigeon family. About the size of a budgerigar, it feeds on the ground, picking up tiny seeds. This species is known also as the cape or masked dove.

SUPERB FRUIT-DOVE
PTILINOPUS SUPERBUS

RANGE: Australia, New Guinea, Solomon Islands, Philippines, Indonesia

SIZE: 8 to 9 in (22 to 24 cm)

DIET: Berries and fruit, especially drupes and palm fruit

Only the male superb fruit-dove is brightly colored, with a purple cap, orange neck, and gray breast. The female is mostly green, with a small blue spot on her head. Figs are another favorite food of this rain forest species.

NICOBAR PIGEON
CALOENAS NICOBARICA

RANGE: India's Nicobar Islands, Myanmar, Thailand, peninsular Malaysia, Cambodia, Vietnam, Indonesia

SIZE: 15 in (40 cm)

DIET: Seeds, fruit, buds

Nicobar pigeons live in large flocks that often roost at night in areas with less food and fewer predators, returning during the day to feed in the lowland rain forest. They may be the closest living relative to the extinct dodo bird.

KINGFISHERS,
HORNBILLS, AND RELATIVES

Though they are found all over the world, kingfishers, hornbills, bee-eaters, and hoopoes are related to each other.

One of the features they share is their shape. All have large heads and beaks relative to their body size, and brightly colored feathers. A second shared feature is the way they kill their food. After catching an insect or fish, they use a branch or the ground to stun or kill it.

For example, when a kingfisher spots a fish, it plunges into the water, grabs it, and flies up to a nearby perch. Once there, it slaps the fish against a branch to stun it before swallowing it. Bee-eaters have a similar behavior. After catching their prey, they fly to a perch and smash the bee to expel the venom in its stinger before eating it. The much larger great Indian hornbill, which eats small mammals, birds, amphibians, and reptiles in addition to fruit, also uses a branch to kill its prey.

Life spans in this group range from up to 18 years for smaller species and 40 years for the larger hornbills.

BIRDS

WREATHED HORNBILL
ACEROS UNDULATUS

RANGE: Northeastern India, Bhutan, Southeast Asia

SIZE: 30 to 32 in (76 to 81 cm)

DIET: Mostly fruit; insects, small reptiles, amphibians during nesting

All hornbills have large, curved bills. Many, like the wreathed hornbill, have an added structure on top known as a casque (CASK). To support the weight of the bill, these birds have two fused neck vertebrae (VER-te-BRAY).

LILAC-BREASTED ROLLER
CORACIAS CAUDATUS

RANGE: Sub-Saharan Africa, southern Arabian Peninsula

SIZE: 14.2 in (36 cm)

DIET: Insects and amphibians

This species is named for the color of its feathers and its courtship display. To attract a mate, the male swoops downward, rocking—or rolling—his body from side to side and calling to the female.

GRAY-HEADED KINGFISHER
HALCYON LEUCOCEPHALA

RANGE: Sub-Saharan Africa

SIZE: 30 to 32 in (76 to 81 cm)

DIET: Insects and small reptiles

Most of the 90 species of kingfishers live in forested areas near rivers and lakes, where they eat mostly fish. But some, like this one, live in dry woodlands, making their diet quite different from that of other kingfishers.

CARMINE BEE-EATER
MEROPS NUBICUS

RANGE: Equatorial and subequatorial Africa

SIZE: 13.5 in (35 cm)

DIET: Bees, grasshoppers, locusts

Bee-eaters perch out in the open, where they have a better chance of catching a meal. The carmine bee-eater uses a moving perch: It hunts for bees and grasshoppers from the back of a much larger bird, the kori bustard.

COMMON HOOPOE
UPUPA EPOPS

RANGE: Africa, Europe, Asia

SIZE: 10.6 in (27 cm)

DIET: Insects

The hoopoe (HOO-poh) nests in tall trees but feeds on the ground, using its long bill to probe for food. It eats mostly crickets, locusts, beetles, and ants, killing them first by beating them on a hard surface.

123

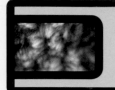

CUCKOOS AND RELATIVES

Cuckoos are secretive birds capable of moving through the forest or brush without making a sound. When they do make noise, it is a distinctive call. Most sound something like *woo-hoo hoo hoooo.*

Their relatives, while not as widely distributed, are also more likely to be seen than heard. These include the roadrunner, ani (aah-NEE), touraco (tu-RAH-koh), and hoatzin (hoh-WAT-zin).

Among the features that distinguish cuckoos and their relatives from the perching birds are their feet. Like woodpeckers and parrots, they have two forward-facing and two rear-facing toes.

Another is a behavior known as brood parasitism. Instead of building their own nest, many cuckoos lay their eggs in the nest of another bird whose eggs look similar. The victim is typically a smaller-size perching bird. When the cuckoo chick hatches, the female who built the nest—not the cuckoo—feeds it. Because the young cuckoo is larger, it gets most of the food and grows faster.

Life spans for cuckoos and their relatives are up to nine years.

LADY ROSS'S TURACO
MUSOPHAGA ROSSAE

RANGE: Central and southern Africa

SIZE: 15 to 18 in (37.5 to 45 cm)

DIET: Fruit, flowers, buds, termites, snails

Turaco feathers contain blue and red pigments not found in other birds. Yet even with its bright coloring, the Lady Ross's is more likely to be heard than seen. Its call sounds as if it is saying *go away.*

GREATER ROADRUNNER
GEOCOCCYX CALIFORNIANUS

RANGE: Mojave, Sonoran, Chihuahuan, and Great Basin deserts in the southwestern United States and Mexico

SIZE: 20.5 to 21.3 in (52 to 54 cm)

DIET: Insects, scorpions, birds, lizards, snakes, rodents, fruit

Roadrunners are a type of ground cuckoo capable of running up to 18.6 miles per hour (36 km/h) after their prey. As omnivores, they eat anything they can find in the desert—even venomous scorpions and snakes.

HOATZIN
OPISTHOCOMUS HOAZIN

RANGE: South America in the Amazon and Orinoco River basins

SIZE: 24 to 26 in (61 to 66 cm)

DIET: Leaves, flowers, fruit

Also called a stinkbird, the hoatzin has a unique digestive system. It eats mostly leaves and has a very large crop that acts like a fermentation vat. The result is a bird that smells like manure and can barely fly.

GREAT BLUE TURACO
CORYTHAEOLA CRISTATA

RANGE: Central and West Africa

SIZE: 28 to 30 in (70 to 76 cm)

DIET: Fruit, flowers, buds, insects

Like all turacos, the great blue is a weak flier. Instead, it runs and jumps among tree branches, using its tail for balance. Turacos also have three forward-facing toes on each foot and a fourth that rotates, giving them an excellent grip.

GUIRA CUCKOO
GUIRA GUIRA

RANGE: Southern South America east of the Andes

SIZE: 13 in (34 cm)

DIET: Insects, frogs, eggs, small birds, rodents

The guira (goo-EAR-ra) cuckoo is a social species. Small flocks feed together in one area, hopping among the tree branches, or from a branch to the ground. These cuckoos also build community nests.

NIGHTJARS, POTOOS, AND RELATIVES

Nightjars and their relatives are very difficult to observe. All are nocturnal and active only in short bursts while hunting. Most fly with their wide mouths held open to trap insects.

During the day, the birds in this group are incredibly well camouflaged. Most roost either on the ground or in trees, where they sit as if frozen. The potoo, a speckled gray-brown color, often perches on the top of broken tree trunks. From a distance, it looks like a branch or piece of the trunk. The common nightjar has speckled brown feathering. It often rests among dried leaves or on a horizontal branch, where it, too, blends right in.

Several species make distinctive calls. One example is a species of nightjar called the whip-poor-will. It is most active on moonlit nights. The male's call sounds like he is saying his name over and over—very loudly.

Another way to find a nightbird is to shine a flashlight and look for two bright dots against a dark background. Like many other nocturnal animals, its eyes reflect the light.

Life spans are up to 15 years.

COMMON POTOO
NYCTIBIUS GRANDIS

RANGE: Tropical Central and South America

SIZE: 13 to 16 in (33 to 41 cm)

DIET: Large flying insects

The female potoo (poo-TOO) lays her egg in a depression on top of a broken tree trunk. She and the male blend right in while they take turns incubating the egg and, later, caring for the chick.

TAWNY FROGMOUTH
PODARGUS STRIGOIDES

RANGE: Australia, Tasmania, southern New Guinea

SIZE: 9 to 21 in (22.9 to 53.3 cm)

DIET: Insects, invertebrates; sometimes mice

Like owls, frogmouths have large eyes and good night vision. Both make noise by clapping their beaks. But the frogmouth hunts differently. It perches and waits for prey to pass by, then grabs it in its beak.

EUROPEAN NIGHTJAR
CAPRIMULGUS EUROPAEUS

RANGE: Europe, Asia; migrates to Africa

SIZE: 10 to 11 in (26 to 28 cm)

DIET: Insects

Nightjars and their eggs are prey for owls, hawks, adders, and foxes. When camouflage fails, these birds create a distraction by pretending to be dead, opening their mouths wide and hissing, or flapping their outstretched wings.

SAND-COLORED NIGHTHAWK
CHORDEILES ACUTIPENNIS

RANGE: North, Central, and South America

SIZE: 8 to 9.2 in (20 to 23 cm)

DIET: Insects

Nighthawks feed on a number of potentially harmful insects, including mosquitoes. As a result, they play an important role in the ecosystem. Yet these birds, which nest on the ground in open areas, are rarely seen.

HUMMINGBIRDS
AND SWIFTS

Hummingbirds are tiny, fast, acrobatic birds with a very high metabolic rate. They rarely perch. Not only can they fly forward at speeds of up to 34 miles per hour (54 km/h), but they can also hover in one place and even fly backward. No other bird can do this.

To maintain this level of activity, they need a constant supply of highly digestible and readily available calories. For this reason, hummingbirds are never far from flowering plants. They are nectarivores, meaning they eat nectar. All have long, narrow beaks adapted to reach deep into a flower. Among the 350 or so species, many are adapted to feed only on certain plants. Their beaks are shaped to fit precisely inside a particular flower.

Though they eat insects, swifts are grouped with hummingbirds because of their wing structure. Both have very stiff elbows and flexible wrists and digits. Swifts also have very unusual feet. All four toes face forward. This arrangement is called paprodactyl (pa-pro-DACK-til).

Life spans for hummingbirds and swifts range up to seven years.

COSTA'S HUMMINGBIRD
CALYPTE COSTAE

RANGE: Canada, United States, Mexico

SIZE: 3 in (7.6 cm)

DIET: Nectar

Costa's hummingbirds live in dry deserts, though they move to cooler areas during the heat of summer. They feed on the nectar of a variety of flowering desert plants, including desert honeysuckle, saguaro cactus, agave, and chuparosa.

CALLIOPE HUMMINGBIRD
STELLULA CALLIOPE

RANGE: Canada, United States, Mexico

SIZE: 3.5 in (9 cm)

DIET: Nectar

The calliope hummingbird is the smallest bird in North America, and the smallest migrating bird in the world. It weighs only 0.1 oz (2 to 3 g) yet it can fly as far as 5,600 miles (9,000 km) to spend the winter in southern Mexico.

WHITE-THROATED SWIFT
AERONAUTES SAXATALIS

RANGE: North and Central America

SIZE: 6.5 in (16.5 cm)

DIET: Insects

Swifts are among the fastest flying animals. All, including the white-throated swift, spend their days in the air, hunting flying insects. At dusk, they gather to spend the night in cavities along cliffs and in large rocks. Hundreds enter the roost at once.

GREAT DUSKY SWIFT
CYPSELOIDES SEN EX

RANGE: Argentina, Brazil, Paraguay

SIZE: 5.5 in (14 cm)

DIET: Insects

Swifts rarely perch, except to roost at night, and even then, their feet never touch the ground. They use their four forward-facing toes to hold on to smooth surfaces like rock walls. In flight, their wings look like boomerangs.

PARROTS

All parrots have relatively large, round heads with curved beaks, colorful feathers, dexterous feet, and noisy social behavior. Most eat a variety of seeds, fruits, and flowers. A few, like the lories and lorikeets, have a specialized tongue used for drinking nectar.

Parrots are found in tropical forests and wooded areas of South America, Africa, and Australia. A few, like the kea and thick-billed parrot, live in cooler climates and can even tolerate snow.

All are experts at eating slippery or difficult-to-reach foods. They often use one foot to perch and the other to bring food to their beaks. Like woodpeckers and toucans, they have a toe arrangement known as zygodactyl (zi-go-DACK-til). Their first and last toes face backward and the middle two face forward.

Their beaks are also much stronger than they look. Even parakeets can crack open a nutshell. Macaws in particular have powerful beaks adapted for eating the fruit, seeds, and nuts of palm trees. When they need to climb, parrots use their beaks like a third limb.

Most parrots form pair bonds for life, but they live in large flocks. Life spans range from 10 years for smaller ones up to 60 years for larger ones.

PINK COCKATOO
CACATUA LEADBEATERI

RANGE: Australia

SIZE: 15.75 in (40 cm)

DIET: Seeds, nuts, grains, fruit, tubers

Also known as Major Mitchell's cockatoo, the male and female of this species look similar. Females are smaller and have more yellow on their crest. They build nests of sticks and stones in hollow trees—and return to the same nests each year.

CUBAN PARROT
AMAZONA LEUCOCEPHALA

RANGE: Cuba, Bahamas, Cayman Islands

SIZE: 13 in (33 cm)

DIET: Fruit, leaves, seeds

There are many species of Amazon parrots. All are mostly green with colorful feathers on their head, wings, and tail. They are very social and noisy, especially while feeding and flying. Cuban Amazon parrots have white foreheads and pale red chins.

AFRICAN GRAY PARROT
PSITTACUS ERITHACUS

RANGE: West and Central Africa

SIZE: 13 in (33 cm)

DIET: Palm nuts, seeds, fruit, leaves

African gray parrots have been studied for their ability to speak and understand human language, solve problems, and mimic sounds. Unfortunately, many have been taken out of the wild to be kept as pets, and their populations are now in trouble.

RED AND GREEN MACAW
ARA CHLOROPTERUS

RANGE: North-central South America

SIZE: 39 in (1 m)

DIET: Fruit, seeds, nuts

Red and green macaws, like most parrots, visit cliffs, where they eat bits of clay and other minerals that help with digestion. Macaws eat a variety of foods that contain toxins, such as cashews and palm.

MANY MALE BIRDS— like the red bird of paradise (*Paradisaea rubra*)—have brightly colored feathers to attract a mate. The vibrant plumes signal to a female that the male is healthy and strong—and will reproduce equally healthy offspring.

WOODPECKERS, TOUCANS, AND RELATIVES

Woodpeckers, toucans, and barbets are forest birds that nest in holes in tree trunks. All are excellent tree climbers, and their feet are adapted for this purpose. Like parrots, these birds are zygodactyls: The first and fourth toes face backward, and the middle two face forward.

Other forest birds with similar feet—and the ability to move with great speed along tree trunks and branches—are the jacamars, honeyguides, and puffbirds. Many of these birds also feed on nectar and nest in termite mounds or on the ground.

Trogons are different. They are also a forest bird that nests in tree holes, but they barely use their feet. The arrangement of their toes is known as heterodactyl (het-er-oh-DACK-til). Their first two toes face backward, and the second two forward, which means they can balance but not grasp. They use their wings to catch and grab their food.

Life spans are up to 12 years for woodpeckers and 20 for toucans.

TOCO TOUCAN
RAMPHASTOS TOCO

RANGE: South America

SIZE: 24 in (61 cm)

DIET: Fruit

Toco toucans use their over-size, colorful bills to pluck fruit from tree branches. Breeding pairs also toss food to each other as part of a breeding display. This bird is always on the move, looking for the next tree full of fruit.

PILEATED WOODPECKER
DRYOCOPUS PILEATUS

RANGE: Northern North America

SIZE: 15.7 to 19.3 in (40 to 49 cm)

DIET: Mostly carpenter ants and beetle larvae; other insects, fruit, nuts

The pileated (PIL-ee-ated) woodpecker is a noisy bird. Both males and females call loudly to each other and drum on tree trunks. They also can be heard pecking at dead wood to find their food.

Did you know?

It takes about three years for male trogons to grow their long tail feathers.

RESPLENDENT TROGON
PHAROMACHRUS MOCINNO

RANGE: Central America

SIZE: 13.8 in (35 cm)

DIET: Fruit, insects, frogs, reptiles

Even with its three-foot-long tail (1 m), the resplendent trogon, or quetzal (ket-SAHL), feeds like other trogons. It hops off its perch, grabs its food—a piece of fruit or an insect—while still in flight, and then swoops back to its perch to eat.

BEARDED BARBET
LIBIUS DUBIUS

RANGE: Africa

SIZE: 10 in (26 cm)

DIET: Fruit, especially figs; insects

Barbets are fruit-eating specialists. They have ridges along the cutting edge of their upper bill that help to tear open fruit, especially figs. Like all fruit-eating forest birds, they play an important role in dispersing seeds.

RATITES

Ostriches, emus, cassowaries, rheas, and kiwis are flightless birds known as ratites (RA-tites), which means raft-like. Their group name refers to their skeletal structure, unique among birds. They lack a keel, the ridge of bone along the breastbone where the flight muscles attach in other birds. The result is that they have very weak wings and cannot fly.

Ratite feathers are also different. They lack tiny hooks, or barbules, that interlock the feathers of other birds. They also have more of what are known as "after feathers"—the light, wispy strands at the base of the feather shaft. As a result, their feathering is overall lighter and fluffier than that of other birds. Ostrich feathers, in particular, are used to decorate hats, fans, and pens. They are also used to make feather dusters.

The larger species—ostriches, emus, and cassowaries—have been traded as well as owned and bred for their meat, leather, oil, and feathers.

Life spans for ratites range from 20 to 30 years.

SOUTHERN CASSOWARY
CASUARIUS CASUARIUS

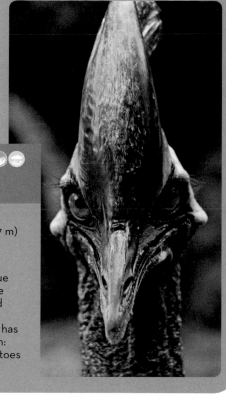

RANGE: New Guinea

SIZE: 3.3 to 5.6 ft (1 to 1.7 m)

DIET: Fruit, insects, vertebrates

The bony crest, or casque (CASK) on the top of the cassowary's head is used to push through dense vegetation. But this bird has a more powerful weapon: its legs, each with three toes and long, sharp claws.

EMU
DROMAIUS NOVAEHOLLANDIAE

RANGE: Australia

SIZE: 5.8 ft (1.7 m)

DIET: Seeds, fruit, flowers, leaves, insects

Emus, the second largest land bird after the ostrich, are known for following the rains in search of their food. They move toward dark rain clouds and the sound of thunder.

Did you know?
Ostriches' eyes are the largest of any land animal.

GREATER RHEA
RHEA AMERICANA

RANGE: Southeastern South America

SIZE: 4.9 ft (1.5 m)

DIET: Plants, seeds, fruit

Compared to other flightless birds, the rhea (REE-yah) has long wings. If chased by a predator, rheas try to dodge the threat by running in a zig-zag pattern, using one wing at a time like a rudder.

OSTRICH
STRUTHIO CAMELUS

RANGE: Asia, Arabian Peninsula, Africa

SIZE: 6.5 ft (2 m)

DIET: Plants

Ostriches live in habitats where the temperatures often vary greatly, by as much as 72°F (40°C). When necessary, they cover the featherless areas on their upper legs to conserve heat and expose them to cool off.

BROWN KIWI
APTERYX AUSTRALIS

RANGE: New Zealand

SIZE: 17.7 to 21.3 in (45 to 54 cm)

DIET: Invertebrates, especially worms, insects, crawfish; also amphibians, eels, fruit

Kiwis are shy birds with strong legs, poor eyesight, good hearing, and an excellent sense of smell. They are the only birds with nostrils at the end of their bill, which they use to poke around in the soil for food.

ANTBIRDS
AND RELATIVES

Antbirds and their relatives are perching birds found in the forests of Central and South America. Most live in the understory—either among the tree branches or on the ground.

The birds in this group are small with strong legs. They have a hooked bill for grabbing insects. Some, like the antthrush, eat mostly ants. Others, like the antshrike and woodcreeper, find their food by following swarms of army ants. These ant-followers eat grasshoppers, the larvae of butterflies and moths, and a variety of other insects.

Mixed flocks are common among antbirds. As the ant swarm goes by, different species position themselves in different locations to grab a meal. Most are much easier to hear than see. Their calls are a simple series of repeated chirps.

Life spans range from two to five years.

BLACK-STRIPED ⚪⚪ ⚫
WOODCREEPER
XIPHORHYNCHUS LACHRYMOSUS

RANGE: Central America

SIZE: 9 in (23 cm)

DIET: Primarily insects

Woodcreepers are ant-followers that feed on insects found in tree trunks. They hunt by hopping short distances or creeping along a tree limb. They also eat spiders, centipedes, millipedes, and even lizards.

RANGE: North and Central America

SIZE: 4.3 to 5.5 in (11 to 14 cm)

DIET: Insects and snails

Ovenbirds forage for insects and snails among leaves on the forest floor. They are named after their nests, which they build on the ground: mounds of woven vegetation with an entrance hole. Their main enemies are chipmunks.

CINEREOUS ⚪⚪ ⚪
ANTSHRIKE
THAMNOMANES CAESIUS

RANGE: South America

SIZE: 18 in (45 cm)

DIET: Insects

Antshrikes are one of the dominant species in a mixed flock of antbirds, meaning they lead the effort to follow army ants. They hunt insects either from a perch, called gleaning, or from the air, called sallying.

PERCHING
BIRDS

Half of all birds are in the order Passeriformes. The 5,000-plus species in this large group are known as "perching birds." All have feet adapted for gripping.

Perching birds have a toe arrangement known as anisodactyl (an-ee-so-DACK-til). They have three toes that face forward and one that faces backward. When wrapped around a perch, these birds have an excellent grip. Their feet also have muscles and tendons that lock their toes in place. As a result, perching birds can hold on with minimal effort to feed, and even sleep.

Because habitats—and perches—vary, there are thousands of species in this group. Perching birds are found all over the world in every type of habitat. All are insectivores; many also eat plants.

The smallest perching bird is the 0.15-ounce (4.2-g) short-tailed pygmy tyrant. The largest is the 57-ounce (1,625-g) raven.

SHORT-TAILED ⚪⚪ ⚫
ANTTHRUSH
CHAMAEZA CAMPANISONA

RANGE: South America

SIZE: 8 in (20 cm)

DIET: Insects, especially ants

The short-tailed antthrush has very strong legs for hopping after its prey and a very short tail that allows it to move quickly over the ground. It rarely flies long distances.

CHESTNUT ⚪⚪ ⚫
CROWNED
GNATEATER
CONOPOPHAGA CASTANEICEPS

RANGE: Central and South America

SIZE: 4.4 in (11.2 cm)

DIET: Insects and larvae

The gnateater is another insect-eater that follows ant swarms. It perches on low branches and jumps down to the ground to grab its prey, which also includes spiders, caterpillars, grasshoppers, and beetles.

FLYCATCHERS

There are about 400 species of tyrant (TY-rant) flycatchers. These are perching birds found in the Americas. They are grouped together because, like antbirds and their relatives, their calls are simple and nonmusical.

The antbirds and New World flycatchers have a simple syrinx (SEAR-inx), the bird equivalent of human vocal cords. The result is that their calls sound like a stream of single notes, rather than a song.

Despite their name, flycatchers eat more than flies. Most of the species found in North America catch their food while in flight. This behavior is called sallying, or hawking. The bird hops onto a perch, grabs an insect out of the air, and returns to the same or a different perch to eat it. Most Central and South American species catch their meals from a standstill, picking the insect off the ground or a leaf. This behavior is called gleaning.

Life spans range from two to five years.

SCISSOR-TAILED FLYCATCHER
TYRANNUS FORFICATUS

RANGE: Central North America and Central America

SIZE: 14.5 in (37 cm)

DIET: Insects

The scissor-tailed flycatcher is found as far north as the central United States. It is the state bird of Oklahoma. It is also known as the Texas bird of paradise because of its long tail feathers and pink coloring.

GREAT KISKADEE
PITANGUS SULPHURATUS

RANGE: Southwestern United States, Central America, South America

SIZE: 8.3 to 10.2 in (21 to 26 cm)

DIET: Fish, frogs, reptiles, insects

The great kiskadee is named for its call, which sounds like *KISK-a-DEE, KISK-a-DEE*. These are the largest of the tyrant flycatchers, and they have the most varied diet.

EASTERN KINGBIRD
TYRANNUS TYRANNUS

RANGE: North, Central, and South America

SIZE: 7.5 to 9.1 in (19 to 23 cm)

DIET: Insects and fruit

The eastern kingbird is a very territorial insect-eater during the breeding season. It will defend its nests even from much larger birds like crows and hawks. In winter, it changes its behavior, becoming a social fruit-eater.

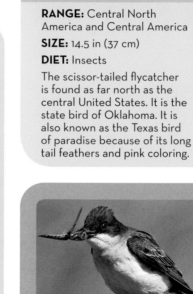

VERMILLION FLYCATCHER
PYROCEPHALUS RUBINUS

RANGE: Southwestern U.S., Central America, central South America, Galápagos Islands

SIZE: 5.1 to 5.5 in (13 to 14 cm)

DIET: Insects

The male vermillion (which means red) flycatcher is more brightly colored than the female. Both feed from a low perch, usually a tree out in the open, sallying out to catch flies, grasshoppers, and beetles in midair.

BLUE-WINGED PITTA
PITTA MOLUCCENSIS

RANGE: Australia and Southeast Asia

SIZE: 8.1 in (21 cm)

DIET: Worms, insects, snails

Pittas live on the forest floor, where they eat by probing with their beak in the leaf litter. Their brightly colored feathers are mostly under their wings and tail, to help hide them from predators.

CROWS
AND RELATIVES

Crows and their relatives—magpies, shrikes, and jays—are large birds known for their social, intelligent behavior. They raise their young together and are found in extended family groups that include a breeding pair and juveniles. Most crows, for example, stay with their parents and help raise new chicks until they are at least five years old. These young birds can be observed playing a variety of games, including "king-of-the-mountain," and learning how to balance sticks or use them as tools to find food.

Birds of paradise, found in New Guinea and parts of Australia, have crow-like bodies with very colorful feathers. Most are found in tropical forests, where they eat fruits and insects.

Vireos are medium-size, mostly dull-green birds found in the Americas. They sing from the treetops, where they also feed on caterpillars and other insects and fruits. Their calls are flute-like and simple.

Life spans are longest for ravens, members of the crow family: up to 15 years.

AMERICAN CROW
CORVUS BRACHYRHYNCHOS

RANGE: North America

SIZE: 15.7 to 20.9 in (40 to 53 cm)

DIET: Grains, seeds, nuts, berries, insects, aquatic animals

The American crow has a distinctive call that sounds like *caaw-caaw, caaw-caaw*. These birds are common because they eat anything, including garbage. Crows also use tools such as sticks or rocks to obtain their food.

COMMON RAVEN
CORVUS CORAX

RANGE: Western and northern North America

SIZE: 22 to 27.2 in (56 to 69 cm)

DIET: Carrion; small animals, including baby tortoises; nestling herons; eggs, insects, fish, plants, human food, garbage

Ravens are usually seen alone or in pairs looking for food. In the air, they are acrobats. In mid-flight, ravens will often drop a stick, and then dive to catch it. They are also excellent mimics.

RED BIRD OF PARADISE
PARADISAEA RUBRA

RANGE: Indonesia

SIZE: 13 in (33 cm)

DIET: Fruit and berries

All birds of paradise have amazingly colorful and elaborate feathers, which they use in breeding displays. The male red bird of paradise does not develop his long red feathers until he is five or six years old.

BLUE JAY
CYANOCITTA CRISTATA

RANGE: North America

SIZE: 9.8 to 11.8 in (25 to 30 cm)

DIET: Insects, nuts, seeds, grain

The blue jay is another social, vocal bird. It communicates using a combination of calls as well as face, crest, and body movements. A jay with its crest up is aggressive. Acorns from oak trees are their preferred food.

FORK-TAILED DRONGO ⚪⚪
DICRURUS ADSIMILIS

RANGE: Sub-Saharan Africa

SIZE: 9.8 in (25 cm)

DIET: Insects

The fork-tailed drongo is known for its ability to mimic other species. It is also an aggressive bird that will attack hawks and other large birds if its young are threatened.

MAGPIE ⚪⚪ SHRIKE
UROLESTES MELANOLEUCUS

RANGE: Sub-Saharan Africa

SIZE: 20 in (50 cm)

DIET: Insects, small birds, reptiles, mammals

The magpie shrike has an intelligent way of capturing its prey: It impales them on thorns or sharp tree branches. It has a hooked beak and can catch insects as well as lizards. By killing its prey first, the magpie shrike avoids stingers and toxins.

WARBLING ⚪⚫⚫ VIREO
VIREO GILVUS

RANGE: North America; migrates to Mexico and Central America

SIZE: 4.7 in (12 cm)

DIET: Insects; also berries

The singing behavior of the warbling vireo is typical of many songbirds. The male arrives in the breeding range first and establishes his territory by singing. Then the females arrive, and he attracts them with his continued singing.

COMMON ⚪⚫ GREEN MAGPIE
CISSA CHINENSIS

RANGE: Asia

SIZE: 14.4 to 15.2 in (37 to 39 cm)

DIET: Invertebrates, small reptiles, mammals, young birds

The green color of the common magpie is a combination of the yellow pigments they contain and the way the feathers are structured to reflect light that looks blue. The yellow and blue combine to make green.

SUPERB ⚪⚪ LYREBIRD
MENURA NOVAEHOLLANDIAE

RANGE: Australia

SIZE: 3.3 ft (1 m)

DIET: Insects

The male superb lyrebird has the most complicated song of any species. It is a combination of his own unique song plus mimicked sounds that may include other birds, koalas, dingos—even chain saws and barking dogs.

WESTERN ⚪⚪⚫ JACKDAW ⚪⚪⚫
CORVUS MONEDULA

RANGE: Europe, North and Central Asia, northwestern Africa

SIZE: 13 to 15 in (34 to 39 cm)

DIET: Plants, invertebrates, garbage

All members of the crow family like to pick up shiny objects. Carl Linnaeus, the scientist who created the animal classification system, named the western jackdaw for this behavior. Their species name comes from the Latin word *moneta*, meaning "money."

Did you know?
With long, strong legs and sturdy feet, the superb lyrebird is a swift runner.

CARDINALS
AND OTHER SONGBIRDS

Songbirds make calls that sound like musical notes and string them together into songs. Most of the perching birds are "songbirds." Cardinals, robins, wrens, thrushes, and blackbirds are among the most well-known songbirds. By comparison, other perching birds, like antbirds, do not sing. Their calls may sound musical, but they are a series of the same note repeated. Songbirds are also called passerines (pas-ser-EENS).

Male songbirds sing to establish their territory and to attract females. Each species has a distinctive courtship call. Learning bird songs is one of the best ways to identify birds. The male cardinal, for example, makes a song that sounds like a two-part whistle that ends in a trill. Both the male and female cardinal make a call that sounds like a flute playing *cheer-cheer-cheer*, followed by *birdie-birdie-birdie*.

Life spans for most songbirds range from five to eight years. Larger birds like mockingbirds can live up to fifteen years.

BLACK-CAPPED CHICKADEE
PARUS ATRICAPILLUS

RANGE: North America

SIZE: 5.9 in (15 cm)

DIET: Insects

Black-capped chickadees live in large flocks, often with other species. They call to each other by singing *chick-a-dee-dee-dee*. When they see a potential predator, they sound an alarm by adding additional high-pitched *dee-dees*.

GOLDEN-BELLIED GROSBEAK
PHEUCTICUS CHRYSOGASTER

RANGE: Colombia, Ecuador, Peru

SIZE: 9 in (23 cm)

DIET: Seeds

The golden-bellied grosbeak is a songbird in the cardinal family and is named for the bright coloration of the male and for the size of its beak— "grosbeak" means "large beak" in French. There are also grosbeaks in the finch family.

CURVE-BILLED THRASHER
TOXOSTOMA CURVIROSTRE

RANGE: Southwestern North America

SIZE: 9.1 in (23 cm)

DIET: Insects, seeds, berries

These birds have a long, curved, dark bill, which they use to dig holes in the soil and probe around looking for insects. This behavior is called thrashing. Curved-billed thrashers build their nests in cholla cactus and other spiny shrubs.

BALI MYNAH
LEUCOPSAR ROTHSCHILDI

RANGE: Bali in Indonesia

SIZE: 8.2 in (25 cm)

DIET: Fruit, seeds, worms, insects

The Bali mynah is an all-white starling, except for black tips on its wings and tail and a bare blue area around its eyes. It lives only on the island of Bali, where it is almost extinct—the result of illegal capture for the pet trade.

INDIGO BUNTING
PASSERINA CYANEA

RANGE: Canada, United States, Central America, Caribbean, Colombia

SIZE: 8.3 to 9.1 in (21 to 23 cm)

DIET: Insects, seeds, berries, buds

Indigo buntings have a fast, whistling song that sounds like *sweet-sweet-chew*. They often call from the tops of trees or telephone poles. These are migratory birds that fly at night, using the stars to find their way.

BARN SWALLOW
HIRUNDO RUSTICA

RANGE: North and South America

SIZE: 5.9 to 7.5 in (15 to 19 cm)

DIET: Insects, especially flies

Barn swallows build nests out of mud, either in caves or in barns. They start by collecting mud in their bills and then build it up to make a cup-shaped nest. Finally, they line it with grass and feathers.

SUPERB STARLING
LAMPROTORNIS SUPERBUS

RANGE: East Africa

SIZE: 7.5 in (19 cm)

DIET: Insects and fruit

The superb starling is very common in East Africa. Similarly, the common myna in Asia and the European starling in Europe and North America are found everywhere. In cities, starlings often use car alarm sounds in their songs.

CACTUS WREN
CAMPYLORHYNCHUS BRUNNEICAPILLUS

RANGE: Southwestern North America

SIZE: 7.1 to 8.7 in (18 to 22 cm)

DIET: Insects and spiders

Cactus wrens feed on the ground, mostly on insects and spiders, but they also eat lizards and frogs and can survive without drinking water. They nest in cactus or thorn trees and will actively attack predators like squirrels.

CEDAR WAXWING
BOMBYCILLA CEDRORUM

RANGE: North America

SIZE: 5.5 to 6.7 in (14 to 17 cm)

DIET: Fruit and insects

This bird is named for its red-tipped wings and for its favorite food: the berries of the red cedar tree, a type of juniper. In winter, cedar waxwings live in large flocks, visiting berry bushes and birdbaths.

NORTHERN CARDINAL
CARDINALIS CARDINALIS

RANGE: North and Central America

SIZE: 8.3 to 9.1 in (21 to 23 cm)

DIET: Seeds, fruit, insects

Many male birds develop brightly colored feathers for the breeding season, and then lose them. Not the male northern cardinal. He is bright red all year—and he sings for much of that time. The female sings, too, mostly in spring.

BIRD SONGS

Have you ever wondered how birds are able to sing their beautiful songs? Birds have a special structure in their throats called a syrinx, which functions similarly to human vocal cords. The syrinx is made of cartilage (the same as your ear) and is located at the base of the trachea, which connects the back of the throat to the lungs. Birds vary the pitch and volume of their voices by relaxing the muscles of the syrinx. This changes the airflow and creates vibrations that come out as sound. Birds with the best control of these movements are called songbirds. Some birds create their own sounds, but others, like mockingbirds, mimic other birds' songs. The nightingale knows more than 300 songs!

NORTHERN MOCKINGBIRD
MIMUS POLYGLOTTOS

RANGE: North America

SIZE: 8.2 to 10 in (20.8 to 25.5 cm)

DIET: Insects, seeds, berries

Male mockingbirds sing nonstop, day and night. In cities, their calls sound like all the neighborhood bird songs combined. They are also very active defenders of their territory and will dive-bomb or fly tight circles around any intruder.

137

ROBINS
AND OTHER SONGBIRDS

Songbirds take advantage of their ability to perch on a treetop, a high branch, or even a tuft of grass to better project—or broadcast—their calls. Most are heard before they are seen. Some may be easier to spot than others. The American robin, for example, is rarely hard to find. In urban areas, these birds often are seen perching on, and singing from, fence posts, telephone wires, and lawn furniture.

Like most other birds, songbirds also make contact calls to each other, and to their chicks, as well as alarm calls. Compared to other birds, even these calls sound like music. Some species also sing a morning song that differs from their daytime song. Others sing all year, even outside the breeding season. Many, like the mockingbird, can learn to mimic other birds.

With more than 4,000 species of songbirds, and many that sound—and even look—alike, the key is to learn the call of the breeding male.

RED-WINGED BLACKBIRD
AGELAIUS PHOENICEUS

RANGE: North America

SIZE: 8.3 to 9.8 in (21 to 25 cm)

DIET: Insects and fruit

Red-winged blackbirds are easy to identify. The males sit on a high perch, flash their red and yellow wing feathers, and sing oak-a-lee. The brown female is harder to find. One male may have up to 15 mates.

EASTERN BLUEBIRD
SIALIA SIALIS

RANGE: Eastern North America, Central America

SIZE: 8.3 in (21 cm)

DIET: Insects, fruit

Male bluebirds have bright, royal blue feathers on their head and wings, contrasting with rust-colored breast feathers. They often are seen perching on low branches, telephone wires, and nest boxes set out just for them.

Did you know?

When they are ready to eat, bluebirds swiftly swoop to the ground and pounce to catch their prey.

ANTILLEAN EUPHONIA
EUPHONIA MUSICA

RANGE: Caribbean islands, especially Hispaniola and islands in the Lesser Antilles

SIZE: 4.7 in (12 cm)

DIET: Fruit of mistletoe; also a few other fruits and seeds

Euphonias are small, colorful seed-eaters related to finches. By feeding on mistletoe, the antillean helps disperse its seeds. Its call sounds like a tiny bell tinkling.

BOAT-TAILED GRACKLE
QUISCALUS MAJOR

RANGE: Canada, United States, Mexico

SIZE: 10 to 17 in (26 to 43 cm)

DIET: Insects, eggs, frogs, seeds, berries, grain, small birds, small fish

The male and female boat-tailed grackle look like separate species. The male has shiny black-purple feathers on his body and greenish black ones on his wings and tail. The female is half his size, with a dark brown body and light brown belly.

OLIVE THRUSH
TURDUS OLIVACEUS

RANGE: East Africa

SIZE: 9.4 in (24 cm)

DIET: Insects, fruit, snails

Olive thrushes are common in East Africa and are readily seen foraging on the ground for food. Their songs are a pleasing mixture of flute-like phrases, whistles, and trills.

WESTERN TANAGER
PIRANGA LUDOVICIANA

RANGE: Western North America

SIZE: 7.5 in (19 cm)

DIET: Insects and fruit

Western tanagers are forest birds that feed on a variety of insects, either by gleaning or hawking. They breed along the west coast of North America from Alaska to California, and migrate during winter to Mexico and Costa Rica.

AMERICAN ROBIN
TURDUS MIGRATORIUS

RANGE: North America

SIZE: 6.3 to 8.3 in (16 to 21 cm)

DIET: Insects, berries, earthworms

American robins sing at the first hint of spring. Their morning song starts before sunrise and is a series of cheery whistles and chirps. Robins are common in urban areas, where they hunt for earthworms on grassy lawns.

GOULDIAN FINCH
ERYTHRURA GOULDIAE

RANGE: Australia

SIZE: 5.9 in (15 cm)

DIET: Grass seeds, especially sorghum

The colorful gouldian finch lives in a specific type of habitat in Australia: open tropical, grassy woodlands with eucalyptus trees. It is endangered due to habitat loss.

WHITE-HEADED BUFFALO WEAVER
DINEMELLIA DINEMELLI

RANGE: East Africa

SIZE: 7.5 in (19 cm)

DIET: Insects, especially beetles and butterflies; also fruit and seeds

This weaver often follows African buffalo, grabbing beetles and butterflies as they are stirred up out of the grass. Like its relatives, the white-headed buffalo weaver builds a tube-like nest that hangs from a tree branch above the ground.

OLIVE-BACKED SUNBIRD
CINNYRIS JUGULARIS

RANGE: Southern Asia to Australia

SIZE: Up to 5 in (12 cm)

DIET: Nectar and insects

Sunbirds are specialized nectar-feeders. Their lifestyles are very similar to that of hummingbirds found in the Americas, and honey-eaters found in Australia. Though they can hover to feed, they usually perch.

COMMON CROSSBILL
LOXIA CURVIROSTRA

RANGE: North America

SIZE: 5.5 to 8.3 in (14 to 21 cm)

DIET: Pinecone seeds

The common crossbill is a type of finch with a very limited diet: pinecone seeds. Instead of meeting perfectly, its upper and lower bills cross. When it bites down on the scale of a pinecone, it uses its tongue to pull out the seed.

139

PENGUINS

Penguins are another group of flightless birds. They have a keel and large shoulder muscles, but instead of flapping their wings to fly, they use them like flippers to swim. Unlike most birds, their wing bones are dense and flattened, and their wrist and elbow joints are stiff. This gives penguins incredible power underwater, which is where they spend most of their time.

On land, penguins look awkward. To stand, they balance on their webbed feet and short tail, using it like a tripod. When they walk, they waddle. For long distances, they slide. They leave the water for extended periods of time only when necessary—during the breeding season.

Penguins are found only in the Southern Hemisphere and mostly in cold waters. Two species, the Adélie and emperor penguins, spend their winter in Antarctica. The others move to warmer waters, following their food: krill, plankton, and small fish. To stay warm, penguins have very dense, short, overlapping feathers and a thick layer of fat.

Life spans for penguins range from 20 to 30 years for larger species; 10 years for smaller ones.

CHINSTRAP PENGUIN
PYGOSCELIS ANTARCTICUS

RANGE: Antarctic Peninsula; South Shetland, South Orkney, and South Sandwich Islands

SIZE: 28 in (71 cm)

DIET: Krill, fish, crustaceans

Chinstrap penguins live in large colonies, usually on icebergs in the open ocean. Compared to other penguins, the chicks of this species mature quickly. They are able to swim and feed on krill by two months of age.

ROCKHOPPER PENGUIN
EUDYPTES CHRYSOCOME

RANGE: Falkland and other sub-Antarctic islands

SIZE: 21.7 in (55 cm)

DIET: Krill, squid, crustaceans

Female rockhoppers typically lay two eggs, one of which is up to 50 percent smaller than the other. The smaller one is usually lost. The male incubates the egg for four months; both parents raise the chick.

YELLOW-EYED PENGUIN
MEGADYPTES ANTIPODES

RANGE: New Zealand's sub-Antarctic islands

SIZE: 23.6 in (60 cm)

DIET: Fish and squid

The yellow-eyed penguin nests in pairs, rather than in large colonies like other penguins. They nest under trees or logs, and only where other birds cannot see them. Their most social time is right after molting, when they often hunt together.

EMPEROR PENGUIN LIFE CYCLE

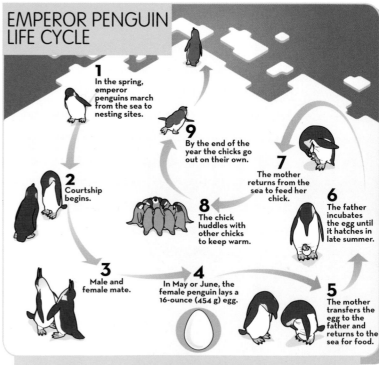

1 In the spring, emperor penguins march from the sea to nesting sites.

2 Courtship begins.

3 Male and female mate.

4 In May or June, the female penguin lays a 16-ounce (454 g) egg.

5 The mother transfers the egg to the father and returns to the sea for food.

6 The father incubates the egg until it hatches in late summer.

7 The mother returns from the sea to feed her chick.

8 The chick huddles with other chicks to keep warm.

9 By the end of the year the chicks go out on their own.

Emperor penguins begin their yearlong reproductive cycle with a very long walk—up to 75 miles (120 km)—from the edge of the ice to their breeding colony.

GENTOO PENGUIN
PYGOSCELIS PAPUA

RANGE: Antarctic Peninsula and sub-Antarctic islands, especially Falkland Islands

SIZE: 29 in (75 cm)

DIET: Fish, crustaceans, cephalopods

Gentoo penguin chicks look like their parents, except for the white patch above the eye and bright orange beak—features that appear when they become adults. These penguins swim faster than any other bird underwater—up to 18.6 miles per hour (30 km/h).

ADÉLIE PENGUIN
PYGOSCELIS ADELIAE

RANGE: Antarctic coast and islands, especially in Ross Sea

SIZE: 27 in (70 cm)

DIET: Krill

Penguins communicate using calls, eye contact, and body language. To attract a mate and establish territory, the male Adélie penguin performs a "salute," a behavior in which he arches his neck, stands tall, and pokes his beak in the air.

LITTLE PENGUIN
EUDYPTULA MINOR

RANGE: Coasts of New Zealand and New South Wales in Australia

SIZE: 11.8 in (30 cm)

DIET: Fish, squid, crustaceans

The chicks of this species are a brighter blue than the adults. The little penguin, also called the fairy blue penguin, is the smallest of the penguins. At hatching, chicks weigh from 1.3 to 1.7 ounces (36 to 47 g).

MAGELLANIC PENGUIN
SPHENISCUS MAGELLANICUS

RANGE: Falkland Islands, southern coasts of Chile and Argentina

SIZE: 24 to 30 in (61 to 76 cm)

DIET: Fish

For much of the year, Magellanic penguins live in the open ocean. During the breeding season, they migrate to the coast of South America and nearby islands, where they nest in dense colonies of up to 200,000.

AFRICAN PENGUIN
SPHENISCUS DEMERSUS

RANGE: Coastal southwest Africa

SIZE: 17.7 in (45 cm)

DIET: Fish, squid, crustaceans

African penguins spend their days in the water feeding on anchovies, pilchards, mackerels, and herring. They swim an average of 68 miles (110 km) on each trip to find food. At night, they come on shore, where they live in large colonies.

EMPEROR PENGUIN
APTENODYTES FORSTERI

RANGE: Antarctic region

SIZE: 43 in (109 cm)

DIET: Crustaceans, fish, cephalopods

During their nine-month breeding cycle, emperor penguins endure long stretches without food and long marches back and forth to the open ocean. Each pair alternates taking care of a single egg and—if all goes well—to a single chick.

FROM THE FIELD:

YVA MOMATIUK & JOHN EASTCOTT

KING PENGUIN

King penguins and other penguin species are tough seabirds that can survive in some of the harshest places on Earth. When my husband, John, and I go to the Antarctic to photograph them, we experience their extreme environment firsthand: frigid, slushy waters, gale-force winds, punishing snowstorms, and jagged, ice-covered terrain. Just getting there is a journey! After flying to the Falkland Islands off South America, we sail for four to five days through stormy seas—a rogue wave once sent me crashing into the wall of our sailboat, and I broke my toe! But to us, it's all worth it when we arrive at South Georgia Island to the buzzing and trumpeting sounds of thousands of waddling birds in their finest black-tie apparel.

Luckily for us, penguins don't fear people. And although we try not to get in their way, we have had a few close encounters. On our first trip to South Georgia, I decided to lie down near some napping penguins. Suddenly, I felt two rubbery feet climb onto my back. It was a curious king penguin (*Aptenodytes patagonicus*) who had come to investigate the foreign object on the beach. It shuffled all around my back, then hopped off and went on its way. John likes to tell people I had a penguin massage!

Husband-and-wife team Yva Momatiuk and John Eastcott are internationally published nature photographers. They have traveled the globe documenting wild places and have photographed penguins from the Antarctic Peninsula to New Zealand.

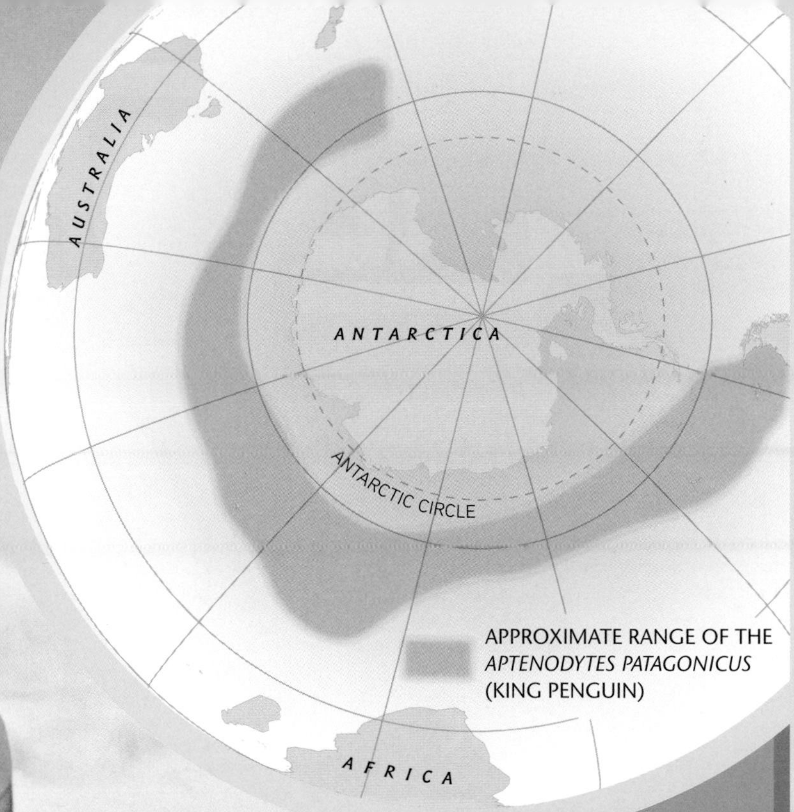

AUSTRALIA

ANTARCTICA

ANTARCTIC CIRCLE

AFRICA

APPROXIMATE RANGE OF THE *APTENODYTES PATAGONICUS* (KING PENGUIN)

OBSERVATION TIPS

1 Let penguins come to you. Be quiet and still, and they may waddle over to investigate. Avoid breeding seals. They won't think twice about sinking their fangs into you!

2 Bundle up! You need extra-warm—and water-proof—coats, hats, and boots on South Georgia.

3 South Georgia beaches are steep. Steer clear of large waves that could scoop you into the sea.

4 Your body works over-time in the Antarctic, so eat plenty of fatty foods and extra desserts!

Penguins raise their chicks in rookeries—groups of hundreds or even thousands of penguin families. Here, parents take turns incubating their eggs and fishing. When the chicks hatch, parents vomit up fish into their open beaks to feed them. Eventually, the chicks huddle into several large crèches, or groups, to keep warm. When an adult returns to the group, all the hungry chicks whistle at it, each hoping the adult is their parent coming home with dinner!

RECORDS

E ver seen an ostrich speed by or a falcon swoop into the water like a rocket out of the sky? Well, these are just some of the amazing things birds can do. Want to know more? Check out these superstar record holders of the bird world!

LONG-DISTANCE TRAVELER
ARCTIC TERN
STERNA PARADISAEA

Each year, the Arctic tern migrates an incredible 44,000 miles (70,811 km) on its way from Greenland to Antarctica and back. These birds, which weigh less than two pounds (0.9 kg), rack up their mileage by flying between the coasts of Africa and South America along the way to avoid flying directly into the wind. Because terns can live up to 30 years, that's 1.5 million miles of travel in one lifetime—roughly three trips to the moon and back.

FASTEST FLIER
PEREGRINE FALCON
FALCO PEREGRINUS

Plunge-diving through the air at speeds of what many believe to be 200 miles an hour (322 km/h), the peregrine falcon is so fast that it has completely stumped scientists. There is much debate about the accuracy of this number, though experiments in several countries have ranged from an impressive 124 miles per hour (200 km/h) to a whopping 217 miles per hour (350 km/h). Whatever the real number may be, scientists aren't sure how they manage to dive that fast without blacking out entirely.

BADDEST BIRD
OSTRICH
STRUTHIO CAMELUS

Measuring up to nine feet (2.7 m) tall and weighing up to 350 pounds (160 kg), ostriches are the biggest birds on Earth. Much of that height is made up of their long legs, which can cover an incredible 16 feet (4.9 m) in one stride! Perhaps that's why ostriches are also the fastest bird on land, reaching speeds of up to 45 miles an hour (72 km/h). And those legs aren't just made for running. One kick from this bad bird can chase a lion away! Top that off with the fact that they travel in herds—this is one bird that's best left alone.

SUPER SWIMMER
GENTOO PENGUIN
PYGOSCELIS PAPUA

Like most penguins, little gentoos are awkward on land. But get them in the water and watch out: These pint-size penguins are diving machines! Standing about 30 inches (76 cm) tall and weighing only 12 pounds (5.4 kg), gentoo penguins easily dive in water at speeds of up to 22 miles per hour (35 km/h)—about the same speed as a bottlenose dolphin. And the impressive stats don't end there. Foraging for food and avoiding predators, gentoo penguins can dive 655 feet deep (220 m) as many as 450 times a day, staying underwater for up to 7 minutes!

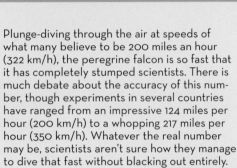

HIGHEST FLIER

→

BAR-HEADED GOOSE
ANSER INDICUS

Look! Up in the sky! It's a bird...it's a plane...no wait, it *is* a bird. And if it's flying *really* high, it just might be a bar-headed goose—the highest flier in the world. These pretty geese frantically flap their wings and reach altitudes of more than 21,000 feet (6,400 m) as they migrate over the Himalaya—the tallest mountain range in the world! Scientists think extra blood vessels in their bodies deliver oxygen to their muscles more quickly than in other birds and may give them the boost they need for the eight-hour, nonstop trek.

SMALLEST BIRD

→

BEE HUMMINGBIRD
MELLISUGA HELENAE

At a maximum length of just over two inches (5 cm) and a weight of a mere .06 ounces (2 g)—about the same as two dimes—the bee hummingbird is named after an insect for a reason. These itty-bitty birds are the smallest in the world, roughly a tenth of the size of the largest hummingbird and less than an inch (2.5 cm) larger than the biggest bee. What it lacks in size it makes up in ability: This humble hummingbird can flap its wings at a rate of 50 to 80 times per second.

WONDERFUL WINGS

→

WANDERING ALBATROSS
DIOMEDEA EXULANS

When it comes to an amazing wingspan, there's no denying that the wandering albatross wins—wings down. This sensational seabird boasts wings that span an incredible 11 feet (3.4 m)—about the length of two adult humans lying end to end. But easy flying is key when you live your life above the ocean, as albatrosses rarely go on land. They spend their days gliding through the air—sometimes never even flapping their massive wings—or resting on the surface of the ocean, waiting for their next meal to swim by.

BIGGEST BILL

→

AUSTRALIAN PELICAN
PELECANUS CONSPICILLATUS

There's no competition in the biggest bill category: The bill of the Australian pelican can be up to 20 inches (50 cm) long. This fierce feeder is not shy when it comes to eating—it even steals fish from other birds' mouths. But it's this pelican's bill that is most impressive. It is super sensitive, which helps the pelican find fish in murky water. There's a hook on the end for stabbing and grabbing. And the huge pouch beneath serves as a net by scooping a "bill-full" of water and fish, and holding the fish while the water drains out.

Want to know where these record-holding birds live around the world? Take a look at this range map to find out.

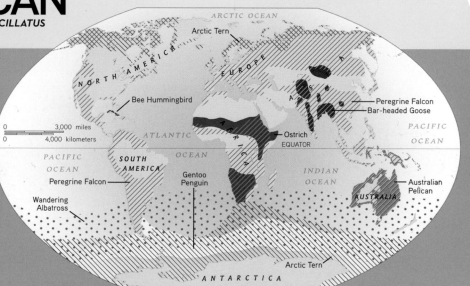

Arctic Ocean
Arctic Tern
NORTH AMERICA
EUROPE
Bee Hummingbird
ASIA
Peregrine Falcon
Bar-headed Goose
Ostrich
EQUATOR
3,000 miles
4,000 kilometers
ATLANTIC OCEAN
PACIFIC OCEAN
PACIFIC OCEAN
SOUTH AMERICA
AFRICA
INDIAN OCEAN
Peregrine Falcon
Gentoo Penguin
AUSTRALIA
Australian Pelican
Wandering Albatross
Arctic Tern
ANTARCTICA

MAP KEY
APPROXIMATE RANGES OF RECORD-SETTING BIRDS
Arctic Tern
Bee Hummingbird
Australian Pelican
Wandering Albatross
Gentoo Penguin
Peregrine Falcon
Ostrich
Bar-headed Goose

145

Most reptiles, like this chameleon, have scales—overlapping layers of skin—covering their bodies. A reptile's scales can protect the animal from a rocky or thorny habitat and lock in moisture to keep it from drying out.

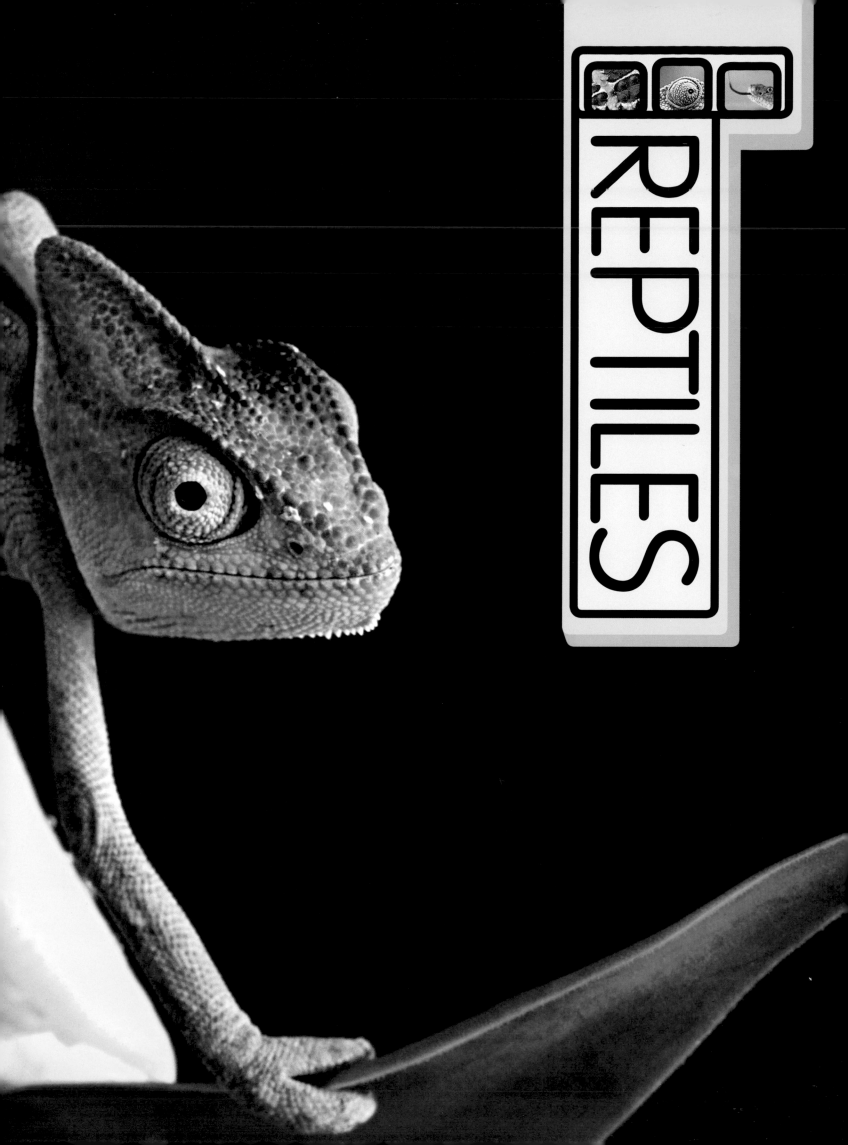

REPTILES

GREEN SEA TURTLE

BEARDED DRAGON

DWARF CROCODILE

KING COBRA

ANOLE LIZARD

TOKAY GECKO

AMERICAN ALLIGATOR

DIAMONDBACK TEXAS RATTLESNAKE

MARINE IGUANA

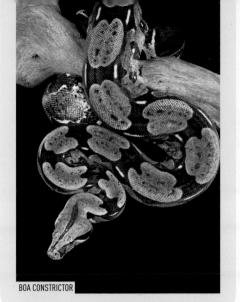
BOA CONSTRICTOR

LIZARD

YELLOW-SPOTTED AMAZON RIVER TURTLE

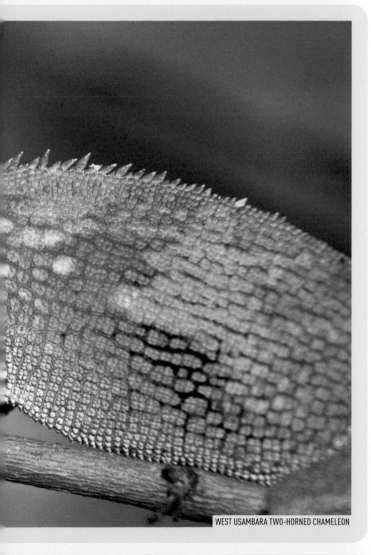
WEST USAMBARA TWO-HORNED CHAMELEON

AMBOINA SAIL-FINNED LIZARD

149

WHAT IS A REPTILE?

REPTILES ARE AIR-BREATHING VERTEBRATES COVERED IN SPECIAL SKIN MADE UP OF SCALES, BONY PLATES, OR A COMBINATION OF BOTH.

They include crocodiles, snakes, lizards, turtles, and tortoises. All regularly shed the outer layer of their skin. Their metabolism depends on the temperature of their environment.

Unlike birds and mammals, reptiles do not maintain a constant internal body temperature. Without fur or feathers for insulation, they cannot stay warm on a cold day, and without sweat glands or the ability to pant, they cannot cool off on a hot one. Instead, they move into the sun or into the shade as needed. During cooler parts of the year they become inactive. Because of their slow metabolism and heat-seeking behavior, reptiles are cold-blooded.

Reptile reproduction also depends on temperature. Only boas and pythons give birth to live young. The other species lay their eggs in a simple nest, and leave. The young hatch days to months later. The soil temperature is critical during this time: It determines how many hatchlings will be male or female. Young reptiles can glide, walk, and swim within hours of birth. Reptiles first appear in the fossil record 315 million years ago and were the dominant animals during the Mesozoic era, which lasted for 270 million years until the extinction of the dinosaurs.

REPTILE TRAITS

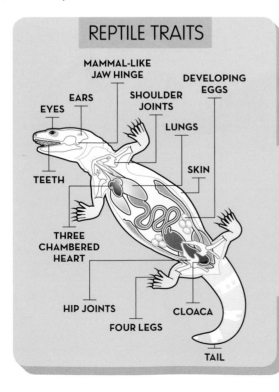

MAMMAL-LIKE JAW HINGE

DEVELOPING EGGS

EARS

SHOULDER JOINTS

EYES

LUNGS

TEETH

SKIN

THREE CHAMBERED HEART

HIP JOINTS

CLOACA

FOUR LEGS

TAIL

All reptiles have scales, or scutes, on their skin and a mammal-like hinged jaw. Lizards also have mammal-like shoulder and hip joints.

The green vine snake is active during the day and sleeps at night. It moves slowly and blends easily into its surroundings, using its unique color and pattern as camouflage.

Did you know? Only a few hundred of the 3,000-plus species of snakes are venomous.

CLASSIFICATION OF REPTILES

There are four reptile orders (see below). There are about 9,500 species of reptiles, with new species being discovered on a regular basis. Most are lizards or snakes.

1 CROCODILES, CAIMANS, AND ALLIGATORS *(CROCODILIA)*

2 SNAKES, LIZARDS, AND WORM LIZARDS *(SQUAMATA)*

3 TURTLES AND TORTOISES *(TESTUDINAE)*

4 TUATARAS *(SPHENODONTIA)*

CROCODILES, CAIMANS, AND ALLIGATORS

Crocodiles, caimans, and alligators—along with birds and sea turtles—are the only living direct descendants of the dinosaurs. The 25 species that exist today also look the same as they did 65 million years ago.

All are semiaquatic, meaning they require dry land to rest and lay their eggs. They spend the rest of their time in the water. They are found only in warmer climates, and most live in fresh water. All have long snouts and tails, a flattened body, a mouth full of peg-like teeth, thick armor-like scales, and webbed feet. With nostrils and eyes on the top of their heads, they are able to stay mostly submerged.

The species in this group are meat- or carrion-eaters. They hunt ambush-style and can bite with power, but cannot chew, which means they either swallow their prey whole, or kill it by drowning it and then eat it by tearing it into smaller pieces. The Nile crocodile, for example, waits along the edge of the river for a thirsty antelope and leaps out to grab it by the neck and pull it under the water.

Crocodiles and their relatives live for a long time. Their life spans range from 40 to 100 years.

NILE CROCODILE
CROCODYLUS NILOTICUS

RANGE: Africa

SIZE: 11 to 20 ft (3.5 to 6 m)

DIET: Zebras, antelopes, buffaloes, fish, birds

Studies show the Nile crocodile has a stronger bite than any other animal tested, including alligators. Instead of chewing their food, they tear it into chunks. As a result, the muscles that open the mouth are surprisingly weak.

AMERICAN ALLIGATOR
ALLIGATOR MISSISSIPPIENSIS

RANGE: Southeastern United States

SIZE: 9.25 to 16 ft (2.8 to 5 m)

DIET: Both small and large prey; generally fish, turtles, snakes, small mammals

American alligators use their powerful jaws to clamp down on prey of all sizes. When hunting larger animals like deer, they float just beneath the surface until the time is right to grab the animal's head, pull it underwater, and drown it.

Did you know? American alligators may take shelter in swimming pools.

SPECTACLED CAIMAN
CAIMAN CROCODILUS

RANGE: Northern South America, Central America, certain parts of the Caribbean

SIZE: 6.5 to 8 ft (2 to 2.5 m)

DIET: Insects, snails, shrimp, crabs, fish, lizards, snakes, turtles, birds, mammals

Spectacled caimans are named for the bony ridge around their eyes, which makes them look as though they are wearing glasses. This adaptable species is found in both fresh and salt water, making it the most common among all crocodilians.

DWARF CAIMAN
PALEOSUCHUS PALPEBROSUS

RANGE: Wetlands of Brazil, French Guiana, Suriname, Guyana, Venezuela, Colombia

SIZE: 3.9 to 4.9 ft (1.2 to 1.5 m)

DIET: Tadpoles, frogs, snails, crabs, shrimp, small fish

Adult dwarf caimans have more bony plates, called osteoderms, covering their bodies than any other crocodilian. These protect them from raccoons and foxes, which prey on caiman eggs, but not from jaguars, large boas, and green anacondas.

SALTWATER CROCODILE
CROCODYLUS POROSUS

RANGE: Northern Australia, Southeast Asia, eastern coast of India

SIZE: Up to 18 ft (5.5 m)

DIET: Fish, reptiles, birds, mammals

This is the largest crocodile, and the largest living reptile. Males weigh up to 2,200 pounds (1,000 kg). Females are about half the size—but no less dangerous. Saltwater crocodiles are known to attack humans.

FALSE GHARIAL
TOMISTOMA SCHLEGELII

RANGE: Western Malaysia, Sumatra, Borneo, Thailand

SIZE: At least 16 ft (5 m)

DIET: Fish, insects, crustaceans, small mammals

Like all crocodilians, false gharials (GAH-ree-yal) have teeth that are constantly replaced throughout their lives. This happens whether or not they lose them while hunting. Underneath each visible tooth, there is a replacement ready in the socket.

YACARE CAIMAN
CAIMAN YACARE

RANGE: Central South America

SIZE: 6.6 to 6.8 ft (2 to 2.5 m)

DIET: Fish, especially piranhas; birds, capybaras

This is the second-smallest species of crocodilian. Despite its size, this caiman is a significant predator. As an adult, it can eat porcupines and large rodents called pacas.

AMERICAN CROCODILE
CROCODYLUS ACUTUS

RANGE: Atlantic and Pacific coasts of Central and South America, Caribbean islands, southeast Florida, U.S.A.

SIZE: 11 to 23 ft (3.50 to 7 m)

DIET: Mostly fish, frogs, turtles; also birds and small mammals

As soon as they hatch, American crocodiles start croaking. The mother responds by uncovering them in the nest and carrying them in her mouth to the water. She will continue to look out for them for several more weeks.

ALLIGATORS VS. CROCS

With massive jaws, sharp teeth, and powerful bodies, crocodilians are among the most dangerous animals on Earth. They include fourteen species of crocodile, one gharial, six caiman, and two species of alligator, the Chinese and the American. So what's the difference between an alligator and a crocodile? The first is that alligators are freshwater animals, whereas crocodiles can tolerate salt water. The second is that alligators have short, broad, U-shaped snouts. Crocodile mouths have a sharper V-shape. But the most telltale sign is the teeth. Alligators have an upper jaw that overlaps the lower jaw, and their teeth are not clearly visible when the mouth is shut. Crocodiles, on the other hand, have interlocking chompers and an oversize fourth tooth that fits outside the mouth when the jaw is closed.

153

CROCODILE

AMERICAN

Crocs are hard animals to catch. They have huge, powerful bodies and bone-crushing jaws, yet they are masters of disguise—a 2,000-pound crocodile can hide in only ten inches (25 cm) of water! But several years ago, I discovered a little secret that has helped me catch thousands of wild crocs.

I was in Costa Rica to relocate some troublesome American crocodiles *(Crocodylus acutus).* There were about 30 of them hanging around the day my colleague and I drained their lake. But when we arrived the next day to move them to their new home, they were nowhere in sight! Then we spotted a burrow in the lake bank. The opening was slightly wider than my shoulders, so I wormed my way down into it to investigate. I shined my light but didn't see anything, so I wiggled back out and let my colleague have a turn. He emerged with eyes as big as saucers! I immediately headed back in, only this time, I heard hissing—and then, four large, green crocodile eyes popped open. The "muddy walls" on either side of my body were actually two giant, mud-covered crocs! We ended up pulling 13 crocodiles out of that burrow. Since then, I've found thousands of crocs in burrows all over the world.

APPROXIMATE RANGE OF THE
CROCODYLUS ACUTUS
(AMERICAN CROCODILE)

0   500 miles
0   500 kilometers

NORTH
AMERICA

PACIFIC
OCEAN

SOUTH
AMERICA

OBSERVATION TIPS

1 Crocs are sneaky animals—a large adult can hide in a mere ten inches (25 cm) of water.

2 Listen carefully. Crocs are extremely vocal—they growl, hiss, pop, bellow, and roar.

3 In the dry season, you are likely to find crocs hiding in underground burrows.

4 Beware of venomous snakes, spiders, and other creepy crawlers that may be lurking inside croc burrows.

Brady Barr, a world-renowned herpetologist, has spent nearly two decades catching and studying crocodilians and working to preserve their habitats. He is the first person to capture and study all 23 species of wild crocodilians.

Crocodiles bury their eggs in the ground or in mounded nests near the water and guard them from predators. When the babies are ready to hatch, they make squeaking noises from inside their eggs. This is the female crocodile's cue to dig up her nest, crack open the eggs, and carry the hatchlings to the water—in her mouth! Newborn crocs are about the size of a Snickers bar and munch on small fish, tadpoles, insects, and snails.

155

TURTLES AND TORTOISES

Turtles and tortoises are the oldest reptiles. Their fossils date from 215 million years ago—long before the dinosaurs appeared—and many species have changed very little since then.

All have a domed shell that encases most of the body. The upper part is the carapace, the lower the plastron. The outer surface is made up of specialized scales known as scutes. The inner surface is attached to the ribs, as well as the spine, shoulder, and pelvis. As a result, turtles and tortoises inhale and exhale by moving their leg muscles.

Another distinctive feature of this group is a bird-like beak that functions more like a set of jaws with teeth than a beak. Turtle and tortoise beaks have horn-like ridges lining the inner surface of the upper and lower beak. Carnivorous species have sharp ridges for slicing, whereas herbivorous ones have serrated, or tooth-like, ridges for cutting through plant stems.

More than half of the species in this group are threatened with extinction, due to habitat destruction and the harvesting of the species for food, traditional Chinese medicine, and the pet trade.

Life spans are generally long. Several giant tortoises have lived more than 150 years.

BROWN TORTOISE
MANOURIA EMYS

RANGE: Southern and southeastern Asia

SIZE: 19.7 to 23.6 in (50 to 60 cm)

DIET: Grasses, leaves, fruit

Like most tortoises, brown tortoises are herbivores that eat grasses, leaves, and fruit. This species lives in temperate, humid areas. On a hot day, it burrows into moist soil to keep cool, or waits until dusk to feed.

EASTERN BOX TURTLE
TERRAPENE CAROLINA

RANGE: Eastern United States

SIZE: 4 to 8.5 in (10 to 21 cm)

DIET: Snails, insects, slugs, worms, roots, flowers, berries, fungi, fish, frogs, salamanders, snakes, birds, eggs

This species is named for the "box" shape it forms when threatened. If a predator approaches, it will pull in its head, legs, and tail, and close the front hinge of its bottom shell until the predator leaves.

TURTLE LIFE CYCLE

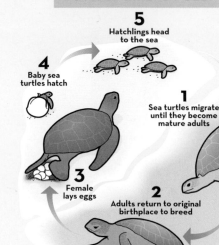

5 Hatchlings head to the sea

4 Baby sea turtles hatch

3 Female lays eggs

1 Sea turtles migrate until they become mature adults

2 Adults return to original birthplace to breed

All seven species of sea turtles follow a similar life cycle, in which young hatch on beaches and find their way to the sea to mature.

LEATHERBACK SEA TURTLE
DERMOCHELYS CORIACEA

RANGE: Worldwide

SIZE: 4.25 to 6 ft (1.3 to 1.8 m)

DIET: Mainly jellyfish and salps

This species lays its eggs on the sands of tropical beaches, but it spends its life at sea in cold waters feeding on jellyfish. Sadly, leatherback turtles mistake plastic debris in the ocean for food. This is one reason they are endangered.

LOGGERHEAD SEA TURTLE
CARETTA CARETTA

RANGE: Worldwide

SIZE: 28 to 39 in (70 to 100 cm)

DIET: Algae; horseshoe crabs, mollusks, sea snails, other invertebrates; fish and fish eggs

Loggerhead sea turtles are named for their large head and strong jaws adapted for crushing hard-shelled invertebrates. Young turtles eat algae and plants, but older ones are carnivores. Their size and rough, scaly skin on their head and neck protect them from predators.

MATA MATA TURTLE
CHELUS FIMBRIATUS

RANGE: Parts of Central America, South America in Amazon and Orinoco River systems; also Trinidad

SIZE: 12 to 18 in (30 to 45 cm)

DIET: Mainly fish and aquatic invertebrates

Mata mata turtles are poor swimmers. Instead, they walk along the river bottom, using their snouts like snorkels to breathe. To find their food, they use the skin flaps on their head and neck to detect the movements of fish and invertebrates.

GALÁPAGOS GIANT TORTOISE
GEOCHELONE NIGRA

RANGE: Galápagos Islands

SIZE: Up to 4 ft (1.2 m)

DIET: Grasses, forbs, leaves on bushes

The Galápagos is the largest tortoise, weighing up to 880 pounds (440 kg). The shape of its shell depends on the vegetation found on the island on which it lives. Tortoises that eat tall plants have a saddle-shaped shell so they can reach up with their necks.

Did you know? Desert tortoises get water from the flowers and grasses they eat.

DESERT TORTOISE
GOPHERUS AGASSIZII

RANGE: Southwest United States, northwest Mexico

SIZE: 10 to 14 in (25 to 36 cm)

DIET: Low-growing plants, leaves, bark, stems, fruit, shrubs, woody vines, grasses

Desert tortoises use their strong front legs and long claws to dig burrows to escape the heat or to hibernate. Some populations create a complicated burrow system big enough to share with others—usually 5, with room for 25.

GIANT SNAKE-NECKED TURTLE
CHELODINA EXPANSA

RANGE: Eastern Australia

SIZE: 34 in (86 cm)

DIET: Aquatic invertebrates, crustaceans, fish

The giant snake-necked turtle is an ambush predator. It waits for its prey, head and neck hidden inside its shell. When it strikes, snake-like, it has its mouth open, which draws in the food like a vacuum.

SNAPPING TURTLE
CHELYDRA SERPENTINA

RANGE: North America

SIZE: 20 to 45 cm (7.87 to 17.72 in)

DIET: Carrion, invertebrates, small mammals, amphibians, fish, birds, aquatic vegetation

The tail of the snapping turtle looks like a saw. Its shell is also smaller than that of other species, which means its head, neck, and legs are more mobile. Snapping turtles will eat anything that fits in their beak-like jaws.

SCIENTISTS can identify different sea-turtle species by the number and pattern of scutes, or horny scales, on their shells. The green sea turtle (*Chelonia mydas*), shown here, has five scutes that run down the middle of its shell. None of these scutes overlap.

IGUANAS,
CHAMELEONS, AND RELATIVES

izards are the most successful group of reptiles, with more than 5,600 species. They are subdivided into four groups: iguanas and relatives, geckos and relatives, skinks and relatives, and monitors and relatives.

All have tails, and most have four legs. They also have excellent vision, which they use to find food and for communication. Like birds, they can see color in both the visible (to humans) and ultraviolet (UV) spectrum.

Body language is especially important among lizards. They use a variety of postures and movements to defend their territories and attract mates. The males, in particular, show off their crests, horns, and brightly colored patches of skin by raising their heads, pointing their tails, and scurrying from one place to another.

Many of these behaviors are used for defense against predators. Some species use another tactic: With a quick jerk, they can release their tail and leave it behind as a distraction. A new tail will eventually grow back.

Iguanas and their relatives, which include chameleons, are tree-living species found in tropical forests.

Life spans for these reptiles range from 5 to 20 years, and up to 30 for the larger iguana species.

VEILED CHAMELEON ◯◯⊕
CHAMAELEO CALYPTRATUS

RANGE: Border of Yemen and Saudi Arabia

SIZE: 10 to 24 in (25.4 to 61 cm)

DIET: Insects, some vertebrates, plants

Veiled chameleons have a very distinctive head crest, or helmet—up to two inches tall in a male. When threatened, it turns dark and curls into a ball. Like all lizards, chameleons shed their skin in patches.

CHAMELEONS AND THEIR **VISION**

Chameleons are amazing lizards. They change color; have very long and sticky tongues, which they use to catch food; and five toes, which help them grab on to tree branches. Another extraordinary trait is their 360-degree vision, which means they can see in every direction! Their eyes are cone-shaped and have an opening in the middle, where the pupil sits. To get a 360-degree view, chameleons move their eyes independently. They can look at two different objects at the same time or do a once-around to see what is going on nearby. Chameleons also can focus both eyes on their food before they quickly extend their long tongues and go in for the kill.

ALLIGATOR LIZARD ◯◯�⟨⟩◯
ELGARIA MULTICARINATA

RANGE: Western United States, Mexico

SIZE: 3.1 to 7.3 in (7.8 to 18.4 cm)

DIET: Insects, spiders, centipedes, scorpions, snails, frog tadpoles, other lizards

Alligator lizards are named for the overlapping bony plates found beneath their scales and their long tails, which can be up to twice as long as their bodies. They are carnivores that eat anything they find.

EASTERN COLLARED LIZARD ◯◯◠
CROTAPHYTUS COLLARIS

RANGE: United States

SIZE: 8 to 14 in (20 to 35 cm)

DIET: Insects and smaller lizards; sometimes plant matter

Female collared lizards are gray with some red speckling, whereas males are bright blue. Both males and females have a black band on their necks. This species is an active predator of its food and can run as fast as 16 miles per hour (26 km/h).

COMMON GREEN IGUANA
IGUANA IGUANA

RANGE: Central and South America, Caribbean islands, coastal eastern Pacific islands

SIZE: 3.3 to 6.5 ft (1 to 2 m)

DIET: Mainly plants

Like other iguanas, green iguanas also vary in color. Their skin turns darker while they bask in the sun (a change that helps them absorb heat) and lighter when it gets too hot or bright. Breeding males also turn orange or gold.

NORTH AFRICAN SPINY-TAILED LIZARD
UROMASTYX ACANTHINURA

RANGE: Northwest Africa

SIZE: 15.75 to 16.93 in (40 to 43 cm)

DIET: Mainly plants; also ants and beetles

This lizard digs burrows up to ten feet (3 m) deep, where it can escape from predators and extreme temperatures. Like other herbivorous desert reptiles, it does not drink but instead obtains water from grasses and desert plants.

THORNY DEVIL
MOLOCH HORRIDUS

RANGE: Great Sandy Desert in Australia

SIZE: 3.0 to 4.3 in (7.6 to 11.0 cm)

DIET: Ants

Thorny devils are covered in cone-shaped gold and brown scales. Their special skin gives them excellent camouflage and protection from predators. But the spines serve another role that is especially important in the Australian desert: water collection and absorption.

PANTHER CHAMELEON
FURCIFER PARDALIS

RANGE: Madagascar

SIZE: 16 to 20.5 in (40 to 52 cm)

DIET: Insects

The panther chameleon is named for its spotted skin. Males are more brightly colored than females, and their coloring varies depending on where they live. Some are mostly red, whereas others are blue, green, or orange.

CUBAN KNIGHT ANOLE
ANOLIS EQUESTRIS

RANGE: Cuba

SIZE: 13 to 19 in (33 to 48 cm)

DIET: Grubs, crickets, spiders, moths

The knight anole is twice the size of most anole lizards (more than 360 species.) All have special toes for clinging to branches and are highly territorial. Males of this species will face off with another male by standing up, turning dark green, gaping, and bobbing.

PINK IGUANA
CONOLOPHUS MARTHAE

RANGE: Isabela Island in the Galápagos

SIZE: 3 to 4 ft (1 to 1.2 m)

DIET: Mainly plants; the fruit of the prickly pear cactus

Pink iguanas look like the Galápagos land iguana, which is yellowish brown in color and much more widespread. Genetic studies confirm the two species are closely related, but the connection is very old. Their common ancestor lived 5.7 million years ago.

GECKOS, SKINKS, AND MONITORS

Geckos are known for their sticky feet, amazing camouflage, and strange-sounding calls. All are nocturnal. At night, they chirp like birds or croak like frogs. When disturbed, they scream or hiss. These are also among the smallest lizards: The ashy gecko is just three inches (7.5 cm) long.

Skinks are the most common lizards. They are generally long and slender. Several have an unusual method of reproduction: Males are not necessary. The female produces clones of herself. This is called parthenogenesis. Some populations of skinks have no males at all!

The monitors are a diverse group that includes the largest lizard, the Komodo dragon; the only venomous lizards, the Gila monster and Mexican beaded lizard; and the legless lizards. All have a forked tongue and excellent sense of smell. Snakes are descended from this group.

Life spans range from 5 to 20 years for most geckos, skinks, and smaller monitors. Komodo dragons live up to 50 years.

GILA MONSTER
HELODERMA SUSPECTUM

RANGE: Southwestern United States and northwestern Mexico

SIZE: 14 to 20 in (35 to 50 cm)

DIET: Small mammals; birds; lizards; eggs of quails, doves, and reptiles

Gila monsters inject venom, produced by salivary glands in their lower jaw, into their prey as they bite down. These lizards eat up to one-third of their body weight at each meal and only feed five to ten times a year.

NILE MONITOR LIZARD
VARANUS NILOTICUS

RANGE: Sub-Saharan Africa

SIZE: Up to 8 ft (2.4 m)

DIET: Frogs, toads, rodents, reptiles, fish, birds and their eggs, beetles, crabs, earthworms, slugs, caterpillars, spiders, millipedes

The Nile monitor is a largely aquatic lizard and one of the biggest lizards in Africa. It has tough skin, which is covered by bead-like scales, and nostrils located high up on its nose—an adaptation for swimming.

CALIFORNIA LEGLESS LIZARD
ANNIELLA PULCHRA

RANGE: California, U.S.A. and Mexico

SIZE: 6 to 9 in (15 to 23 cm)

DIET: Insects, insect larvae; termites, beetles, spiders, other invertebrates

This is one of many species of legless lizards. Though this reptile may look like a snake, it has several features shared by most lizards. These include eyelids, external ear openings, and a short body with a very long tail.

TOKAY GECKO
GEKKO GECKO

RANGE: Northeast India, southeast Indonesia, western New Guinea

SIZE: 7 to 14 in (18 to 36 cm)

DIET: Other tokays, insects, other small vertebrates

For small animals, tokays make very loud sounds. Their mating call sounds like a frog croaking, interspersed with a person calling out their name, *too-kay, too-kay*. Males are more colorful than females.

DON'T TRY THIS AT **HOME**

Of all the awesome reptiles in the world, climbing geckos have got to be at the top of the list for outrageous abilities. Why? These little lizards seem to defy gravity by climbing straight up walls and walking upside down across the ceiling! You might think the secret to their skill involves suction cups on each foot, but the truth is it's more like built-in Velcro than anything else. Climbing geckos have toe pads that are made up of millions of microscopic structures. The structures are so small (only a few thousandths of a millimeter) that they fit into the spaces in between the smallest irregularities in the surface of the object they are climbing. This gives them quite an advantage over their ground-dwelling counterparts: No bug can escape to the ceiling to avoid becoming lunch!

GOLD DUST DAY GECKO
PHELSUMA LATICAUDA

RANGE: Madagascar

SIZE: 9 to 12 in (22 to 30 cm)

DIET: Insects, spiders, crustaceans; sometimes sweet fruit or nectar

Like all geckos (there are more than 1,500 species) the gold dust gecko can cling to any surface. They have special toe pads and muscles that allow them to bend their toes upward—so they can peel their feet off a flat surface.

BLUE-TAILED SKINK
CRYPTOBLEPHARUS EGERIAE

RANGE: Christmas Island and Australia

SIZE: 1.6 to 3 in (4 to 8 cm)

DIET: The skink's bright blue tail is the first thing a predator sees. To escape being eaten, these lizards whip their tail so quickly that it breaks off. They leave it behind as a distraction, and then grow a new one.

BLUE-TONGUED SKINK
TILIQUA SCINCOIDES

RANGE: Australia

SIZE: 18 to 20 in (45 to 50 cm)

DIET: Insects, other reptiles, snails, carrion; some plant material, fruit, berries

Like most of its relatives (there are 1,200 skink species), the blue-tongued skink has a very short neck and legs. It moves snake-like, with its belly on the ground. The blue tongue is used for defensive displays against predators.

SPINY-TAILED GECKO
STROPHURUS SPINIGERUS

RANGE: Northwest Australia

SIZE: 3 to 5 in (8 to 13 cm)

DIET: Insects and other invertebrates

Instead of eyelids, geckos have clear membranes over their eyes, which they clean with their tongues. Most species, including the spiny-tailed gecko, have another unusual behavior: They can shake their tail and break it off, leaving it behind to distract a predator.

SOLOMON ISLANDS SKINK
CORUCIA ZEBRATA

RANGE: Solomon Islands

SIZE: Up to 30 in (75 cm)

DIET: Mainly fruits and leaves

Unlike most other skinks, the Solomon Islands skink has a prehensile tail and long toes, adaptations for its life in the trees. This lizard is unusual in another way: It is one of the very few social reptiles.

SNAKES

nakes are highly successful predators. Yet they lack features shared by most other vertebrate hunters. They cannot chew, they have no limbs, their hearing is limited, and their vision is poor. They cannot hunt or digest their food unless the temperature in their environment is just right.

One reason for their success is their incredible sense of smell, which they use to locate prey. When a snake flicks its forked tongue, it is sampling the air, bringing various scents into its mouth, where they are picked up by special nervous tissue called Jacobson's organ. Some species, like pit vipers, also have a sixth sense: sensors under their eyes that can pick up body heat.

Another reason is their unique anatomy. Snakes have incredibly flexible jaws, elastic skin, and expandable stomachs. These features combined make it possible for them to open their mouths wider than the width of their bodies, and swallow prey of all shapes and sizes. This is particularly true for constrictors like the boas and pythons.

Finally, some species have a powerful weapon: venom. The most dangerous of these are the cobras and sea kraits (Elapid family), and the vipers, adders, and rattlesnakes (Viper family).

Life spans range up to 40 years.

ADDER
VIPERA BERUS

RANGE: Western Europe, Asia north to Arctic Circle and south to Mediterranean Sea

SIZE: 26 to 35 in (65 to 90 cm)

DIET: Primarily small rodents and lizards

Also known as the common viper, this shy snake has less toxic venom and is less aggressive when surprised than most vipers. Widespread in Europe and Asia, adders play an important role in controlling mice and rat populations in urban areas.

EYELASH PIT VIPER
BOTHRIECHIS SCHLEGELII

RANGE: Mexico and Central America

SIZE: 18 to 30 in (45 to 75 cm)

DIET: Lizards, frogs, small rodents

Pit vipers, including this one, use heat detection to find their prey. The pit organ is a narrow opening in the scales between the eye and the nose. Inside the opening is a heat-sensitive membrane that transmits signals to the brain.

SNAKE DIGESTION

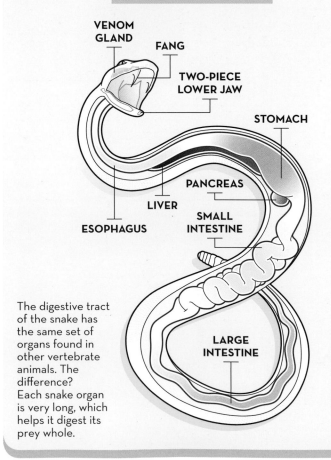

VENOM GLAND

FANG

TWO-PIECE LOWER JAW

STOMACH

PANCREAS

LIVER

SMALL INTESTINE

ESOPHAGUS

LARGE INTESTINE

The digestive tract of the snake has the same set of organs found in other vertebrate animals. The difference? Each snake organ is very long, which helps it digest its prey whole.

BOA CONSTRICTOR
BOA CONSTRICTOR

RANGE: Mexico and Central and South America

SIZE: 3.2 to 13 ft (1 to 4 m)

DIET: Mostly birds and mammals

Boa constrictors hunt by ambush, often while hanging from a tree limb, and kill by constriction. They grab the animal in their mouth and coil around the rest of it, squeezing until it dies by suffocation. Boas will eat any animal that is not too big to swallow.

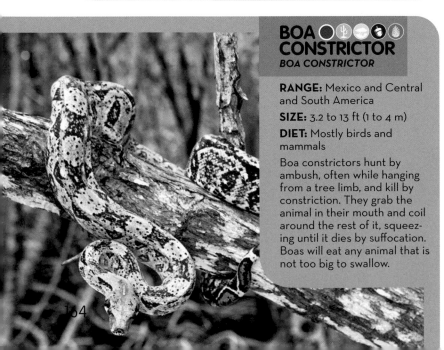

EASTERN BLACK NECK GARTER SNAKE
THAMNOPHIS CYRTOPSIS OCELLATUS

RANGE: Southwestern United States, Mexico

SIZE: 20 in (51 cm)

DIET: Small fish, frogs, other snakes, invertebrates, including earthworms

Found across North America, garter snakes are one of the few snakes that give birth to live young—from 3 to 80 babies in each litter. They also have mild venom, which is released only when they chew on their prey.

BALL PYTHON
PYTHON REGIUS

RANGE: West and Central Africa

SIZE: 3.3 to 6 ft (1 to 1.8 m)

DIET: Rodents

Ball pythons prey almost entirely on rats and mice, which they either kill by constriction and swallow, or swallow alive. They are nocturnal snakes that spend most of their time in burrows. When threatened, they curl up into a ball.

COTTONMOUTH
AGKISTRODON PISCIVORUS

RANGE: Southeastern United States

SIZE: 2.2 to 6.2 ft (0.7 to 1.9 m)

DIET: Mostly fish and frogs; also mammals, snakes, birds

Also called water moccasins, cottonmouths are semiaquatic pit vipers—the only ones in the world. Most live in freshwater swamps, shallow lakes, and slow-moving streams, but they also are found in brackish and salt water. They mostly prey on fish and frogs.

SCARLET KINGSNAKE
LAMPROPELTIS ELAPSOIDES

RANGE: Eastern United States

SIZE: 14 to 20 in (35.5 to 50.8 cm)

DIET: Small lizards such as skinks; also rodents, other snakes

Kingsnakes vary in coloration, and in the southeastern U.S. can resemble the coral snake. The rhyme "red on black, friend of Jack" is one way to identify these harmless scarlet kingsnakes.

TIMBER RATTLESNAKE
CROTALUS HORRIDUS

RANGE: Eastern United States

SIZE: 3 to 5 ft (0.9 to 1.5 m)

DIET: Mice, rats, squirrels, rabbits; sometimes birds

Rattlesnakes are venomous pit vipers found only in the Americas. They are named for their rattle, a series of button-like scales at the end of their tail. When threatened, rattlesnakes shake their tail, making a noise intended to scare potential predators.

EASTERN GREEN MAMBA
DENDROASPIS ANGUSTICEPS

RANGE: Coastal southern and eastern Africa

SIZE: 4.6 to 7.9 ft (1.4 to 2.4 m)

DIET: Birds, eggs, frogs, lizards, rodents, small mammals

Mambas are highly venomous snakes related to cobras. The green mamba, which is strictly arboreal, is much less aggressive when surprised or provoked, compared to its larger relative, the black mamba. Both snakes have a deadly bite.

VIPER

GABOON

Venomous reptiles possess one of nature's deadliest weapons: toxic cocktails that evolved over millions of years to immobilize and kill prey and predators. But these deadly toxins also can save human lives. Scientists study their effects on the body and borrow the toxins' blueprint to develop drugs that treat diseases like heart disease and diabetes. I've traveled all over the world capturing deadly snakes and extracting their tissues—a source for the toxins' blueprint. On one trip, Baaka pygmies of the Congo basin rain forest guided me on my search for the Gaboon viper *(Bitis gabonica)*—a snake that likely produces the most venom of any animal species.

About a week after the rainy season set in, one of the guides yelled at me to come quick. After a half-hour sprint through the forest, we stopped to stare at the ground. One of the largest vipers I have ever seen was lying barely above the leaf litter. Its head was too big to fit in the tube I had brought to shield my hands from its fangs, so I had to hold its head with my bare hands! After my assistant managed to extract a piece of tissue from the tail, we released the snake, grateful for the millions of years of potentially life-saving information locked inside the sample.

APPROXIMATE RANGE OF
THE *BITIS GABONICA*
(GABOON VIPER)

0   1,000   miles

0   1,000   kilometers

A F R I C A

OBSERVATION
TIPS

1 Know your surroundings: Learn everything you can about the animals, environment, people, and culture *before* heading into the forest.

2 Vipers tend to be most active at the beginning of the rainy season and in the spring—and you may find them wandering into open areas at night, which is when they hunt.

3 Viper venom can easily kill a human. You must have years of experience and be prepared for an emergency when dealing with venomous snakes.

4 Watch your step. Even the largest vipers disappear into rain forest leaf litter—and beware of charging forest elephants!

Zoltan Takacs began catching snakes in kindergarten. His fascination with venomous reptiles inspired him to co-invent a revolutionary technology that screens millions of toxin blueprints for potential use in making medicines.

Gaboon vipers are fearsome predators—they produce two teaspoons of venom that deliver a violent, multipoint attack on blood circulation and inject it via two-inch fangs! They hide motionless, camouflaged among leaf litter, to ambush their prey—including rodents and even small monkeys and antelopes! Males fight before mating—hissing and striking with closed mouths, each trying to force the other's head down—and females typically give birth to 10 to 30 live young. Born with deadly venom and fangs, the baby vipers soon disperse to live on their own.

RECORDS

E ver heard a crocodile roar like a lion? Or see a snake smaller than a worm? If you thought you knew everything about reptiles, you had better think again. Check out these superstars of the reptile world!

LONGEST LIVING →

ALDABRA GIANT TORTOISE
DIPSOCHELYS DUSSUMIERI

While it's difficult to know for sure the life span of certain animals, scientists believe that the giant tortoise lives the longest. Several species are known to live more than 150 years. But the tortoise with the longest life lived more than 200 years! His name was Adwaita, and he was originally brought from the Seychelles Islands to the Calcutta Zoo in India in 1875. When he died in 2006, a technique known as carbon dating was used to determine his age. Adwaita was 255 years old!

SMALLEST SNAKE →

BARBADOS THREADSNAKE
LEPTOTYPHLOPS CARLAE

The Barbados threadsnake was identified for the first time in 2008, and it's easy to see why it went unnoticed for so long. It averages a four inches (10 cm) in length and is as thin as a spaghetti noodle. Unlike most snakes, which lay many eggs at a time, the threadsnake lays just one. The hatchling is also relatively large compared to the mother—about half her size. The reason has to do with space. The snake's body cavity must have room for all of the organs, including reproductive tract, and the egg must be large enough to house the tiniest known snake form: a baby threadsnake.

FASTEST SNAKE →

BLACK MAMBA
DENDROASPIS POLYLEPIS

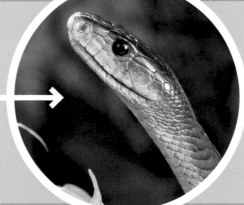

If snakes were cars, the black mamba would be a Corvette. These aggressive snakes can grow to an impressive 14 feet (4.3 m) in length and are capable of raising their heads 4 feet (1.2 m) in the air. When cornered, they are aggressive and explosive. As a result, black mambas are the most feared snake in Africa. But it's not only their size and temperament that make them scary, it's their speed: They are able to move in bursts of up to 12.5 miles per hour (20 km/h). Good luck outrunning this swift snake!

WEIRDEST →

TEXAS HORNED LIZARD
PHRYNOSOMA CORNUTUM

There's no doubt about it. When it comes to self-defense, the Texas horned lizard of North America is the king. With several tricks up their sleeves, these lizards can change color to blend in with their surroundings. When threatened by a predator, they inflate themselves to look more threatening. But that's not the strange part. As a last resort, the horned lizard can actually squirt blood from its eyeballs a distance of three feet (.9 m) to thwart attackers. Now, *that's* weird.

LARGEST LIZARD

KOMODO DRAGON
VARANUS KOMODOENSIS

Thought dragons only exist in fairy tales? Think again. The Komodo dragon is real, terrifying, and not afraid to take down a water buffalo twice its size. At ten feet (3 m) in length and weighing more than 300 pounds (136 kg), this largest of all lizards has bacteria-ridden saliva that seeps into the bite wounds of its victims, causing a slow, painful death. Komodo dragons are known to deliver their deadly bite, and then follow their victims for miles while they slowly succumb to blood poisoning. Yikes!

SMELLIEST

STINKPOT TURTLE
STERNOTHERUS ODORATUS

If you're like many reptile-lovers and keep one of these guys as a pet, you know where they get their name. At a maximum of about five inches (12.7 cm), the stinkpot turtle doesn't have much of a chance defending itself in the wild based on size alone. But it does have one feature that might keep attackers away. When threatened, the stinkpot turtle releases a foul-smelling oily substance to deter predators. Startle these turtles, and you'll certainly pay the price.

NOISIEST

AMERICAN ALLIGATOR
ALLIGATOR MISSISSIPPIENSIS

Crocodilian species are famous for lurking in muddy waters with only their eyes and snouts above the surface, barely visible to unsuspecting prey. But if you thought these reptiles were silent killers, you thought wrong. All crocodilians are able to hiss, snort, moan, and bellow, with American alligators being the loudest. Said to resemble a lion's roar, an alligator's bellow can easily be heard 500 feet (152.4 m) away. Individual alligators can even be identified by their call, much like humans can be identified by their voice.

LONGEST TONGUE

Chameleons have the longest tongues, relative to body size, in the entire animal world. These lizards keep their sticky, mucus-covered tongues bunched up at the back of their mouths until needed, then shoot them out a distance of one and a half times their body length to catch an insect. It's all over in about half a second.

VEILED CHAMELEON
CHAMAELEO CALYPTRATUS

Want to know where these record-holding reptiles live around the world? Take a look at this range map to find out.

MAP KEY
APPROXIMATE RANGES OF RECORD-SETTING REPTILES

- Aldabra Giant Tortoise
- American Alligator
- Barbados threadsnake
- Black Mamba
- Komodo Dragon
- Stinkpot Turtle
- Texas Horned Lizard
- Veiled Chameleon

The name "amphibian" comes from a Greek word that means "living a double life." The term refers to the ability of some of these animals to live on land and in water. Bullfrogs are amphibians that begin life underwater but head to land when they mature.

AMPHIBIANS

ROBBER FROG

AMERICAN TOAD

PETERS' TOADLET

PACIFIC TREE FROG

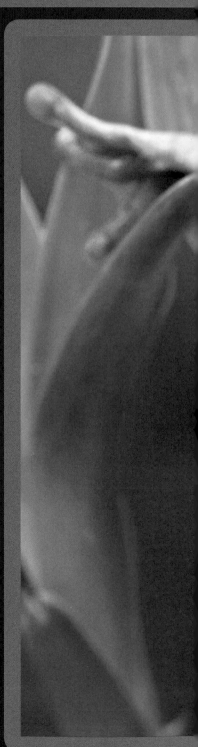

AUSTRALIAN GREEN TREE FROGS

BICOLOR CAECILIAN

AFRICAN BULLFROG

GLASS FROG EGGS

HARLEQUIN FLYING FROG

RED-LEGGED FROG

GRAY TREE FROG

RED-EYED TREE FROG

GOLFODULCEAN POISON FROG

SPOTTED SALAMANDER

173

WHAT IS AN AMPHIBIAN?

AMPHIBIANS ARE SMALL VERTEBRATES THAT NEED WATER, OR A MOIST ENVIRONMENT, TO SURVIVE.

The species in this group include frogs, toads, salamanders, and newts. All can breathe and absorb water through their very thin skin.

Amphibians also have special skin glands that produce useful proteins. Some transport water, oxygen, and carbon dioxide either into or out of the animal. Others fight bacteria or fungal infections. And at least one—in each species—is used for defense.

To warn potential predators, the most toxic amphibians are also the most brightly colored. Curare [kyoo-RAW-ree], for example, is found on the skin of colorful poison dart frogs. Another special feature of most amphibians is their egg-larva-adult life cycle. The larvae are aquatic and free-swimming—frogs and toads at this stage are called tadpoles. At a certain size, the young develop limbs and lungs. Some also lose their tails. Eventually, they hop or climb out of the water as adults, and spend the rest of their lives on land. This process is known as metamorphosis.

Like reptiles, amphibians are cold-blooded. Because of their special skin, they require very specific living conditions. Too much sun can damage their cells. Too much wind can dry their skin and dehydrate the animal. As a result, amphibians are the first to die off when their habitats are disturbed or contaminated with chemicals like weed killers. This is the main reason over half of all frog species are in danger of extinction.

AMPHIBIAN TRAITS

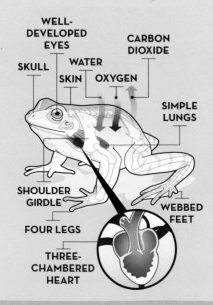

WELL-DEVELOPED EYES

CARBON DIOXIDE

SKULL

WATER

SKIN   OXYGEN

SIMPLE LUNGS

SHOULDER GIRDLE

WEBBED FEET

FOUR LEGS

THREE-CHAMBERED HEART

Frogs, like all amphibians, have very delicate skin that allows water, oxygen, carbon dioxide, and chemicals to pass right through.

CLASSIFICATION OF AMPHIBIANS

Amphibians appear in the fossil record more than 370 million years ago. They were the first four-legged vertebrates to live on land and are considered descendants of fish and ancestors of terrestrial reptiles. They were once much larger than they are today. There are more than 6,500 species. These are the three amphibian orders:

1   SALAMANDERS AND NEWTS (CAUDATA)

2   FROGS AND TOADS (ANURA)

3   CAECILIANS (GYMNOPHIONA)

Did you know? A group of frogs is called a chorus.

The black spots on the back of blue poison dart frogs are unique to each frog. Like finger-prints, they help identify individual frogs.

SALAMANDERS
AND NEWTS

Salamanders have smooth, slimy skin compared to newts, which have rough skin. All require moist habitats such as caves, wetlands, streams, and forests. They are aquatic, terrestrial, or both, depending on their life cycle. One-third of all salamanders are found in North America, with the highest density in the Appalachian Mountains.

Most, like the tiger salamander, begin life as aquatic larvae with external gills, then change, through a process called metamorphosis, to terrestrial adults with simple lungs. Others, such as axolotl (AXE-oh-lot-til), are aquatic animals throughout their life cycle. Some, such as the eastern red-spotted newt, are terrestrial while they mature, then aquatic as adults. Finally, there are lungless salamanders, which are completely terrestrial.

All are carnivorous. For defense, they produce toxins in their skin and their bright colors warn predators. Life spans range from 10 to 15 years.

AXOLOTL
AMBYSTOMA MEXICANUM

RANGE: Southern Mexico

SIZE: 9 to 12 in (20 to 30 cm)

DIET: Anything that it can catch, such as mollusks, fish, arthropods

The axolotl is an aquatic salamander that does not go through a complete metamorphosis. The adults look like the larval form. They have external gills, a dorsal fin, and short, undeveloped legs. They also are able to regrow lost limbs.

ITALIAN NEWT
LISSOTRITON ITALICUS

RANGE: Italy

SIZE: Up to 3 in (8 cm)

DIET: Plankton and other invertebrates

The rate of development of the Italian newt depends on the temperature of its environment, which is true for all amphibians. In this species, metamorphosis from larvae to juvenile takes four to six weeks in warm water, and several months in cold water.

SPOTTED-TAIL CAVE SALAMANDER
EURYCEA LUCIFUGA

RANGE: Central eastern United States

SIZE: 4 to 6 in (10 to 15 cm)

DIET: Variety of invertebrates

There are more than a dozen species of salamanders that live in caves. The spotted-tail cave salamander is found near the entrance. It lives under rocks and in rock crevices, and has a long, prehensile tail that it uses to climb.

RIO GRANDE LESSER SIREN
SIREN INTERMEDIA

RANGE: Eastern United States and northern Mexico

SIZE: 7 to 27 in (18 to 68 cm)

DIET: Aquatic invertebrates, including crustaceans, insect larvae, worms, snails

Most of the time, lesser sirens are buried in mud and debris at the bottom of slow-moving streams. If its habitat dries up temporarily, this species can survive by secreting a protective layer of mucus, like a cocoon.

ARBOREAL SALAMANDER ○○○
ANEIDES LUGUBRIS

RANGE: California, U.S.A.

SIZE: 4 to 7.25 in (10 to 18.4 cm)

DIET: Variety of invertebrates

This tree-climbing salamander is found in the black oak-yellow pine forests of the Sierra Nevada foothills. It has a prehensile tail and has been found as high as 60 feet (18 m) above ground! Males have visibly sharp teeth.

LONG-TOED SALAMANDER ○○○○○ ○○ ○○○
AMBYSTOMA MACRODACTYLUM

RANGE: Northwestern United States, Canada

SIZE: Up to 4 in (10 cm)

DIET: Worms, tadpoles, insects, small fish

The long-toed salamander can survive in all kinds of habitats, as long as there is water nearby. The adults are seen only during the breeding season. Most of the time they stay moist underground in burrows created by rodents, or under rocks and rotten logs.

HELLBENDER ○○
CRYPTOBRANCHUS ALLEGANIENSIS

RANGE: United States

SIZE: 11 to 29 in (28 to 74 cm)

DIET: Crayfish, insects, fish, worms

The three species of giant salamanders—Chinese, Japanese, and American, or hellbender—are all aquatic as adults. Lacking gills, they breathe through long folds of skin. Hellbenders can weigh as much as 5.5 pounds (2.5 kg).

EMPEROR NEWT ○○○○
TYLOTOTRITON SHANJING

RANGE: Southern China

SIZE: 6 to 8 in (15 to 20 cm)

DIET: Small insects

The orange spots on the sides of this newt are filled with a toxic poison that is highly dangerous for potential predators like mice. They also have a relatively thick skull. These adaptations are for defense, not offense.

EASTERN RED-SPOTTED NEWT ○○○○○
NOTOPHTHALMUS VIRIDESCENS

RANGE: Eastern North America

SIZE: 2.8 to 4.9 in (7 to 12.4 cm)

DIET: Small invertebrates

The larval form of this species is light green. The terrestrial, immature form is bright orange-red with spots and is called an "eft." The mature form is aquatic, with olive-green skin and the same orange-red spots.

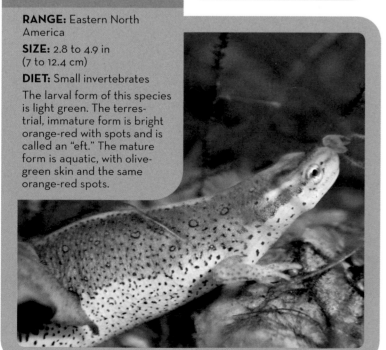

WESTERN TIGER SALAMANDER ○○○○ ○
AMBYSTOMA MAVORTIUM

RANGE: Southwestern Canada, western United States, northern Mexico

SIZE: 6 to 8.5 in (15.2 to 22 cm)

DIET: Small insects, slugs, worms; sometimes small frogs, lizards, small mice, snakes

To escape temperature extremes and dry air, tiger salamanders spend their days underground in deep burrows they dig in the soil. At night, they come out to feed, using their sticky tongues to catch prey. This tiger salamander is one of the largest in North America.

THE LONG-TAILED salamander (*Eurycea longicauda*) belongs to an order of amphibians that has cylinder-shaped bodies, limbs, and tails. Like its name suggests, this salamander has a very long tail. It measures up to four inches (10 cm)—that's two-thirds the length of the animal's body.

TOADS

Toads—and frogs—are named because of the way they look. And they look different because of where they live.

A toad is a type of frog that needs relatively little water. Because they are adapted to drier habitats, they look different. Instead of wet skin, long legs, and webbed feet, toads have dry skin, short legs, and stubby bodies (see diagram on p. 181).

Otherwise, toads are very similar to other frogs. They have breathable skin, sac-like lungs, and a four-stage life cycle. They also lack tails. All frogs and toads are in the order Anura, which means "tailless" in Greek.

Of the 33 frog families, one contains mostly toads, the Bufonid (boo-FON-id) family. The animals in this group include the cane toad, green toad, smooth-sided toad, Panamanian golden frog, and the Limosa harlequin frog. All share one trait: They lack teeth.

Though the distinction between a frog and a toad is important, in some cases, the differences are no more than skin deep.

Life spans for true toads range from seven to ten years.

EUROPEAN GREEN TOAD
BUFO VIRIDIS

RANGE: Europe, Asia, northern Africa

SIZE: 4 to 6 in (1.6 to 2.4 cm)

DIET: Insects, worms, butterflies, moths, caterpillars

These toads vary in color. Some are white with speckled green; others are brown, red, or black. They live in open areas near open bodies of water or places that flood seasonally.

CANE TOAD
RHINELLA MARINA

RANGE: Texas, U.S.A.; South America to the central Amazon and parts of Peru

SIZE: 6 to 7 in (15 to 17.5 cm)

DIET: Ants, beetles, earwigs; sometimes dragonflies, grasshoppers, crustaceans, plant matter, true bugs

The cane toad was introduced to the Caribbean, Hawaii, and Australia to control sugarcane beetles. Instead, it became an invasive species, preying on native frogs. Its skin secretions are also very toxic.

SONORAN DESERT TOAD
BUFO ALVARIUS

RANGE: Southwestern United States and northern Mexico

SIZE: 4.3 to 7.4 in (11 to 18.7 cm)

DIET: Snails, beetles, spiders, grasshoppers, lizards, mice, smaller toads

Like many toads, this species has salivary glands known as parotid glands with chemicals toxic enough to kill a dog. In people, these poisons produce hallucinations. The Sonoran Desert toad is one of the largest in North America.

PANAMANIAN GOLDEN FROG
ATELOPUS ZETEKI

RANGE: Panama

SIZE: 1.4 to 2.5 in (3.5 to 7 cm)

DIET: Variety of small invertebrates

Golden frogs are symbols of good luck in Panama. They are also symbols of extinction. The numbers of this species have declined drastically in the wild as a result of pollution, habitat loss, overcollecting, and a fungal skin disease spread by global trade.

KIHANSI SPRAY TOAD
NECTOPHRYNOIDES ASPERGINIS

RANGE: Tanzania

SIZE: 0.4 to 0.7 in (1 to 1.8 cm)

DIET: Insects and small invertebrates

Before this tiny toad became extinct in the wild in 2003, it lived only near the Kihansi waterfall in Tanzania. Today, it survives only in captivity. Conservation organizations are working to reintroduce them.

FROGS VS. TOADS

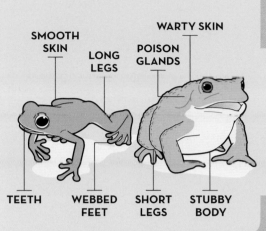

SMOOTH SKIN

LONG LEGS

WARTY SKIN

POISON GLANDS

TEETH

WEBBED FEET

SHORT LEGS

STUBBY BODY

Unlike frogs, toads have short rear legs; thick skin that is dull, dry, and covered with warts; poison glands; and no teeth.

AMERICAN TOAD
BUFO AMERICANUS

RANGE: Eastern Canada south to all U.S. Gulf Coast states except Florida

SIZE: 2 to 4 in (5 to 10.2 cm)

DIET: Insects

American toads are thriving in urban areas. As long as this species has water during the breeding season, it can survive in almost any habitat, including forests, gardens, and agricultural fields. During bouts of cold weather, they hibernate.

SMOOTH-SIDED TOAD
BUFO GUTTATUS

RANGE: Northern South America

SIZE: 9 in (23 cm)

DIET: Insects and small mammals

The patchy light- and dark-brown colors of this toad help it blend in with the leaf litter on the forest floor. Smooth-sided toads are still common in South American rain forests, but they can be very hard to find.

RED-SPOTTED TOAD
ANAXYRUS PUNCTATUS

RANGE: Southwestern United States and northern Mexico

SIZE: 1.5 to 2.5 in (3.8 to 6.4 cm)

DIET: Small arthropods, such as spiders and insects

Unlike so many of its relatives, populations of red-spotted toads remain stable. This toad lives in streams that run through deserts and dry areas, including grazing lands. It also likes cattle water tanks!

LIMOSA HARLEQUIN FROG
ATELOPUS LIMOSUS

RANGE: Panama

SIZE: 1 to 1.8 in (2.6 to 3 cm)

DIET: Invertebrates

In this species, the female is not only larger than the male but also has brighter coloring, with a red or orange belly. The Limosa harlequin frog is another amphibian in trouble. It has largely disappeared from higher elevations in its range.

HOUSTON TOAD
BUFO HOUSTONENSIS

RANGE: Southeastern Texas, U.S.A.

SIZE: 1.8 to 3.5 in (4.5 to 8.8 cm)

DIET: Ground beetles; small ants and toads

Some species of frogs and toads have small ranges, which can make them even more vulnerable to extinction. The Houston toad is one of them. It is found only in southeastern Texas and has been on the endangered species list since 1974.

AMPHIBIANS

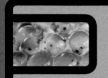

FROGS

Frogs—there are almost 5,000 species—are found everywhere except the open ocean and Antarctica.

Their lifestyles differ depending on their habitats, but all require access to a moist environment, especially during the breeding season. More than half of the world's frogs are found in tropical rain forests.

Compared to toads, frogs have a shorter body, webbed feet, smoother skin, and long rear legs that allow them to swim and leap. Most also have protruding eyes and teeth on their upper jaws. Like all amphibians, frogs produce a variety of skin secretions. Poison frogs, for example, secrete chemicals known as alkaloids. The source of these toxins is the frog's (wild) insect diet, particularly ants. Other skin secretions act naturally to help the frog fight off infections from bacteria and fungi. Several of these chemicals have been developed into promising medicines for humans.

Life spans range from four to six years for smaller frogs and up to ten for larger ones.

STRAWBERRY POISON DART FROG
OOPHAGA PUMILIO

RANGE: Nicaragua, Panama, Costa Rica

SIZE: 0.67 to 0.94 in (1.7 to 2.4 cm)

DIET: Small arthropods; mostly ants but also mites

Among the 170 poison frogs in the Dendrobatid (den-dro-BAY-tid) family, all are toxic, some more than others. A few, including the strawberry poison dart frog, are so poisonous they are used to coat the tips of hunting arrows.

GOLDEN POISON FROG
PHYLLOBATES TERRIBILIS

RANGE: Pacific coast of Colombia

SIZE: 1.85 to 2.17 in (4.7 to 5.5 cm)

DIET: Ants; also other small invertebrates such as termites and beetles

Like the strawberry poison dart frog, skin secretions from this species are used to coat arrow tips. It is, by far, the most toxic of the poison frogs. Poison from a single frog is enough to kill 10 to 20 humans.

AMERICAN BULLFROG
RANA CATESBEIANA

RANGE: Eastern and central North America (has been introduced to South America, Europe, and Asia)

SIZE: Up to 8 in (20.3 cm)

DIET: Frogs and tadpoles; snakes, insects, worms, crustaceans

Bullfrogs eat the tadpoles of other frogs and are large enough to escape predation by fish. As a result, they are rapidly increasing in number and moving west into new habitats, such as ponds stocked with fish.

SOUTH AMERICAN HORNED FROG
CERATOPHRYS CORNUTA

RANGE: Amazon basin

SIZE: 2.9 to 4.7 in (7.2 to 12 cm)

DIET: Mostly ants and beetles; other frogs, small reptiles, small mammals

The shape and coloration of this terrestrial frog give it near-perfect camouflage. Horned frogs bury themselves in the leaves on the rain forest floor and wait to ambush their unsuspecting prey.

Did you know? A frog's tongue is at the front of its mouth, which helps it grab prey.

COMMON COQUI
ELEUTHERODACTYLUS COQUI

RANGE: Puerto Rico

SIZE: 0.9 to 2.2 in (2.4 to 5.5 cm)

DIET: Mostly small arthropods

Frogs fill their vocal sacs, located under the throat, with air to make their calls louder. The frog's size determines the pitch of the call. Smaller ones, like the tiny tree frog known as the coqui (ko-KEE), make high-pitched calls.

BLUE POISON FROG
DENDROBATES AZUREUS

RANGE: Suriname and Brazil

SIZE: 1.18 to 1.77 in (3 to 4.50 cm)

DIET: Insects and other arthropods, especially ants, flies, mites, spiders, beetles, termites, maggots, caterpillars

Like the other species in its family, the blue poison frog is small and colorful and has toxic skin. It is a very territorial animal that will readily chase off or fight with intruders, of the same or different species.

RED-EYED TREE FROG
AGALYCHNIS CALLIDRYAS

RANGE: Southern Mexico, Central America

SIZE: 1.5 to 2.8 in (4 to 7 cm)

DIET: Insects, especially crickets, moths, flies, grasshoppers; sometimes smaller frogs

These brightly colored tree frogs have tiny suction cups on the bottom of their toes that allow them to cling to anything. They often rest by hanging from the underside of leaves—with their toes.

AFRICAN CLAWED FROG
XENOPUS LAEVIS

RANGE: Southern Africa

SIZE: 1.8 to 5.8 in (4.6 to 14.7 cm)

DIET: Insects; other vertebrates, especially anurans, fish, birds, small mammals

This aquatic frog thrives in warm, stagnant water. Instead of a tongue or teeth, it has claws on its rear feet, which it uses to break up its prey. Then it pumps water along with tiny bits of food into its mouth.

TOMATO FROG
DYSCOPHUS INSULARIS

RANGE: Madagascar

SIZE: 2 to 4 in (5 to 10 cm)

DIET: Invertebrates, especially crickets and waxworms; mice

When a predator grabs a tomato frog, it is in for a nasty surprise. The frog puffs up its body and secretes an irritating, thick mucus. In response, the predator—a stork, crocodile, or snake—often drops the frog.

FROG LIFE CYCLE

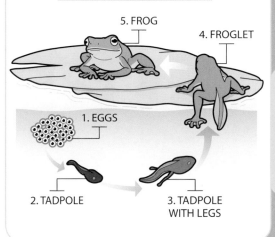

5. FROG

4. FROGLET

1. EGGS

2. TADPOLE

3. TADPOLE WITH LEGS

Like all amphibians, frogs and toads require water to complete their life cycle, from egg to tadpole to adult.

EMERALD GLASS FROG
ESPADARANA PROSOBLEPON

RANGE: Central America and South America

SIZE: 0.8 to 1.2 in (2.1 to 3.1 cm)

DIET: Insects

Glass frogs are found in humid rain forests. They are named for the transparent skin covering the belly. This skin is so glass-like that it is possible to see the internal organs.

FROM THE FIELD:
MARK MOFFETT

FROG

GOLDEN POISON

Touching neon-colored dart frogs is not a good idea—especially if you have a scratch or open wound. Your fingers could go numb, or worse. The golden poison frog that lives around the Embera Choco village in Colombia is so poisonous that one touch can kill. Scientists call this tiny, inch-long (2.5 cm) frog *terribilis*. The Embera people rub the tips of their blowgun hunting darts over *terribilis*'s back to coat the darts with poison. I wanted to photograph this formidable frog, and I needed these people to help me find one.

My assistant and I flew to Guapi, Colombia, and hired a speedboat to ferry us to the village. A trip that should have taken two hours took two days. The river was too low for a boat—even a canoe—so we were forced to hike with all our gear to the village. My pale legs blistered under the boiling sun, making me walk like Frankenstein! But it was worth it because when we finally arrived, the Embera people agreed to help us find the golden frog. After wrapping my blistered legs in plastic, we whacked our way through thick jungle brush and waist-deep mud until our guide spotted a brilliant yellow blotch in the leaf litter. It was *terribilis!* I dropped to my belly and pointed my camera at the deadly frog, just inches from its face. Instead of hopping away, *terribilis* came right toward me! Luckily, my assistant slid me out of its way in the nick of time—*after* I snapped the photo.

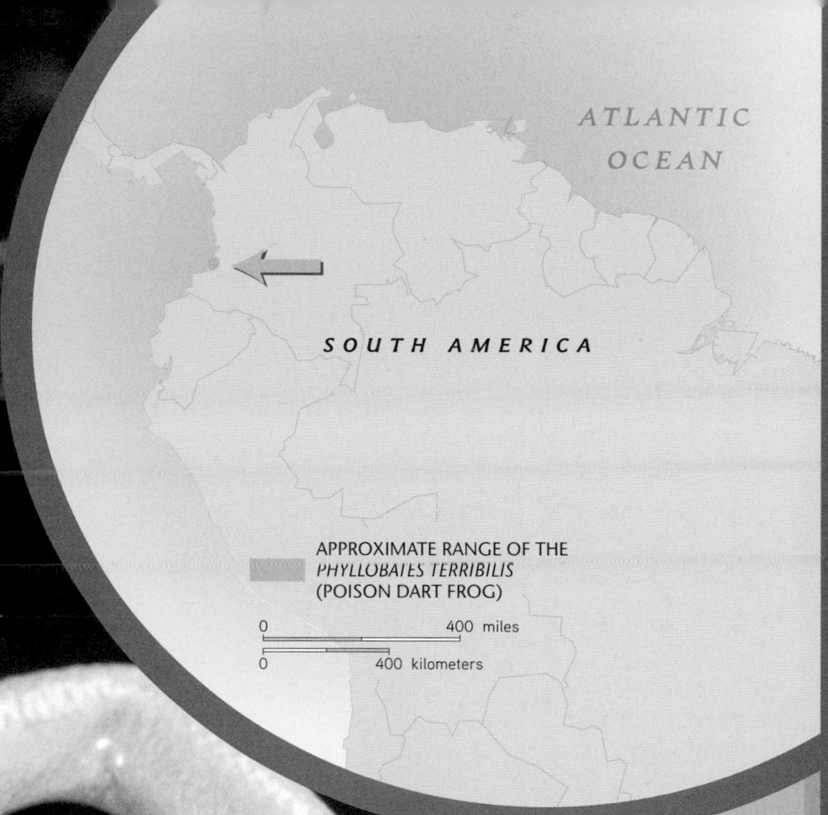

ATLANTIC
OCEAN

SOUTH AMERICA

APPROXIMATE RANGE OF THE
PHYLLOBATES TERRIBILIS
(POISON DART FROG)

0   400 miles
0   400 kilometers

OBSERVATION TIPS

1 Dart frogs hang out in leaf litter on the rain forest floor. Mid-day is the best time to see them hopping around.

2 Never, ever touch a neon-colored frog—it's likely to be poisonous!

3 To keep creepy crawlies from getting inside your clothes, tuck in your shirt and pull your socks over your pantlegs. And beware of South American bullet ants. They are the biggest ants in the rain forest and have terrifying stings!

4 Be on the lookout for movement. It can signal a possible threat—like a snake! Practice by looking for small animals moving around in your own backyard.

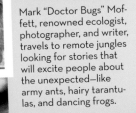

Mark "Doctor Bugs" Moffett, renowned ecologist, photographer, and writer, travels to remote jungles looking for stories that will excite people about the unexpected—like army ants, hairy tarantulas, and dancing frogs.

Female dart frogs lay their eggs on the rain forest floor. After the tadpoles hatch, they wiggle onto their mother's back to be carried to a water source up in the trees to complete their development. The mother checks on her tadpoles every few days, and some dart frog mothers lay eggs as food for their babies to eat. Soon the tadpoles grow legs, lose their tails, and climb down to the forest floor to live as adults.

RECORDS

E ver heard of a salamander that's as big as an adult human or a frog that can soar in the air? There are tons of incredible things amphibians can do, so hop in and check out these wet and wild record holders of the amphibian world!

LARGEST AMPHIBIAN

→

GIANT CHINESE SALAMANDER
ANDRIAS DAVIDIANUS

Measuring up to six feet (1.8 m) in length and weighing 24 pounds (11 kg), the giant Chinese salamander can grow to be roughly the length of an adult human. This weird and wonderful amphibian has prehistoric origins, with a family lineage dating all the way back to the age of the dinosaurs. Unfortunately, today the giant Chinese salamander is considered to be one of the most endangered amphibians, as its existence is being threatened by overpopulation, pollution, and hunting.

SMALLEST AMPHIBIAN

→

PAEDOPHRYNE AMAUENSIS

Discovered as recently as 2012, *Paedophryne amauensis* is not just the world's smallest frog; it is currently the world's smallest vertebrate. Measuring a maximum of 0.3 inches (7.7 mm), this itty-bitty amphibian is roughly the size of a housefly. It beat out the previous smallest vertebrate title-holder, a species of fish, by a mere 0.01 inches (0.2 mm). Talk about winning by a hair!

LOUDEST AMPHIBIAN

→

AMERICAN BULLFROG
LITHOBATES CATESBEIANUS

The American bullfrog, the largest frog in North America, has a big, bellowing call to match its substantial size. Measuring up to eight inches (20.3 cm) in length and weighing up to 1.5 pounds (0.7 kg), this loudmouth amphibian's croak is said to resemble a cow's *moo*, which is how "bull" became part of its name. Active mostly at night, the bullfrog's deep-pitched call can be heard more than a quarter-mile (0.4 km) away.

MOST TOXIC FROG

→

GOLDEN POISON FROG
PHYLLOBATES TERRIBILIS

Don't be fooled by this frog's cute and friendly appearance. That bright yellow color means "stay away." The golden poison frog stands out from its green-and-brown surroundings for a reason: Just one touch can bring on muscle paralysis and even death in a matter of minutes. Its skin contains a toxin that's so potent, one two-inch (1.6-cm) frog has enough toxins to kill at least ten full-grown men.

FANCIEST FLIER

→ WALLACE'S FLYING FROG
RHACOPHORUS NIGROPALMATUS

Okay, so you know frogs can't really fly—but if you saw this one, you might think twice about that. The Wallace's flying frog, native to Borneo, doesn't defy the laws of gravity, but it is an accomplished glider, able to soar up to 50 feet (15.2 m) in the air from tree to tree. How does it do it? Easy. Super-webbed feet and extra skin folds help this frog catch air and glide to a halt in the trees or on the ground. Now, that is some fancy flying!

COOLEST CAMOUFLAGE

EUPEMPHIX NATTERERI

This frog doesn't have eyes in the back of its head, but it sure looks that way! The *Eupemphix nattereri* is a tiny amphibian native to South America that has one very cool feature. Two splotches on its hind end resemble the eyes of a much larger animal. If this fearless frog becomes threatened, it will raise up its rear and send predators running!

GREATEST GETAWAY

→ MOUNT LYELL SALAMANDER
HYDROMANTES PLATYCEPHALUS

What it lacks in size, the Mount Lyell salamander certainly makes up in style. A true rock-and-roller, this slippery salamander turns itself into a rubbery ball to get away from predators. If disturbed, it shuts its eyes, tucks in its arms and legs, and takes on a tire-like shape for a quick escape down a rocky slope.

LARGEST FROG

GOLIATH FROG
CONRAUA GOLIATH

It may seem like nothing compared to the six-foot (1.8-m) giant Chinese salamander, but imagine a frog the size of a housecat and try not to be impressed! The Goliath frog, native to rain forests in Africa, measures up to 12.5 inches (32 cm) in length and weighs a whopping 7.2 pounds (3.3 kg). What does it take to satisfy a frog this size? A lot of insects, fish, other amphibians, and—in some cases—bats!

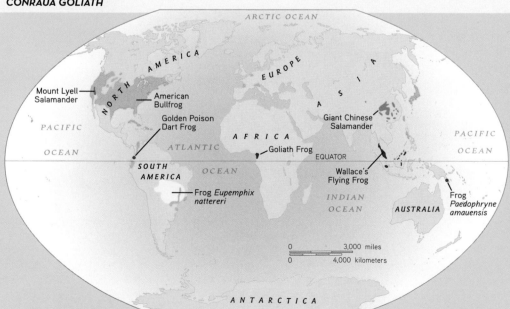

ARCTIC OCEAN

NORTH AMERICA

EUROPE

ASIA

Mount Lyell Salamander

American Bullfrog

Golden Poison Dart Frog

Giant Chinese Salamander

PACIFIC OCEAN

AFRICA

ATLANTIC OCEAN

Goliath Frog

EQUATOR

PACIFIC OCEAN

SOUTH AMERICA

Frog *Eupemphix nattereri*

Wallace's Flying Frog

INDIAN OCEAN

AUSTRALIA

Frog *Paedophryne amauensis*

ANTARCTICA

0   3,000 miles
0   4,000 kilometers

Want to know where these record-holding amphibians live around the world? Take a look at this range map to find out!

MAP KEY

APPROXIMATE RANGES OF RECORD-SETTING AMPHIBIANS

- Wallace's Flying Frog
- Goliath Frog
- American Bullfrog
- Frog *Eupemphix nattereri*
- Mount Lyell Salamander
- Golden Poison Dart Frog
- Giant Chinese Salamander
- Frog *Paedophryne amauensis*

All fish live in water and have a backbone, but as a group they are very diverse. Fish include four classes of animals and 32,000 species.

FISH

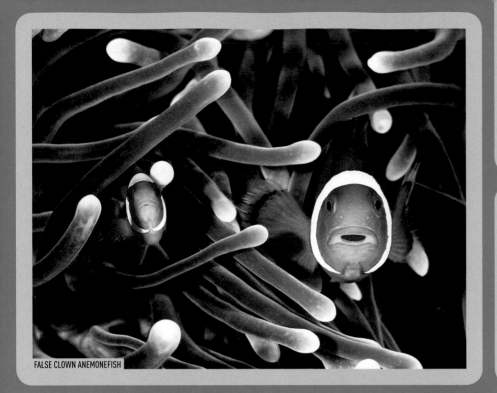

FALSE CLOWN ANEMONEFISH

CORAL GROUPER

MOONTAIL BULLSEYE

TOMATO GROUPER

BULLETHEAD PARROTFISH

LEOPARD CORAL GROUPER

BULL SHARK

NEON GOBY

SPOTTED TRUNKFISH

HARLEQUIN TUSK WRASSE

ORANGE FAIRY BASSLETS AND STONY CORAL

LONGSPINED PORCUPINEFISH AND SEA FAN

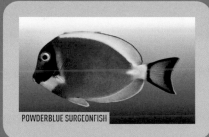
POWDERBLUE SURGEONFISH

SILVERSIDES

FISH

REDCAP ORANDA GOLDFISH

BLUE SPOTTED FANTAIL STINGRAY

WHALE SHARK AND REMORA

GREEN MORAY EEL STINGRAY

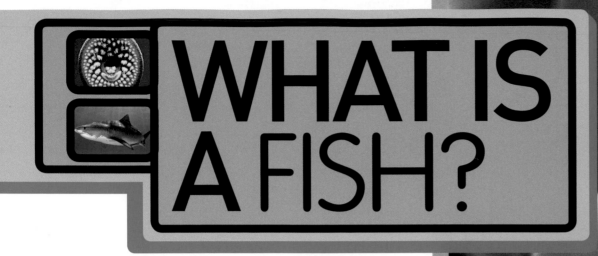

WHAT IS A FISH?

ALL FISH SHARE TWO TRAITS: THEY LIVE IN WATER AND THEY HAVE A BACKBONE—THEY ARE VERTEBRATES.

Apart from these similarities, however, many of the species in this group differ markedly from one another. Fin fish like salmon have gills, are covered in scales, and reproduce by laying eggs. Eels, by contrast, have worm-like bodies and exceedingly slimy skin. Lungfish gulp air. Whale sharks, the largest fish, give birth to live young and eat only tiny fish, squid, and plankton. Some species, such as the weedy sea dragon, are so bizarre they seem almost unreal.

Fish have developed special senses, too. Because water transmits sounds, disperses chemicals, and conducts electricity better than air, fish rely less on their vision and more on their hearing, taste, and smell. Many can detect motion in the water using a special row of scales with sensors known as the lateral line. Others can find their prey and even navigate by detecting electrical charges.

One reason fish are so diverse is that 70 percent of the planet is covered in water. The animals in this group live in a variety of habitats ranging from coral reefs and kelp forests to rivers, streams, and the open ocean. Another is that fish are very old on the evolutionary scale. According to fossil records, they have been on Earth for more than 500 million years! The total number of living fish species—about 32,000—is greater than the total of all other vertebrate species (amphibians, reptiles, birds, and mammals) combined.

FISH TRAITS

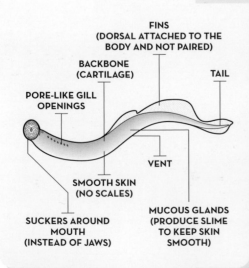

FINS (DORSAL ATTACHED TO THE BODY AND NOT PAIRED)

BACKBONE (CARTILAGE)

TAIL

PORE-LIKE GILL OPENINGS

VENT

SMOOTH SKIN (NO SCALES)

SUCKERS AROUND MOUTH (INSTEAD OF JAWS)

MUCOUS GLANDS (PRODUCE SLIME TO KEEP SKIN SMOOTH)

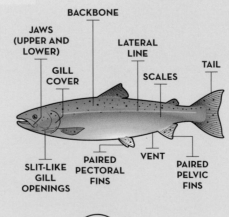

BACKBONE

JAWS (UPPER AND LOWER)

LATERAL LINE

GILL COVER

SCALES

TAIL

SLIT-LIKE GILL OPENINGS

PAIRED PECTORAL FINS

VENT

PAIRED PELVIC FINS

BARBELS (WHISKERS SPECIFIC TO CATFISH)

These diagrams point out the unique body parts that allow both primitive and nonprimitive fish to thrive underwater.

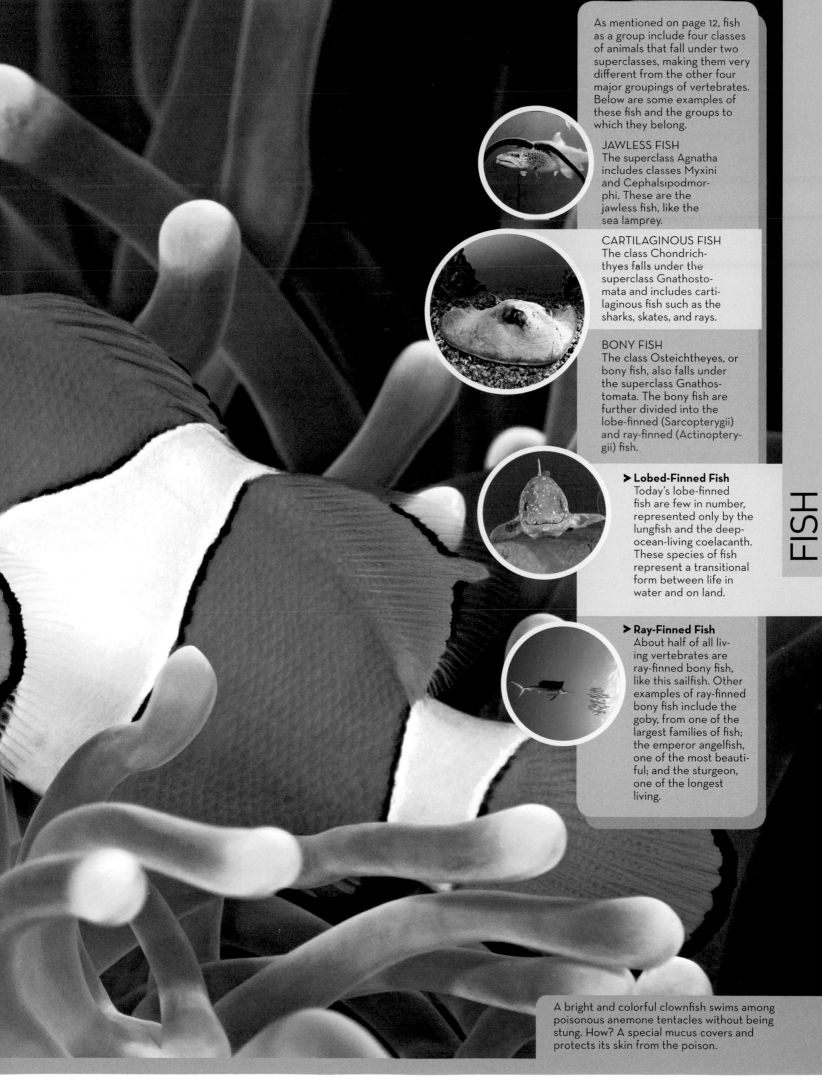

As mentioned on page 12, fish as a group include four classes of animals that fall under two superclasses, making them very different from the other four major groupings of vertebrates. Below are some examples of these fish and the groups to which they belong.

JAWLESS FISH
The superclass Agnatha includes classes Myxini and Cephalsipodmorphi. These are the jawless fish, like the sea lamprey.

CARTILAGINOUS FISH
The class Chondrichthyes falls under the superclass Gnathostomata and includes cartilaginous fish such as the sharks, skates, and rays.

BONY FISH
The class Osteichtheyes, or bony fish, also falls under the superclass Gnathostomata. The bony fish are further divided into the lobe-finned (Sarcopterygii) and ray-finned (Actinopterygii) fish.

> **Lobed-Finned Fish**
Today's lobe-finned fish are few in number, represented only by the lungfish and the deep-ocean-living coelacanth. These species of fish represent a transitional form between life in water and on land.

> **Ray-Finned Fish**
About half of all living vertebrates are ray-finned bony fish, like this sailfish. Other examples of ray-finned bony fish include the goby, from one of the largest families of fish; the emperor angelfish, one of the most beautiful; and the sturgeon, one of the longest living.

FISH

A bright and colorful clownfish swims among poisonous anemone tentacles without being stung. How? A special mucus covers and protects its skin from the poison.

 # PRIMITIVE FISH

Based on studies of the fossil record, the species known as lungfish, arowana, sturgeon, and gar are some of the oldest known fish—about 200 million years old.

Two species are even older—the hagfish and the lamprey. These are the world's only remaining jawless fish. They first appear in the fossil record 500 million years ago.

Together, these species are considered "primitive fish" because they share relatively few features with modern-day fish. For example, sturgeon and gar have fins with rays like the bony fish, but their skeletons are made up mostly of cartilage. Their scales are interocking bony plates that look like body armor. Like lungfish, gar are capable of gulping air if the oxygen levels in the water are too low.

Arowana and arapaima are bony-tongued fish. Instead of teeth in their lower jaw, they have a tongue-like structure made of bone and rimmed with teeth. Their gills also are nonfunctional. These fish must surface every few minutes to take a gulp of air.

Life spans range from 15 years for jawless fish to 100 or more for sturgeons and lobe-finned fish.

ALLIGATOR GAR
ATRACTOSTEUS SPATULA

RANGE: United States and the Gulf of Mexico

SIZE: Up to 10 ft (3 m)

DIET: Fish, ducks, turtles, small mammals, carrion

The alligator gar is one of the largest freshwater fish in North America. Because of its size and body armor, it has few natural predators. This species was once common but is declining because of overfishing and habitat loss.

CALIFORNIA HAGFISH
EPTATRETUS STOUTII

RANGE: Pacific Ocean

SIZE: 2 ft (0.6 m)

DIET: Dead or dying fish and mammals; marine invertebrates, including worms

Hagfish are also called slime eels. Like lampreys, they have a skull but no jaw. Worms are their main diet, but they will feed on—even swim into—dying or dead animals. When threatened, they excrete large amounts of slime.

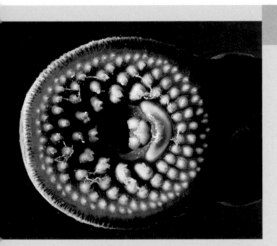

SEA LAMPREY
PETROMYZON MARINUS

RANGE: Atlantic coasts of Europe, North America, and the western Mediterranean Sea

SIZE: 4 ft (1.2 m)

DIET: Blood and skin of other fish

This parasitic fish latches on to the skin of another fish using the rim of suckers around its mouth. It then feeds on blood and flesh. It is invasive in the Great Lakes region of North America, where it preys on lake trout.

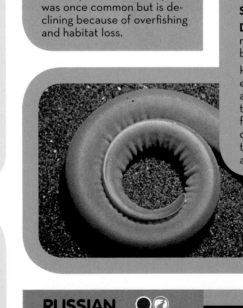

AROWANA
OSTEOGLOSSUM BICIRRHOSUM

RANGE: Amazon drainage system, South America

SIZE: Up to 3.9 ft (1.2 m)

DIET: Insects, spiders, cras, fish, snails, birds, monkeys, snakes, plant material

Arowana are ambush-style hunters. They hide beneath low-lying tree branches, and will jump out of the water to grab a bird or insect. These fish are mouthbrooders, which means they hold their eggs and young in their mouth.

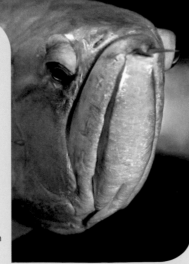

RUSSIAN STURGEON
ACIPENSER GUELDENSTAEDTII

RANGE: Russia; parts of Eastern Europe; Central Asia; Caspian, Black, and Azov Sea basins

SIZE: Up to 6 ft (1.8 m)

DIET: Mollusks, fish, crustaceans

Russian sturgeon live in salt water and breed in freshwater rivers. In recent years, most of their spawning sites have been lost due to dam construction for hydroelectric power. They are also in trouble from overfishing for their eggs.

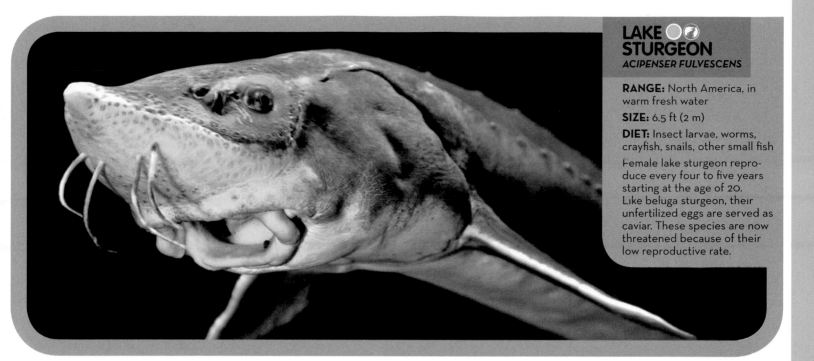

LAKE STURGEON
ACIPENSER FULVESCENS

RANGE: North America, in warm fresh water

SIZE: 6.5 ft (2 m)

DIET: Insect larvae, worms, crayfish, snails, other small fish

Female lake sturgeon reproduce every four to five years starting at the age of 20. Like beluga sturgeon, their unfertilized eggs are served as caviar. These species are now threatened because of their low reproductive rate.

LIVING FOSSIL FISH

Most of today's fish look very different from their 200- to 250-million-year-old ancestors. But a few have changed so little that they are called "living fossils." They include lungfish, arowana, sturgeon, and gar.

Lungfish (six species) are of special interest in piecing together evolutionary history. They are in a group known as the lobe-finned fish because of their large, fleshy fins. These fins are much more mobile than the fins of other fish, and they attach to the body like the limbs of terrestrial animals. Lungfish also breathe by gulping air. Their gills are too small to be useful. These features give these fish the ability to live in shallow water with low oxygen content—and even survive out of water, buried in mud. For these reasons, the lungfish are considered close relatives of the first vertebrate animals to live on land.

LONGNOSE GAR
LEPISOSTEUS OSSEUS

RANGE: United States and Canada

SIZE: 0.25 to 6 ft (.08 to 1.8 m)

DIET: Mostly fish, small crustaceans, insects

The longnose gar hunts mostly at night. It attacks its fish prey from the side, grabbing them with rows of teeth on its long, narrow snout. Their eggs are poisonous to other animals—including humans.

ARAPAIMA
ARAPAIMA GIGAS

RANGE: Brazil, Guyana, Peru

SIZE: Up to 9 ft (2.75 m)

DIET: Crustaceans and fish

The arapaima is one of the largest species of freshwater fish. An air breather, it often is found in warm, shallow water. The way to find this fish is to watch the surface of the water until it comes up for a breath, which it does every ten minutes or so.

WEST AFRICAN LUNGFISH
PROTOPTERUS ANNECTENS

RANGE: Africa

SIZE: 3.3 ft (1 m)

DIET: Mollusks, frogs, fish, seeds, aquatic vegetation

Lungfish are considered the closest relatives of four-legged terrestrial animals. They breathe by gulping air, swim like eels, crawl in the mud like salamanders, and survive for months out of water buried in mud burrows.

195

SHARKS

Sharks are a group of about 400 marine fish. All have torpedo-shaped bodies, skeletons made of cartilage, exposed gill slits, powerful tails, teeth that are replaced throughout their lives, and (airplane) wing-like pectoral fins.

Most are predators with highly developed senses for hunting prey. Sharks have good underwater vision and acute senses of taste and smell. They can detect tiny amounts of chemicals in the water—as little as one drop of blood. They have lateral line pores for sensing sound and motion. They can pick up electrical signals as tiny as those created by the muscles of their prey.

Sharks are almost always on the move. For one thing, they are hungry. But many must swim to avoid sinking because they lack an air bladder, which helps other fish stay afloat when not moving. Others cannot pump water over their gills, so they cannot breathe unless they swim.

Life spans range from 20 to 30 years for most species. The dogfish and whale shark can live up to 100 years.

GREAT WHITE SHARK
CARCHARODON CARCHARIAS

RANGE: Cold and tropical waters around the world

SIZE: 26 ft (7.9 m)

DIET: Bony fish, sharks, rays, seals, sea lions, dolphins, sea turtles, squid, sea birds

This shark is an ambush hunter that rams its prey. It has a long, spongy snout to absorb the impact and massive jaws supported by layers of hard tissue called tesserae (TES-ser-ray), which act like bone.

HAMMERHEAD SHARK
SPHYRNA LEWINI

RANGE: Warm tropical and temperate waters

SIZE: 6.5 to 7.5 ft (2 to 2.3 m)

DIET: Lobster, shrimp, crab, fish, squid

Hammerhead sharks have an excellent prey detection system: their huge heads. The skin is covered in electrical sensors and the eyes on either side allow the shark to see above and below at once. When bottom hunting, they also use the hammer to pin down stingrays.

BASKING SHARK
CETORHINUS MAXIMUS

RANGE: North and South Pacific and Atlantic Oceans

SIZE: 29.5 ft (9 m)

DIET: Zooplankton

Basking sharks are filter feeders—and the second largest shark. They feed by swimming through plankton-rich water with their huge mouths open. The water flows through their gill slits, where brush-like filaments called gill rakers trap the plankton.

SPINY DOGFISH
SQUALUS ACANTHIAS

RANGE: Atlantic Ocean and Indo-Pacific region

SIZE: Up to 5.2 ft (1.6 m)

DIET: Fish and crustaceans

Spiny dogfish have two spines, one in front of each dorsal fin, each containing a supply of mild venom. This small, predatory shark is found worldwide and is a major source of food, shark oil, and shark cartilage.

Did you know? The smallest sharks live in the deepest parts of the ocean.

CARTILAGINOUS
FISH

Sharks, rays, and skates are called cartilaginous (CART-el-AJ-in-us) fish because their skeletons are made entirely of cartilage. This is a lightweight material that gives them an advantage in the water over bony fish. They weigh less, which means they use less energy while swimming.

These fish also have ridges on their scales, called dermal denticles, that reduce turbulence. If you rub their skin one way, it feels smooth; rub it the other way, it feels like sandpaper. They also have wing-like pectoral fins that allow them to swim bird-like, gliding underwater.

Another feature of sharks, rays, and skates is their slow reproductive rate. Most do not begin to reproduce until they are several years old, and some have very long gestation periods. The dogfish shark, for example, is pregnant for 24 months, longer than the Asian elephant! This is one reason overfishing has led to the decline of so many of these species.

LEOPARD SHARK
TRIAKIS SEMIFASCIATA

RANGE: Indian and Pacific Oceans, Australian coast

SIZE: 6.5 ft (2 m)

DIET: Crab, shrimp, bony fish, fish eggs

Leopard sharks were once in trouble from overfishing. The good news is fishing regulations worked, and their numbers are stable. The bad news is dozens of other species are declining rapidly in number for the same reason: They are used as food in shark fin soup.

WHALE SHARK
RHINCODON TYPUS

RANGE: Tropical and warm waters worldwide

SIZE: 36 to 39 ft (11 to 12 m)

DIET: Plankton, squid, small fish

The whale shark is the largest fish in the world, yet it is a filter feeder. Like the basking shark, it has gill rakers for trapping its food. Whale sharks migrate, often timing their movement with the spawning of corals.

WHITETIP REEF SHARK
TRIAENODON OBESUS

RANGE: Indian and Pacific Oceans

SIZE: 5.2 ft (1.6 m)

DIET: Fish, octopuses, crab, lobsters

The whitetip reef shark specializes in squeezing into crevices, cracks, and caves, looking for fish. It feeds at night, using its sense of smell to find fish hidden in the reef. Multiple sharks often hunt in the same area.

HORN SHARK
HETERODONTUS FRANCISCI

RANGE: Eastern Pacific Ocean

SIZE: 4 ft (1.2 m)

DIET: Fish, sea urchins, crabs

Unlike most sharks, horn sharks are oviparous. They reproduce by laying eggs in the water enclosed in a leathery case that often washes onto shore. Other sharks are ovoviviparous: They give birth to live young that develop in eggs inside the adult's body.

NURSE SHARK
GINGLYMOSTOMA CIRRATUM

RANGE: Tropical and subtropical waters in western Atlantic, eastern Atlantic, and eastern Pacific Oceans

SIZE: 14 ft (4.3 m)

DIET: Lobster, shrimp, crabs, sea urchins, squid, octopuses, stingrays, bony fish

Nurse sharks are nocturnal predators. Unlike other sharks, this species can actively pump water across its gills. Like other fish, it can breathe without swimming and is often found resting on the bottom of the ocean during the day.

TIGER SHARK

Encountering a tiger shark (*Galeocerdo cuvier*) in the ocean anymore is rare. You're more likely to bump into a lemon or reef shark. And you can't track a tiger shark by following its footprints like you would a lion or a leopard, so when my diving partner Jennifer and I really need to photograph them, we head to Tiger Beach in the Bahamas—a protected patch of ocean known to harbor these gorgeous, silvery striped sharks. Even here it's rare to see more than one or two of them in a week—but on one assignment a few years ago, we hit the jackpot.

Toward the end of a weeklong expedition, we slipped into the shallow water at Tiger Beach and were instantly greeted by about 30 curious lemon sharks. As they milled about our ankles like puppies, we spotted several large, gray shapes looming in the distance. Out of the gloom one tiger shark emerged, then two, and suddenly a half dozen 12- to 15-foot (3.6- to 4.6-m) tiger sharks surrounded us. Hardly able to believe our luck, Jennifer and I drifted with our cameras to a nearby grassy area, hoping the tiger sharks would follow—and they did. A 15-foot (4.6-m), blunt-nosed behemoth swam right toward me, nudged the dome of my camera, and made a grand sweeping circle around us. The others joined in this game we call "bump-and-go," and for the next two hours we became the center pole of a giant shark carousel. It was one of the most exhilarating experiences of our lives, and we were able to make beautiful photographs of a rare group of tiger sharks for our new book.

APPROXIMATE RANGE OF THE *GALEOCERDO CUVIER* (TIGER SHARK)

NORTH AMERICA
EUROPE
ATLANTIC OCEAN
AFRICA
PACIFIC OCEAN
SOUTH AMERICA
ANTARCTICA

ASIA
PACIFIC OCEAN
INDIAN OCEAN
AUSTRALIA
ANTARCTICA

OBSERVATION **TIPS**

1 If you ever encounter a tiger shark, keep your eyes fixed on it at all times. These animals, while beautiful and captivating, can be aggressive and unpredictable.

2 Tiger sharks are typically slow and sluggish; so if you see one swimming fast or making sharp movements, calmly exit the water.

3 Human flesh can look like bait to a tiger shark. When diving, it's important to cover your skin from head to toe—including your neck, feet, and ankles.

4 Dive with a buddy and swim back-to-back so a shark can't sneak up on you from behind.

FISH

David Doubilet is an internationally acclaimed underwater photographer, and his wife and diving partner, Jennifer Hayes, is an aquatic biologist, author, and photojournalist. Together, they photograph marine life around the world.

Tiger sharks are among the largest and most fearsome predators in the sea. They can reach lengths of more than 20 feet (6 m), and their powerful jaws and sharp, jaggy teeth crunch through whale carcasses and sea turtle shells with ease. Adult tiger sharks are mostly solitary, but juveniles stick together. They live in shallow-water nurseries that offer abundant food for growing tiger sharks, and their natural defenses—gray stripes for camouflage, sharp teeth for snatching prey, and swift speed for escaping predators—help them survive on their own.

SKATES AND RAYS

Skates and rays have flat bodies, long tails, skeletons made of cartilage, and (bird) wing-like pectoral fins. Like all fish, they breathe through their gills, but instead of taking water in through their mouths, they use a small opening behind each eye called a spiracle.

Most of the 500 species in this group are marine predators that feed along the ocean floor. Skates have small teeth for feeding on small fish in deeper water. Rays have plate-like teeth for crushing snails, crabs, and other prey in shallower water.

Skates and rays are common prey for sharks and whales. For defense, skates have large, thorn-like scales on their backs and sides. Rays have sharp spines about a third of the way down the length of their long tails. In stingrays, these are venomous.

Skates lay eggs in cases; rays give birth to live young. Life spans range from 15 to 20 years.

COWNOSE RAY ○○○
RHINOPTERA BONASUS

RANGE: Atlantic Ocean

SIZE: Disc width up to 3.6 ft (1.1 m); length 3.9 ft (1.2 m)

DIET: Invertebrates, including crustaceans and mollusks

Cownose rays often travel in schools of up to 10,000. They also hunt together by flapping their pectoral fins at the same time. The result is an underwater sandstorm that leaves their food exposed and easy to find.

GIANT MANTA RAY ○○○
MANTA BIROSTRIS

RANGE: Tropical waters worldwide

SIZE: Disc width 22 ft (6 m); length 14.7 ft (4.5 m)

DIET: Plankton and fish

The giant manta ray is exceptional. It is the largest member of this group, weighing up to 3,100 pounds (1,400 kg). Its pectoral fins have extensions that look like paddles. It is an open-ocean filter feeder, like whales and basking sharks.

YELLOW STINGRAY ○○
UROBATIS JAMAICENSIS

RANGE: Coastal waters of western Atlantic Ocean and the Gulf of Mexico

SIZE: Disc width up to 1.2 ft (0.4 m); length 2.2 ft (0.7 m)

DIET: Worms, crabs, small fish

Yellow stingrays vary in color and pattern. The two most common are a dark green or brown ray with tiny white and yellow spots, or the reverse—a white background with tiny dark-green or brown spots.

COMMON STINGRAY ○○
DASYATIS PASTINACA

RANGE: Northeastern Atlantic Ocean, and Mediterranean and Black Seas

SIZE: Width up to 4.6 ft (1.4 m); length up to 8.2 ft (2.5 m)

DIET: Fish, crustaceans, mollusks

Like all stingrays, the common stingray has a venom gland at the base of its spine, which is used for defense. Though this ray looks as though it has a large eye, the large oval structure is the spiracle. Their eyes are in front.

Did you know?

The tiny hedgehog skate is less than 20 in (50 cm) long.

STARRY SKATE
RAJA STELLULATA

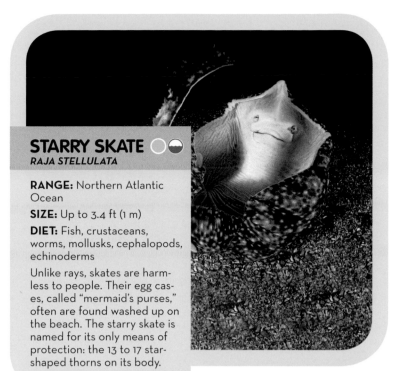

RANGE: Northern Atlantic Ocean

SIZE: Up to 3.4 ft (1 m)

DIET: Fish, crustaceans, worms, mollusks, cephalopods, echinoderms

Unlike rays, skates are harmless to people. Their egg cases, called "mermaid's purses," often are found washed up on the beach. The starry skate is named for its only means of protection: the 13 to 17 star-shaped thorns on its body.

BLUE-SPOTTED STINGRAY
DASYATIS KUHLII

RANGE: Indonesia, Japan, northern Australia, continental waters of Asia

SIZE: Disc width 1.4 ft (0.4 m); length 2.3 ft (0.7 m)

DIET: Shrimp, small bony fish, mollusks, crabs, worms

Blue-spotted stingrays have very long tails and two venomous spines, one longer than the other. Its bright blue coloration is a warning to potential predators. This species is a favorite prey of hammerhead sharks and killer whales.

AUSTRALIAN THORNBACK SKATE
DENTIRAJA LEMPRIERI

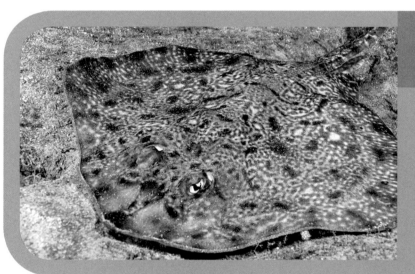

RANGE: Australia

SIZE: 1.8 ft (0.5 m)

DIET: Crabs, lobsters, octopuses; sometimes fish

The Australian thornback skate relies on camouflage for protection from potential predators such as large bony fish. It also surprises its prey—mostly crabs. Like all skates, it catches its prey by pouncing on and trapping it.

SOAKING UP SOME "RAYS"!

With an ominous name and an even more ominous-looking tail, stingrays might seem like a sea creature you'd want to steer clear of. But the truth is that they are particularly gentle animals, and certainly not out to harm you. As friendly as they are, however, stingrays are still armed with some pretty heavy defenses, which they use only if they feel threatened.

Stingrays have long, whip-like tails that can be covered with more than one knife-sharp, serrated barb. Additionally, they produce venom that can be toxic to humans. If a stingray comes in contact with a predator, it will whip its tail around and pierce the perceived threat with the sharp point, then a thin layer of skin called a sheath will break, injecting the venom into the wound of the unlucky victim.

SPOTTED EAGLE RAY
AETOBATUS NARINARI

RANGE: Tropical and warm temperate waters worldwide

SIZE: 8.2 ft (2.5 m), not including the tail; 16.4 ft (5 m) with tail

DIET: Small fish, shrimp, crab

Though it feeds in shallow water, the spotted eagle ray swims long distances through open water—often in large schools. Named for the graceful way it swims, it looks as though it is flying.

 EELS

Eels are bony fish with elongated bodies, a reduced number of fins, and, instead of scales, thick skin covered in mucus. Most are ambush predators. This group includes the electric eels and about 800 species of "true eels."

True eels, such as the moray eel, cannot swallow. Instead, they have two sets of teeth: one along the leading edge of their jaws, and one in the back of their throat. They use the front set to tear their prey into smaller pieces and the rear to pull it into their mouths.

They also have an unusual life cycle. Eggs hatch into transparent larvae called glass eels. As these mature, they darken and are called elvers. These young eels are usually found in the open ocean. They become adults after several years.

Life spans for these animals may be as long as 75 years.

LEOPARD SKINNED GARDEN EEL ⬤⬤
GORGASIA SILLNERI

RANGE: Indian Ocean and Red Sea
SIZE: Up to 33 in (84 cm)
DIET: Crustaceans, small fish

Garden eels are small, social eels that live in burrows under the seafloor. At times, they are completely invisible; to feed, they poke their heads out and look like stems growing from the ground—like a garden.

SPOTTED ⬤⬤
MORAY EEL
GYMNOTHORAX MORINGA

RANGE: Western and eastern Atlantic Ocean
SIZE: 6.6 ft (2 m)
DIET: Fish and crustaceans

Like all eels, spotted morays have poor vision and no lateral line pores. They find their food by smell. Divers have been injured because the eel cannot distinguish a fish from a finger. Their jaws also do not release.

STARRY ⬤⬤
MORAY EEL
GYMNOTHORAX NUDIVOMER

RANGE: Indo-Pacific region
SIZE: 5.9 ft (1.8 m)
DIET: Fish, crustaceans, squid

Like all true eels, the starry moray has a narrow head with wide jaws. When a moray catches prey too big to fit down its throat, it ties itself in a knot, restraining the fish or crustacean so it can tear it into smaller pieces.

ZEBRA ⬤⬤
MORAY EEL
GYMNOMURAENA ZEBRA

RANGE: Indo-Pacific region, eastern central Pacific Ocean
SIZE: 4.9 ft (1.5 m)
DIET: Crabs, crustaceans, mollusks, sea urchins

Most morays eat anything that fits in their mouths. The zebra moray eel is unusual because it specializes in eating crabs. Otherwise, its behavior is similar. It waits in a hole or crevice to ambush its prey.

ELECTRIC EEL ⬤⬤⬤
ELECTROPHORUS ELECTRICUS

RANGE: Northeastern South American waters
SIZE: 8.2 ft (2.5 m)
DIET: Invertebrates, fish, small mammals

Electric eels produce two types of electricity: a weak pulsating signal for navigation, communication, and prey detection, and a strong signal—up to 650 volts—for stunning prey. Like lungfish, they are air breathers.

RAY-FINNED BONY FISH

Half of all vertebrates—animals with a backbone—and 95 percent of all fish species are ray-finned bony fish. All have skeletons made of bone and fins made of webbed skin with bony or horny spines.

There are 25,000 species of ray-finned bony fish. They exist in all sizes, shapes, and colors, and are found all over the world. They do share some common behaviors, though.

One is migration. Though distances vary, many species in this group migrate to find food, avoid predators, or breed. Some move from salt water to fresh water, and back again. A second common behavior is shoaling, when fish move together in a group. Schooling is a specific type of shoaling, when the grouped fish are doing the same thing, such as swimming fast to avoid a predator. A third is aggression. The fish in this group tend to fight for access to food, mates, or territory.

ANCHOVIES, HERRINGS, AND RELATIVES

Anchovies, herrings, and their relatives (shads, sardines, and menhadens) are referred to as baitfish because of their place in the food web. They feed on plankton and, in turn, are eaten by bigger fish, marine mammals and birds, and people. They are the most numerous fish in the world.

These species are found in all oceans. Some also live in the brackish water of estuaries and bays. They are small- to medium-size fish, long and slender, with a single dorsal fin and a forked tail. They feed by swimming with their mouths open, collecting plankton on filaments in their gills. Most are schooling fish that swim together in large numbers to escape being eaten. As a result, many of the world's largest commercial fisheries depend on them.

Life spans range from 3 years for anchovies to up to 25 years for herrings and sardines.

EURPOEAN ANCHOVY ◐ ○
ENGRAULIS ENCRASICOLUS

RANGE: Eastern Atlantic Ocean and Mediterranean Sea

SIZE: 7.9 in (20 cm)

DIET: Plankton

Anchovies live in a wide range of salty waters and water temperatures. The European anchovy is a coastal species, also found in large schools like its relatives. These fish often move into lagoons, estuaries, and lakes during spawning.

ATLANTIC HERRING ○ ◐ ○
CLUPEA HARENGUS

RANGE: North Atlantic Ocean

SIZE: 1.5 ft (0.5 m)

DIET: Plankton

Atlantic herrings are found in large schools—up to several billion fish—that often stretch for miles. Their many predators include cod, bass, tuna, salmon, dogfish sharks, porpoises, whales, seals, puffins, terns, and humans.

SOUTH AMERICAN PILCHARD ○ ◐
SARDINOPS SAGAX

RANGE: Indian and Pacific Oceans

SIZE: 1.3 ft (0.4 m)

DIET: Plankton

There are many fish species called sardines. The South American pilchard is harvested in the greatest numbers for human use. Most of these sardines are processed into fish meal used for animal food.

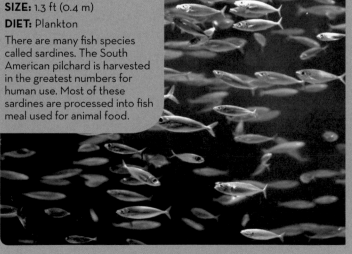

SOME FISH are as small as a dime, whereas others—like this whale shark *(Rhincodon typus)*—are as big as a school bus! To support its hefty frame, the whale shark sucks in about 160 gallons (605,000 L) of plankton-rich water each hour. The plankton gets trapped on bristle-like structures called rakers inside the shark's body, and is eventually digested. Meanwhile, the water is expelled through the shark's gills.

COD AND RELATIVES

Cod and their relatives are medium-size fish found in cooler, deeper waters. They are bottom dwellers and are sometimes referred to as groundfish. All are marine, meaning they live in saltwater environments, except for the burbot. Their prey include baitfish like anchovies and herrings, eels, and each other. They are eaten by sharks, seals, and people.

Many species of cod and their relatives are popular foods because of their mild-tasting, flaky white meat. They are used to make cod liver oil and other nutritional supplements as well. As a result, many have become extremely rare due to overfishing.

Groundfish like cod are caught using a method known as trawling, in which large numbers of fish—including young fish that have not had time to reproduce—are swept up in nets dragged along the ocean bottom. Some populations of Atlantic cod, for example, may never recover.

The life span for cod and cod-like fish ranges from 12 to 25 years.

HADDOCK ◐◐
MELANOGRAMMUS AEGLEFINUS

RANGE: Northeastern Atlantic Ocean

SIZE: 3.7 ft (1.2 m)

DIET: Small crustaceans, mollusks, echinoderms, worms, fish

Haddock have the same body shape and fin arrangement as cod, but with a black lateral line and a black patch behind their gill flaps. Their prey are mostly bottom-dwelling, meaning they live at or near the surface of the ocean floor.

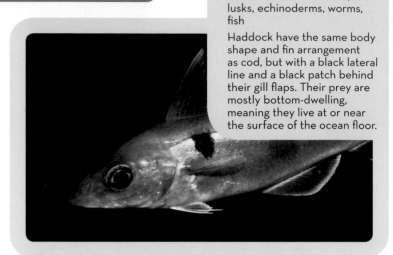

EUROPEAN ◐◐ HAKE
MERLUCCIUS MERLUCCIUS

RANGE: Mediterranean and Black Seas, eastern Atlantic Ocean

SIZE: 4.6 ft (1.4 m)

DIET: Fish and squid

The European hake can be found living at depths of up to 3,300 feet (1,000 m). Like its relatives, it feeds on a variety of fish, but as an adult, it will also eat smaller hakes and hake eggs.

ATLANTIC ◐◐ COD
GADUS MORHUA

RANGE: North Atlantic Ocean

SIZE: 6.6 ft (2 m)

DIET: Invertebrates and fish

Atlantic, Pacific, and Greenland cod are closely related. All have rounded dorsal fins, pelvic fins that are placed very far forward, a white lateral line, and a single whisker, or barbel, on their chin used to feel for their prey.

COMMON LING ◐◐
MOLVA MOLVA

RANGE: Atlantic Ocean and Mediterranean Sea

SIZE: Up to 6.6 ft (2 m)

DIET: Lobster, fish, starfish, squid

Like Atlantic and Pacific cod, ling have a mild taste and delicate white meat. Caught in the open ocean, they are eaten fresh, as well as dried and salted—both methods used to preserve fish. The salted eggs, or roe, of ling are a favorite food in Spain.

Did you know? Atlantic cod make a type of antifreeze to keep their blood from freezing.

BURBOT ◐◐
LOTA LOTA

RANGE: Cold fresh water in the Northern Hemisphere

SIZE: 5 ft (1.5 m)

DIET: Fish

The burbot is the only freshwater cod relative. This fish moves into deeper, cooler water during the warmer months and will burrow under mud or rocks for shelter. It also spawns during winter—under the lake ice.

DEEP-SEA FISH

The largest group of deep-sea fish are the dragonfish, lightfish, and their relatives. These species are found in deep oceanic waters worldwide, from the tropics to the Antarctic. Many migrate up the water column during the day to feed on plankton and small fish.

Finding food in the depths of the ocean, where it is cold and dark and where food is scarce, is a challenge. Deep-sea fish have adapted to their unique environment in several ways.

Many are opportunistic feeders with long, sharp teeth; large mouths; and jaws that unhinge. Some have large, light-sensitive eyes. Most have reduced fins because they need only to move up or down.

Light-producing organs called photophores are their most distinctive feature. This light, known as bioluminescence, varies in color from yellow to white, violet, or red. The fish use it to communicate, find their food, and avoid predators.

Life spans are unknown for most of these species.

FLASHLIGHT FISH
PHOTOBLEPHARON STEINITZI

RANGE: Red Sea and Indian Ocean

SIZE: 4.3 in (11 cm)

DIET: Zooplankton and coral

Flashlight fish are capable of bioluminescence. They have a pocket beneath each eye that contains bacteria that give off a green light. These fish live in coral caves during the day and move up to the surface to feed on coral reefs at night.

NORTHERN LAMPFISH
STENOBRACHIUS LEUCOPSAURUS

RANGE: Northern Pacific Ocean

SIZE: 5 in (13 cm)

DIET: Plankton and fish

The northern lampfish, one of 250 species of lanternfish, is named for its photophores, which give off light. All eat plankton, are common in the deep sea, and are an important food source for whales, dolphin, salmon, tuna, sharks, and seabirds.

SLOANE'S VIPERFISH
CHAULIODUS SLOANI

RANGE: All tropical and temperate oceans

SIZE: 11 to 24 in (30 to 60 cm)

DIET: Shrimp, crustaceans, other fish, squid

Viperfish are found as deep as 9,000 feet (4,400 m). Their teeth are so long they overlap the jaws. This fish catches its prey by piercing it. Like its relatives, it has a row of photophores under its belly.

SCALY DRAGONFISH
STOMIAS BOA FEROX

RANGE: Atlantic Ocean

SIZE: 12 in (30 cm)

DIET: Fish and crustaceans

The scaly dragonfish is also known as the boa dragonfish because of its long, slender shape. It lives at depths of 3,300 feet (1,000 m) or more. Like many deep-sea fish, it migrates toward the surface of the water at night to find food.

Did you know?

A female angler has a pole-like dorsal fin stemming from its mouth.

ANGLER
LOPHIUS PISCATORIUS

RANGE: Eastern Atlantic Ocean

SIZE: 6.6 ft (2 m)

DIET: Fish and seabirds

The angler has a huge head and mouth and, instead of a dorsal fin, several long, thin spines. The first is used as a lure to catch its prey. This fish ambushes its prey by burying itself in the sand or hiding in seaweed.

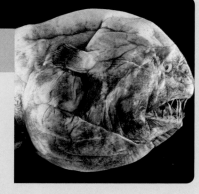

TROUT AND SALMON

Trout and salmon are medium-size fish with long bodies, pointed snouts, and a rounded fatty fin just in front of the tail. All spend the first part of their lives in fresh water, then return to where they hatched to breed, or spawn. After spawning, most die.

Between hatching and spawning, some species migrate to the open ocean and spend several years at sea. They return to fresh water when ready to spawn. By detecting magnetic fields beneath the ocean floor and using their sense of smell, they find their way to their home stream. Then they swim upstream, a behavior known as a run.

Life spans range from 7 years for species that migrate to 30 years for nonmigrating species.

SOCKEYE SALMON
ONCORHYNCHUS NERKE

RANGE: Both sides of the northern Pacific Ocean

SIZE: 2.8 ft (84 cm)

DIET: Plankton

Sockeye salmon are also called red and blueback salmon for the bright coloration they develop during spawning. Those that remain in fresh water for their entire lives are called kokanee salmon.

ATLANTIC SALMON
SALMO SALAR

RANGE: Both sides of the North Atlantic Ocean

SIZE: 4.9 ft (1.5 m)

DIET: Squid, fish, shrimp

Young Atlantic salmon have purple and red spots for camouflage. Adults at sea are silvery with a few black spots. During spawning, they turn dull brown or yellow, and the males develop hooked jaws.

BROOK TROUT
SALVELINUS FONTINALIS

RANGE: Eastern North America

SIZE: 2.8 ft (0.9 m)

DIET: Mayflies, leeches, worms, mollusks, salamanders; anything else it can catch

Brook trout, or char, are found only in fast-running streams with clear, cold water. Most do not migrate. Those that do swim only a few miles out to sea and stay there for only a few months. They are called sea-run brook trout.

Did you know? The biggest rainbow trout recorded weighed almost 60 pounds (27 kg).

RAINBOW TROUT
ONCORHYNCHUS MYKISS

RANGE: Pacific coast of North America

SIZE: 3.9 ft (1.2 m)

DIET: Invertebrates and small fish

Some rainbow trout migrate to the sea; others do not. Adults look different depending on where they live. Because of their silver color, ocean-living rainbow trout are called steelhead trout, even though they are the same species.

SALMON LIFE CYCLE

1 Newly hatched salmon are called sac fry, or alevin. They live off their yolk sacs.

2 Soon the tiny fish leave the nest and begin to feed on aquatic insects. As they grow, they develop spots for camouflage and are called fry, or parr.

3 After one to two years, parr go through a process called smolting, which prepares them for life in salt water.

4 Smolt swim downstream and into the open ocean, where they mature into adults. They are a silvery color at this stage.

5 After one to five years, mature salmon migrate back to fresh water to reproduce. Some species swim as far as 3,000 miles (4,828 km).

6 As they swim upstream, breeding salmon turn a darker color. The adults die soon after spawning.

Most salmon are anadromous, meaning they are born in fresh water, migrate to the ocean, where they live for several years, and return to fresh water to reproduce.

CATFISH, PIRANHAS, AND RELATIVES

Catfish, carp, piranhas, tetras, and their relatives are grouped together because of one feature: a connection between the inner ear and the swim bladder. Because of this connection, they have excellent hearing. They can make sounds for communication, too. Most species in this group share another feature: They live in fresh water.

Catfish are the exception. They are found on every continent except Antarctica, in coastal brackish water and salt water, as well as in fresh water in ponds, lakes, rivers, streams, caves, and even underground. At least 1 in 20 vertebrate animals is a catfish!

One reason for their success is diet: They are bottom feeders that eat just about anything—aquatic plants, other fish, decaying vegetation, fish eggs, crayfish, snails, aquatic bugs, carrion, leeches, and worms. Larger catfish also eat frogs, rodents, and ducks. A catfish has no teeth. Instead, it surrounds its prey with its pectoral fins, opens its mouth, and gulps.

Life spans for these fish range up to 40 years.

CHANNEL CATFISH
ICTALURUS PUNCTATUS

RANGE: North America and parts of Europe

SIZE: 4.3 ft (1.3 m)

DIET: Fish, crustaceans, insects

Another reason for the success of catfish as a group is their skin. Instead of scales, some are armored, but many, like the channel catfish, have only a mucous covering. This allows them to breathe through their skin, like frogs.

STERBA'S CORYDORAS CATFISH
CORYDORAS STERBAI

RANGE: Central Brazil and Bolivia

SIZE: 2.6 in (6.8 cm)

DIET: Algae

Like all catfish, corydoras use their skin sensors to taste the water and their cat-like whiskers, or barbels, to feel for food. These fish are an example of an armored catfish because their skin is protected by bony plates, or scutes.

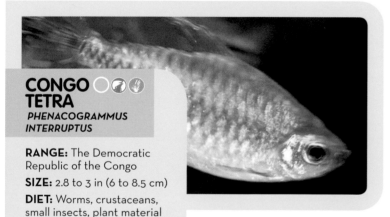

CONGO TETRA
PHENACOGRAMMUS INTERRUPTUS

RANGE: The Democratic Republic of the Congo

SIZE: 2.8 to 3 in (6 to 8.5 cm)

DIET: Worms, crustaceans, small insects, plant material

Tetras have six fins. The two pelvic fins under the belly are paired. The name "tetra," which means "four," refers to the single fins: the tail, dorsal, adipose, and anal fins. When the fish swims, it uses these fins like wings.

RED PIRANHA
PYGOCENTRUS NATTERERI

RANGE: South America

SIZE: 20 in (50 cm)

DIET: Insects and fish

Piranhas have sharp, interlocking teeth for puncturing and tearing into their food. While feeding, these fish gather in vegetation in groups of up to 30 to wait for their prey.

GOLDFISH
CARASSIUS AURATUS

RANGE: Worldwide

SIZE: Up to 16 in (41 cm)

DIET: Crustaceans, insects, plants

Goldfish are domesticated Prussian carp. There are now over 300 breeds of different shapes and colors. Like other carp, goldfish have teeth set way back in their mouths, attached to their gills instead of their jaws.

FROM THE FIELD:

ZEB HOGAN

TAIMEN

Taimen *(Hucho taimen)* will eat pretty much anything they can wrap their mouths around. These megafish can grow to more than six feet (1.8 m) and weigh more than 200 pounds (90.7 kg). But they're disappearing from many rivers where they once thrived, and catching a taimen that large is unheard of these days. The species' best hope for survival may be in remote river basins in Russia and Mongolia. So for the past five years, I have traveled with a team of researchers to an isolated stretch of river in northern Mongolia to catch, measure, tag, and release taimen back into the river to collect data that could help protect them from extinction.

A couple weeks into our first expedition, an aggressive taimen lunged at my fishing lure. It nabbed the bait, and I pulled hard on the line, but the fish fought like a giant. It swam for cover under a pile of floating tree branches next to the bank, so my colleague fired up the boat's motor and steered toward the opposite shore. My arms trembled and sweat streamed down my face as I wrestled the fish for nearly 30 minutes before we hit land. Finally, I jumped into the water to weigh and measure the monster taimen. It was a 5-foot (1.5 m), 70-pound (31.8-kg) megafish! We collected the data and released the fish. Seeing it was proof that we still have a chance to save this species.

APPROXIMATE RANGE OF THE
HUCHO TAIMEN (TAIMEN)

0   1,000 miles

0   1,000 kilometers

Zeb Hogan is an aquatic ecologist. Through his Megafishes Project, he travels the globe and works with local and international organizations to study and protect the world's largest—and often critically endangered—freshwater fish.

OBSERVATION **TIPS**

1 If you're in a boat, turn off the motor and peer into the water. It can be quite shocking to see a five-foot (1.5-m)-long fish looming below!

2 Taimen hide in pools where the river flows from shallow to deep water. You may spot them under fallen tree branches, too, waiting to nab a mouse or squirrel that wanders near the water.

3 Be patient. Hours could pass before you spot a taimen, but typically where you see one you'll see more.

4 Pack your warmest hats, sweaters, and gloves. Temperatures in northern Mongolia can plunge to several degrees below zero, even in the spring and fall.

FISH

Taimen are aggressive feeders that explode out of the water to snatch smaller fish, mammals, and birds. They even eat each other! Female taimen dig nests in the gravel with their tails when they're ready to spawn, and their mates fight off other males who dare to approach. Then, the male and female swim together over the nest, and the female releases her eggs. Once the tiny larvae hatch, it can take 50 years for them to grow to the size of a megafish!

211

PERCH
AND RELATIVES

Perch and their relatives form a very large group: 40 percent of all bony fish, known Perciformes (PER-see-FOR-meez). They are also known as spiny-rayed fish because of the organization of their fins.

Fish in this group are found all over the world and in every type of aquatic habitat. Many are favorite food fish, like bass, snapper, and tilapia. Others are found on coral reefs and range in size from tiny gobys and gouramies to large groupers.

The reason for so much diversity within a single grouping of fish is that species classification is based on more than one piece of information. Physical features, like scale color and the shape of the skeleton, are important. So is behavior: where the fish lives, what it eats, how it reproduces, and whether it lives alone or in groups. Genetic information is also used determine how species are related.

Life spans for these fish range from 5 to 30 years.

YELLOW PERCH
PERCA FLAVESCENS

RANGE: North America
SIZE: 4 to 10 in (10 to 25.5 cm)
DIET: Fish and invertebrates

Yellow perch are in the middle of the food chain. They eat invertebrates and smaller fish and are, in turn, eaten by bigger fish, such as bass, sunfish, and lake trout. Cormorants and other water birds also prey on yellow perch.

DOLPHINFISH
CORYPHAENA HIPPURUS

RANGE: Tropical and subtropical Atlantic, Pacific, and Indian Oceans
SIZE: 6.6 ft (2 m)
DIET: Sargassum weeds

Though not related to dolphins, which are mammals, this fish has a dolphin-like shape, with a large head and narrow body. Dolphinfish are marine fish that eat plants. They typically grow up to 30 pounds (13.6 kg) and are known as mahi-mahi, or dorado.

SPINY-RAYED FISH

Spiny-rayed fish are ray-finned bony fish with spines in both their dorsal and anal fins and sometimes in their pectoral fins. Perch and their relatives are generally referred to as spiny-rayed fish.

The part of the fin with spines is always closer to the head. It is stiff and sharp, made up of larger bony spines covered by skin. The softer part of the fin is closer to the tail. It is flexible, made up of tiny bones covered by a web of skin.

Most spiny-rayed fish also have scales with a spiny edge. These are thin, overlapping scales that feel rough, like tiny teeth. They are called ctenoid (TEN-noyd) scales.

There are other fish with spines. The difference is in how they are arranged. Catfish, for example, have a sharp spine on their dorsal fin and both pectoral fins.

Did you know?

Dolphinfish can swim up to 40 miles (64 km) an hour.

BLACKBANDED SUNFISH
ENNEACANTHUS CHAETODON

RANGE: North America
SIZE: 1.9 to 4.9 in (4.8 to 10 cm)
DIET: Smaller fish, insects

Though they look different, these sunfish are related to smallmouth bass. In both species, the male builds the nest, a depression in the mud, using his tail. After the female lays the eggs, he guards them.

SMALLMOUTH BASS
MICROPTERUS DOLOMIEU

RANGE: Temperate waters of North America
SIZE: 1.25 to 1.7 ft (0.4 to 0.5 m)
DIET: Crayfish, insects, smaller fish, amphibians

Smallmouth bass are top predators that eat smaller fish. Their size as adults depends on how much time they have to eat during the summer months. The largest bass are found in places with long, hot summers.

LEOPARD FLOUNDER
BOTHUS PANTHERINUS

RANGE: Indo-Pacific region

SIZE: 1.3 ft (39 cm)

DIET: Small fish and invertebrates

Flounder are a type of flatfish. The adults have a strange adaptation for living on the seafloor: Both eyes are on one side of the head. Some species are right-eyed; others are left-eyed.

Did you know?
At about four years old, female striped bass start growing faster than males.

STRIPED BASS
MORONE SAXATILIS

RANGE: Atlantic coast of the United States

SIZE: 1.5 to 4.6 ft (0.5 to 1.4 m)

DIET: Zooplankton, insects, small crustaceans, other fish

Striped bass are popular sport fish. Also called striper, rock, or rockfish, they are caught from boats, bridges, beaches, creeks, streams, and rivers using a variety of baits. Natural populations are anadromous, meaning they are marine fish that spawn in fresh water.

PEACOCK SOLE
PARDACHIRUS PAVONINUS

RANGE: Indo-Pacific region

SIZE: 10 in (25 cm)

DIET: Crustaceans and other bottom-dwelling invertebrates

Like all flatfish, a peacock sole starts life as fish larvae with one eye on either side of its head. As it matures, one eye moves so that both are on the same side of the head—the up side. All adult soles are right-eyed.

CALIFORNIA FLOUNDER
PARALICHTHYS CALIFORNICUS

RANGE: Eastern Pacific Ocean and west coast of North America

SIZE: 60 in (152 cm)

DIET: Mostly anchovies

California flounder have large mouths compared to other flatfish and very sharp teeth. They are known to bite! They are a favorite food and can grow quite large. The record is 5 feet (1.5 m) long and 72 pounds (33 kg).

STRIPED MULLET
MUGIL CEPHALUS

RANGE: Worldwide tropical and subtropical waters

SIZE: 3.3 ft (1 m)

DIET: Zooplankton, algae, fish

These schooling fish gather in large numbers during the fall to swim offshore to spawn. They are known for their impressive jumps, moves made to avoid predators. Mullet are eaten by sharks, dolphins, pelicans, sea trout, and people.

TUNA, MARLIN, SWORDFISH, AND RELATIVES

Tuna are among the fastest-swimming fish in the world. Streamlined for speed, they have torpedo-shaped bodies with stiff tails and tiny fins, or finlets, that decrease water turbulence. They fold their dorsal fins into grooves while they swim. They also have darker muscles than other fish, the result of high amounts of a molecule known as myoglobin, which binds oxygen.

Tuna are schooling fish that prey on smaller schooling fish, including smaller tunas and relatives like mackerel. Some swim with larger fish for protection. Yellowfin tuna, for example, school with dolphins to avoid their main predators: sharks.

Marlin, swordfish, and their relatives, which include sailfish and barracuda, are equally fast swimmers. Tuna are among their prey.

Life spans range from 9 years for swordfish up to 30 years for some species of marlin.

ATLANTIC BLUEFIN TUNA
THUNNUS THYNNUS

RANGE: Atlantic Ocean

SIZE: 4.6 ft (1.4 m)

DIET: Crustaceans, fish, squid

Bluefin tuna swim at high speed for great distances. They are also one of the largest fish in the open ocean. Using heat generated by their muscles, they keep their body temperature above that of the water, a rare ability among fish.

SWORDFISH
XIPHIAS GLADIUS

RANGE: Atlantic, Indian, and Pacific Oceans

SIZE: 14.9 ft (4.5 m)

DIET: Crustaceans, fish, squid

Swordfish use their sword-like snouts to slash and injure their prey. During the day, they move to deep water. At night, they move up to the surface to feed. Swordfish typically weigh 30 to 700 pounds (140 to 320 kg).

ATLANTIC SAILFISH
ISTIOPHORUS ALBICANS

RANGE: Atlantic Ocean

SIZE: 10.3 ft (3.1 m)

DIET: Smaller fish

To make its body more streamlined, the sailfish folds its huge, spiny-rayed fin into a ridge on its back while it swims. It then unfolds the fin to surprise and herd its fish prey. It can reach speeds of 68 miles an hour (110 km/h).

GREAT BARRACUDA
SPHYRAENA BARRACUDA

RANGE: Indo-Pacific region and eastern Atlantic Ocean

SIZE: 6.6 ft (2 m)

DIET: Fish, cephalopods, shrimp

Barracuda are predators that use bursts of speed to swim up to their fish prey and then take bites out of them with their sharp, fang-like teeth. Adults are solitary, whereas young often live together in shallow mangroves and reefs.

SCORPIONFISH AND SCULPINS

F ound worldwide, scorpionfish and sculpins are spiny, venomous fish. Most are found in shallow water, and most are marine. All are bottom dwellers that feed on crustaceans, small fish, and invertebrates.

The fish in this group have spines with venom glands located at the base, near the skin. There are at least a dozen of these spines in the dorsal fin and more in the anal and pectoral fins. They are used only for self-defense. When pressure is applied to a spine, it releases venom. These spines are so effective that most species have few predators. Among them are sharks, rays, and moray eels.

Scorpionfish and sculpins hunt by hiding or sneaking up on their prey. They are extremely well camouflaged, with fleshy bumps and skin tags on their heads and blotchy coloration.

Life spans range from two to ten years.

BANDED SCULPIN
COTTUS CAROLINAE

RANGE: Central United States
SIZE: 7 in (18 cm)
DIET: Invertebrates

Sculpins have flat bodies for burrowing under the sand and large pectoral fins for holding onto rocks so they can stay in one place in fast-moving water. These fish are also capable of surviving out of water for several hours.

RED LIONFISH
PTEROIS VOLITANS

RANGE: Indo-Pacific region
SIZE: 15 in (38 cm)
DIET: Fish and crustaceans

The red lionfish is a colorful and bold marine fish. Unfortunately, it is also an invasive species in the Caribbean and off the Florida coast. Where there were once many snapper and grouper, there are now mostly lionfish.

SMALL RED SCORPIONFISH
SCORPAENA NOTATA

RANGE: Eastern Atlantic Ocean
SIZE: 9 in (24 cm)
DIET: Crustaceans and small fish

Like its relatives, the small red scorpionfish lives in shallow marine habitats, including coral reefs. It sneaks up on its prey, corners them with its pectoral fins, and then vacuums them up.

REEF STONEFISH
SYNANCEIA VERRUCOSA

RANGE: Indo-Pacific region
SIZE: 16 in (40 cm)
DIET: Crustaceans, small fish

Reef stonefish are the world's most venomous fish. They are well hidden on the seafloor and can be fatal to people if stepped on. The amount of venom injected through the dorsal spines depends on the amount of pressure applied.

REEF FISH AND SEAHORSES

Coral reefs are often called rain forests of the sea. They are home to a huge amount of life, including 25 percent of all marine fish. Yet there are relatively few coral reef ecosystems. They represent less than 1 percent of the ocean surface and are found only in tropical parts of the world, where the water, depth, current, and light conditions favor the growth of coral.

Unlike the open ocean, where silvery, streamlined bodies are common, reef fish exist in all shapes, sizes, and colors, from tiny gobys to huge groupers. Many are strangely long, narrow, flat, or round with extra, fewer, or modified fins so they can dart in and out of holes or hide under ledges. Some have spines and venom for defense; others, like the seahorses, have incredible camouflage. All are competing for the same resources: food, shelter, room to move, and a chance to breed.

The life spans vary from 60 days for some gobys to 40 or more years for the goliath grouper.

LEAFY SEADRAGON ○○
PHYCODURUS EQUES

RANGE: Eastern Indian Ocean to southern Australia

SIZE: 13.8 in (35 cm)

DIET: Crustaceans

This seahorse is shaped to give it near-perfect camouflage in seaweed. But the leaf-like structures are not used for swimming. To move, this species uses two fins—one pectoral and one dorsal—that are so thin they are almost transparent.

YELLOWTAIL SNAPPER ○○
OCYURUS CHRYSURUS

RANGE: North American coast of the western Atlantic Ocean

SIZE: 34 in (86.3 cm)

DIET: Crabs, shrimp, cephalopods, worms, fish, plankton

Yellowtail snapper are reef fish that tend to stay in the same area in small groups. These smaller snapper are prey for larger snapper as well as for top predators like barracudas, groupers, and sharks.

FIRE CLOWNFISH ○○
AMPHIPRION MELANOPUS

RANGE: Pacific Ocean

SIZE: 4.7 in (12 cm)

DIET: Planktonic crustaceans

Fire clownfish live among the tentacles of sea anemones. Each protects the other from predators, and each provides food, either in the form of leftovers or excrement. The fish also keeps the anemone free of parasites.

LONG-SNOUTED SEAHORSE ○○
HIPPOCAMPUS GUTTULATUS

RANGE: Caribbean Sea and the western North Atlantic Ocean

SIZE: 9.8 in (25 cm)

DIET: Zooplankton, shrimp, very small fish, plants

The long-snouted seahorse has a crown on top of its head, a very long tail, and a thick nose. It can change color for better camouflage and to attract mates. It can be black, yellow, red, orange, or brown.

ATLANTIC GOLIATH GROUPER
EPINEPHELUS ITAJARA

RANGE: Atlantic Ocean

SIZE: 98.4 in (250 cm)

DIET: Crustaceans, spiny lobsters, turtles, fish, stingrays

Goliath groupers are large, predatory fish that weigh several hundred pounds. They are also very defensive around their home caves. They open their mouths, quiver, and contract their swim bladders to make a rumbling sound.

ALLIGATOR PIPEFISH
SYNGNATHOIDES BIACULEATUS

RANGE: Indo-Pacific region

SIZE: 11.4 in (29 cm)

DIET: Zooplankton

Like its relatives the seahorses and seadragons, the alligator pipefish has a fused jaw. It cannot open its mouth, so it feeds by using its long snout like a suction tube to inhale food.

LINED SEAHORSE
HIPPOCAMPUS ERECTUS

RANGE: Western North Atlantic Ocean

SIZE: 6.9 in (17.5 cm)

DIET: Crustaceans and other small invertebrates

Seahorses do not have scales. Instead, their skin is attached to rings of bone. These rings give the fish its shape and, along with its spines and changeable skin coloration, help protect it from predators.

NAPOLEON WRASSE
CHEILINUS UNDULATUS

RANGE: Indo-Pacific region

SIZE: 90 in (229 cm)

DIET: Mollusks, fish, sea urchins, crustaceans, other invertebrates

Also called the humphead wrasse, this fish feeds on invertebrate animals found along the ocean floor that many others avoid. These include sea urchins, mollusks, and toxic species like sea hares and crown-of-thorn starfish.

ORBICULAR BATFISH
PLATAX ORBICULARIS

RANGE: Tropical waters of the Indo-Pacific region

SIZE: 19.7 in (50 cm)

DIET: Algae, invertebrates, small fish

Batfish have a distinctive shape: They are extremely thin and very round. The roundface batfish is silvery gray in color, with darker vertical bands and a black spot in front of its pectoral fin. They are often found together in schools.

SEAHORSE LIFE CYCLE

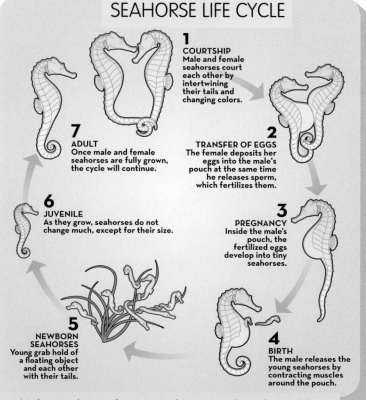

1 COURTSHIP
Male and female seahorses court each other by intertwining their tails and changing colors.

2 TRANSFER OF EGGS
The female deposits her eggs into the male's pouch at the same time he releases sperm, which fertilizes them.

3 PREGNANCY
Inside the male's pouch, the fertilized eggs develop into tiny seahorses.

4 BIRTH
The male releases the young seahorses by contracting muscles around the pouch.

5 NEWBORN SEAHORSES
Young grab hold of a floating object and each other with their tails.

6 JUVENILE
As they grow, seahorses do not change much, except for their size.

7 ADULT
Once male and female seahorses are fully grown, the cycle will continue.

Seahorses begin their reproductive cycle with an elaborate courtship dance. Then the female deposits her eggs into the male's pouch, where they develop into young.

GRAY ANGELFISH

One of my most memorable experiences exploring coral reefs was living in an underwater habitat for two weeks with four other researchers. Our habitat was like a hotel—it had bunk beds and warm showers and a stove to cook meals—only it was on the ocean floor, and our backyard was filled with fish and other sea critters! We studied the reef day and night and became intimately acquainted with our new neighbors.

Each day, we'd wake before sunrise and slip into the sea through a hatch at the bottom of the habitat. And every morning, just as we approached the reef's edge, five gray angelfish (*Pomacanthus arcuatus*) swam over to greet us! The largest was maybe a foot (30.5 cm) across and the smallest only six inches (15 cm). They cruised the reef, grazing on seaweed and nibbling on sponges, but they were also curious and followed us around like puppies. On one occasion, I could see that I could actually tell them apart—that they had unique faces and personalities. Three were shy and hung back, while the other two swam within inches of our scuba masks. One day, a bold angelfish even nibbled a sprig of alga I held in my hand! We collected a lot of new and exciting scientific data over the two weeks, but I'll never forget those five curious angelfish that taught me that fish, like humans, are each unique and special.

APPROXIMATE RANGE OF
THE *POMACANTHUS PARU*
(GRAY ANGELFISH)

0   1,000 miles
0   1,000 kilometers

NORTH
AMERICA

PACIFIC
OCEAN

SOUTH
AMERICA

OBSERVATION
TIPS

FISH

1 Go out and get wet. Put on a face mask and snorkel around coral reefs to explore a world brimming with sea life.

2 Keep your hands to yourself. Touching coral can harm the reef, and its sharp edges can easily pierce skin.

3 Angelfish are popular reef fish and are among the first you're likely to see cruising around.

4 Reef fish—angel or otherwise—can be curious and may swim over to investigate *you!* Just be sure to respect their space.

Sylvia Earle is a world-renowned oceanographer, explorer, and author. A pioneer of underwater exploration, she researches marine algae and deep-water ecosystems, with a focus on new technology for reaching and studying the deep sea.

Adult gray angelfish typically cruise coral reefs in pairs. They nibble on sponges and algae during the day and tuck into reef crevices at night. Females swim above the reef to release their eggs, and newly hatched larvae float on plankton, where they transform into tiny angelfish. Juveniles, with their black bodies and yellow stripes, look quite different from adults. They hang out around shallow patch reefs and grassy areas and often eat parasites that latch on to the bodies of other fish.

RECORDS

Did you know there is a species of fish that can fit on your fingertip? Or that some fish can swim as fast as a car? Want to find out more? Then check out these fabulous fish record holders!

WORLD'S BIGGEST FISH

WHALE SHARK
RHINCODON TYPUS

A whale shark measures up to 40 feet (12 m) in length with an average weight of 41,200 pounds (18,688 kg). If you saw one coming toward you in the water, you would probably swim for your life. Then it would open its five-foot-wide mouth (1.5 m), and you'd really think you're a goner. Fortunately, this giant of the sea is a gentle one, feeding only on plankton and small fish. Whale sharks suck huge amounts of water into their mouths and then strain it out through its gills, trapping the small organisms inside.

BIGGEST FRESHWATER FISH

MEKONG GIANT CATFISH
PANGASIANODON GIGAS

When some people think of catfish, they think of something that fits perfectly on a dinner plate. But not the Mekong giant catfish! Measuring up to nine feet long (2.7 m) and weighing up to 646 pounds (293 kg)—this river monster can grow to the size of a grizzly bear! The largest ever recorded was recently found in northern Thailand, where efforts are under way to protect giant fish in the river because many are considered critically endangered. It is rumored there are bigger fish out there, but this is the only confirmed discovery in recorded history.

SMALLEST FISH

PAEDOCYPRIS PROGENETICA

This barely there fish is so tiny that it went undiscovered until the last decade or so. Measuring a mere 0.3 inches long (8 mm), *Paedocyrpis progenetica* is a little fish with some funky features. First is a see-through body with no skeleton in the head, leaving the brain unprotected. Next is that it lives in very acidic water, and boasts fins that can grasp on to things. Little is known about this strange fish, which until 2012 was thought to be the smallest vertebrate in the world. Now that honor goes to a tiny frog named *Paedophryne amauensis*.

FASTEST FISH

Racing through the water at speeds topping 68 miles per hour (110 km/h), an Atlantic sailfish sighting might be a case of "now you see it, now you don't." This sleek speedster has a compressed body perfect for darting through the water, and a long bill and jaws that help with its fancy way of fishing. Sailfish generally follow a school of fish slowly, until they are ready to attack. Then they charge full speed ahead into the school, darting left and right to stun their prey.

ATLANTIC SAILFISH
ISTIOPHORUS PLATYPTERUS

MOST POISONOUS FISH

REEF STONEFISH
SYNANCEIA VERRUCOSA

If you're ever in the water off the coast of Australia, beware the sinister stonefish. This fiendish fish is aptly named for its resemblance to a rock which is what makes it particularly dangerous. It's 13 venomous spines can cause pain, paralysis, and even death. Particularly vulnerable are bottom-feeding sharks and rays, and humans who accidentally step on it. Be sure to wear thick-soled shoes and walk very carefully.

FIERCEST FANGS

FANGTOOTH
ANOPLOGASTER CORNUTA

Lurking in depths of up to 16,000 feet deep (4,876 m) there are some strange sights to behold. Fish that glow; fish that dangle anglers above their heads to attract prey; and, of course, the fangtooth. The fangtooth is not a large fish, only about six inches in length (15 cm), but what it lacks in size it makes up for in teeth. The largest two fangs in this weird-looking fish's mouth are located on the lower jaw. They are so long that there are actually two sockets on either side of the fangtooth's brain so its teeth have somewhere to go when its mouth is shut. Fortunately, this freaky fish feasts only on shrimp and other fish, so you can sleep easy tonight.

HEAVIEST BONY FISH

OCEAN SUNFISH
MOLA MOLA

When it comes to size, the ocean sunfish may have nothing on a whale shark, but compared to its bony fish friends it is most definitely large and in charge. That's because it maxes out at a whopping 5,000 pounds (2,268 kg)! And while it might not be the fastest fish in the sea, it certainly does get around. Sunfish are known to stay near the surface of the water to soak up some rays, but recent research shows they are quite good divers and can migrate long distances. And because they are downright puny as guppies, they also boast the biggest growth rate throughout their life-times—increasing in size about 60 million times!

MOST SHOCKING

ELECTRIC EEL
ELECTROPHORUS ELECTRICUS

With more than five times the electric voltage of your average household electrical outlet, the electric eel is not to be messed with. These river-dwellers are air breathers, meaning they must surface often for oxygen. Get too close to this feisty fish and zap! Two of the eel's organs produce an electric pulsating current. The shock is not meant to be deadly, though— just to scare predators away.

FISH

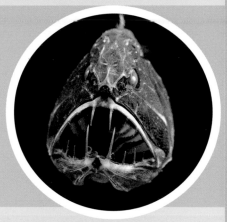

MAP KEY
APPROXIMATE RANGES OF RECORD-SETTING FISH

- Fangtooth
- Mekong Giant Catfish
- Reef Stonefish
- Ocean Sunfish
- Atlantic Sailfish
- Whale Shark
- Electric Eel
- Fish *Paedocypris progenetica*

ARCTIC OCEAN

Ocean Sunfish

Fangtooth

NORTH AMERICA

EUROPE

ASIA

PACIFIC

Atlantic Sailfish

Mekong Giant Catfish

AFRICA

EQUATOR

SOUTH AMERICA

Electric Eel

Fish *Paedocypris progenetica*

AUSTRALIA

OCEAN

Whale Shark

OCEAN

Fangtooth

Reef Stonefish

0   3,000 miles
0   4,000 kilometers

ANTARCTICA

Want to know where these record-holding fish live around the world? Take a look at this range map to find out.

Ninety-seven percent of the world's animals lack a backbone. To support their frames, these spineless animals—or invertebrates—have skeletons made of protein fibers. For some invertebrates, like this octopus, not having a backbone has its advantages. It allows the animal to squeeze into tight places.

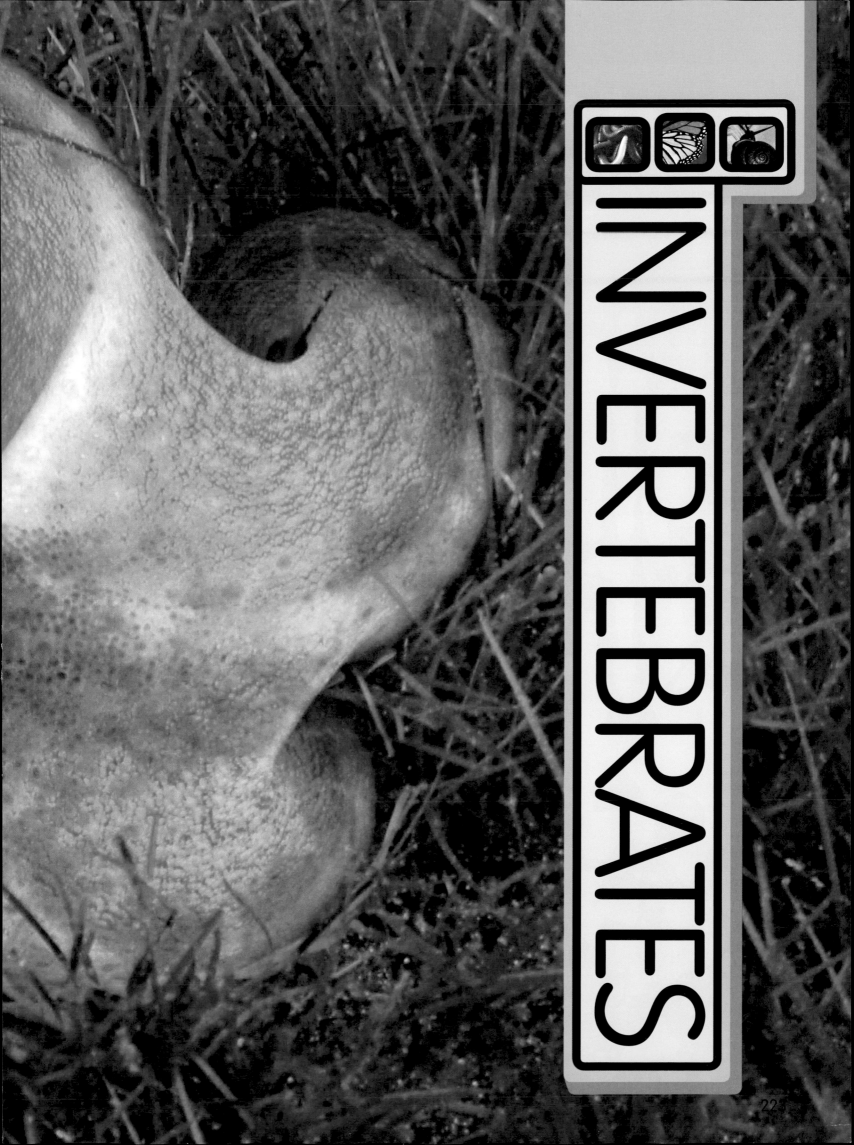

INVERTEBRATES

JUMPING SPIDER

GHOST CRAB

EARTHWORMS

MONARCH BUTTERFLIES

GREEN BEETLE

SNAIL

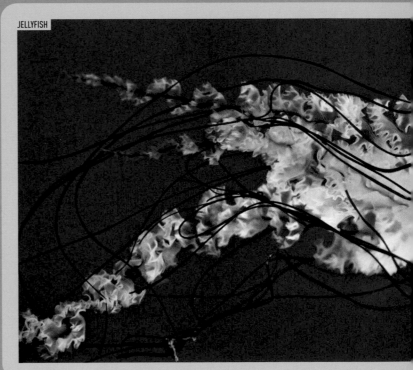
JELLYFISH

STINKBUGS WITH EGGS

FLY

BEES

AZURE WEEVIL

224

STARFISH

ECITON HAMATUM ARMY ANTS

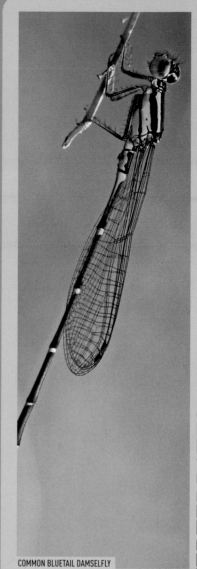

CAIRNS BIRDWING BUTTERFLY

BANANA SLUG

COMMON BLUETAIL DAMSELFLY

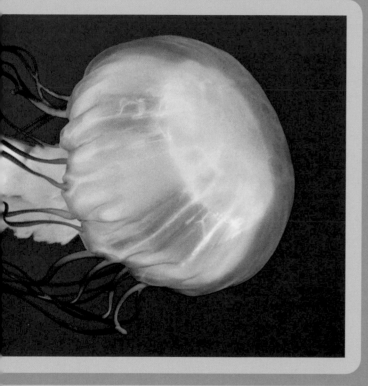

ATLANTIC SEA NETTLE

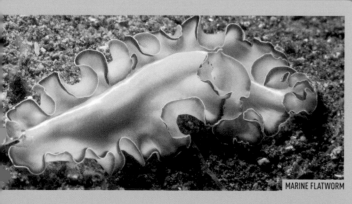
MARINE FLATWORM

ONGWING BUTTERFLY

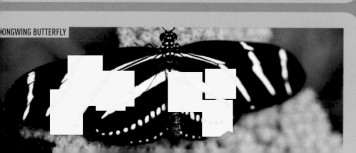

WHAT IS AN INVERTEBRATE?

INVERTEBRATES ARE ANIMALS WITHOUT A BACKBONE OR BONY SKELETON.

They range in size from microscopic mites and almost invisible flies to giant squid with soccer-ball-size eyes.

This is by far the largest group in the animal kingdom: 97 percent of all animals are invertebrates. So far, 1.25 million species have been described, most of which are insects, and there are millions more to be discovered. The total number of invertebrate species could be 5, 10, or even 30 million, compared to just 60,000 vertebrates.

One reason for the success of invertebrates is how quickly they reproduce. Sponges and corals, for example, produce both eggs and sperm. Social insects such as ants and bees lay eggs that can develop without fertilization—they become the workers.

Insects in particular are successful because they are so adaptable. They are opportunistic eaters, feeding on plants, animals, and decaying organic material. They are able to survive in extreme environments, including very hot, dry habitats. And many can fly—either to escape predators or to find new sources of food, water, and shelter.

Like vertebrates, invertebrates are classified based upon their body structure, life cycle, and evolutionary history.

INVERTEBRATE TRAITS (ANT)

WINGS
ABDOMEN
THORAX
HEAD
HEART
ANTENNAE
DIGESTIVE TRACT
STINGER
STOMACH
NERVE CORD
MOUTH-PARTS
COMPOUND EYES

Any animal without a backbone is considered an invertebrate. As this ant diagram shows, compared to vertebrates, invertebrates have much simpler nervous, circulatory, and digestive systems.

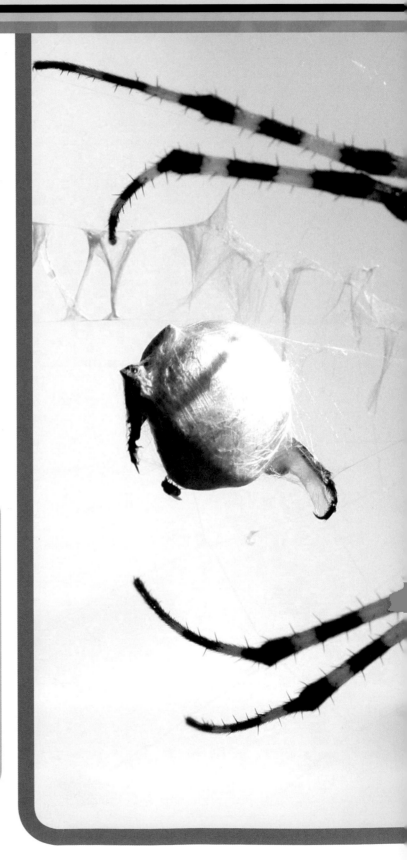

CLASSIFICATION OF INVERTEBRATES

Invertebrate animals belong to one of eight large groups, listed below. These groups are each known as a phylum (FYE-lum).

1 INSECTS, ARACHNIDS, CENTIPEDES AND MILLIPEDES, CRUSTACEANS, AND HORSESHOE CRABS (*ARTHROPODA*)

2 SQUID, OCTOPUSES, CUTTLEFISH, AND SNAILS (*MOLLUSCA*)

3 JELLYFISH, CORALS, AND HYDRAS (*CNIDARIA*)

4 EARTHWORMS, LEECHES, AND POLYCHAETES (*ANNELIDA*)

5 FLUKES AND TAPEWORMS (*PLATYHELMINTHES*)

6 ROUNDWORMS (*NEMATODA*)

7 STARFISH, SEA URCHINS, AND SEA CUCUMBERS (*ECHINODERMATA*)

8 SPONGES (*PORIFERA*)

INVERTEBRATES

Wasp spiders (*Argiope bruennichi*), like the one shown here, weave orb, or circular, webs, and females have a distinctive yellow-and-black striped abdomen that resembles the markings of a wasp.

SPONGES

Sponges are the oldest animals by far—they appear in the fossil record 600 to 760 million years ago.

Most are marine animals. They look like colorful globs of plant material. Some grow like tubes; others grow as crusts over hard surfaces. They have no organs and a very simple body structure.

The outer surface of a sponge is full of holes called pores. The inner surface of each pore is lined by cells that draw in water and catch food like bacteria. "Porifera," the name of the sponge phylum, means "pore-bearing." Their bodies are supported by a very delicate skeleton of calcium or other minerals.

Though they do not have nerves, sponges can change their body shape by coordinating the movements of their cells. They do this to pump out water that has been filtered, along with any waste, through an exit hole. Some sponges have multiple exit holes. Others have just one.

Life spans for sponges range from a few years to thousands. Most are extremely slow-growing.

AZURE VASE SPONGE
CALLYSPONGIA PLICIFERA

RANGE: Waters of the Caribbean Sea, Bahamas, and south Florida, U.S.A.

SIZE: 6 to 18 in (15 to 45 cm)

DIET: Bacteria and tiny marine organisms

This tube-like sponge also has folds in its body. These give it extra surface area, which creates room for more pores and more ways to filter food. The azure vase sponge grows as a single pink or purple tube.

STOVE-PIPE SPONGE
APLYSINA ARCHERI

RANGE: Atlantic Ocean, Caribbean Sea, coastal waters of Venezuela

SIZE: 59 in (150 cm)

DIET: Bacteria and tiny marine organisms

The stove-pipe sponge and many other tube-like sponges filter water for food and oxygen by taking it in through pores close to the bottom of the tube. Then they pump out the extra water through a large hole at the top.

Did you know?
Sponge skeletons and fingernails are made of similar material.

FRESHWATER SPONGE
SPONGILLA LACUSTRIS

RANGE: North America, Europe, Asia

SIZE: 0.07 in to 3.2 ft (2 mm to 1 m)

DIET: Bacteria and tiny marine organisms

Like corals, many freshwater sponges have algae growing in their cells that give them a green color. The sponge benefits from the energy produced by the algae (by photosynthesis), and the algae have a place to live.

DEAD MAN'S FINGER SPONGE
NEOESPERIOPSIS SP.

RANGE: Tropical waters

SIZE: 19.7 in (50 cm)

DIET: Bacteria and tiny marine organisms

These sponges are free-standing, like the barrel and vase sponges, and are recognized by their finger-like projections. They vary in color from dull brown or gray to orange.

BARREL SPONGE
XESTOSPONGIA TESTUDINARIA

RANGE: Tropical waters of the western Pacific

SIZE: Up to 6 ft (1.8 m)

DIET: Bacteria and tiny marine organisms

Barrel sponges are among the largest sponges in the world. They are long-living and sometimes called the "redwoods of the deep." A related species, the giant barrel sponge, can grow big enough to fit a car inside.

WORMS

There are three groups of worms: flatworms, segmented worms—which include earthworms and leeches—and roundworms.

Flatworms are the simplest worms, with no body cavity and simple organs. They take up oxygen and food directly through their skin. For this reason, they are small and flat. Examples are turbellarians, parasitic worms like flukes (trematodes) and tapeworms (cestodes), and nonparasitic worms like planarians. Life spans range from one year to unlimited in the case of planarians, which can regenerate.

Segmented worms have a body cavity and a simple digestive tract. Leeches live in water and feed on animal blood. Earthworms live in soil and feed on decaying plants. Life spans range from four to eight years.

Roundworms have a body cavity, digestive tract, and more complex lifestyles. Many are parasites, which could explain why they may be the single most numerous animals on land and in the sea. Thousands may be found inside a single cow, for example. Life spans range from one to two years.

SHOVEL-HEADED GARDEN WORM
BIPALIUM SIMROTHI

RANGE: United States

SIZE: Up to 20 in (8 cm)

DIET: Earthworms and other invertebrates

This garden worm is a terrestrial, carnivorous flatworm. It feeds on other invertebrates, including earthworms, snails, slugs, and insects, by wrapping around its prey, then releasing mucus that digests it.

COMMON EARTHWORM
LUMBRICUS TERRESTRIS

RANGE: Native to Europe; introduced to North America and Australia

SIZE: 8 to 10 in (20 to 25 cm)

DIET: Soil and decomposing matter such as leaves and roots

The common earthworm has been introduced to forests all over the world. Because they eat a lot of leaf litter in a short time, they are changing these habitats, disrupting the lives of native animals and plants.

LEECH
HIRUDO MEDICINALIS

RANGE: Western and southern Europe

SIZE: 8 in (20 cm)

DIET: Blood

Among the 700 species of leeches, some have been used to remove blood from human patients as a way to get rid of toxins. These species have a sucker on one end and a tiny, three-part jaw with sharp teeth on the other.

C-ELEGANS
CAENORHABDITIS ELEGANS

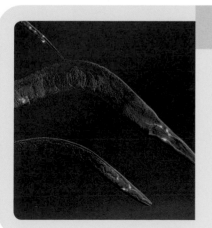

RANGE: Temperate climates

SIZE: Microscopic: 0.04 in (1 mm)

DIET: Bacteria and decaying vegetable matter

This tiny, transparent roundworm has been studied extensively in the lab and was the first multicellular animal to have its genome sequenced (1998). It has also been to the International Space Station and back.

WANDERING BROADHEAD PLANARIAN
BIPALIUM ADVENTITIUM

RANGE: Asia; introduced to U.S.

SIZE: 4 in (11 cm)

DIET: Earthworms and other invertebrates

This worm, also known as the hammerhead, was introduced to the United States in potted plants and is now very common. It finds earthworms by following their chemical trails.

INVERTEBRATES

CORALS

Corals, sea anemones, and jellyfish are in the phylum Cnidaria (ni-DAIR-ee-uh). All have stinging cells, and all are much more complex than they seem.

Corals are colonies of tiny animals called polyps (POL-ips). Each has a sac-like body. One end is attached to a calcium skeleton; the other end is open and surrounded by tentacles. Corals can't move, so they depend on currents to flush nutrients in and wastes out.

Most corals use their stinging cells to feed on plankton and small fish at night. During the day, shallow-water corals also get energy from symbiotic algae that live in their stomachs. Using sunlight and waste products from the coral, the algae carry out photosynthesis. The energy and oxygen created help the coral grow and build the calcium structures known as coral reefs. These algae also give corals their color, which is why the most colorful corals—and the largest reefs—are found in shallow water.

Coral life spans range from 20 to hundreds of years.

MAT ZOANTHID
ZOANTHUS PULCHELLUS

RANGE: Caribbean Sea; Bahamas; Florida, U.S.A.

SIZE: 0.5 in (1.3 cm)

DIET: Energy from photosynthesis by symbiotic algae; small fish; plankton

The corals in the zoanthid (zoe-AN-thid) group live as single polyps, long strands, or soft mats in a variety of marine habitats. The mat-like structure is made up of many individual coral polyps attached to bits of sand and rock.

CAULIFLOWER CORAL
POCILLOPORA GENUS

RANGE: Indian and Pacific Oceans

SIZE: 20 in (50 cm)

DIET: Energy from photosynthesis by symbiotic algae; small fish; plankton

This coral looks like cauliflower when its polyps are extended and active. Also called brush corals, cauliflower corals may be either domed or branched. Their colors range from pink to brown.

BUBBLE CORAL
PLEROGYRA SINUOSA

RANGE: Mostly found in Indian and Pacific Oceans; also Red Sea, Gulf of Aden, East China Sea, the waters off Southeast Asia and Japan

SIZE: 16 in (40 cm)

DIET: Energy from photosynthesis by symbiotic algae; small fish; plankton

Bubble corals, like all shallow-water corals, rely on their algae for energy during the day. Their polyps contract, or deflate, at night when their stinging tentacles become active. Bubble corals have extra tentacles called sweepers.

STAGHORN CORAL
ACROPORA CERVICORNIS

RANGE: Caribbean; Bahamas; Florida, U.S.A.

SIZE: 1 to 8 ft (30 to 240 cm)

DIET: Energy from photosynthesis by symbiotic algae; small fish; plankton

Many coral species take years to grow one inch. But staghorn coral can grow as fast as eight inches (20 cm) a year. This species is endangered because of habitat damage, pollution, collecting, and an infection called white-band disease.

Did you know? Some corals grow in the direction of the water current.

WHIP CORAL
CIRRHIPATHES (GENUS)

RANGE: Indian and Pacific Oceans

SIZE: 3 m (10 ft)

DIET: Energy from photosynthesis by symbiotic algae; small fish; plankton

Whip corals look a bit like barbed wire and cannot retract their polyps. Their calcium skeleton is also dark. Depending on their algae, they may be green, yellow, brown, or gray.

ANEMONES AND JELLYFISH

A nemones (a-NEM-o-neez) are animals with a polyp body shape like corals, but they are much bigger. Most are the size of a large flower. They also hold onto the seafloor or coral reef using a muscular foot.

Some anemones feed only on plankton; many have symbiotic algae. The majority also capture larger animals with their stinging tentacles, including mussels, crabs, sea urchins, and even small fish.

Life spans for sea anemones range from 10 to 80 years.

Jellyfish are not fish at all! They are free-floating, upside-down polyps, a body shape known as medusa. They have three cell layers like corals and anemones. The difference is the middle layer is greatly expanded with a jelly-like substance. They move by contracting and expanding their umbrella-like bell.

Some jellyfish are so small they are barely visible. The largest—the giant Nomura's jellyfish—can weigh 440 pounds (200 kg). All feed on plankton, crustaceans, fish, and other jellyfish.

Life spans for jellyfish range from a few hours to six months, though there may be a few long-living species.

GIANT GREEN ANEMONE
ANTHOPLEURA XANTHOGRAMMICA

RANGE: Pacific Ocean along North America; also Panama

SIZE: 7 by 12 in (17.5 by 30 cm); crown diameter: 10 in (25 cm)

DIET: Mussels, small fish, crabs, sea urchins

Green anemones are found in cooler water often in shallow tide pools. Their bright green color is a combination of pigmented cells and the color of the algae that live in their cells. Mussels are their preferred food.

MEDITERRANEAN JELLYFISH
COTYLORHIZA TUBERCULATA

RANGE: Mediterranean, Aegean, and Adriatic Seas

SIZE: Diameter: up to 14 in (35 cm)

DIET: Plankton

This jellyfish is also known as the fried egg jellyfish because of the way it looks from above. It is able to move on its own, rather than depending on the water current.

FISH-EATING ANEMONE
URTICINA PISCIVORA

RANGE: Alaska to California's Channel Islands, U.S.A.

SIZE: Height: 8 in (20 cm); crown diameter: 4 in (10 cm)

DIET: Shrimp, small fish, plankton

Fish-eating anemones are a common cool-water species often found in kelp forests. Like many of their relatives, they capture shrimp and small fish using their tentacles to pierce and stun their prey.

PURPLE TUBE ANEMONE
CERIANTHUS MEMBRANACEUS

RANGE: Indo-Pacific waters

SIZE: 1 to 15 in (3 to 40 cm)

DIET: Plankton

Tube anemones are close relatives of sea anemones and live partially buried in the ocean floor. Their tentacles secrete a mucus that hardens to form a tube, which it uses like a burrow. They are nocturnal and feed on plankton and debris.

DEADLY JELLIES

Jellyfish can be found in bodies of water all around the world. They often are feared for their painful sting, though some species don't actually sting at all. But there are a select few that pack a potent punch.

The sea wasp (*Chironex fleckeri*), a type of box jellyfish, is the most venomous marine animal in the world. With tentacles stretching ten feet (3 m) long, it has a powerful toxin that attacks the nervous system, heart, and skin. Each tentacle contains 20,000 stinging cells, and one jellyfish has enough venom to kill 20 grown humans!

Another dangerous box jelly is the much smaller Irukandji (*Malo kingi*), which measures roughly one inch (2.5 cm), including the tentacles. It can fire its stingers at its victims. The result usually is not death, but symptoms called the Irukandji syndrome: intense backache, head-ache, nausea, and anxiety.

231

MANY WATER-DWELLING invertebrates migrate for food. Some travel from deep water to the surface; others travel hundreds of miles across the sea. The golden jellyfish *(Mastigias papua etpisoni)* makes a daily migration across a saltwater lake, following the sun's arc. The sun's rays provide nourishment to algae-like organisms on which the jellyfish feed.

SNAILS AND SLUGS

Gastropods—snails and slugs—are the most common type of mollusks, and the second-most-common group of animals after insects! At least 60,000 species have been discovered so far.

Slugs have either no shell or a very tiny one, whereas all snails have shells, which they use for protection. Many can close off the entrance to their shell with a horny plate known as an operculum (o-PER-cyoo-lum).

All gastropods have a head with eyespots and tentacles, a digestive tract that runs the length of their body, and a muscular foot. These features give this group its name. "Gastropod" means "stomach foot" in Greek.

Snails and slugs are found worldwide and in all habitat types. Some are herbivores; others are carnivores. Two-thirds live in salt water, a few live in fresh water, and the rest are terrestrial. Many are edible, such as the abalone and conch. Life spans range from three to eight years.

PACIFIC SIDEBAND SNAIL
MONADENIA FIDELIS

RANGE: Pacific coast of North America

SIZE: 0.9 to 1.4 in (2.2 to 3.6 cm)

DIET: Decaying material

Land snails have either two or four sensory tentacles on their heads to detect smells, and two eyespots to detect motion. The eyes are located either at the end of two of the tentacles or, as in the Pacific sideband, at the base.

YELLOW BANANA SLUG
ARIOLIMAZ COLUMBIANUS

RANGE: Pacific Northwest of North America

SIZE: Up to 63.5 in (25 cm)

DIET: Leaves, dead plant material, fungi, animal droppings

Even though they are one of the largest land slugs, banana slugs can move fast—up to 6.5 inches (16.5 cm) per minute. Their bodies are more streamlined without a shell. To keep their skin moist, they secrete a slimy mucus.

RED SLUG
ARION RUFUS

RANGE: Europe; introduced in United States

SIZE: .06 to 7 in (1.5 to 18 cm)

DIET: Plants, decaying material, feces, carrion

The red slug is an omnivorous land slug native to Europe that has been introduced in the United States, where it has become a big problem. It eats anything, including crops like strawberries, cabbage, and clover.

WHITE-LIPPED SNAIL
CEPAEA HORTENSIS

RANGE: Western and central Europe

SIZE: Shell height: 0.6 to 0.63 in (1.5 to 1.6 cm)

DIET: Leaves, wood, bark, stems, fruit, flowers, insects

The white-lipped snail is found in woods, grasslands, and sandy shores. As in most shelled gastropods, it has a coiled shell with an opening on the right side. The shell is used for protection from predators and the environment.

NUDIBRANCH
DENDTONOTUS FRONDOSUS

RANGE: North Atlantic and Pacific Oceans, waters around the British Isles

SIZE: 4 in (10 cm)

DIET: Sponges, anemones, other invertebrates

Nudibranchs are a type of sea slug. They are carnivores, and most release toxic chemicals when disturbed. Their bright colors are a warning to predators to stay away.

CLAMS, OYSTERS, MUSSELS, AND SCALLOPS

Clams, oysters, mussels, and scallops have two cup-like shells connected by a hinge. This is the reason for the name bivalve, which means "two shells." Like gastropods, they have a strong foot muscle. Instead of using it to move, however, they use it to close their shell.

Most bivalves are filter feeders. They have two siphons: one that pumps water in, and one that pumps water out over the gills, which trap plankton. Most bury themselves under the sea or riverbed. A few attach themselves to rocks. Some, like scallops, swim using their siphons.

Oysters and freshwater mussels often produce pearls. These begin as grains of sand that lodge in the mantle, a very thin tissue that covers the body and secretes the shell. In response, the animal covers the sand with the same material it uses to produce the inner surface of its shell. The result is a smooth, usually white, pebble-like structure.

Life spans range from 2 to 40 years for smaller species and longer for larger ones.

NUTTAL'S COCKLE
CLINOCARDIUM NUTTALLII

RANGE: Offshore of British Isles

SIZE: Up to 3.9 in (10 cm)

DIET: Plankton

With its shell closed and viewed from the side, this clam is shaped like a heart. Most of the time, it lies buried under the sand or mud with only a part of its shell visible. Younger clams are lighter in color compared to older ones.

BIG MOLLUSKS

There are three types of mollusks: gastropods, bivalves, and cephalopods. All share two features: a nervous system and muscular feet, or arms. Many also have shells, usually for protection.

Mollusk shells are made of calcium carbonate, the same material as coral reefs. It is much harder than chitin, the protein found in the exoskeletons of insects and crustaceans.

Bivalves, like clams, oysters, and mussels, have two external shells joined by a hinge. Among the gastropods, land snails have a single external shell.

Only a few cephalopods have shells. The nautilus has an external shell, the cuttlefish has an internal shell called a cuttlebone, and the vampire squid has a vestigial, or remnant, internal shell called a gladius.

FIRE CLAM
CTENOIDES ALES

RANGE: Indo-Pacific waters

SIZE: 1 in to 3.1 ft (2.5 cm to 1 m)

DIET: Plankton

Also called the flashing fire shell and the electric scallop, this clam uses bioluminescence to turn its lips—the tissue just under each half of its shell—a bright color, like a flash of light.

BAY SCALLOP
ARGOPECTEN IRRADIANS

RANGE: Atlantic Ocean

SIZE: 2.2 to 3.5 in (5.5 to 9 cm)

DIET: Plankton

Populations of bay scallops have been decreasing because sharks are being overfished. In the food web, sharks eat rays, and rays eat scallops. Fewer sharks means there are more rays to eat more scallops.

WAVY-RAYED LAMP MUSSEL
LAMPSILIS FASCIOLA

RANGE: Great Lakes of North America

SIZE: Up to 3.15 in (8 cm)

DIET: Plankton

When the eggs of the wavy-rayed lamp mussel hatch, they release larvae that attach to the gills of the smallmouth bass. There, they develop into juveniles, drop off, and mature to adults on the lake bottom.

OCTOPUSES
AND RELATIVES

n Greek, "cephalopod" (SEF-a-low-pod) means "head foot." The animals in this group have large heads and strong, muscular feet—lots of them! The octopus, for example, has eight. Its feet are called arms because they attach to the head, not the body.

Some cephalopods have external shells, like the nautilus, whereas others have internal ones, like squid and cuttlefish. The only hard part of the octopus's body is its beak. This soft body allows it to squeeze through tiny holes.

All cephalopods are predators that feed on marine animals, grabbing their prey with their arms and pushing it into their mouths. They have well-developed eyes and excellent vision. They also can change the color of their skin to match their environment.

When threatened, most of these animals secrete a black, milky substance known as ink. This gives them time to hide or jet away from the predator.

Life spans range from six months to five years.

GIANT PACIFIC OCTOPUS
ENTEROCTOPUS DOFLEINI

RANGE: Pacific Ocean

SIZE: 20 to 24 in (50 to 60 cm)

DIET: Clams, crab, fish, squid

The giant Pacific octopus has six-foot (1.8-m)-long arms, each with hundreds of touch- and taste-sensitive suckers. Since it hunts at night, the octopus relies on its vision to find a place to feed and on its arms to find prey.

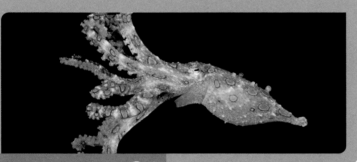

CARIBBEAN REEF SQUID
SEPIOTEUTHIS SEPIOIDEA

RANGE: Florida, U.S.A.; Caribbean, Central America, northern South America

SIZE: 8 in (20 cm)

DIET: Fish and shrimp

This squid takes water into its head and shoots it out the siphon to move quickly to catch food or escape a predator. It can even jet itself into the air.

GREATER BLUE-RINGED OCTOPUS
HAPALOCHLAENA LUNULATA

RANGE: Northern Australia and tropical western Pacific Ocean

SIZE: Up to 8 in (20 cm)

DIET: Fish, crabs, mollusks

The saliva of this octopus contains highly toxic venom—not ink—that is made from bacteria in its salivary glands. One bite paralyzes the octopus's prey.

OVAL SQUID
SEPIOTEUTHIS LESSONIANA

RANGE: Indo-Pacific waters

SIZE: 1.5 to 13 in (3.8 to 33 cm)

DIET: Crustaceans and fish

The oval squid has pigmented cells in its skin, especially around its eyes. In the light, some of these cells turn metallic red and green. Others turn the same color as the light shining on them.

CUTTLEFISH
SEPIA OFFICINALIS

RANGE: North Atlantic Ocean, English Channel, Mediterranean Sea

SIZE: 12 to 20 in (30 to 49 cm)

DIET: Crustaceans and fish

Like octopus, cuttlefish have eyes that can see both forward and backward at the same time. In addition to eight arms, they have two long tentacles used for grabbing prey.

ECHINODERMS

The name "echinoderm" (ee-KINE-o-derm) means "spiny skin" in Greek. The animals in this group are found only in salt water and include sea stars, brittle stars, sea urchins, sand dollars, and sea cucumbers. All have a delicate skeleton made of calcium; skin that is prickly, bumpy, or covered with spines; and tube-like feet. They are mostly herbivores that feed on algae and scavengers that eat decomposing animal and plant material. Some also eat other invertebrates.

Though they may not look like it, all echinoderms are shaped like a bicycle wheel with spokes. The mouth is in the center, and there are usually five arms, or rays. This form is easy to see in sea stars—also called starfish—except they are not fish! The rays of a sea urchin can be seen in the animal's bare skeleton, which often washes up on beaches. Sea cucumbers have tentacles around their mouth, also arranged in rays.

Life spans are up to 5 years for sea cucumbers, 35 for sea stars, and 100 or more for sea urchins.

SWIMMING SEA CUCUMBER
ENYPNIASTES EXIMIA

RANGE: All oceans

SIZE: Up to 12 in (30 cm)

DIET: Dead organisms, bottom sediment, algae

The swimming, or pink, sea cucumber is more mobile than other sea cucumbers. It swims up the water column—as far as 3,280 feet (1,000 m) above the ocean floor—and back down. When threatened, it produces bioluminescence, and then sheds its brightly lit skin.

RED SLATE PENCIL URCHIN
HETEROCENTROTUS MAMMILLATUS

RANGE: Indo-Pacific waters, including Hawaii

SIZE: 5 to 10 in (15 to 25 cm)

DIET: Mainly algae

The spines of the red slate pencil urchin were once used to write on slate boards—like blackboards. Like all urchins, it has tiny bones in its mouth that function like teeth to scrape up its food. It is a nocturnal feeder.

BLUE SEA STAR
LINCKIA LAEVIGATA

RANGE: Indo-Pacific waters

SIZE: 12 in (30 cm)

DIET: Dead organisms and algae

The blue sea star has tubular, rounded arms. Like many other sea stars, it can regrow a damaged arm. It also can detach one as a way to distract predators, such as other sea stars, shrimp, and sea anemones.

CHOCOLATE CHIP STARFISH
PROTOREASTER NODOSUS

RANGE: Indo-Pacific waters

SIZE: 12 in (30 cm)

DIET: Mainly mussels

Like other sea stars, the chocolate chip starfish feeds mostly on mussels. It uses its arms to open the mussel shell just enough so it can fit its mouth inside—then inserts its entire stomach. This species is named for its resemblance to cookie dough.

BLUE SEA URCHIN
ECHINOTHRIX DIADEMA

RANGE: Indo-Pacific waters

SIZE: Diameter: 3 in (8 cm)

DIET: Mainly algae

Sea urchins are an important source of food for sea otters, wolf eels, and triggerfish. The urchin's spines are for protection and are not venomous, though some species have short stingers in between the spines that can be toxic.

INVERTEBRATES

CRABS, SHRIMP, AND LOBSTERS

SPANISH SLIPPER LOBSTER
SCYLLARIDES AEQUINOCTIALIS

RANGE: Caribbean; Bahamas; South Florida, U.S.A.

SIZE: 6 to 12 in (15 to 30 cm)

DIET: Dead and decomposing animals and plants

This species is named for its slipper-like antennae. Like true lobsters, it is long-living and caught for food. But it lacks large claws and lives in warm water.

Crustaceans (cruss-TAY-shunz) have five pairs of walking legs. The animals in this group are lobsters, crabs, shrimp, barnacles, and crayfish. Most have claws on their first legs that they use for feeding and antennae that they use to detect tastes and smells. In some species, like the mantis shrimp, antennae are used for catching prey, too. All have two body parts: a head and abdomen. Barnacles and hermit crabs also have shells. Barnacles make their own, whereas hermit crabs have to find one—usually left over from a snail.

Like all arthropods, crustaceans go through a molt, which means they shed their exoskeleton and grow a new one. Crabs and lobsters are most likely to be eaten during this stage. Hermit crabs look for new shells, often trading them among one another.

Horseshoe crabs are in their own group, with just five species. They have five legs, a large domed shell, and a long tail.

Life spans range from 20 to 50 years.

OCONEE BURROWING CRAYFISH
CAMBARUS TRUNCATUS

RANGE: Southeastern United States off the coast of Georgia

SIZE: 6 to 12 in (15 to 30 cm)

DIET: Dead and decomposing animals and plants

All crayfish dig burrows to stay moist, especially the burrowing crayfish. This species is from the southeastern United States, home to the greatest diversity of crayfish anywhere. If the soil is moist, these animals do not need to visit water.

HORSESHOE CRAB
LIMULUS POLYPHEMUS

RANGE: Atlantic coast of North America, from Nova Scotia to the Yucatán Peninsula

SIZE: 10 to 20 in (25 to 50 cm)

DIET: Worms, small mollusks, algae

Horseshoe crabs have five legs arranged around their mouth, each with spines used to crush clams. Many other animals live attached to their shells, including algae, worms, and barnacles.

ARTHROPODS

All arthropods have segmented bodies covered with a hard outer skeleton, or exoskeleton, and several pairs of legs. Insects have three pairs of legs; millipedes have hundreds. The name of this group means "jointed foot" in Greek. Most have claws, bristles, or pads instead of feet, and many can fly.

Insects are by far the most numerous types of arthropods, but there are four others: crustaceans, which include lobsters, shrimp, and crabs; arachnids, which include spiders, ticks, and mites; centipedes and millipedes; and horseshoe crabs.

Because of their hard bodies, arthropods are more likely to fossilize than most other invertebrates. Another feature shared by many arthropods is mass migration. Some, like spiny lobsters, move in response to seasonal changes. Others, like ladybugs, move in search of places to hibernate.

STRAWBERRY HERMIT CRAB
COENOBITA PERLATUS

RANGE: Indo-Pacific waters and central Pacific Ocean

SIZE: 3.15 in (8 cm)

DIET: Dead and rotting material along the seashore

Though most of its relatives are aquatic, the strawberry hermit crab is terrestrial. It lives in coastal areas, visiting the sea at night to refill its shell with water, feeding along the way. These crabs live in groups and trade shells among one another.

COLEMAN SHRIMP ○○
PERICLIMENES COLEMANI

RANGE: West Pacific Ocean

SIZE: 0.8 in (2 cm)

DIET: Parasites, algae, plankton

Many smaller shrimp feed on parasites found on fish. They are known as cleaner shrimp. They wait inside a sea anemone or, as in the case of the Coleman shrimp, a sea urchin, and pick their meals off the fish that visit.

PEACOCK MANTIS SHRIMP ○○○
ODONTODACTYLUS SCYLLARUS

RANGE: Indo-Pacific waters

SIZE: 1.2 to 7.1 in (3 to 18 cm)

DIET: Snails, slugs, other crustaceans, bivalves

Peacock mantis shrimp use their club-shaped feet to smash open hard prey like snails and mussels. They also have excellent color vision used in mating and for spotting predators like barracuda. Females carry their eggs under their tails.

Did you know?
A female lobster carries its eggs under its abdomen.

SMOOTH GOOSENECK BARNACLE ○○
LEPAS ANATIFERA

RANGE: Tropical and subtropical ocean waters

SIZE: Shell size: up to 1.2 in (3 cm)

DIET: Plankton

All barnacles make their own shells, unlike hermit crabs, which have to find one. They also make a glue-like chemical to attach their head to a rock, dock, or even a whale; they then wave their feet in the water to catch plankton.

SPOTTED SPINY LOBSTER ○○
PANULIRUS GUTTATUS

RANGE: Caribbean Sea; Bahamas; Florida, U.S.A.

SIZE: 5 to 18 in (13 to 45 cm)

DIET: Snails, clams, crabs, sea urchins, carrion

Instead of claws, this lobster has spiny antennae. These animals migrate in large groups along the seafloor. They communicate with each other and ward off predators by rubbing their antennae on their bodies to make different sounds.

SALLY LIGHTFOOT CRAB ○○
GRAPSUS GRAPSUS

RANGE: Pacific coast of Mexico; Central and South America, including Galápagos Islands

SIZE: 3 in (8 cm)

DIET: Mostly algae; also dead and decomposing animals and plants

This species is named for the way it moves: very quickly on the tips of its claws, changing directions in a flash. On the Galápagos Islands, the Sally Lightfoot crab has a symbiotic relationship with the marine iguana: It picks off the iguana's ticks for food.

SPIDERS,
SCORPIONS, TICKS, AND MITES

Spiders, scorpions, ticks, and mites are called arachnids (a-RACK-nidz), which is Greek for "spider." All have eight legs. Many of the 100,000 species in this group are venomous, but only 25 species of scorpions are dangerous to people. Spiders also have glands that produce silk, which they use for building webs to capture insects, for building egg sacs, and for climbing.

Some arachnids look as though they have more than eight legs. This is because they have two pairs of leg-like structures. The first, called chelicerae (kuh-LIS-eh-ree), are used for feeding and defense. The second, called pedipalps (PEH-duh-palps), are used for capturing food, walking, and reproduction. Scorpions, for example, have a set of claws they use to grab and crush their prey.

Except for mites, the animals in this group predigest their food. They mix digestive juices with bits of food in their mouths and swallow the liquid, spitting out any hard parts.

Life spans range from 7 to 25 years.

BOLD JUMPING SPIDER
PHIDIPPUS AUDAX

RANGE: North America and parts of Central America

SIZE: 0.5 to 0.8 in (1.3 to 2 cm)

DIET: Insects

Bold jumping spiders are identified by their bright-green or blue chelicerae, or chewing mouthparts. All jumping spiders have large forward-facing eyes that give them very good depth perception for jumping to catch their insect prey.

GIANT VELVET MITE
DINOTHROMBIUM GENUS

RANGE: Southwestern United States

SIZE: 0.2 to 0.6 in (4 to 15 mm)

DIET: Young: parasitic on grasshoppers; adults: termite eggs

The giant velvet mite is much larger than other mites and their close relatives, ticks. The result is they are easy to see in the soil.

VINAGAROON
MASTIGOPROCTUS GIGANTEUS

RANGE: Southern United States, Mexico

SIZE: 2 in (5 cm) without whip

DIET: Soft-bodied insects such as termites, cockroaches, crickets

The vinagaroon is a type of whip scorpion. Instead of a venomous stinger, it has a long, whip-like structure that it uses to spray an irritating chemical called acetic acid, or vinegar—hence its name.

BARK SCORPION
CENTRUROIDES SCULPTURATUS

RANGE: Southwestern United States

SIZE: 3.1 in (8 cm)

DIET: Crickets, cockroaches

Bark scorpions are found anywhere there is shade and a large supply of their favored prey: insects, especially crickets and roaches. As a result, they often are found in people's homes. Their sting is painful but not fatal.

ROCKY MOUNTAIN WOOD TICK
DERMACENTOR ANDERSON

RANGE: Rocky Mountains, U.S.A., southwestern Canada

SIZE: Up to 0.25 in (6 mm)

DIET: Blood of mammals

This tick requires three hosts to complete its life cycle. Larvae feed on small mammals, nymphs feed on slightly larger ones, and adults feed on deer and dogs—sometimes even people.

CENTIPEDES AND MILLIPEDES

Centipedes and millipedes are arthropods with lots of legs! Each has dozens to hundreds of body segments. Centipedes have one pair of legs for each segment except for the first and last. Millipedes have two pairs. Both types of animals have simple digestive tracts and breathe through tiny holes in their skin called spiracles (SPIR-uh-kulz).

Millipedes feed on decaying plants and fruits and are found all over the world in a variety of habitats. They can open or close their spiracles, depending on the amount of moisture in their environment. They lack eyes and find food using their antennae.

Centipedes prey on insects, which they kill by using their first pair of legs to inject venom. Unlike millipedes, they cannot close their spiracles and are found only in moist habitats or where they can find shelter. They also are flatter, with longer legs, which makes them very fast movers.

Life spans are up to seven years for centipedes and millipedes.

NORTH AMERICAN MILLIPEDE
NARCEUS AMERICANUS

RANGE: North America

SIZE: 3 in (8 cm)

DIET: Decaying plants and insects

North American millipedes are usually found under logs or piles of wet leaves. They feed at night and are a favorite food of shrews as well as of frogs, lizards, beetles, and some birds.

Did you know?
Despite its name, no millipede has a thousand legs.

HOUSE CENTIPEDE
SCUTIGERA COLEOPTRATA

RANGE: Mediterranean; also introduced across Europe, Asia, North America

SIZE: 0.4 to 2.4 in (1 to 6 cm)

DIET: Worms, snails, fly larvae, bedbugs, other arthropods

There are several species of house centipedes, so named because they are very common in people's homes, where they feed on bedbugs, cockroaches, and other insects. With a rigid body and 15 pairs of long legs, they run as fast as some insects fly.

AFRICAN GIANT MILLIPEDE
ARCHISPIROSTREPTUS GIGAS

RANGE: Africa

SIZE: 15.2 in (38.5 cm)

DIET: Decaying plants

When millipedes are threatened, they curl up into a spiral so only their hard, outer covering, or exoskeleton, is exposed. They also secrete an irritating liquid from holes in their skin. The African giant millipede has 256 legs.

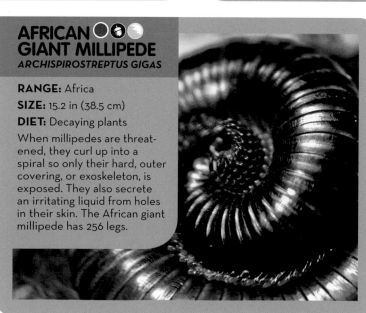

GIANT DESERT CENTIPEDE
SCOLOPENDRA HEROS

RANGE: Southern United States and northern Mexico

SIZE: 6.5 to 8 in (17 to 20 cm)

DIET: Small arthropods, toads, small snakes

This centipede is also known as the giant redheaded centipede because some have dark-blue bodies with red heads; others are all reddish brown. Its stinging front legs are long, curled, and always light tan.

241

FROM THE FIELD:
ROBERT JACKSON

JUMPING SPIDER

Jumping spiders use sharp vision and a keen sense of smell to hunt and stalk their prey. They creep up to an insect and pounce, injecting it with deadly venom. The jumping spider my collaborator Fiona Cross and I study, called *Evarcha culicivora*, prefers to pounce on mosquitoes. We call it the mosquito terminator! This spider is found only around Lake Victoria in East Africa, so we travel from our university in New Zealand to a research station by this lake in Kenya to study them. Being bitten by a jumping spider is very unlikely, and they're typically not considered dangerous to humans—so our houses double as labs, and we collect and study thousands of jumping spiders while we're there. For six months of the year, we literally live among spiders!

The mosquito terminator prefers to eat mosquitoes that feed on blood—they can actually *smell* blood-carrying mosquitoes—and often wander into houses to look for them. One year, a male jumping spider made himself right at home in my house, as though he was our little guest! One morning, he strolled across the computer keyboard while Fiona was typing. Then he shuffled down the side of her desk and scurried into the next room. Later that day, the same spider sauntered across the kitchen counter near my coffee mug! A few days later, we were working with our lab spiders and spotted our fuzzy guest hanging out on the living room wall. He must have liked us, because he stayed in my house the rest of the time we were in Kenya. But we didn't mind. A roaming mosquito terminator meant fewer mosquitoes to bite *us*!

APPROXIMATE RANGE OF
THE *EVARCHA CULICIVORA*
(JUMPING SPIDER)

AFRICA

Lake Victoria

0   1,000   miles

0   1,000   kilometers

OBSERVATION TIPS

1 To find jumping spiders, look for movement in tall grass and under rocks, leaves, and bark—and even in your house!

2 Most jumping spiders would fit on your pinky fingernail. You'll know you've spotted one if it looks back at you with large, forward-facing eyes.

3 Move *very* slowly. Jumping spiders have excellent eyesight. If they see you, they'll run—or jump—away!

4 Be aware of your surroundings. In Kenya, we once found ourselves surrounded by baboons!

Robert Jackson is a professor of zoology at the University of Canterbury in New Zealand. Fiona Cross is a postdoctoral fellow at the university and has spent a decade studying jumping spiders. They do their fieldwork in Kenya.

INVERTEBRATES

Instead of spinning webs to trap insects like most spiders, *Evarcha culicivora* stalks its prey and pounces like a jungle cat! It prefers to eat plump mosquitoes that have just fed on human blood. Blood acts like perfume, making the spider more attractive to potential mates. The male uses his best dance moves to impress a female. After they mate, the female lays about ten eggs in a nest she weaves out of silk.

INSECTS

nsects are by far the most numerous animals on Earth, and the largest type of arthropod. About a million have been described so far.

The main insect groups are beetles, butterflies and moths, flies, bees and wasps, and ants. Other, smaller groups—still large relative to the rest of the animal world—are grasshoppers, mantises, walking sticks, cockroaches, termites, earwigs, and wingless insects such as fleas, lice, and silverfish.

They are found in every habitat worldwide and are important in the food web as pollinators, pests, parasites, food, and carriers of disease. The only place where there are relatively few insects is the ocean, where other arthropod groups are dominant.

Insects are identified by a three-part body (head, thorax, and abdomen), three pairs of legs, large eyes, and two antennae. Most have wings. Many have complicated life cycles, where the larval form takes years to become an adult.

Life spans (including all stages of the life cycle) range from 60 days for fruit flies to 17 years for cicadas.

HORSELUBBER GRASSHOPPER
TAENIOPODA EQUES

RANGE: Southwestern United States, Mexico

SIZE: 2.5 in (6.4 cm)

DIET: Plants; sometimes carrion or other insects

The horselubber grasshopper cannot fly and can barely jump, unlike most other grasshoppers, crickets, katydids, and locusts. For defense, it eats toxic plants so it tastes nasty to any animal that tries to eat it.

GIANT DEAD LEAF MANTIS
DEROPLATYS DESICCATA

RANGE: Southeast Asia

SIZE: 6 in (15 cm)

DIET: Flying insects

Like all mantises, the giant dead leaf mantis uses camouflage to surprise its prey and to protect itself from predators, such as bats. If disturbed, it will fall to the ground and stay motionless, like a leaf.

PRAYING MANTIS
MANTIS RELIGIOSA

RANGE: Europe; introduced to North America

SIZE: 2 to 3 in (5 to 7.5 cm)

DIET: Caterpillars, flies, butterflies, bees, moths

The praying mantis is used to control plant pests in gardens and nurseries. An ambush predator, it hunts by sight—it can swivel its head 180 degrees in each direction. It uses its forelegs to capture its insect prey.

GIANT PRICKLY STICK INSECT
EXTATOSOMA TIARATUM

RANGE: Australia

SIZE: 6 to 8 in (15 to 20 cm)

DIET: Plants, especially eucalyptus, raspberry, oak, rose

Stick insects are vegetarians that, like mantises, use camouflage to hide from predators. The female giant prickly stick insect is larger than the male and unable to fly, so she has sharp spines on her head as an extra means of protection.

GIANT COCKROACH
BLABERUS GIGANTEUS

RANGE: Central America

SIZE: 3.5 in (9 cm)

DIET: Plants and sometimes animal material

Cockroaches communicate with one another by releasing chemicals in the air and leaving a trail of feces. The result is a swarm of these insects. They are nocturnal insects that run away from light. Most eat almost anything.

BEETLES

Almost half (up to 400,000) of all named insect species are beetles. They are found in all habitats except marine and polar ones, and they are potential prey for all kinds of animals. For protection, they have an armor-like exoskeleton and an outer set of wings that protects their true flying wings. Most beetles fly. There are also aquatic species that dive, often taking an air bubble down with them.

Most beetles have additional forms of defense. These include camouflage, mimicking wasps and other stinging insects, and the ability to spray nasty-smelling chemicals from glands in their abdomen. The bombardier beetle takes this one step further: It has two chemicals in separate glands that it mixes to create a popping sound and a burst of heat.

The feeding habits of beetles range from species that are general herbivores, insectivores, or scavengers, to those that specialize in eating certain plants, pollen, fungi, or dung. Many eat aphids and other insects that are damaging to crops. There are also more than 1,000 species of beetles that parasitize, eat, or live with ants.

Life spans (including all stages of the life cycle) range from weeks to 12 years.

MULTICOLORED ASIAN LADY BEETLE
HARMONIA AXYRIDIS

RANGE: Native to Asia; introduced worldwide

SIZE: 0.2 to 0.4 in (5 to 8 mm)

DIET: Insects, insect larvae and eggs, ripe fruit

Commonly called ladybugs, they are not bugs at all. This beetle and other species were introduced to control aphids.

TEXAS DUNG BEETLE
ONTHOPHAGUS GAZELLA

RANGE: Texas, U.S.A.

SIZE: Up to 1.3 in (3.3 cm)

DIET: Dung; also fungi, carrion, decomposing plants

All species of dung beetles eat animal manure, or dung. The Texas dung beetle is especially good at cleaning up after cows. Males and females work in pairs to bury food for later use and to feed their young.

WASP MIMIC BEETLE
CLYTUS RURICOLA

RANGE: Eastern North America

SIZE: 0.4 to 0.6 in (10 to 15 mm)

DIET: Larvae: decaying hardwood trees; adults: pollen, nectar

Although harmless, this beetle looks—and acts—as if it could sting. Like many wasps, it is found on flowers and makes a buzzing noise when disturbed. This type of mimicking is called Batesian mimicry.

FIGEATER BEETLE
COTINIS MUTABILIS

RANGE: Southwestern United States, Mexico

SIZE: 1.25 in (3 cm)

DIET: Ripe fruit, sap

This beetle's favorite fruit is figs. Like all beetles, it has two prominent antennae, claws on its feet, and two pairs of wings. The second flying pair is protected by the first, which is hard, like the exoskeleton.

CICADA

Cicadas live almost their entire lives underground. Then, when they're ready to mate, they burrow to the surface and climb up the nearest tree, shrub, house, fence, or signpost. There they molt, shedding their skins for the last time, and emerge as winged adults. There are some 2,500 species of cicadas worldwide. One special type of cicada—the *Magicicada*, or periodical cicada—surfaces only every 13 or 17 years. I was really excited to photograph them, so I went to the Washington, D.C., area because of its reputation for having the largest numbers of emerging adults. I found a schoolyard north of the city that was loaded with old trees—perfect for mating cicadas—and littered with dime-size holes in the ground, a telltale sign that cicadas were in the area and about to emerge.

That evening, I packed a sandwich, grabbed my flashlight and blanket, and headed to the school. I set up camp and shined my flashlight over the holes. Then I waited and waited. Finally, right after dark on the third night, one tiny cicada head popped out of the ground! Then another and another, and soon thousands of cicadas flooded the schoolyard! But the wildest part came a few days later, when thousands of male cicadas began singing to the females. It was a deafening sound that vibrated through my body. I felt like I was going to be beamed up to outer space! The whole experience was one I'll never forget. I was able to photograph cicadas crawling out of their burrows, shedding their skins, and transforming from juveniles into adults to carry out their final stage of life.

APPROXIMATE RANGE OF THE
MAGICICADA SEPTENDECIM (CICADA)

0   500 miles

0   500 kilometers

OBSERVATION **TIPS**

1 *Magicicadae* live beneath older neighborhoods and forests filled with old trees.

2 Most types of cicadas emerge at night. Shine a flashlight on the bases and trunks of trees to look for molting cicadas.

3 Bring a tape recorder so that you can record the deafening sound made by the male mating call.

4 If you find a cicada, get a good look at its face. It has five eyes!

Darlyne Murawski is an internationally published photographer, writer, and biologist. She showcases the lives and habitats of some of the planet's smallest critters—including insects, fungi, and parasites—in hopes of motivating young people to care about and explore their natural world.

Magicicadae crawl out of their burrows and climb the nearest vertical surfaces. They attach themselves to trees, fence posts, and even light poles to shed their skins and pump their wings full of blood. Their bodies change color from white to black, and they begin mating. The females make tiny slits in tree branches and lay their eggs inside. Both parents die before their eggs hatch. After the ant-size nymphs emerge, they drop to the ground and burrow deep into the earth, where they will stay for another 13 or 17 years, depending on the type of *Magicicada*.

BUGS

The main types of bugs are cicadas and relatives; aphids and relatives; and typical bugs, which include the water bugs.

All bugs have sucking mouthparts used to pierce their food and ingest the fluid inside. Most are plant-sap eaters. The exceptions are in the typical bug group. Pond skaters and assassin bugs, for example, prey on insects. Bedbugs and kissing bugs feed on blood.

Typical bugs are distinguished from other bugs by their wings. Their forewings are thicker and leathery where they attach to the body. The rest of the wing is soft and clear, like a membrane. At rest, the tips of the forewings cross over and are held flat across the back. If these bugs have a second set of wings, they are also soft and clear. Other bugs either have completely clear, membrane-like wings that rest on their backs, as in the cicada, or no wings.

Life spans range from 30 days for aphids to 17 years for cicadas.

BROWN MARMORATED STINK BUGS
HALYOMORPHA HALYS

RANGE: Asia; introduced to the United States

SIZE: 0.5 to 0.7 in (12 to 17 mm)

DIET: Plants

Stinkbugs are now major agricultural pests in countries where they are not native but have been introduced. Like all true bugs, they suck fluid out of plants and leave them damaged. They release a stinky chemical as a means of defense.

RED APHID
ACYRTHOSIPHON PISUM

RANGE: Worldwide

SIZE: 0.16 in (4 mm)

DIET: Sap of legumes such as peas, clover, alfalfa, beans

The aphid's ability to reproduce rapidly makes it a worldwide cause of crop damage. Most aphids are produced from un-fertilized eggs and are born live at a rate of about 100 a month. Each new aphid comes with babies ready to be born!

MAGIC CICADA
MAGICICADA SEPTENDECIM

RANGE: North America

SIZE: 1.5 in (3.8 cm)

DIET: Juices from the roots of plants, especially deciduous trees

Newly hatched magic cicadas burrow underground to feed on tree roots. They climb back out 17 years later to breed! They molt into adults, and the males start singing to attract a mate. Within six weeks, eggs are layed, and the adults die.

POND SKATER
GERRIDAE

RANGE: Worldwide except polar regions

SIZE: 0.3 in (8 to 10 mm)

DIET: Insects

Pond skaters have thousands of tiny hairs that cover their body and repel water. They use their front legs to detect ripples in the water made by their prey—struggling insects that cannot walk on water, like spiders and bees.

MILKWEED ASSASIN BUG
ZELUS LONGIPES

RANGE: Southern North America; Central America; most of South America; parts of the Caribbean

SIZE: Up to 0.7 in (18 mm)

DIET: Soft-bodied insects

This bug hides in leaves until an insect lands on its sticky front legs. It inserts its mouthparts to paralyze, then digest the food.

Did you know?

A water bug uses its middle legs for rowing and back legs for steering.

FLIES

The main groups of flies are true flies, dragonflies and damselflies, mayflies, and relatives. All are found worldwide and require access to water or a moist environment for reproduction.

Examples of true flies are horseflies, gnats, midges, mosquitoes, fruit flies, and—the most common of all flies—the housefly. These insects have only one set of wings. Their feeding styles and mouthparts vary, though. Some are plant-sap eaters; others suck blood or feed on carrion.

Some true flies have larvae that are parasitic, meaning they require a living host. The screwworm fly, for example, lays its eggs near open wounds. After the larvae hatch, they feed on living tissue. Other flies, like the greenbottle fly, have parasitic larvae—often called maggots—that feed on dead tissue.

Dragonflies and damselflies are predators that feed on mosquitoes and other insects. Mayflies feed on plants as larvae.

Life spans range from 21 days for houseflies to 1 year for mayflies.

COMMON HORSEFLY
TABANUS BOVINUS

RANGE: Worldwide

SIZE: 0.3 to 1 in (8 to 25 mm)

DIET: Flower, nectar, pollen; blood of vertebrates

Male horseflies feed on nectar and pollen, but females require a blood meal for reproduction. They usually choose a mammal, like a horse, and in the process they can transmit disease.

COMMON BLUE DAMSELFLY
ENALLAGMA CYATHIGERUM

RANGE: Worldwide

SIZE: 5 in (13.5 cm)

DIET: Mostly insects, but will eat anything they can digest

Damselflies are closely related to dragonflies. Both have compound eyes that give them a wide-angle view for hunting insects. Damselfly eyes are widely spaced; dragonfly eyes are so large they touch each other.

BLUE DASHER
PACHYDIPLAX LONGIPENNIS

RANGE: Most of the U.S., southern Canada, northern Mexico

SIZE: 1 to 1.7 in (25 to 43 mm)

DIET: Small flying insects

Dragonflies catch their prey in mid-air. They are capable of flying up to 60 miles per hour (97 km/h) with their very distinctive, membrane-like wings. The second pair is wider than the first and both are held out to the sides.

MAYFLY
POTAMANTHUS LUTEUS

RANGE: Worldwide; many in North America

SIZE: 0.04 to 1.2 in (1 to 30 mm)

DIET: Plant material, algae, debris

Young mayflies are aquatic insects for a long period of time: months to years. During this time, they feed on algae. Once they mature into adults, they mate almost immediately and die within a day.

HOUSEFLY
MUSCA DOMESTICA

RANGE: Worldwide

SIZE: 0.3 to 0.4 in (8 to 12 mm)

DIET: Decaying fruit and vegetables

Like all true flies, houseflies have a single pair of flight wings attached to their mid section, or thorax, and a tiny pair of nonfunctional wings, or halteres, behind those. True flies are in the order Diptera, which means "two wings" in Greek.

BUTTERFLIES
AND MOTHS

Butterflies and moths are flying insects with colorful scales on their wings. Their patterned, and often brightly colored, wings are used for defense as well as breeding and territorial displays. Many have eyespots to confuse predators. Others contain toxic chemicals from eating specific plants. Some look like toxic species, but are not. These are called mimics.

Butterflies and moths go through a similar life cycle known as metamorphosis: egg-larvae-pupa-adult. Larvae, or caterpillars, feed on leaves; adults feed on flower nectar or pollen and are important pollinators.

Butterflies and moths differ in a number of ways. Butterflies have thin antennae with clubs at the ends, are more likely to be active during the day, and rest with their wings closed. The pupa is a clear membrane and is called a chrysalis (KRIS-uh-lis). Moths have thicker, fuzzy antennae, are more active at night, and rest with their wings open. The pupa is either buried or wrapped in silk and is known as a cocoon.

Life spans for adult butterflies and moths range from a day to a year.

MONARCH BUTTERFLY ● ○ ●
DANAUS PLEXIPPUS

RANGE: North and South America, Caribbean, Australia, New Zealand, western Europe, islands of the Pacific and Atlantic Oceans

SIZE: Wingspan: 3.4 to 4.9 in (8.6 to 12.4 cm)

DIET: Milkweed plant, nectar

The monarch's orange color warns predators of its nasty taste, caused by milkweed toxins. Monarchs migrate between Canada and Mexico, a journey that requires several generations.

SIX-SPOT ● ● BURNET MOTH
ZYGAENA FILIPENDULAE

RANGE: Europe

SIZE: 1.2 to 1.6 in (30 to 40 mm)

DIET: Adult: flower nectar; caterpillar: leaves of lotus plants and clover

The six-spot burnet moth belongs to a group of day-flying moths in which the adults as well as the caterpillars are toxic. The bright spots warn predators that the moth contains hydrogen cyanide, a very toxic chemical.

LUNA MOTH ● ●
ACTIAS LUNA

RANGE: North America

SIZE: 1 in (2.54 cm); wingspan: 4 to 5 in (10 to 12.7 cm)

DIET: Caterpillar: foliage of hickory, walnut, sweetgum, other kinds of trees

Adult luna moths do not eat—they do not even have mouthparts. The adults live for only one week in order to breed. They reproduce once a year in cooler areas and up to three times a year—every eight to ten weeks—in warmer areas.

SILKMOTH ● ●
BOMBYX MANDARINA

RANGE: Asia; introduced worldwide

SIZE: 4 in (10 cm)

DIET: Mulberry tree leaves

The silkmoth was first bred in China for its silk 5,000 years ago. As its larva, called a silkworm, enters the pupa stage, it wraps itself in silk to form a cocoon. To make one pound of silk requires 2,000 to 3,000 cocoons.

ZEBRA SWALLOWTAIL BUTTERFLY
EUPROTOGRAPHIUM MARCELLUS

RANGE: Eastern United States and southeastern Canada

SIZE: 4 in (10 cm)

DIET: Pawpaw and dwarf pawpaw

Like many moth and butterfly species, the zebra swallowtail feeds on a specific group of plants. Caterpillars feed on the leaves of the pawpaw; adults feed on the tree's flower nectar. These butterflies are found only in areas where pawpaws grow.

GLASS WING BUTTERFLY
GRETA OTO

RANGE: Mexico to Panama

SIZE: Wingspan: 2.2 to 2.4 in (5.6 to 6 cm)

DIET: Flower nectar

Instead of using their wings to scare predators with bright colors, the glass wing butterfly uses its wings to hide. Their wings are clear, except for the borders and the veins that support them. These butterflies are also called little mirrors.

Did you know?
Blue morphos spend most of their 115-day lives as caterpillars.

BLUE MORPHO BUTTERFLY
MORPHO PELEIDES

RANGE: Tropical forests of Latin America, from Mexico to Colombia

SIZE: 8 in (20 cm)

DIET: Adult: rotting fruit, tree sap, fungi, wet mud; caterpillar: plants from the pea family

The males of the blue morpho butterfly are brightly colored; the females are brown and yellow. Males use their bright colors both for defense—to scare away birds—and to establish their territory during the breeding season.

POLYPHEMUS MOTH
ANTHERAEA POLYPHEMUS

RANGE: North America

SIZE: 6 in (15 cm)

DIET: Adult: does not eat; caterpillar: leaves of broadleaf trees and shrubs such as sweetgum, birch, hickory, maple, rose

Male and female polyphemus moths look similar in many ways. Both have purple eye-spots. But the male has thicker, fuzzier antennae, and the female has a larger body for carrying eggs. As in all moths, the cocoon is made of silk.

RED CRACKER BUTTERFLY
HAMADRYAS AMPHINOME

RANGE: Tropical Americas from central Mexico and Cuba south to Argentina

SIZE: Wingspan: 3 in (7.6 cm)

DIET: Adult: rotting fruit and other nonfloral resources; caterpillar: leaves

Wing color is only one of the features used to identify butterflies. For example, red cracker butterflies are related to glass wing butterflies because both are four-footed. They have six legs like all insects, but the first pair is very short.

ORNATE MOTH
UTETHEISA ORNATRIX

RANGE: Nova Scotia to Florida, U.S.A.; west to Minnesota, Kansas, and Texas, U.S.A.

SIZE: Wingspan: 1.2 to 1.6 in (3 to 4 cm)

DIET: Flowering plants

The larvae of ornate moths feed on plants like sweet clover that contain chemicals toxic to birds. By the time the adult emerges from the cocoon, it has high levels of these toxins in its saliva, which it spits for defense.

Bees and wasps are closely related to ants. All have long antennae with at least ten segments. Females also lay eggs using a leg-like structure called an ovipositor. In some species, the ovipositor is also a stinger used for paralyzing prey or for defense. All bees, wasps, and ants go through complete metamorphosis. Adults are usually found on flowers and feed their young either stored pollen or other insects.

Bees are pollen gatherers—and pollinators. There are more than 20,000 species. Most are solitary, meaning they live in small groups with a single breeding female and her offspring. Pollen is gathered to feed the young; sometimes it is mixed with nectar to make a paste.

Seven species of bees are called honeybees because they convert nectar to honey and store it in large amounts. Honeybees are able to do this because they are highly social, or eusocial, meaning they live in large groups called colonies that include a queen bee and thousands of offspring with specific duties. Honeybees also do a "waggle dance" to let other bees know which direction to go to search for nectar.

Most wasps are parasites of other insects. Some are eusocial like honeybees, but they hunt other insects. These include paper wasps, yellow jackets, and hornets.

Life spans range from two to five years.

PARASITIC WASP
ICHNEUMONIDAE CREMASTINAE

RANGE: North America

SIZE: 0.5 in (1.3 cm)

DIET: Other insects

Most parasitic wasps are highly specialized and feed only on a specific insect. Many have wings but cannot fly. For this reason, they are used to control insect problems, such as aphid infestations, on farms and in gardens.

DISAPPEARING BEES

Beginning in 2006, beekeepers noticed that entire colonies of their bees were mysteriously disappearing, abandoning their hives overnight. The phenomenon was so great they gave it a name: Colony Collapse Disorder. It's not just happening in managed bee colonies. Wild honeybees are at risk, too. So what's going on? For starters, food is harder for bees to come by because people are cutting down the weed flowers on which bees feed. The use of chemicals called insecticides, intended to keep insects from destroying crops, are detrimental to honeybee populations as well. In addition, pollution, mites, and diseases can kill entire bee colonies.

This is a big problem because honeybees play an important role in our ecosystem. Wild bees pollinate at least 80 percent of all plants, including crops. They, along with managed honeybees, are needed to grow many of the foods we eat; without them we wouldn't have foods such as apples, carrots, cucumbers, and almonds.

ORCHID BEE
EULAEMA BOMBIFORMUS

RANGE: Brazil, Paraguay, Argentina

SIZE: 0.125 to 1 in (0.3 to 2.7 cm)

DIET: Pollen and nectar

Orchid bees are known for their long tongues, which measure up to 1.6 inches (4 cm). They pollinate hundreds of species of orchid flowers in tropical forests and use their tongues to access hard to reach flower nectar.

EUROPEAN HONEYBEE
APIS MELLIFERA

RANGE: Europe, western Asia, Africa

SIZE: 0.39 to 0.79 in (10 to 20 mm)

DIET: Pollen and nectar

The European honeybee was first domesticated 6,000 years ago and is used worldwide for honey production and pollination. Workers are non-breeding females that build the nest, gather pollen, and make honey. The males, or drones, fertilize females.

PAPER WASP
POLISTES FUSCATUS

RANGE: Temperate areas of North America

SIZE: 0.59 to 0.83 in (15 to 21 mm)

DIET: Nectar, other insects

These wasps are named for the material they use to make their nests: a mix of plant fibers and their own saliva. In addition to nectar, this social species feeds on flies, caterpillars, and beetle larvae.

ANTS

A nts look like a lot like wasps. All have stingers and many have wings during the breeding stage. But ants have bent, or elbowed, antennae and a waist, which makes their rear end look large. Unlike wasps, all ant species are either highly social—or eusocial—or they parasitize other eusocial ants. Eusocial means that ants live in large colonies in which different types of ants have different jobs. For example, there are nonbreeding, wingless females that are called workers that dig tunnels and find food; soldier ants that protect the colony; and winged males and females, or queens, that breed. The males and queen ant look very different from each other, so ant species are identified based on the worker females.

Ants nest on the ground and in trees. Most are predators or scavengers that also eat nectar and fruit if available. Some, like leafcutter ants, eat fungi they farm. Adults eat only liquid food because of their narrow necks. Larvae eat solid food and will sometimes regurgitate—bring back up—liquid food for adults.

Life spans range from 1 to 20 years.

WEAVER ANT ● ●
OECOPHYLLA SMARAGDINA

RANGE: Africa, Asia, Australia
SIZE: Major workers: 0.3 to 0.39 in (8 to 10 mm)
DIET: Insects and nectar

Weaver ants build unusual nests made of silk and leaves woven together. Often, hundreds of nests are built in just a few trees. Unlike many ants in their particular group, weaver ants don't sting; they spray formic acid, an irritating chemical.

RED WOOD ANT ● ●
FORMICA RUFA

RANGE: Europe
SIZE: 0.4 in (10 mm)
DIET: Insects

Red wood ants live in forests and feed on aphids and other insects, including other ants. They build large, dome-shaped nests, usually in clearings on the forest floor. Each colony may have hundreds of egg-producing females.

EASTERN CARPENTER ANT ● ● ● ●
CAMPONOTUS PENNSYLVANICUS

RANGE: Worldwide
SIZE: Up to 0.7 in (18 mm)
DIET: Nectar, aphids, other soft-bodied insects

Carpenter ants nest in damp or dead wood, including wood in houses, and destroy it. Termites also destroy wood in homes, but they leave holes packed with mud. Carpenter ants leave sawdust.

LEAFCUTTER ANT ● ● ●
ATTA SEXDENS

RANGE: Central and South America
SIZE: 0.12 to 0.94 in (3 to 24 mm)
DIET: Fungi

Worker leafcutter ants carry leaves from the forest back to their nest along an obvious trail. The leaves are food for fungi that they farm and eat. They build large underground nests with as many as 2,000 chambers growing the fungi.

INSIDE AN ANTHILL

EGG CHAMBER

FOOD CHAMBER

WASTE CHAMBER

LARVAE CHAMBER

QUEEN'S CHAMBER

Worker ants haul bits of soil to the colony entrance and leave them there, eventually creating a mound, or anthill.

RECORDS

D id you know that some invertebrates live more than 200 years, or that some are more toxic than any other animals in the world? Check out these record-holding rock stars of the invertebrate world to learn more.

BIGGEST
GIANT SQUID
ARCHITEUTHIS DUX

Perhaps one of the most curious creatures of the deep, the giant squid is one interesting invertebrate. This super-size squid can grow to a massive 18 feet (5.5 m) long and weigh almost a ton (900 kg)! Not only that, it boasts the largest eye of any animal on Earth—about 10 inches (25.4 cm) in diameter—roughly the size of a volleyball. Scientists don't know a lot about this mysterious monster, mostly because it lives at depths of 660 to 2,300 feet (201 to 671 m), but they do know that it can go into battle with a huge sperm whale and win.

BEST BITE
TRAP-JAW ANT
ODONTOMACHUS BAURI

The teeny-tiny trap-jaw ant might not be much to look at, but when it snaps its jaws shut—watch out. Those chompers are closing at speeds anywhere from 62 to 145 miles per hour (100 to 233 km/h)! Some scientists even estimate their jaws can snap shut about 2,300 times faster than humans can blink their eyes. Not only that, the force behind that bite is estimated to be 300 times the ant's body weight. That means that if it were the size of the average adult human, its bite would be strong enough to easily crush a refrigerator.

MOST INTELLIGENT
COMMON OCTOPUS
OCTOPUS VULGARIS

In a classification of animals not known for beauty or brains, you probably wouldn't imagine the race to the head of the class would be so tight. But for scientists, the smartest selection is kind of a toss-up between the octopus and squid, with the common octopus inching ahead just slightly. Part of an elite group of slimy mollusks called cephalopods, octopuses and squids have big brains relative to their body sizes and can do things that scientists once thought only "intellectual" animals could do. The common octopus can complete simple mazes, solve problems, and even play—kind of like a slimy, eight-armed puppy dog.

MOST TOXIC
BOX JELLYFISH
CHIRONEX FLECKERI

If you've spent your life avoiding venomous spiders, beware! There are far more dangerous invertebrates out there. Fortunately, you're completely safe from them on land. The box jellyfish, which lives off the coast of Australia, is believed to be the most toxic animal in the world. With 60 15-foot (4.6-m)-long tentacles, one jellyfish contains enough venom to kill 60 adult humans. Despite that, one animal will stare a box jellyfish in the tentacles and live to tell the tale: Sea turtles are completely immune to the venom. In fact, they eat these jellies as a snack!

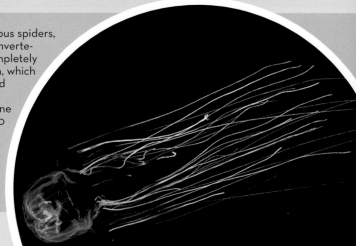

STRONGEST →
HERCULES BEETLE
DYNASTES HERCULES

Close your eyes and picture the strongest animal in the world. Are you thinking of the mighty African elephant, with its powerful tusks and massive body? If so, you need to think smaller—*much* smaller—because the strongest animal in the world is one that you can actually hold in one hand. The Hercules beetle, native to Central and South America, can lift an incredible 850 times its own body weight. The African elephant can only lift 25 percent of its body weight. So while the elephant might take the top prize in a tree-trunk-throwing contest, the Hercules beetle still wins the strongman title, hands down.

FASTEST GROWING →
GIANT TUBE-WORMS
RIFTIA PACHYPTILA

Deep in the darkest depths of the ocean lives the fastest-growing animal on Earth—the giant tubeworm! These icky invertebrates grow near hydrothermal vents one to three miles (1.6 to 4.8 km) under the ocean surface. Not only can they survive the crushing pressure and boiling temperatures, they thrive, growing up to 33 inches (84 cm) per year. Amazingly, giant tubeworms can grow to a maximum of six feet (1.8 m) long, even though they have no mouth or digestive system!

LONGEST LIVING →
OCEAN QUAHOG
ARCTICA ISLANDICA

The oldest tortoise might live a couple of centuries, but it's got nothing on the ocean quahog, a species of clam. This magnificent mollusk lives 200 years or more, though the oldest specimen ever found was estimated to be around 500 years old. Scientists could tell its age by looking at "growth lines" in the shell—ridges that appear annually. That means the clam was born only a decade or two after Columbus stumbled upon the Americas!

LEGGIEST →
ILLACME PLENIPES

The *Illacme plenipes* might not have the longest legs in the animal kingdom but it certainly has the most. Millipedes, contrary to their name ("millipede" comes from the words "thousand" and "legs" in Latin), do not have a thousand legs. But this one comes pretty close. Female *Illacme plenipes*, which are native to California, have an estimated 750 legs—at least 50 more than other millipede species—and males have about half that number. Which do you think would win in a race?

Want to know where these record-holding invertebrates live around the world? Take a look at this range map to find out.

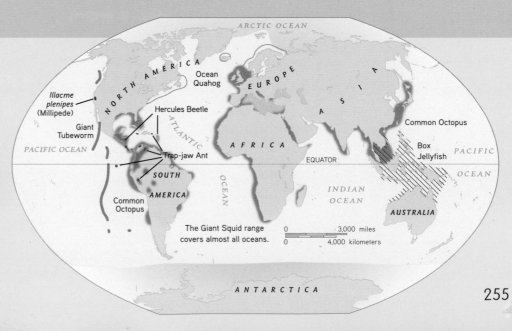

The Giant Squid range covers almost all oceans.

0   3,000 miles
0   4,000 kilometers

MAP KEY
APPROXIMATE RANGES OF RECORD-SETTING INVERTEBRATES

- Box Jellyfish
- *Illacme plenipes* (Millipede)
- Ocean Quahog
- Giant Squid
- Hercules Beetle
- Giant Tubeworm
- Trap-jaw Ant
- Common Octopus

255

With more than 1,000 additional animals in one easy-to-read list, this section introduces even more amazing creatures. Dig in and discover fast facts about everything from what a green sea turtle eats to where a bamboo rat lives, and so much more.

 GRASSLAND/OPEN AREA/SHRUBLAND
 CONIFEROUS FOREST/ WOODLAND
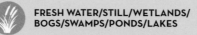 FRESH WATER/STILL/WETLANDS/ BOGS/SWAMPS/PONDS/LAKES
 URBAN AREAS/CITIES/ INDOOR/PARKS/GARDENS

 DESERT/DRY/DRY AND ROCKY
 MOUNTAINS/HIGHLANDS/ SLOPES/TEMPERATE & TROPICAL
 OCEANS/INSHORE AREAS & OPEN SEA
 OUTDOOR/FARMLAND/ RURAL AREAS

 TROPICAL FOREST/ RAIN FOREST
 POLAR REGIONS/ARCTIC/ TUNDRA & ANTARCTIC
 COASTAL AREAS INCLUDING MANGROVE SWAMPS

TEMPERATE FOREST/ WOODLAND
FRESH WATER/FLOWING/RIVERS & STREAMS/LAKES/ RIVERS & WETLANDS
CORAL REEFS

MAMMALS

- ● ALERT
- ● IN TROUBLE
- ● STABLE
- ● DOMESTICATED
- ● UNDER STUDY
- ● NOT LISTED

	COMMON NAME	SCIENTIFIC NAME	SIZE	RANGE	HABITAT	DIET
	MONOTREMES AND MARSUPIALS					
●	Long-beaked echidna	Zaglossus bruijni	11.01 to 36.3 lb (5 to 16.5 kg)	New Guinea		insects
●	Tiger or spotted-tail quoll	Dasyurus maculatus	8.8 to 13 lb (4 to 6 kg)	Australia		mostly small and medium-size mammals, birds, invertebrates, reptiles
●	Numbat	Myrmecobius fasciatus	0.7 to 1.2 lb (0.3 to 0.6 kg)	southern Australia		termites, ants, other invertebrates
●	Red kangaroo	Macropus rufus	up to 198 lb (90 kg)	Australia		plant-eaters: grasses and dicotyledonous flowering plants
●	Tammar wallaby	Macropus eugenii	9 to 20 lb (4 to 9 kg)	Australia and New Zealand		herbivorous: grasses
●	Parma wallaby	Macropus parma	7 to 13 lb (3.2 to 5.9 kg)	Australia and New Zealand		herbivorous: reedy grasses, herbaceous plant parts
●	Goodfellow's tree kangaroo	Dendrolagus goodfellowi	16.3 lb (7.4 kg)	Indonesia and Papua New Guinea		fruit, flowers, grasses
●	Long-nosed potoroo	Potorous tridactylus	1.5 to 4 lb (0.7 to 1.8 kg)	Australia		plants, roots, fungi, insects
●	Sugar glider	Petaurus breviceps	3.9 oz (110 g)	Australia, Indonesia, Papua New Guinea		omnivorous: pollen, nectar, insects (and their larvae), arachnids, small vertebrates
●	Leadbeater's possum	Gymnobelideus leadbeateri	3.5 to 6 oz (100 to 170 g)	Australia		small invertebrates and tree juices
●	Ringtail possum	Pseudocheirus peregrinus	18 to 35 oz (500 to 1,000 g)	Australia		folivorous: mainly eucalyptus leaves; also flowers, buds, nectar, fruit
●	Gray cuscus	Phalanger orientalis	2 to 11 lb (1 to 5 kg)	Indonesia and southwest Pacific Islands		leaves, fruit, other plant material
●	Common or coarse-haired wombat	Vombatus ursinus	33 to 77 lb (15 to 35 kg)	Australia		herbivorous: native grasses, roots of shrubs and trees, sedges, mat rushes, fungi
●	Eastern barred bandicoot	Perameles gunnii	23 oz (640 g)	Australia and Tasmania		mainly invertebrates such as earthworms, grubs, beetles; small vertebrates; some plants
	MOUSE-LIKE RODENTS					
●	Greater cane rat	Thryonomys swinderianus	6.6 to 19.8 lb (3 to 9 kg)	Africa		mainly grasses and cane
●	Small five-toed jerboa	Allactaga elater	2.1 oz (58.7 g)	Asia Minor		seeds, insects, succulent parts of plants
●	Common or black-bellied hamster	Cricetus cricetus	17.9 oz (506.7 g)	Eurasia from Belgium to Siberia		seeds, grains, roots, potatoes, green plants, insect larvae
●	Bank vole	Myodes glareolus	0.6 to 0.7 oz (17 to 20 g)	Europe through Central Asia		leaves; seeds, grains, nuts; fruit
●	Brown lemming	Lemmus sibiricus	1.6 to 4.6 oz (45 to 130 g)	Siberia and North America		live plant parts
●	Tree shrew	Tupaia glis	5 oz (142 g)	Southeast Asia		insects, spiders, seeds, buds
●	Woodland jumping mouse	Napaeozapus insignis	0.6 to 1.2 oz (17 to 35 g)	northeastern North America		arthropods; worms; leaves, roots, tubers; seeds, grains, nuts; fruit; bryophytes
●	Armored rat	Hoplomys gymnurus	0.5 to 1.8 lb (0.2 to 0.8 kg)	Central and South America		seeds, grains, nuts; fruit, insects
●	Bamboo rat	Rhizomys sumatrensis	1.1 to 8.8 lb (0.5 to 4 kg)	southern China, Nepal, eastern India		bamboo, plants, seeds, fruit

COMMON NAME	SCIENTIFIC NAME	SIZE	RANGE	HABITAT	DIET
CAVY AND SQUIRREL-LIKE RODENTS					
Eurasian beaver	*Castor fiber*	28.6 to 77.1 lb (13 to 35 kg)	Europe and Asia		bark, leaves, plants
Lowland paca	*Cuniculus paca*	8.8 to 26.4 lb (4 to 12 kg)	east-central Mexico south to Paraguay		fruit, leaves, buds, flowers
Brazilian agouti	*Dasyprocta leporina*	6.6 to 13 lb (3 to 5.9 kg)	South America		seeds, fruit
Desmarest's hutia	*Capromys pilorides*	2.2 to 19.8 lb (1 to 9 kg)	Cuba		leaves, fruit, bark; some vertebrates including lizards
Patagonian mara	*Dolichotis patagonum*	17.9 lb (8.1 kg)	Argentina		plant material: grasses, low shrubs
North African crested porcupine	*Hystrix cristata*	22 to 66.1 lb (1 to 30 kg)	Italy and Mediterranean coast of Africa		herbivorous: bark, roots, tubers, rhizomes, bulbs, fallen fruit, cultivated crops
North American porcupine	*Erethizon dorsatum*	11 to 30.8 lb (5 to 14 kg)	North America		buds, twigs, bark; roots and stems of flowering plants
Rock cavy	*Kerodon rupestris*	31.7 to 35.2 oz (900 to 1,000 g)	northeastern Brazil		leaves, buds, flowers, bark
Damara mole rat	*Cryptomys damarensis*	3.03 to 7.12 oz (86 to 202 g)	southwestern and central Africa		herbivorous: mostly roots, bulbs, tubers, aloe leaves; also some invertebrates
Guinea pig	*Cavia porcellus*	24.7 to 38.8 oz (700 to 1,100 g)	no longer exist in the wild		lettuce, cabbage, grasses, fruit
Plains viscacha	*Lagostomus maximus*	4.4 to 17.6 lb (2 to 8 kg)	Paraguay, Argentina, Bolivia		any kind of vegetation; seeds, grasses
Northern viscacha	*Lagidium peruanum*	2 to 3.5 lb (0.9 to 1.6 kg)	Andes		tough grasses, lichens, mosses
Degu	*Octodon degus*	6 to 10.6 oz (170 to 300 g)	west-central Chile		plants, bulbs, tubers
Coypu	*Myocastor coypus*	11.01 to 22.03 lb (5 to 10 kg)	South America		aquatic vegetation; stems, leaves, roots, bark
Douglas's squirrel	*Tamiasciurus douglasii*	5 to 11 oz (141 to 312 g)	Pacific coast of North America		pine seeds; also twigs, sap, leaves, buds, acorns and other nuts, mushrooms, fruit, berries
White-tailed antelope squirrel	*Ammospermophilus leucurus*	3.4 to 4.1 oz (96 to 117 g)	Western U.S.		leaves; seeds, grains, nuts; fruit; insects
Red squirrel	*Tamiasciurus hudsonicus*	4.9 to 8.8 oz (140 to 250 g)	North America		primarily seeds of conifer trees
Golden-mantled ground squirrel	*Spermophilus lateralis*	4.2 to 13.9 oz (120 to 394 g)	Canada and the United States		fungi, nuts, acorns, seeds, forbs, flowers, bulbs, fruit, shrubs, leafy greens
Siberian flying squirrel	*Pteromys volans*	4.6 oz (130 g)	Scandinavia, Russia, Asia, China		green plants, young branches, berries, seeds, nuts, catkins, pinecones, pine needles
Hoary marmot	*Marmota caligata*	17.6 to 22.03 lb (8 to 10 kg)	North America		mostly herbivorous: sedges, fescues, mosses, lichens, willows; also flowers
Olympic marmot	*Marmota olympus*	6.8 to 24.2 lb (3.1 to 11 kg)	Olympic National Park of Washington (U.S.A.)		meadow flora, including avalanche lilies, sub-alpine lupine, mountain buckwheat; grasses
Himalayan marmot	*Marmota himalayana*	8.8 to 20.3 lb (4 to 9.2 kg)	Asia, Europe, North America		herbivorous: flowering plants
Eastern chipmunk	*Tamias striatus*	2.8 to 5.3 oz (80 to 150 g)	eastern North America		nuts, acorns, seeds, mushrooms, fruit, corn; insects, bird eggs, mice, other small vertebrates
Chinchilla	*Chinchilla lanigera*	1.1 to 1.8 lb (0.5 to 0.8 kg)	mountains of Northern Chile		mainly grass and seeds
BATS					
Egyptian fruit bat	*Rousettus aegyptiacus*	2.8 to 6 oz (80 to 170 g)	Africa and the Middle East		pulp and juice of very ripe fruit; also fruit from trees, such as lilac, fig, baobab, mulberry
Pacific flying fox	*Pteropus tonganus*	6.7 to 38.7 oz (191 to 1,099 g)	American Samoa, Fiji, other Pacific islands		fruit, flowers, nectar, pollen
Long nosed nectar bat	*Leptonycteris yerbabuenae*	0.81 oz (23 g)	Central and North America		nectar and pollen from night-blooming flowers; cactus fruit
Greater bulldog bat	*Noctilio leporinus*	2.1 to 2.8 oz (60 to 78 g)	South and Central America		fish, crustaceans, stinkbugs, crickets, scarab beetles, moths, winged ants, other insects
False vampire bat	*Vampyrum spectrum*	6 to 6.3 oz (170 to 180 g)	South and Central America		birds, rodents, bats
Big brown bat	*Eptesicus fuscus*	0.8 oz (23 g)	North, Central, and South America		insects, especially beetles
Hoary bat	*Lasiurus cinereus*	0.7 to 1.2 oz (20 to 35 g)	North, Central, and South America		moths, flies, beetles, small wasps and their relatives, grasshoppers, termites, dragonflies
Red bat	*Lasiurus borealis*	0.25 to 0.5 oz (7 to 13 g)	eastern U.S.		insects
RABBITS AND RELATIVES					
Brown hare	*Lepus europaeus*	6.6 to 11.01 lb (93 to 5 kg)	Europe to Central Asia		leaves, buds, roots, fruit, berries, fungi, twigs, bark
European rabbit	*Oryctolagus cuniculus*	3.3 to 5.5 lb (1.5 to 2.5 kg)	Every continent except Asia and Antarctica		grasses, leaves, buds, tree bark, roots
Marsh rabbit	*Sylvilagus palustris*	2.7 to 4.9 lb (1,200 to 2,200 g)	Southeastern U.S.		herbivorous: blackberries, rhizomes, bulbs, cattails, water hyacinths, other marsh plants
Antelope jackrabbit	*Lepus alleni*	6 to 10.4 lb (2.7 to 4.7 kg)	Western coast of Mexico and southern Arizona U.S.		leaves, grasses, plants
Large-eared pika	*Ochotona macrotis*	0.26 lb (0.12 kg)	Central Asia		grasses, sedges, twigs, flowers
SHREWS AND SMALL INSECTIVORES					
Large-eared tenrec	*Geogale aurita*	0.18 to 0.30 oz (5 to 8.5 g)	Madagascar		insectivorous: especially termites
Short-eared elephant shrew	*Macroscelides proboscideus*	1.4 to 1.8 oz (40 to 50 g)	Botswana, Namibia, South Africa		insects, especially termites and ants; other small invertebrates

COMMON NAME	SCIENTIFIC NAME	SIZE	RANGE	HABITAT	DIET
Southern African hedgehog	*Atelerix frontalis*	5 to 20 oz (150 to 555 g)	Southern Africa and Angola		mainly insects; also carrion, fungi, frogs, lizards, bird eggs and chicks, small mice
Western European hedgehog	*Erinaceus europaeus*	28 to 42 oz (800 to 1,200 g)	Europe and Central Asia		worms, slugs, caterpillars, other invertebrates; frogs; berries; bird eggs and chicks
Rock hyrax	*Procavia capensis*	up to 9.5 lb (4.3 kg)	Africa and Arabian Peninsula		leaves, grasses, small plants, berries, fruit

ANTEATERS, ARMADILLOS, AND SLOTHS

COMMON NAME	SCIENTIFIC NAME	SIZE	RANGE	HABITAT	DIET
Southern three-banded armadillo	*Tolypeutes matacus*	3.08 to 3.52 lb (1.4 to 1.6 kg)	South America		ants and termites
Nine banded armadillo	*Dasypus novemcinctus*	8 to 17 lb (3.6 to 7.7 kg)	North, Central, and South America		insects, spiders, small reptiles, amphibians, eggs
Giant armadillo	*Priodontes maximus*	41 to 71 lb (18.7 to 32 kg)	northern South America		termites, ants, some other small animals
Aardvark	*Orycteropus afer*	88.1 to 180.6 lb (40 to 82 kg)	Africa		insects, especially ants and termites

DOGS, WOLVES, AND RELATIVES

COMMON NAME	SCIENTIFIC NAME	SIZE	RANGE	HABITAT	DIET
African wild dog	*Lycaon pictus*	40 to 80 lb (18 to 36 kg)	Africa		small antelope such as impala and bush duiker; old, sick, or injured larger animals
Dingo dog	*Canis lupus spp. dingo*	21 to 43 lb (9.5 to 19.5 kg)	western and central Australia		sheep, rabbits, rats, wallabies, birds, reptiles, human garbage
Maned wolf	*Chrysocyon brachyurus*	44.05 to 50.66 lb (20 to 23 kg)	Brazil		large rodents, including pacas and agoutis; birds, reptiles, frogs, insects, snails
Red wolf	*Canis rufus*	88.11 to 180.62 lb (40 to 82 kg)	southeastern United States		rodents, ungulates; other small mammals, including raccoons, white-tailed deer, muskrats
Crab-eating fox	*Cerdocyon thous*	11 to 17.6 lb (5 to 8 kg)	South America		small rodents (mice and rats); lizards, frogs, crabs, insects, fruit
Bat-eared fox	*Otocyon megalotis*	6.6 to 11.7 lb (3 to 5.3 kg)	Africa		insects, other arthropods; also small rodents, lizards, bird eggs and chicks; plants
Gray fox	*Urocyon cinereoargenteus*	4.4 to 19.8 lb (2 to 9 kg)	North, Central, and South America		omnivorous: small vertebrates, fruit, invertebrates
Arctic fox	*Vulpes lagopus*	183.3 oz (5,200 g)	Eurasia, North America, Greenland, Iceland		ground-dwelling birds; lemmings and other small mammals; insects, berries, carrion
Kit fox	*Vulpes macrotis*	3.5 to 6 lb (1.6 to 2.7 kg)	southwestern U.S. and Mexico		primarily rodents and rabbits, including prairie dogs and kangaroo rats
Red fox	*Vulpes vulpes*	6.6 to 30.8 lb (3 to 14 kg)	Northern Hemisphere		rodents, rabbits, hares, birds, insects, invertebrates; fruit; berries

SKUNKS AND STINK BADGERS

COMMON NAME	SCIENTIFIC NAME	SIZE	RANGE	HABITAT	DIET
Western hog-nosed skunk	*Conepatus leuconotus*	4.4 to 9.9 lb (2 to 4.5 kg)	southern U.S. and Mexico		insects, grubs, snakes, small mammals, fruit
Pygmy spotted skunk	*Spilogale pygmaea*	5 to 11 oz (150 to 320 g)	Pacific coast of Mexico		insects, fruit, berries, small mammals, birds, reptiles
Sunda stink badger	*Mydaus javanensis*	3.08 to 7.93 lb (1.4 to 3.6 kg)	Indonesian islands of Sumatra, Java, and Borneo		insects, worms, grubs, plants

OTTERS, WEASELS, AND RELATIVES

COMMON NAME	SCIENTIFIC NAME	SIZE	RANGE	HABITAT	DIET
Chinese ferret-badger	*Melogale moschata*	2.2 to 6.6 lb (1 to 3 kg)	China, Taiwan, Southeast Asia		small rodents, amphibians, insects and other invertebrates; sometimes fruit
Hog badger	*Arctonyx collaris*	15.4 to 30.8 lb (7 to 14 kg)	Southeast Asia		worms, invertebrates, fruit, roots
Eurasian badger	*Meles meles*	14.5 to 36.8 lb (6.6 to 16.7 kg)	Ireland, Spain, Russia, China, Japan		earthworms, small animals, bulbs, fruit, nuts
North American river otter	*Lontra canadensis*	11.01 to 30.8 lb (5 to 14 kg)	Canada and the United States		amphibians; fish; turtles; crayfish, crabs, and other invertebrates
Southern river otter	*Lontra provocax*	39.4 to 45.7 in (100 to 160 cm)	Chile and parts of Argentina		fish, crustaceans, mollusks, birds
Sea otter	*Enhydra lutris*	30.8 to 99.1 lb (14 to 45 kg)	East Asia to North America		clams, mussels, snails, abalone, and other mollusks; sea urchins
European otter	*Lutra lutra*	237.9 oz (6,750 g)	Eurasia south of the tundra line and North Africa		fish; crustaceans; clams; small mammals, amphibians, birds; eggs; insects; worms
Spotted-necked otter	*Hydrictis maculicollis*	8.8 lb (4 kg)	central Africa		mainly fish; also frogs, crabs, mollusks, aquatic insects, larvae
Hairy-nosed otter	*Lutra sumatrana*	11 to 13 lb (5 to 5.9 kg)	Southeast Asia		fish, crustaceans
Marine otter	*Lontra felina*	6.6 to 11 lb (3 to 5 kg)	Pacific coast of South America		crustaceans, mollusks, other invertebrates; fish; also birds, small mammals
Cape clawless otter	*Aonyx capensis*	23.4 to 46.3 lb (11 to 21 kg)	Africa		crabs, mollusks, fish, reptiles, frogs, birds, small mammals
Tayra	*Eira barbara*	6.6 to 13.2 lb (3 to 6 kg)	Central and South America		omnivorous; small mammals, especially the spiny rat
Greater grison	*Galictis vittata*	2.2 to 6.6 lb (1 to 3 kg)	Central and South America		small mammals, such as chinchillas, viscachas, agoutis, mice; frogs; worms
Striped polecat or zorilla	*Ictonyx striatus*	32.1 oz (910 g)	Africa		carnivorous: small rodents, frogs, lizards, snakes, birds, bird eggs, beetles
American marten	*Martes americana*	9.9 to 45.8 oz (280 to 1,300 g)	North America		squirrels; small animals and insects; fruit; nuts
Black-footed ferret	*Mustela nigripes*	22.7 to 39.7 oz (645 to 1,125 g)	North America		mainly prairie dogs; sometimes mice, ground squirrels, other small animals
American mink	*Neovison vison*	24.7 to 56.4 oz (700 to 1,600 g)	United States		crayfish; small frogs; rabbits, mice, other small mammals; fish; ducks, other waterfowl
Long-tailed weasel	*Mustela frenata*	2.8 to 15.9 oz (80 to 450 g)	North America		small rodents

CIVETS, FOSSAS, AND RELATIVES

COMMON NAME	SCIENTIFIC NAME	SIZE	RANGE	HABITAT	DIET
African palm civet	*Nandinia binotata*	3.7 to 4.6 lb (1.7 to 2.1 kg)	sub-Saharan Africa		rodents, insects, birds, fruit bats, eggs, carrion, pineapples, fallen fruit

COMMON NAME	SCIENTIFIC NAME	SIZE	RANGE	HABITAT	DIET
Large spotted genet	Genetta tigrina	1.85 to 7.05 lb (0.84 to 3.20 kg)	southern Africa		seeds, fruit, insects, rodents, snakes, skinks, geckos
Yellow mongoose	Cynictis penicillata	1.8 lb (0.5 kg)	southern Africa		insects, grasses, seeds, birds, reptiles, amphibians
MONGOOSES					
Indian gray mongoose	Herpestes edwardsi	1.1 to 8.8 lb (0.5 to 4 kg)	Arabia, Nepal, India, Pakistan, Sri Lanka		mice, rats, lizards, snakes, beetles
RACCOONS, RED PANDAS, AND RELATIVES					
White-nosed coatimundi	Nasua narica	6.6 to 11 lb (3 to 5 kg)	Arizona, Central America, Colombia, Ecuador		omnivorous: prefers all types of insects; will eat fruit and small mammals
Cacomistle	Bassariscus sumichrasti	31.7 oz (900 g)	Central America		omnivorous: fruit, eggs, lizards, insects, tree frogs, birds, mice
Northern raccoon	Procyon lotor	4 to 23 lb (2 to 10 kg)	North America and northern South America		aquatic animals, small land animals, birds, nuts, seeds, turtle eggs, fruit, corn
Olingo	Bassaricyon gabbii	2.1 to 3.3 lb (1 to 1.5 kg)	Nicaragua to Bolivia		small vertebrates, insects, nectar, flowers, fruit
HYENAS AND AARDWOLVES					
Brown hyena	Hyaena brunnea	75 to 160 lb (34 to 73 kg)	Angola and southern Africa		carrion, birds, melon
BEARS					
Spectacled bear	Tremarctos ornatus	132.2 to 440.5 lb (60 to 200 kg)	South America		mainly leaves, fruit, and roots; berries, cacti, shrubs, honey, sugarcane
American black bear	Ursus americanus	85.9 to 900.9 lb (39 to 409 kg)	North America		fruit, berries, nuts, roots, honey, insects, small mammals, fish, carrion
LARGE CATS					
Asiatic lion	Panthera leo ssp. Persica	295 to 340 lb (135 to 155 kg)	Gir Forest, India		sambar and chital deer, wild boar, water buffalo, livestock
Sumatran tiger	Panthera tigris sumatrae	295 to 340 lb (135 to 155 kg)	Indonesia		wild pigs, deer, cattle; other mammals, such as sloth bears
SMALL AND MEDIUM CATS					
Asiatic golden cat	Pardofelis temminckii	26.5 to 33.1 lb (12 to 15 kg)	Asia		small animals, including muntjacs, snakes, squirrels and other rodents, reptiles, birds
Domestic cat	Felis catus	9 to 11.9 lb (4.1 to 5.4 kg)	every continent except Antarctica		most depend on human-supplied food; feral cats may hunt rodents, birds
Jungle cat	Felis chaus	8.8 to 35.3 lb (4 to 16 kg)	Middle East and Asia		rodents, frogs, birds, hares, fish, lizards, snakes, insects, livestock, fruit (in winter)
Wild cat	Felis silvestris	7.7 to 11 lb (3.50 to 5 kg)	Europe, Asia, Africa		small rodents, ground-dwelling birds
Geoffroy's cat	Leopardus geoffroyi	6.6 to 11 lb (3 to 5 kg)	southern half of South America		wide variety of animals, especially hamsters and hares
Kodkod	Leopardus guigna	3.3 to 6.6 lb (1.50 to 3 kg)	Chile		carnivorous: primarily small rodents, reptiles, birds, large insects
African golden cat	Profelis aurata	7.72 to 39.68 lb (3.5 to 18 kg)	equatorial Africa		mid-size mammals, including tree hyraxes, red duikers, small antelopes, monkeys, birds
Marbled cat	Pardofelis marmorata	5.28 to 11 lb (2.40 to 5 kg)	Himalaya, Burma, southeast Asia		primarily birds and arboreal small mammals
Spanish lynx	Lynx pardinus	24.25 to 33.07 lb (11 to 15 kg)	western Europe		small mammals, primarily European rabbits
Leopard cat	Prionailurus bengalensis	6.61 to 15.43 lb (3 to 7 kg)	Asia		small terrestrial vertebrates such as rodents and lizards; small birds
Cougar	Puma concolor	63.8 to 264 lb (29 to 120 kg)	North and South America		mammals, including moose, elk, deer, caribou, squirrels, muskrats, rabbits; also birds
Jaguarundi	Puma yagouaroundi	9.9 to 19.8 lb (4.50 to 9 kg)	southern Texas and Arizona (U.S.A.) to northern Argentina		carnivorous: small mammals, reptiles, birds, frogs, fish
Caracal	Caracal caracal	17.6 to 41.8 lb (8 to 19 kg)	Africa; Central Asia and southwestern Asia		mammals: hyraxes, hares, rodents, antelopes, small monkeys; birds; reptiles
SEALS, SEA LIONS, AND FURRED SEALS					
New Zealand fur seal	Arctocephalus forsteri	66.1 to 396.5 lb (30 to 80 kg)	New Zealand and Australia		aquatic species, including arrow squid, octopus, barracuda, jade mackerel
New Zealand sea lion	Phocarctos hookeri	299.6 to 903.1 lb (136 to 410 kg)	New Zealand		small fish, crabs, octopus, mussels, penguins
South American sea lion	Otaria flavescens	308.4 to 770.9 lb (140 to 350 kg)	South American coastlines		carnivorous: fish, cephalopods, crustaceans, other invertebrates
Australian sea lion	Neophoca cinerea	231.3 to 660.8 lb (105 to 300 kg)	Australia		fish, including whiting, rays, small sharks; squid; cuttlefish; fairy penguins
Gray seal	Halichoerus grypus	330.4 to 484.6 lb (150 to 220 kg)	sub-Arctic waters of the North Atlantic Ocean		fish; some crustaceans and mollusks
Hooded seal	Cystophora cristata	352.4 to 660.8 lb (160 to 300 kg)	eastern coast of North America north of Maine		fish, such as redfish, herring, polar cod, flounder; also octopus and shrimp
Weddell seal	Leptonychotes weddellii	881.1 to 1,321.6 lb (400 to 600 kg)	Antarctic continent		notothenioid (Antarctic) fish, squid, crustaceans
Harbor seal	Phoca vitulina	110.1 to 374.5 lb (50 to 170 kg)	North Atlantic and North Pacific Oceans		crustaceans, mollusks, squid, fish
Harp seal	Pagophilus groenlandicus	264.3 to 297.4 lb (120 to 135 kg)	Arctic and northern Atlantic Oceans		fish, crustaceans
SEA COWS					
Amazonian manatee	Trichechus inunguis	1,057 lb (479 kg)	Amazon Basin in South America		aquatic grasses and flowers, water lettuce
African manatee	Trichechus senegalensis	790 lb (360 kg)	west coast of Africa		aquatic vegetation

COMMON NAME	SCIENTIFIC NAME	SIZE	RANGE	HABITAT	DIET
COWS, SHEEP, AND GOATS					
Gaur	*Bos frontalis*	1,432 to 2,203 lb (650 to 1,000 kg)	Nepal, India to Indochina, Malay Peninsula		green grasses; also coarse, dry grasses; forbs, leaves
Water buffalo	*Bubalus bubalis*	551 to 2,643 lb (250 to 1,200 kg)	widespread		grasses; also herbs, aquatic plants, leaves, crops, vegetation along rivers and streams
African or cape buffalo	*Syncerus caffer*	1,101 to 1,982 lb (500 to 900 kg)	middle of the African continent		herbivorous: grasses
Europen bison or wisent	*Bison bonasus*	661 to 2,026 lb (300 to 920 kg)	mainland Europe		primarily grazers; also browsers, eating leaves, ferns, twigs, bark, acorns
ANLETOPES AND PRONGHORNS					
Greater kudu	*Tragelaphus strepsiceros*	264 to 693 lb (120 to 315 kg)	Africa		herbivorous: leaves, herbs, fruit, vines, flowers, some new grasses
Impala	*Aepyceros melampus*	99 to 132 lb (45 to 60 kg)	Africa		grasses, leaves, flowers, fruit
Topi	*Damaliscus lunatus*	198 to 323.4 lb (90 to 147 kg)	Africa		almost entirely grasses
Springbok	*Antidorcas marsupialis*	72.6 to 101.2 lb (33 to 46 kg)	South Africa		leaves of shrubs and bushes; grasses
Blackbuck	*Antilope cervicapra*	70.4 to 94.6 lb (32 to 43 kg)	India, U.S., Argentina		grasses
Dorcas gazelle	*Gazella dorcas*	30.8 to 39.6 lb (14 to 18 kg)	northern Africa		flowers, leaves, pods of Acacia trees; also fruit and leaves
Kirk's dik-dik	*Madoqua saltiana*	4.4 to 13.2 lb (2 to 6 kg)	Africa		leaves of scrub and bushes; buds; plants; flowers; fruit; herbs
Sable antelope	*Hippotragus niger*	484 to 523.6 lb (220 to 238 kg)	Africa		foliage and herbs; grasses
Arabian oryx	*Oryx leucoryx*	220 to 462 lb (100 to 210 kg)	Middle East		grasses and shrubs
Nilgai	*Boselaphus tragocamelus*	264 to 528 lb (120 to 240 kg)	India		browsers: grasses; also fruit and sugarcane
Steenbok	*Raphicerus campestris*	15.4 to 35.2 lb (7 to 16 kg)	Africa		grasses, roots, tubers of some plants; shoots of bushland trees and shrubs
Saiga	*Saiga tatarica*	66 to 99 lb (30 to 45 kg)	Asia		grasses, low-growing shrubs
Sitatunga	*Tragelaphus spekii*	110 to 275 lb (50 to 125 kg)	Africa		grazers and browsers: especially foliage of alchornea cordifolia
Bongo	*Tragelaphus eurycerus*	462 to 891 lb (210 to 405 kg)	Africa		grazers and browsers: leaves, flowers, twigs, thistles, garden produce, cereals
Defassa waterbuck	*Kobus ellipsiprymnus*	352 to 660 lb (160 to 300 kg)	Africa		variety of grasses, long and short
Yellow-backed duiker	*Cephalophus silvicultor*	99.1 to 176.2 lb (4 to 80 kg)	Africa		fruit, leaves, seeds, buds, bark, shoots
DEER AND ELK					
Marsh deer	*Blastocerus dichotomus*	195.8 to 275 lb (89 to 125 kg)	South America		herbivorous: mainly aquatic and riparian vegetation
Andean deer taruca	*Hippocamelus antisensis*	150 lb (68.6 kg)	Argentina, Chile, Peru		herbivorous: sedges and grasses
Mule deer	*Odocoileus hemionus*	94.6 to 330 lb (43 to 150 kg)	western North America		woody and herbaceous forage; acorns, legume seeds, fleshy fruits
Chital	*Axis axis*	60 to 100 lb (27 to 45 kg)	India		grasses; flowers; fruit; sedges
Tufted deer	*Elaphodus cephalophus*	37.4 to 110.1 lb (1 to 50 kg)	China, Myanmar		grasses, other plant material; leaves, twigs, fruit; sedges, forbs, woody growth
Indian muntjac	*Muntiacus muntjak*	30.8 to 77 lb (14 to 35 kg)	southern and southeastern Asia		omnivorous: herbs, fruit, bird eggs, small animals, sprouts, seeds, grasses
Sambar	*Rusa unicolor*	239.8 to 572 lb (109 to 260 kg)	southern Asia		leaves, berries, grasses, bark from young trees, fallen fruit, herbs, buds
Javan rusa	*Rusa timorensis*	162.8 to 352 lb (74 to 160 kg)	southern Asia		primarily grasses and leaves
Chinese water deer	*Hydropotes inermis*	26.4 to 40.7 lb (12 to 18.5 kg)	only true deer to lack antlers; has tusks		reeds, coarse grasses, beets, other vegetation
Himalayan musk deer	*Moschus leucogaster*	24 to 40 lb (10 to 18 kg)	Himalaya		herbivorous: grasses, forbs, mosses, lichen, twigs, shoots, plant leaves
Water chevrotain	*Hyemoschus aquaticus*	15.4 to 33 lb (11 to 18 kg)	Africa		grasses, leaves, fruit; some insects, crabs, fish, worms, small mammals
Greater mouse-deer	*Tragulus napu*	11 to 17.6 lb (5 to 8 kg)	southern Asia		fallen fruit and berries, aquatic plants, leaves, buds, shrubs, grasses
GIRAFFES					
Giraffe	*Giraffa camelopardalis*	2,599.12 to 4,251.10 lb (1,180 to 1,930 kg)	Africa, south of Sahara		Acacia tree foliage, buds, fruit; grasses; plants; grains; leaves; flowers; seed pods
HIPPOS AND PIGS					
Pygmy hippopotamus	*Hexaprotodon liberiensis*	352 to 605 lb (160 to 275 kg)	West Africa		leaves, swamp vegetation, fallen fruit, roots, tubers
Bushpig	*Potamochoerus larvatus*	118.8 to 253 lb (54 to 115 kg)	Africa		roots, rhizomes, bulbs, tubers, fruit, insect larvae; invertebrates, small vertebrates, carrion
Giant hog	*Hylochoerus meinertzhageni*	396 to 605 lb (180 to 275 kg)	Africa		grasses, plants, leaves, buds, roots, berries, fruit
Pygmy hog	*Sus salvanius*	17.6 lb (8 kg)	northwestern Assam, India		roots, tubers, other plant parts; insects, eggs, young birds, reptiles
Babirusa	*Babyrousa babyrussa*	94.6 to 220 lb (43 to 100 kg)	Indonesia		roots, berries, tubers, leaves, fallen fruit, fungi
Chacoan peccary	*Catagonus wagneri*	63.9 to 107.9 lb (29 to 49 kg)	Paraguay, Bolivia, southern Brazil		cacti, seeds of leguminous plants

COMMON NAME	SCIENTIFIC NAME	SIZE	RANGE	HABITAT	DIET
● White-lipped peccary	*Tayassu pecari*	55.1 to 88.1 lb (25 to 40 kg)	southern Mexico and South America		fruit, leaves, roots, seeds, mushrooms, worms (Annelida), insects
CAMELS AND RELATIVES					
● Llama	*Lama glama*	286 to 341 lb (130 to 155 kg)	North America, Europe, Australia		low shrubs, lichens, mountain vegetation
● Alpaca	*Lama pacos*	121 to 143 lb (55 to 65 kg)	central and southern Andes		herbivorous: grasses, plants, woody shrubs
HORSES AND RELATIVES					
● Przewalski's horse	*Equus ferus*	440.5 to 660.8 lb (200 to 300 kg)	original species: steppe zone of Europe and Asia		herbivorous: grasses, plants, fruit; sometimes bark, leaves, buds
● Grevy's zebra	*Equus grevyi*	768.7 to 993.4 lb (349 to 451 kg)	northern Africa and southern Ethiopia		herbivorous grazers: tough grasses and forbs; leaves
● Mountain zebra	*Equus zebra*	528 to 818.4 lb (240 to 372 kg)	South and Southwest Africa		primarily grasses
● Kulan	*Equus hemionus*	440.5 to 572.7 lb (200 to 260 kg)	southern Mongolia, Russia, China, Iran, India		herbivorous: perennial grasses, herbs, bark
TAPIRS					
● Mountain or woolly tapir	*Tapirus pinchaque*	300 to 400 lb (136 to 182 kg)	Northern Andes, Peru, Ecuador, Colombia		herbivorous: tough, fibrous leaves of shrubs; myrtle trees; pampas grass
WHALES AND DOLPHINS					
● Bowhead whale	*Balaena mysticetus*	165,000 to 220,000 lb (75,000 to 100,000 kg)	Northern Hemisphere		planktonic crustaceans; epibenthic organisms; some benthic organisms
● Blue whale	*Balaenoptera musculus*	418,502 lb (190,000 kg)	All oceans		mostly krill; other planktonic crustaceans
● North Atlantic right whale	*Eubalaena glacialis*	121,145 to 209,251 lb (55,000 to 95,000 kg)	North Atlantic and north Pacific Oceans		aquatic crustaceans, zooplankton
● Humpback whale	*Megaptera novaeangliae*	66,000 lb (30,000 kg)	Arctic Sea; Atlantic, Indian, Pacific Oceans		planktonic crustaceans, fish
● Pygmy right whale	*Caperea marginata*	9,912 lb (4,500 kg)	Atlantic, Indian, and Pacific Oceans		krill
● Long-finned pilot whale	*Globicephala melas*	3,968 to 8,378 lb (1,800 to 3,800 kg)	All oceans except Poles; Med. and Black Seas		squid; fish such as cod and turbot
● Beluga whale	*Delphinapterus leucas*	2,976 to 3,307 lb (1,350 to 1,500 kg)	Arctic Sea, Atlantic and Pacific Oceans		smelt, flounder, sculpins, salmon, cod; invertebrates such as crab, octopus, squid
● Narwhal	*Monodon monoceros*	1,982 to 3,524 lb (900 to 1,600 kg)	Arctic Sea and Atlantic Ocean		squid, crabs, shrimp, fish
● Sperm whale	*Physeter macrocephalus*	77,093 to 110,132 lb (35,000 to 50,000 kg)	All oceans except Poles; Med. and Black Seas		large, deep-water squid; some fish, lobsters, other marine life
● Cuvier's beaked whale	*Ziphius cavirostris*	6,608 lb (3,000 kg)	All oceans except Poles; Med. and Black Seas		squid; deep-water fish
● False killer whale	*Pseudorca crassidens*	2,018 to 4,056 lb (916 to 1,842 kg)	All oceans except Poles; Med. and Black Seas		primarily fish and squid
● Common dolphin	*Delphinus delphis*	220 to 299 lb (100 to 136 kg)	All oceans except Poles; Med. and Black Seas		small fish; squid and octopus
● Risso's dolphin	*Grampus griseus*	661 to 1,102 lb (300 to 500 kg)	All oceans except Poles; Med. and Black Seas		fish, krill, crustaceans, cephalopods; greater argonaut (paper nautilus)
● Common porpoise	*Phocoena phocoena*	99 to 132 lb (45 to 60 kg)	All oceans except Poles; Med. and Black Seas		smooth, nonspiny fish; cephalopods
● Gulf porpoise	*Phocoena sinus*	66 to 121 lb (30 to 55 kg)	Pacific Ocean		tuna and other teleost fish; squid
● Atlantic white sided dolphin	*Lagenorhynchus acutus*	396 to 550 lb (180 to 250 kg)	Atlantic Ocean		shrimp, smelt, hake, squid, herring
● Irrawaddy dolphin	*Orcaella brevirostris*	251 to 293 lb (114 to 133 kg)	Indian and Pacific Oceans		fish, cephalopods, crustaceans
● Amazon River dolphin	*Inia geoffrensis*	217 to 407 lb (99 to 185 kg)	South America		fish; some crustaceans
● Ganges River dolphin	*Platanista gangetica*	112 to 196 lb (51 to 89 kg)	southern Asia		variety of aquatic animals; fish, crustaceans
LEMURS					
● Aye-aye	*Daubentonia madagascariensis*	6 lb (3 kg)	Madagascar		insect larvae, plant shoots, fruit, eggs
● Gray mouse lemur	*Microcebus murinus*	2.11 oz (60 g)	Madagascar		insects, small reptiles, plants, fruit, flowers
● Fork-marked lemur	*Phaner furcifer*	0.6 to 1 lb (0.3 to 0.5 kg)	coastal and western Madagascar		gum of temperate deciduous trees
● Indri	*Indri indri*	15 to 22 lb (7 to 10 kg)	northeastern Madagascar		leaves, shoots, fruit
● Diademed sifaka	*Propithecus diadema*	11 to 15 lb (5 to 7 kg)	eastern Madagascar		leaves, shoots, fruit, flowers
● Woolly lemur	*Avahi laniger*	1.3 to 2.9 lb (0.6 to 1.3 kg)	northwestern and eastern Madagascar		fruit, leaves, buds
● Black lemur	*Eulemur macaco*	4.4 to 5.5 lb (2 to 2.5 kg)	Madagascar and nearby islands		mainly fruit; reportedly mushrooms and millipedes; flower nectar; seed pods
● Bamboo lemur	*Hapalemur griseus*	1.5 to 2 lb (0.7 to 0.9 kg)	Madagascar		mainly bamboo; also grasses, fruit, leaves
POTTOS, LORISES, AND GALAGOS					
● Lesser bushbaby	*Galago senegalensis*	0.2 to 0.6 lb (0.09 to 0.27 kg)	sub-Saharan Africa		insects, spiders, scorpions, young birds, lizards, seeds, fruit, nectar
● Greater galago	*Otolemur crassicaudatus*	2.2 to 4.4 lb (1 to 2 kg)	East Africa		insects, reptiles, birds, bird eggs, plant material
● Slow loris	*Nycticebus coucang*	4.4 lb (2 kg)	Southeast Asia		insects, bird eggs, small birds, fruit, shoots

COMMON NAME	SCIENTIFIC NAME	SIZE	RANGE	HABITAT	DIET
● Slender loris	*Loris tardigradus*	0.28 to 0.5 lb (0.13 to 0.23 kg)	Sri Lanka		insects, small birds, bird eggs, lizards, leaves, shoots
● Potto	*Perodicticus potto*	1.3 to 3.5 lb (0.6 to 1.6 kg)	equatorial Africa		insects, snails, fruit, leaves
MONKEYS					
● Sooty mangabey	*Cercocebus atys*	12 to 22 lb (5.5 to 10.2 kg) (males)	coastal West Africa		omnivorous: fruit, seeds, small animals
● Drill	*Mandrillus leucophaeus*	24 to 55 lb (11 to 25 kg) (males)	Cameroon		plant matter, fruit, leaves; insects, small invertebrate and vertebrate animals
● Mona monkey	*Cercopithecus mona*	4.4 to 13.2 lb (2 to 6 kg)	southwest Africa		mostly fruit; also sprouts, young leaves, invertebrates
● Blue monkey	*Cercopithecus mitis*	8.8 to 13.2 lb (4 to 6 kg)	equatorial Africa		mainly fruit and leaves; also slow-moving slugs and worms
● De Brazza's monkey	*Cercopithecus neglectus*	8.8 to 15.4 lb (4 to 7 kg)	Africa, especially east		leaves, shoots, fruit, berries, insects, lizards
● Crowned guenon	*Cercopithecus pogonias*	5.7 to 9.9 lb (2.6 to 4.5 kg)	West Africa		fruit; also insects, leaves
● Patas monkey	*Erythrocebus patas*	14.3 to 27.3 lb (6.5 to 12.4 kg)	sub-Saharan Africa		fruit, seeds, roots, leaves, lizards, insects, bird eggs
● Grey-cheeked mangabey	*Lophocebus albigena*	24 to 55 lb (11 to 25 kg) (males)	Central Africa		mainly fruit and seeds
● Gelada baboon	*Theropithecus gelada*	28 to 46 lb (13 to 21 kg)	Ethiopia, Eritrea		herbivorous: grasses, seeds
● Yellow baboon	*Papio cynocephalus*	24 to 57 lb (11 to 26 kg)	East Africa		grasses, pods, seeds, fruit, roots, leaves, buds, bark, flowers, insects, meat
● Hamadryas baboon	*Papio hamadryas*	20 to 47 lb (9 to 21 kg)	northern Africa		omnivorous: birds, mammals; reptiles; eggs; leaves, roots, tubers, seeds, grains, nuts, fruit
● Japanese macaque	*Macaca fuscata*	19 to 25 lb (8.4 to 11.3 kg)	Japan		mainly nuts, berries, buds, leaves, bark
● Stump-tailed macaque	*Macaca arctoides*	16 to 23 lb (7 to 10.4 kg)	Southeast Asia		leaves, fruit, roots, crops
● Liontail macaque	*Macaca silenus*	6 to 22 lb (3 to 10 kg)	India, Western Ghats mountains		fruit; also leaves, stems, flowers, buds, fungi; some insects, lizards, frogs, small mammals
● Bonnet macaque	*Macaca radiata*	8 to 15 lb (4 to 7 kg)	India, Western Ghats mountains		leaves, fruit, nuts, seeds, insects, eggs; sometimes lizards
● Western red colobus	*Procolobus badius*	15 to 27 lb (7 to 12 kg)	West Africa		primarily leaves; also shoots, fruit, flowers
● Proboscis monkey	*Nasalis larvatus*	15 to 48 lb (7 to 22 kg)	Borneo		fruit, seeds, young leaves, shoots of mangrove; also some invertebrates
● Mitred leaf monkey	*Presbytis melalophos*	13.22 lb (6 kg)	Malay Peninsula, Sumatra, western Borneo		leaves, seeds, fruit, flowers, roots
● Douc langur	*Pygathrix nemaeus*	21 lb (9.6 kg)	Vietnam, Cambodia		mainly leaves; also unripe fruit, their seeds and flowers
● Hanuman langur	*Semnopithecus entellus*	22 to 29 lb (10 to 13 kg)	South and Central Asia		leaves, fruit, flowers, insects; also bark, gum, soil
● Chinese golden snub-nosed monkey	*Rhinopithecus roxellana*	36 lb (16.1 kg)	southwestern China		leaves from broadleaf trees; fir and pine needles; also buds, bark, fruit seeds
● Northern owl monkey	*Aotus trivirgatus*	1.75 lb (0.8 kg)	tropical South America		fruit; leaves, insects, spiders; also some small mammals and birds
● Black spider monkey	*Ateles paniscus*	11 to 22 lb (5 to 10 kg)	South America north of Amazon River		mainly fruit; some flowers, mature seeds, tips of roots, fungi
● Humboldt's woolly monkey	*Lagothrix lagotricha*	6 to 22 lb (3 to 10 kg)	Central and South America		fruit; also leaves, seeds, some insects
● Brown capuchin monkey	*Cebus apella*	2.9 to 10.6 lb (1.3 to 4.8 kg)	South America		fruit; also vegetation, seeds, pith, eggs, birds, small mammals, insects, reptiles
● Geoffroy's tamarin	*Saguinus geoffroyi*	0.75 to 1 lb (0.3 to 0.4 kg)	Central and South America		insects and fruit; also small lizards; flowers; nectar found in secondary growth
● Black-mantled tamarin	*Saguinus nigricollis*	1 lb (0.45 kg)	South America		insects, leaves, fruit
● Golden-headed lion tamarin	*Leontopithecus chrys-omelas*	0.8 to 1.6 lb (0.3 to 0.7 kg)	Brazil		insectivorous, frugivorous; also invertebrates such as spiders and snails
● Common marmoset	*Callithrix jacchus*	10.6 to 12.69 oz (300 to 360 g)	Brazil		tree sap; also insects, spiders, fruit flowers, nectar
● White-eared marmoset	*Callithrix aurita*	10.78 oz (306 g)	Brazil		insectivorous: ants, termites, larvae, caterpillars, insect galls, large-winged insects
● Goeldi's marmoset	*Callimico goeldii*	13.85 to 30.31 oz (393 to 860 g)	northern Amazon forests of South America		plant matter, including berries; insects; small vertebrates
● Bolivian titi monkey	*Callicebus donacophilus*	33.5 oz (950g)	Bolivia, Brazil		primarily frugivorous; also leaves, seeds, insects
● Brown bearded saki monkey	*Chiroptes satanas*	5.7 to 7 lb (2.6 to 3.2 kg)	Northern Amazonian and Guianas, South America		seeds of fruit and nuts; also fruit, flowers, leaf stalks, insects
APES AND TARSIERS					
● Western lowland gorilla	*Gorilla gorilla*	396.48 lb (180 kg)	West Africa		plant material, such as leaves, buds, berries, stalks, bark, ferns
● Red-cheeked gibbon	*Nomascus gabriellae*	15.4 to 24.2 lb (7 to 11 kg)	southeastern Asia		leaves, flowers, shoots, insects
● Hoolock gibbon	*Hoolock hoolock*	13 to 15 lb (6 to 6.8 kg)	southern Asia		fruit, leaves, shoots; sometimes spiders, insects, larvae, bird eggs
● Spectral tarsier	*Tarsius tarsier*	2.82 to 5.81 oz (80 to 165 g)	Indonesia		ants, beetles, cockroaches, scorpions, lizards, bats, snakes, birds, small mammals

● ALERT	● DOMESTICATED				
● IN TROUBLE	● UNDER STUDY				
● STABLE	● NOT LISTED				

COMMON NAME	SCIENTIFIC NAME	SIZE	RANGE	HABITAT	DIET
DUCKS, GEESE, AND SWANS					
Mandarin duck	*Aix galericulata*	16 to 19.3 in (41 to 49 cm)	China, eastern Siberia, Japan		aquatic plants, rice
Mallard duck	*Anas platyrhynchos*	19.7 to 25.6 in (50 to 65 cm)	worldwide		insects, aquatic invertebrates and vegetation, seeds, grains
Northern pintail duck	*Anas acuta*	20.1 to 29.9 in (51 to 76 cm)	worldwide		grains, seeds, aquatic insects, crustaceans
American black duck	*Anas rubripes*	21.3 to 23.2 in (54 to 59 cm)	Canada to the Gulf Coast and Bermuda		seeds, roots, grains, aquatic plants, fish
Speckled teal	*Anas flavirostris*	14.6 to 16.9 in (37 to 43 cm)	eastern South America		seeds, insects, vegetation
Eurasian wigeon	*Anas penelope*	16.5 to 20.5 in (42 to 52 cm)	Europe, Asia, Africa, United States		seeds, insects, vegetation
Northern shoveler	*Anas clypeata*	17.3 to 20.1 in (44 to 51 cm)	Europe, Asia, Africa, North America		seeds and insects
White-winged scoter	*Melanitta fusca*	18.9 to 22.8 in (48 to 58 cm)	Europe, Asia, Canada, coastal U.S.		mollusks, crustaceans, insects
Canvasback duck	*Aythya valisineria*	18.9 to 22 in (48 to 56 cm)	Mexico, United States, western Canada		seeds, vegetation, insects
Surf scoter	*Melanitta perspicillata*	17 to 19 in (44 to 48 cm)	Canada, U.S., Baja California, British Isles		freshwater invertebrates
Bufflehead	*Bucephala albeola*	12.6 to 15.7 in (32 to 40 cm)	Canada, U.S., northern Mexico		seeds and aquatic invertebrates
Lesser scaup	*Aythya affinis*	15.4 to 18.1 in (39 to 46 cm)	Canada, U.S., Central America, Caribbean		aquatic vegetation and insects, seeds, crustaceans
Hawaiian goose	*Branta sandvicensis*	21 to 27 in (53 to 69 cm)	Hawaiian Islands		grasses, seeds, berries, flowers
Egyptian goose	*Alopochen aegyptiaca*	25 to 29 in (63 to 73 cm)	Africa and Europe		grains and vegetation, some insects
Greylag goose	*Anser anser*	29.92 to 35.04 in (76 to 89 cm)	Europe, western Russia, northern Africa		grasses, plants, aquatic animals
Tundra swan	*Cygnus columbianus*	47.2 to 57.9 in (120 to 147 cm)	Siberia, Alaska, Canada, Europe, Asia, U.S.		aquatic plants, seeds, grains
Northern screamer	*Chauna chavaria*	34 in (86 cm)	northwestern Venezuela and northern Colombia		aquatic vegetation
Southern screamer	*Chauna torquata*	32 to 37 in (81 to 95 cm)	much of South America		plants, seeds, leaves
Magpie goose	*Anseranas semipalmata*	27.6 to 35.4 in (70 to 90 cm)	Australia and New Guinea		seeds and grasses
CHICKENS, TURKEYS, AND RELATIVES					
Vulturine guineafowl	*Acryllium vulturinum*	24 to 28 in (61 to 71 cm)	central East Africa		seeds, roots, insects
Northern bobwhite quail	*Colinus virginianus*	8 to 9.7 in (20.3 to 24.7 cm)	from southeastern Ontario to Mexico		vegetation, fruit, invertebrates
Bearded-wood partridge	*Dendrortyx barbatus*	13.4 in (34 cm)	Mexico, mainly along the Gulf Coast		fruit, nuts, vegetation
Chukar	*Alectoris chukar*	13 to 14 in (32 to 35 cm)	Greece to Asia; U.S., Hawaii, New Zealand		grasses, seeds, fruit
Black francolin	*Francolinus francolinus*	13.4 to 14.3 in (34 to 36 cm)	Middle East, South Asia		vegetation and insects
Indian peafowl	*Pavo cristatus*	59 in (150 cm)	Asia, Australia, New Zealand, U.S., Bahamas		vegetation, insects, worms, frogs, snakes
Himalayan monal pheasant	*Lophophorus impejanus*	24.8 to 28.3 in (63 to 72 cm)	South Asia and China		vegetation, seeds, insects
Domestic chicken	*Gallus gallus domesticus*	14 to 34 in (35.6 to 86.4 cm)	worldwide		insects, seeds, grains, mice, small reptiles
Satyr tragopan	*Tragopan satyra*	24.02 to 28 in (61 to 71 cm)	central and eastern parts of Himalaya		vegetation, berries, fruit
Temminck's tragopan	*Tragopan temminckii*	25.2 in (64 cm)	China, India, Myanmar, Vietnam		vegetation, seeds, insects
Spruce grouse	*Falcipennis canadensis*	15.4 to 15.7 in (39 to 40 cm)	Canada and northern U.S.		pine and spruce needles; invertebrates
Willow ptarmigan	*Lagopus lagopus*	13.8 to 17.3 in (35 to 44 cm)	Arctic North America, Greenland, Europe, Asia		insects, willow buds, grasses, roots, flowers seeds
Greater prairie chicken	*Tympanuchus cupido*	16.9 in (43 cm)	midwestern United States		leaves, buds, fruit, insects
Chacalaca, plain	*Ortalis vetula*	21.7 in (55 cm)	Central America, Mexico, southern Texas (U.S.A.)		leaves, berries, buds
Wattled curassow	*Crax globulosa*	32.3 in to 35 in (82 to 89 cm)	northern half of South America		fish, insects, fruit, seeds
Blue-throated piping guan	*Pipile cumanensis*	27.2 in (69 cm)	northern half of South America		fruit and flowers
Maleo scrub fowl	*Macrocephalon maleo*	21.7 to 23.6 in (55 to 60 cm)	Sulawesi and Buton Islands of Indonesia		fruit, seeds, insects
Hamerkop	*Scopus umbretta*	22 in (56 cm)	Africa, Saudi Arabia, Yemen		frogs, fish, insects

COMMON NAME	SCIENTIFIC NAME	SIZE	RANGE	HABITAT	DIET
NIGHTJARS, POTOOS, AND RELATIVES					
Lyre-tailed nightjar	*Uropsalis lyra*	23.6 in (60 cm)	mountains of South America		insects
Common paraque	*Nyctidromus albicollis*	8.7 to 11.8 in (22 to 30 cm)	Texas (U.S.A.), Mexico, Cent. and South America		insects
Common nighthawk	*Chordeiles minor*	8.7 to 9.4 in (22 to 24 cm)	North, Central, and South America		insects
Whip-poor-will	*Caprimulgus vociferus*	8.7 to 10.2 in (22 to 26 cm)	Canada to Central America		insects
Oilbird	*Steatornis caripensis*	16.1 to 19.3 in (41 to 49 cm)	Panama and northern half of South America		insects
HUMMINGBIRDS AND SWIFTS					
Blue-throated hummingbird	*Lampornis clemenciae*	4.5 to 5.3 in (11.5 to 13.5 cm)	Arizona to New Mexico; Texas (U.S.A.)		nectar
Rufous-tailed hummingbird	*Amazilia tzacatl*	4 to 4.8 in (10 to 12 cm)	Central-east Mexico to Ecuador		nectar
Ruby-throated hummingbird	*Archilochus colubris*	2.8 to 3.5 in (7 to 9 cm)	North America to Costa Rica and Caribbean		nectar
Allen's hummingbird	*Selasphorus sasin*	3.3 to 3.8 in (7.5 to 9 cm)	Pacific coast of North America to Mexico		nectar
Common swift	*Apus apus*	6.3 to 6.7 in (16 to 17 cm)	Europe to North Africa; east to Siberia and China		insects
White-throated swift	*Aeronautes saxatalis*	6.5 in (16.5 cm)	western U.S., Mexico, Central America		insects
Fork-tailed swift	*Apus pacificus*	7.1 to 8.3 in (18 to 21 cm)	Southeast Asia, eastern Russia, south to Australia		insects
Chimney swift	*Chaetura pelagica*	4.7 to 5.9 in (12 to 15 cm)	North and South America		insects
PARROTS					
Salmon-crested cockatoo	*Cacatua moluccensis*	19.7 in (50 cm)	South Maluku, Indonesia		seeds, fruit, nuts, insects
Sulfur-crested cockatoo	*Cacatua galerita*	23.6 in (60 cm)	Australia, New Zealand, New Guinea		seeds, fruit, nuts, insects
Cockatiel	*Nymphicus hollandicus*	12.8 in (32 cm)	throughout Australia; introduced to Tasmania		fruit, berries, insects
Violet-necked lory	*Eos squamata*	10.6 in (27 cm)	Maluku Islands, Indonesia		fruit and insects
Kakapo	*Strigops habroptila*	25.2 in (64 cm)	southernmost New Zealand		fruit, seeds, vegetation
Kea	*Nestor notabilis*	18.9 in (48 cm)	mountains of South Island, New Zealand		leaves, buds, nuts
Fischer's lovebird	*Agapornis fischeri*	5 to 5.9 in (12.7 to 15 cm)	north-central Tanzania		seeds and fruit
Sun conure	*Aratinga solstitialis*	11.8 in (30 cm)	northern Brazil and the Guianas into Venezuela		seeds, fruit, berries
Eclectus parrot	*Eclectus roratus*	13.8 in (35 cm)	New Guinea region		seeds, fruit, nuts, berries
Puerto Rican Amazon parrot	*Amazona vittata*	11.8 in (30 cm)	Puerto Rico		fruit, flowers, leaves, seeds
Thick-billed parrot	*Rhynchopsitta pachyrhyncha*	15 in (38 cm)	western Sierra Madres of Mexico		pine nuts
Hyacinth macaw	*Anodorhynchus hyacinthinus*	37.4 to 39.4 in (95 to 100 cm)	Eastern Amazon in Brazil; east Bolivia, Paraguay		nuts and seeds
Scarlet macaw	*Ara macao*	31.5 to 38.4 in (80 to 96.5 cm)	southern Mexico, Central and South America		fruit and nuts
Brown-throated parakeet	*Aratinga pertinax*	9.8 in (25 cm)	northernmost South America into Panama		seeds, fruit, nuts, insects
Budgerigar	*Melopsittacus undulatus*	5.9 to 7.9 in (15 to 20 cm)	Australia, southwest Florida (U.S.A.)		grasses and crop plants
Sun parakeet	*Aratinga solstitialis*	11.8 in (30 cm)	northern Brazil and the Guianas into Venezuela		seeds, nuts, fruit, insects
Senegal parrot	*Poicephalus senegalus*	7.9 to 9.8 in (20 to 25 cm)	western sub-Saharan Africa		fruit, seeds, grains
WOODPECKERS, TOUCANS, AND RELATIVES					
Acorn woodpecker	*Melanerpes formicivorus*	7.5 to 9.1 in (19 to 23 cm)	U.S., Mexico, and Central America		insects, acorns, sap, fruit
Arizona woodpecker	*Picoides arizonae*	7.1 to 7.9 in (18 to 20 cm)	Sierra Madre Mts. in U.S., Mexico to Arizona, U.S.		insects, larvae, fruit, acorns
Black-backed woodpecker	*Picoides arcticus*	9.1 in (23 cm)	Alaska to New England region in U.S.		larvae and insects
Lemon-throated barbet	*Eubucco richardsoni*	5.1 to 6.3 in (13 to 16 cm)	northwestern South America		insects and fruit
Scarlet-hooded barbet	*Eubucco tucinkae*	6.7 in (17 cm)	eastern Peru, slightly into Brazil and Bolivia		insects and fruit
Keel billed toucan	*Ramphastos sulfuratus*	17 to 22 in (42 to 55 cm)	southern Mexico to Colombia and Venezuela		fruit, small reptiles, tree frogs
Channel-billed toucan	*Ramphastos vitellinus*	19.7 in (50 cm)	northern South America		fruit, small reptiles, tree frogs
Collared aracari	*Pteroglossus torquatus*	16.1 in (41 cm)	Southern Mexico to Colombia and Venezuela		insects, eggs, fruit
Saffron toucanet	*Pteroglossus bailloni*	13.8 to 15.4 in (35 to 39 cm)	southern Brazil and just into Paraguay		fruit

COMMON NAME	SCIENTIFIC NAME	SIZE	RANGE	HABITAT	DIET
Whitehead's trogon	*Harpactes whiteheadi*	11.4 in (29 cm)	northern Borneo (island in Southeast Asia)		insects
Guanan puffbird	*Notharchus macrorhynchos*	11.4 in (29 cm)	Guianas into Brazil and Venezuela		insects and other invertebrates
Black-fronted nunbird	*Monasa nigrifrons*	9.8 in (25 cm)	Amazon River region of South America		insects and other invertebrates
Three-toed jacamar	*Jacamaralcyon tridactyla*	5.5 to 13 in (14 to 34 cm)	southeastern Brazil		insects

RATITES					
Slaty-breasted tinamou	*Crypturellus boucardi*	10.8 in (27.5 cm)	parts of Central America just into Mexico		insects, fruit, seeds
Great spotted kiwi	*Apteryx haastii*	17.7 to 19.7 in (45 to 50 cm)	South Island, New Zealand		insects, snails, spiders, earthworms, crayfish, fruits

GULLS, PUFFINS, AND SANDPIPERS					
Tufted puffin	*Fratercula cirrhata*	14.2 to 15.7 in (36 to 40 cm)	northern Pacific Ocean		fish
Black guillemot	*Cepphus grylle*	12.6 to 14.9 in (32 to 38 cm)	north Atlantic and Arctic Oceans		fish
Ancient murrelet	*Synthliboramphus antiquus*	7.9 to 9.4 in (20 to 24 cm)	north Pacific coasts		fish
Cassin's auklet	*Ptychoramphus aleuticus*	9.1 in (23 cm)	Pacific coasts of North America		insects
Marbled auk	*Brachyramphus marmoratus*	9.4 to 9.8 in (24 to 25 cm)	Pacific coasts of North America		fish
Eurasian stone curlew	*Burhinus oedicnemus*	15.7 to 17.3 in (40 to 44 cm)	Europe, Asia, northern Africa		invertebrates and small mammals
Killdeer	*Charadrius vociferus*	7.9 to 11 in (20 to 28 cm)	North America; Central America to South America		insects, other invertebrates
Black-bellied plover	*Pluvialis squatarola*	11 to 11.4 in (28 to 29 cm)	Arctic; all tropical and subtropical coasts		insects, other invertebrates
Southern lapwing	*Vanellus chilensis*	12.6 to 15 in (32 to 38 cm)	most of South America		insects, other invertebrates
Snowy sheathbill	*Chionis albus*	13.4 to 16.1 in (34 to 41 cm)	Antarctic Peninsula, eastern Argentina		invertebrates and carrion
Burchell's courser	*Cursorius rufus*	9.4 in (24 cm)	Angola, Botswana, Namibia, South Africa		insects and seeds
Australian pratincole	*Stiltia isabella*	7.5 to 9.4 in (19 to 24 cm)	Australia to Indonesia and New Guinea		insects and spiders
Black oystercatcher	*Haematopus bachmani*	16.5 to 18.5 in (42 to 47 cm)	Pacific coast of North America to Baja California		mussels and limpets
Northern jacana	*Jacana spinosa*	6.7 to 9 in (17 to 23 cm)	Mexico to Panama, including Caribbean		insects
Californian gull	*Larus californicus*	18. to 21.3 in (4 to 54 cm)	parts of North America to Mexico; Canada		fish, insects, small mammals, grains
Western gull	*Larus occidentalis*	22 to 26 in (56 to 66 cm)	Pacific coast of North America to Baja California		marine invertebrates and fish
Elegant tern	*Sterna elegans*	15.4 to 16.5 in (39 to 42 cm)	Pacific coast of the Americas		fish and invertebrates
Plains wanderer	*Pedionomus torquatus*	5.9 to 7.5 in (15 to 19 cm)	Australia		seeds, invertebrates, leaves
Double-banded sandgrouse	*Pterocles bicinctus*	7.1 in (18 cm)	southern Africa		seeds
Hawaiian stilt	*Himantopus mexicanus knudseni*	13.8 to 15.4 in (35 to 39 cm)	eastern Hawaiian Islands		small fish, seeds, insects
Painted snipe	*Rostratula australis*	8.7 to 9.8 (22 to 25 cm)	eastern Australia		invertebrates, insects, seeds
Spotted sandpiper	*Actitis macularia*	7.1 to 7.9 in (18 to 20 cm)	Americas, including Caribbean		invertebrates, small fish, insects
Sanderling	*Calidris alba*	7.1 to 7.9 in (18 to 20 cm)	Arctic areas; coastlines of all oceans and seas		invertebrates
Black turnstone	*Arenaria melanocephala*	8.7 to 9.8 in (22 to 25 cm)	North American coasts; Ecuador		aquatic invertebrates
Marbled godwit	*Limosa fedoa*	16.5 to 18.9 in (42 to 48 cm)	Canada; coasts of the U.S. and Mexico		insects
Sandpiper stilt	*Calidris himantopus*	7.9 to 9.1 in (20 to 23 cm)	Arctic; U.S., Cent. and S. Am., Caribbean		insects
Long-billed curlew	*Numenius americanus*	19.7 to 25.6 in (50 to 65 cm)	Canada, U.S., and Mexico		insects, crustaceans, other invertebrates
Africa-Greater yellowlegs	*Tringa melanoleuca*	11.5 to 16 in (29 to 40 cm)	Canada, U.S., Mex., Cent. and S. Am., Caribbean		invertebrates, frogs, seeds, berries
Long-tailed jaeger	*Stercorarius longicaudus*	15 in (38 cm)	North Pole, South America, South Africa		rodents, small birds, insects
Least seedsnipe	*Thinocorus rumicivorus*	5.9 in (15 cm)	South America		seeds and vegetation

ALBATROSSES, PELICANS, AND RELATIVES					
Oriental darter	*Anhinga melanogaster*	28 to 31.1 in (71 to 79 cm)	South and Southeast Asia		fish
Brandt's cormorant	*Phalacrocorax penicillatus*	27.6 to 31.1 in (70 to 79 cm)	Pacific coast of North America		fish and squid
Pelagic cormorant	*Phalacrocorax pelagicus*	20.1 to 29.9 in (51 to 76 cm)	Pacific coasts of Asia and North America		fish and marine invertebrates
Red-tailed tropicbird	*Phaethon rubricauda*	30.7 to 31.9 in (78 to 81 cm)	tropical waters of the Indian and Pacific Oceans		fish and squid

COMMON NAME	SCIENTIFIC NAME	SIZE	RANGE	HABITAT	DIET
Masked booby	Sula dactylatra	29.1 to 33.9 in (74 to 86 cm)	tropical waters worldwide		fish and squid
Red-footed booby	Sula sula	27.2 to 31.1 in (69 to 79 cm)	tropical and subtropical waters worldwide		fish and squid
Wandering albatross	Diomedea exulans	3.5 to 4.4 ft (1.1 to 1.3 m)	oceans south of the Tropic of Capricorn		fish and squid
Royal albatross	Diomedea epomophora	42.1 to 48 in (107 to 122 cm)	southern oceans worldwide		cephalopods, fish, crustaceans
Magellanic diving petrel	Pelecanoides magellani	7.48 in (19 cm)	southern South America and Falkland Islands		crustaceans, other aquatic invertebrates, small fish
Polynesian storm petrel	Nesofregetta fuliginosa	9.4 to 10.2 in (24 to 26 cm)	tropical Pacific Ocean islands		fish, cephalopods, crustaceans
Cory's shearwater	Calonectris diomedea	18.1 in (46 cm)	Atlantic Ocean to Gulf of Mexico; Med. Sea		squid, crustaceans, fish
Northern flicker	Colaptes auratus	11 to 12.2 in (28 to 31 cm)	North and Central America; Greater Antilles		insects, fruit, seeds
HERONS, FLAMINGOS, AND RELATIVES					
Yellow-crowned night heron	Nyctanassa violacea	21.7 to 27.6 in (55 to 70 cm)	U.S., Mex., Cent. and S. America, Caribbean		crustaceans, reptiles, small mammals
Black crowned night heron	Nycticorax nycticorax	22.8 to 26 in (58 to 66 cm)	North America, Africa; Europe into Asia		invertebrates, fish, rodents, lizards
Little blue heron	Egretta caerulea	22 to 29.1 in (56 to 74 cm)	North America to South America		small fish, frogs, invertebrates
Boat-billed heron	Cochlearius cochlearius	21.3 in (54 cm)	Mexico to northern half of South America		fish, crustaceans, insects
Snowy egret	Egretta thula	22 to 26 in (56 to 66 cm)	North, Central, and South America		fish, crustaceans, insects
Reddish egret	Egretta rufescens	27.6 to 31.5 in (70 to 80 cm)	Caribbean; Mexico to Cent. and S. America		small fish, frogs, crustaceans
Wood stork	Mycteria americana	33.5 to 45.3 in (85 to 115 cm)	Mexico, Caribbean, Cent. and S. America		small fish; frogs; insects, other invertebrates
Sacred ibis	Threskiornis aethiopicus	25.5 to 29.5 in (65 to 75 cm)	sub-Saharan Africa to Iraq; Europe		frogs, reptiles, fish
Speckled mousebird	Colius striatus	14 in (35.6 cm)	most of sub-Saharan Africa		fruit, leaves, buds
PIGEONS AND DOVES					
White-tipped dove	Leptotila verreauxi	9.8 to 12.2 in (25 to 31 cm)	Mexico; Central and South America		seeds, fruit, invertebrates
African-collared dove	Streptopelia roseogrisea	10.2 to 10.6 in (26 to 27 cm)	the Arabian Peninsula and northern Africa		seeds
Common ground dove	Columbina passerina	5.9 to 7.1 in (15 to 18 cm)	southern U.S. to northern South America		seeds and vegetation
Domestic dove	Streptopelia risoria	12 in (30.5 cm)	Africa, Caribbean, U.S.		grains and seeds
Band-tailed pigeon	Columba fasciata	13 to 5.7 in (33 to 40 cm)	British Columbia, Canada to Argentina		seeds, fruit, flowers
Mauritius pink pigeon	Nesoenas mayeri	13 in (32 cm)	Mauritius		buds, leaves, flowers, fruit, seeds
White-crowned pigeon	Columba leucocephala	13 to 13.8 in (33 to 35 cm)	Caribbean and Bahamas to south Florida		fruit and berries; sometimes insects
White-naped pigeon	Columba albinucha	13.4 in (34 cm)	Africa: Lake Albert region and Cameroon		berries and fruit
Inca dove	Columbina inca	7.1 to 9.1 in (18 to 23 cm)	southwestern U.S. and northern Central America		seeds
KINGFISHERS, HORNBILLS, AND RELATIVES					
Amazon kingfisher	Chloroceryle amazona	11.4 to 11.8 in (29 to 30 cm)	Mexico, Central America, South America		insects and amphibians
African pygmy kingfisher	Ceyx pictus	4.7 in (12 cm)	sub-Saharan Africa except southwestern tip		insects and amphibians
Lilac-cheeked kingfisher	Cittura cyanotis	11 in (28 cm)	central Indonesia		insects
Woodland kingfisher	Halcyon senegalensis	7.9 to 9.1 in (20 to 23 cm)	sub-Saharan Africa except southern tip		invertebrates, insects, fish, other birds
Blue-winged kookaburra	Dacelo leachii	11 to 17 in (28 to 42 cm)	northern Australia; southern New Guinea		snakes and invertebrates
Laughing kookaburra	Dacelo novaeguineae	17.7 in (45 cm)	Eastern and southern Australia; Tasmania		fish, invertebrates, insects, reptiles
Southern yellow billed hornbill	Tockus leucomelas	18.9 to 23.6 in (48 to 60 cm)	Southern Africa		small animals, fruit, insects
Northern ground hornbill	Bucorvus abyssinicus	39.3 in (100 cm)	belt across Africa from Mauritania to Ethiopia		reptiles, mammals, insects
Indian roller	Coracias benghalensis	12.6 to 13.5 in (32 to 34 cm)	India east to northern Southeast Asia		insects and amphibians
Dollarbird	Eurystomus orientalis	9.8 to 11.4 in (25 to 29 cm)	eastern Asia to Australian coasts		insects
Rainbow bee-eater	Merops ornatus	7.4 to 10.6 in (19 to 27 cm)	Australia; eastern Indonesia to Solomon Islands		bees and wasps
Blue-crowned motmot	Momotus momota	15.7 in (40 cm)	northeastern Mexico to northern Argentina		insects and fruit
Green wood hoopoe	Phoeniculus purpureus	17 in (43.2 cm)	sub-Saharan Africa except Congo River basin		insects and spiders
Jamaican tody	Todus todus	3.5 to 4.3 in (9 to 11 cm)	Jamaica		insects and fruit

COMMON NAME	SCIENTIFIC NAME	SIZE	RANGE	HABITAT	DIET
CUCKOOS AND RELATIVES					
Common cuckoo	*Cuculus canorus*	13 in (33 cm)	Europe, Asia, sub-Saharan Africa		insects
Striped cuckoo	*Tapera naevia*	11.8 in (30 cm)	southern Mexico to South America		insects
Yellow-billed cuckoo	*Coccyzus americanus*	10.2 to 11.8 in (26 to 30 cm)	Canada, U.S., Mexico; Caribbean, South America		insects and reptiles
Smooth billed ani	*Crotophaga ani*	11.8 to 14.2 in (30 to 36 cm)	Caribbean into South America		insects, lizards, fruit
Livingstone's turaco	*Tauraco livingstonii*	17.7 in (45 cm)	southeastern Africa from Tanzania to South Africa		fruit
White-bellied go-away bird	*Corythaixoides leucogaster*	13.8 to 29.5 in (35 to 75 cm)	horn of Africa south to Tanzania		fruit, invertebrates, seeds
Gray turaco	*Corythaixoides concolor*	18.1 to 20.1 in (46 to 51 cm)	across southern Africa except southern tip		fruit, flowers, leaves, insects
Prince Ruspoli's turaco	*Tauraco ruspolii*	15.7 in (40 cm)	southern Ethiopia		fruit
EAGLES, FALCONS, HAWKS, AND OWLS					
African fish eagle	*Haliaeetus vocifer*	24.8 to 30.3 in (63 to 77 cm)	sub-Saharan Africa		fish
Golden eagle	*threskiornis aethiopicus*	27.5 to 33 in (78 to 80 cm)	Europe, Asia, Africa, North America		mammals, birds, reptiles
Tawny eagle	*Aquila rapax*	25.5 to 28.3 in (65 to 72 cm)	Romania to Mongolia, India, and Africa		small animals, carrion, insects
Harpy eagle	*Harpia harpyja*	35 in (89.9 cm)	Mexico through northern South America		sloths, primates, reptiles, birds, small mammals
Common black hawk	*Buteogallus anthracinus*	21 in (53 cm)	U.S. to South America; Cuba; Isle of Pines		snakes, frogs, fish, crabs
Roadside hawk	*Buteo magnirostris*	12.2 to 16.1 in (31 to 41 cm)	Mexican coasts, Central America, South America		insects and small mammals
Swallow tailed kite	*Elanoides forficatus*	22.8 in (58 cm)	southeastern U.S. and northern South America		insects, snakes, frogs
Secretary bird	*Sagittarius serpentarius*	34 in (86.4 cm)	sub-Saharan Africa		insects and small mammals
Northern goshawk	*Accipiter gentilis*	21.6 to 24 in (55 to 61 cm)	parts of North America; Europe; parts of Asia		birds, mammals, invertebrates, reptiles
Common turkey vulture	*Cathartes aura*	25.2 to 31.8 in (64 to 81 cm)	throughout the Americas except Canada		carrion, rotten fruit and vegetables, insects, reptiles
King vulture	*Sarcoramphus papa*	27.9 to 31.8 in (71 to 81 cm)	Mexico to South America		carrion
Merlin	*Falco columbarius*	9.4 to 11.8 in (24 to 30 cm)	parts of Northern Hemisphere		small birds
Peregrine falcon	*Falco peregrinus*	14.1 to 22.8 in (36 to 58 cm)	worldwide except rain forests and arctic regions		birds
Lesser kestrel	*Falco naumanni*	11.8 to 14.2 in (30 to 36 cm)	Europe and Asia; most of sub-Saharan Africa		small mammals
Common kestrel	*Falco tinnunculus*	11.8 to 14.1 in (30 to 36 cm)	Europe, Asia, sub-Saharan Africa		small mammals, reptiles, amphibians
Crested caracara	*Caracara cheriway*	20.9 to 22.8 in (53 to 58 cm)	U.S.–Mexico border to Panama		insects, fish, invertebrates
Long-eared owl	*Asio otus*	13.8 to 15.7 in (35 to 40 cm)	North America and Eurasia		small mammals
Eurasian eagle-owl	*Bubo bubo*	22.8 in (58 cm)	Eurasia except polar regions and southern Asia		mammals and birds
Barred owl	*Strix varia*	16.9 to 19.7 in (43 to 50 cm)	eastern U.S. and southern Canada		mammals, birds, amphibians, reptiles
Spotted owl	*Strix occidentalis*	18.5 to 18.9 in (47 to 48 cm)	western North America		small mammals
Boreal owl	*Aegolius funereus*	8.3 to 11 in (21 to 28 cm)	Alaska, Canada, northern Eurasia		small mammals, birds, insects
Elf owl	*Micrathene whitneyi*	4.9 to 5.6 in (12.4 to 14.2 cm)	southwestern U.S. through western Mexico		insects, small mammals, reptiles
Tawny owl	*Strix aluco*	15 in (38 cm)	Europe to Asia; Himalaya to coast of China		small mammals, birds, insects
Northern hawk-owl	*Surnia ulula*	15.5 in (39.4 cm)	Alaska and Canada; northern Eurasia		small mammals
Mottled owl	*Strix virgata*	12.2 in (31 cm)	Mexico; Central and South America		insects, small mammals, birds, reptiles
LOONS AND GREBES					
Arctic loon	*Gavia arctica*	15.7 to 31.8 in (40 to 81 cm)	Arctic to Baja California; Med., East China Sea		fish
White or yellow billed diver loon	*Gavia adamsii*	35 in (88.9 cm)	Arctic North Am., Europe, Asia, Gulf of Alaska		fish and other aquatic animals
Pacific loon	*Gavia pacifica*	22.8 to 29.1 in (58 to 74 cm)	western coast of U.S.; northern Canada; Alaska		fish and other aquatic animals
CRANES, BUSTARDS, AND RELATIVES					
Sunbittern	*Eurypyga helias*	18.5 in (47 cm)	South America to Central America and Mexico		fish, amphibians, crustaceans, insects
Masked finfoot	*Heliopais personatus*	22 in (56 cm)	Bangladesh to Sumatra in Indonesia		small fish and insects
Limpkin	*Aramus guarauna*	25.2 to 28.7 in (64 to 73 cm)	U.S.; Caribbean; Mexico to Argentina		snails and mussels

BIRDS

COMMON NAME	SCIENTIFIC NAME	SIZE	RANGE	HABITAT	DIET
Red-legged seriema	*Cariama cristata*	35.4 in (90 cm)	South America		insects, rodents, lizards, birds
Wattled crane	*Bugeranus carunculatus*	68.9 in (175 cm)	eastern Africa from Ethiopia to South Africa		vegetation and insects
Siberian crane	*Grus leucogeranus*	45.3 in (115 cm)	Russia to western Siberia; Iran, India, China		insects, small mammals, fish
American coot	*Fulica americana*	15 in (38 cm)	southern Canada and the U.S.		aquatic plants and insects
King rail	*Rallus elegans*	15 to 18.9 in (38 to 48 cm)	Eastern U.S. to Mexico and Caribbean		crustaceans, small fish, insects
Subdesert mesite	*Monias benschi*	11.8 to 12.6 in (30 to 32 cm)	Madagascar		invertebrates, seeds, fruit

ANTBIRDS AND RELATIVES

COMMON NAME	SCIENTIFIC NAME	SIZE	RANGE	HABITAT	DIET
Olivaceous woodcreeper	*Sittasomus griseicapillus*	5.2 to 7.6 in (13.1 to 19.3 cm)	South and Central America		invertebrates
Rufous-fronted antthrush	*Formicarius rufifrons*	7.1 in (18 cm)	Bolivia, Brazil, Peru		invertebrates
Giant antpitta	*Grallaria gigantea*	10.4 in (26.5 cm)	Colombia, Ecuador		insects and larvae
Zimmer's tapaculos	*Scytalopus zimmeri*	3. to 5.5 in (10 to 14 cm)	Argentina, Bolivia		insects
Black-chinned antbird	*Hypocnemoides melanopogon*	4.3 to 4.7 in (11 to 12 cm)	South America		insects

FLYCATCHERS

COMMON NAME	SCIENTIFIC NAME	SIZE	RANGE	HABITAT	DIET
Acadian flycatcher	*Empidonax virescens*	5.9 in (15 cm)	eastern United States and northern South America		insects and larvae
Olive-sided flycatcher	*Contopus cooperi*	7.1 to 7.9 in (18 to 20 cm)	North, Central, and South America		insects
Yellow-bellied flycatcher	*Empidonax flaviventris*	5.1 to 5.9 in (13 to 15 cm)	northern U.S., Canada, Central Mexico		insects and fruit
Hammond's flycatcher	*Empidonax hammondii*	4.7 to 5.5 in (12 to 14 cm)	western U.S. and Canada, Central America		insects
Black phoebe	*Sayornis nigricans*	6.3 in (16 cm)	southern U.S., Mexico, northern South America		insects, small fish, berries
Rose-throated becard	*Pachyramphus aglaiae*	6.3 to 7.1 in (16 to 18 cm)	Central America, coastal Mexico		insects, berries, seeds
Red-capped manakin	*Pipra mentalis*	3.9 in (10 cm)	Central America, northern South America		fruit
Andean cock-of-the-rock	*Rupicola peruvianus*	12.6 in (32 cm)	Andes		fruit and insects

CROWS AND RELATIVES

COMMON NAME	SCIENTIFIC NAME	SIZE	RANGE	HABITAT	DIET
Common raven	*Corvus corax*	27.17 in (69 cm)	North and Central America; Europe; Africa; Asia		amphibians, reptiles, birds, small mammals, carrion
Green jay	*Cyanocorax yncas*	11.4 in (29 cm)	Texas (U.S.A.) to Honduras; South America		arthropods, invertebrates, fruit
Western scrub-jay	*Aphelocoma californica*	11 to 11.8 in (28 to 30 cm)	western United States and parts of Mexico		insects, fruit, nuts
Black-billed magpie	*Pica hudsonia*	17.7 to 23.6 in (45 to 60 cm)	western North America; parts of southwest U.S.		invertebrates, grains, acorns, carrion
Magnificent bird of paradise	*Diphyllodes magnificus*	6.3 to 10.2 in (16 to 26 cm)	mountains of New Guinea		fruit and insects
Blue bird of paradise	*Paradisaea rudolphi*	11.8 in (30 cm)	mountains of Papua New Guinea		fruit
Loggerhead shrike	*Lanius ludovicianus*	7.9 to 9.1 in (20 to 23 cm)	southern Canada; United States; Mexico		insects, amphibians, reptiles, birds
White-eyed vireo	*Vireo griseus*	5 in (12.7 cm)	eastern U.S., eastern Mexico; Belize; Caribbean		insects
Elepaio monarch flycatcher	*Chasiempis sandwichensis*	5.5 in (14 cm)	island of Hawaii		insects and spiders

SONGBIRDS

COMMON NAME	SCIENTIFIC NAME	SIZE	RANGE	HABITAT	DIET
Horned lark	*Eremophila alpestris*	6.3 to 7.9 in (16 to 20 cm)	North America; arctic Eurasia; Europe to China		seeds and insects
Mountain chickadee	*Poecile gambeli*	4.3 to 5.5 in (11 to 14 cm)	Canada and U.S.		insects and spiders
Tufted titmouse	*Baeolophus bicolor*	5.5 to 6.3 in (14 to 16 cm)	eastern half of United States		insects, berries, nuts
Brown creeper	*Certhia americana*	4.7 to 5.5 in (12 to 14 cm)	U.S., Canada, Mexico, Central America		insects, spiders, invertebrates
Sedge wren	*Cistothorus platensis*	3.9 to 4.7 in (10 to 12 cm)	U.S., Canada, Central and South America		insects and spiders
Wood thrush	*Hylocichla mustelina*	6.3 to 6.7 in (16 to 17 cm)	eastern N. America; Central America to Mexico		insects and fruit
Western bluebird	*Sialia mexicana*	7.5 to 8.3 in (19 to 21 cm)	western North America		insects and fruit
American dipper	*Cinclus mexicanus*	7.9 to 11 in (2 to 28 cm)	western North America through Central America		invertebrates and fruit
Black-and-white warbler	*Mniotilta varia*	4.3 to 4.7 in (11 to 12 cm)	Canada, U.S., Caribbean; Mex.; Cent. and S. Am.		insects and spiders
Sage thrasher	*Oreoscoptes montanus*	7.9 to 9.1 in (20 to 23 cm)	southwestern Canada, western U.S., Mexico		insects and berries
European starling	*Sturnus vulgaris*	8.5 in (21.5 cm)	Eurasia, Africa; N. America, Aust., New Zealand		insects, spiders, berries

COMMON NAME	SCIENTIFIC NAME	SIZE	RANGE	HABITAT	DIET
Rothschild's mynah	Leucopsar rothschildi	9.8 in (25 cm)	Bali and Nusa Penida in Indonesia		insects, seeds, fruit
Red-billed oxpecker	Buphagus erythrorhynchus	7.5 to 8.7 in (19 to 22 cm)	eastern Africa		insects
Brown-eared bulbul	Ixos amaurotis	11 in (28 cm)	Japan, Korean peninsula, coastal China		insects, fruits, seeds
Golden-fronted leafbird	Chloropsis aurifrons	5.9 in (15 cm)	Himalayas to India, Sri Lanka, and southern Asia		nectar, insects, fruit
Bananaquit	Coereba flaveola	4.1 to 4.5 in (10.5 to 11.5 cm)	South America, southern Mexico and Caribbean		nectar
Varied bunting	Passerina versicolor	8. to 9.8 in (21 to 25 cm)	most of Mexico into southwest Texas (U.S.A.)		seeds, grasses, fruit
Dark-eyed junco	Junco hyemalis	4.9 to 6.5 in (12.5 to 16.5 cm)	North America and southern Mexico		seeds, insects, non-insect arthropods
White-throated towhee	Pipilo albicollis	8.3 to 9.8 in (21 to 25 cm)	Mexico		insects, seeds, fruit
Chestnut-collared longspur	Calcarius ornatus	8.3 to 10.2 in (21 to 26 cm)	U.S. to Canada and Mexico		aquatic insects and seeds
Rusty blackbird	Euphagus carolinus	6.7 to 7.5 in (17 to 19 cm)	Alaska and across Canada; eastern U.S.		insects, fruit, nectar
Altimira oriole	Icterus gularis	15 to 18.1 in (38 to 46 cm)	Gulf coast of Mexico; parts of Central America		insects, other invertebrates, reptiles
Baltimore oriole	Icterus galbula	10.2 to 14.6 in (26 to 37 cm)	North, Central and South America; the Caribbean		invertebrates, frogs, fruit
Common grackle	Quiscalus quiscula	7.9 in (20 cm)	North America east of the Rockies		seeds and insects
Boat-tailed grackle	Quiscalus major	15 to 20.1 in (38 to 51 cm)	Atlantic and Gulf coasts of the United States		fruit and insects
Bronzed cowbird	Molothrus aeneus	6.3 in (16 cm)	Central America, Mexico, U.S.		berries, fruits, seeds, insects
American goldfinch	Spinus tristis	4.5 in (11.5 cm)	U.S. into southern Canada and Mexico		seeds
Oahu Amakihi	Hemignathus flavus	4.7 to 5.1 in (12 to 13 cm)	Honolulu, Hawaii		seeds and insects
'I'iwi	Vestiaria coccinea	4.7 in (12 cm)	Hawaiian Islands		nectar, insects, other invertebrates
Common waxbill	Estrilda astrild	4.7 in (12 cm)	sub-Saharan Africa; Americas, Med., Oceania		seeds
Pin-tailed whydah	Vidua macroura	5.5 in (14 cm)	sub-Saharan Africa		seeds
Red wattlebird	Anthochaera carunculata	13.8 in (35 cm)	southern Australia		nectar
Malaysian rail babbler	Eupetes macrocerus	11 to 11.8 in (28 to 30 cm)	Malay Peninsula, Sumatra, and Borneo		insects and spiders
Whipbird	Psophodes nigrogularis	7.9 to 9.8 in (20 to 25 cm)	isolated pockets in southern Australia		insects and spiders
Satin bowerbird	Ptilonorhynchus violaceus	11.8 in (30 cm)	east coast of Australia		fruit, leaves, insects
Brown treecreeper	Climacteris picumnus	6.2 to 7 in (16 to 18 cm)	eastern Australia		insects and insect larvae
Lark sparrow, lark	Chondestes grammacus	6.7 in (17 cm)	U.S., except eastern; Canada; most of Mexico		seeds
Sunbird	Aethopyga duyvenbodei	4.6 in (12 cm)	Sangihe, Indonesia		nectar and invertebrates
Wood thrush	Hylocichla mustelina	7.5 to 8.3 in (19 to 21 cm)	North America and Central America		snails, small salamanders, insects, fruit
Hermit thrush	Catharus guttatus	6.8 in (17 cm)	North America and Central America		insects, fruit, shrubs, plants
PENGUINS					
King penguin	Aptenodytes patagonicus	33.5 to 37.4 in (85 to 95 cm)	islands surrounding Antarctica		cephalopods, small fish, squid
Royal penguin	Eudyptes schlegeli	27.6 in (70 cm)	Macquarie Island, Australia		fish, squid, crustaceans
Humboldt penguin	Spheniscus humboldti	15 in (38 cm)	coastal Peru and Chile and offshore islands		fish and crustaceans
Galápagos penguin	Spheniscus mendiculus	20.9 in (53 cm)	Galápagos Islands		small fish
Snares penguin	Eudyptes robustus	19.7 to 23.6 in (50 to 60 cm)	the Snares Islands, New Zealand		krill, squid, fish
Fiordland penguin	Eudyptes pachyrhynchus	21.7 in (55 cm)	southern New Zealand islands		crustaceans, fish, squid

REPTILES

COMMON NAME	SCIENTIFIC NAME	SIZE	RANGE	HABITAT	DIET
CROCODILES, CAIMANS, AND ALLIGATORS					
Black caiman	*Melanosuchus niger*	20 ft (6 m)	northern and central South America		mollusks; fish, other aquatic vertebrates; also terrestrial vertebrates, including capybara
Muggar crocodile	*Crocodylus palustris*	13 to 16.4 ft (4 to 5 m)	India, Pakistan, Sri Lanka		crustaceans, fish, frogs, birds, monkeys, squirrels
Cuban crocodile	*Crocodylus rhombifer*	up to 10.5 feet (3.5 m)	Zapata and Lanier Swamps in Cuba		primarily turtles, fish, small mammals
Siamese crocodile	*Crocodylus siamensis*	about 9.8 ft (3 m)	Southeast Asia		fish; also amphibians, reptiles, small mammals
African dwarf crocodile	*Osteolaemus tetraspis*	about 6.3 ft (1.9 m)	west central Africa		fish, crustaceans, amphibians
African slender-snouted crocodile	*Crocodylus cataphractus*	up to 13 ft (4 m)	central Africa		fish, frogs, snakes, shrimp, crabs, waterbirds, mammals
Tuatara	*Sphenodon punctatus*	15.7 to 23.5 in (50 to 60 cm)	Islands off the coast of New Zealand		spiders, insects, worms
Chinese alligator	*Alligator sinensis*	4.6 to 7.2 ft (1.4 to 2.2 m)	Lower Yangtze River basin in China		snails, clams, fish, waterfowl, small mammals
TURTLES					
Pig-nose turtle	*Carettochelys insculpta*	21.7 to 27.6 in (55 to 70 cm)	New Guinea and Northern Australia		fruit of pandanus and figs; also mollusks, worms, crustaceans
Red-bellied short-necked turtle	*Emydura subglobosa*	5.2 to 10 in (13.3 to 25.5 cm)	coastal Australia and New Guinea		omnivorous: fish, mollusks, crustaceans, phytoplankton, worms, algae, leaves, flowers, carrion
Green sea turtle	*Chelonia mydas*	2.3 to 5 ft (71 to 153 cm)	tropical and subtropical oceans worldwide		mostly herbivorous: sea algae, shallow-water grasses
Hawksbill sea turtle	*Eretmochelys imbricata*	24 to 45 in (62.5 to 114 cm)	tropical regions of Atlantic and Pacific Oceans		sponges, sea jellies, other coelenterates; also mollusks, fish, crustaceans, algae
Olive ridley sea turtle	*Lepidochelys olivacea*	2.5 ft (0.7 m)	Indian and southern Atlantic Oceans		carnivorous: invertebrates and protochordates such as jellyfish, snails, shrimp, crabs
Kemp's ridley sea turtle	*Lepidochelys kempii*	22 to 30 in (55 to 75 cm)	Atlantic Ocean to Gulf of Mexico		floating crabs, shrimp, jellyfish, mollusks, some vegetation
Flatback sea turtle	*Natator depressus*	about 3 ft (about 90 cm)	east Indian Ocean, southwest Pacific Ocean		seafloor life such as cuttlefish, hydroids, soft corals, crinoids, mollusks, jellyfish
Alligator snapping turtle	*Macrochelys temminckii*	31.1 to 39.8 in (79 to 101 cm)	Southern and Midwest United States		fish, mollusks, and other turtles
European pond turtle	*Emys orbicularis*	4.7 to 15 in (12 to 38 cm)	Europe, Africa, Middle East, Asia		generalist carnivore: small aquatic animals; worms, insects, frogs, fishes
Diamondback terrapin	*Malaclemys terrapin*	5.5 to 9 in (14 to 23 cm)	eastern United States		snails, other mollusks, fish, insects, crustaceans, carrion
Common slider	*Trachemys scripta*	4.9 to 11.4 in (12.5 to 29 cm)	southeastern U.S., Central and South America		aquatic insects, fish, crustaceans, snails, tadpoles, mollusks; also plant matter
Painted turtle	*Chrysemys picta*	3.5 to 9.8 in (8.8 to 24.8 cm)	North America		mainly plants, small animals (fish, crustaceans, aquatic insects), some carrion
North American wood turtle	*Clemmys insculpta*	6.3 to 9.8 in (16 to 25 cm)	eastern Canada, northeastern United States		omnivorous: slugs, snails, worms, insects, tadpoles, leaves, berries, other plant food
Bog turtle	*Glyptemys muhlenbergii*	3.1 to 4.5 in (8 to 11.4 cm)	eastern United States		omnivorous: small invertebrates such as insects, snails, worms; seeds, berries, vegetation
River cooter	*Pseudemys concinna*	9 to 12 in (23 to 30 cm)	eastern United States		mainly herbivorous: eelgrass, elodea, algae; also small fish, insects, other animal food
American red-bellied turtle	*Pseudemys rubriventris*	10.2 to 12.5 in (26 to 32 cm)	Mid-Atlantic United States		mostly aquatic vegetation and algae; also crayfish, snails, fish, and tadpoles
Southeast Asian box turtle	*Cuora amboinensis*	8 in (20 cm)	Southeast Asia		omnivorous: vegetables, fruit, mushrooms, aquatic plants; also waxworms, fish, insects
False map turtle	*Graptemys pseudogeographica*	3.5 to 10.6 in (9 to 27 cm)	Midwest United States		omnivorous: mollusks, insects, fish carrion; some vegetation
Central American wood turtle	*Rhinoclemmys pulcherrima*	7 to 8 in (18 to 20 cm)	Central America		omnivorous: wildflowers, grasses, fruit, insects, worms, fish
Black-breasted leaf turtle	*Geoemyda spengleri*	about 4.5 in (11.5 cm)	China, Vietnam		little documented; possibly snails, slugs, earthworms, other forest-floor invertebrates
Yellow mud turtle	*Kinosternon flavescens*	4 to 6 in (10.2 to 15.2 cm)	Midwest United States, northern Mexico		snails, worms, insects, tadpoles
Eastern mud turtle	*Kinosternon subrubrum*	2.8 to 4.9 in (7 to 12.5 cm)	eastern United States		omnivorous: mostly insects, mollusks, crustaceans, amphibians, carrion
Giant South American river turtle	*Podocnemis expansa*	42 in (107 cm)	northern South America		plant food
Madagascan big-headed turtle	*Erymnochelys madagascariensis*	about 20 in (50 cm)	Madagascar		mainly herbivorous: plants overhanging water; also small vertebrates
African helmeted turtle	*Pelomedusa subrufa*	5.9 to 7.1 in (15 to 18 cm) upper shell	western and southern Africa		frogs, tadpoles, mollusks, invertebrates, carrion
Big-headed turtle	*Platysternon megacephalum*	6 to 7 in (15 to 18 cm)	southeastern Asia		carnivorous: small marine and terrestrial animals including fish, mollusks, worms
TORTOISES					
Leopard tortoise	*Stigmochelys pardalis*	11.8 to 27.5 in (30 to 70 cm)	Africa		primarily herbivorous; berries and other fruits when available
Radiated tortoise	*Astrochelys radiata*	up to 16 inches (40 cm)	southern Madagascar		herbivorous: grasses, fruit, plants

COMMON NAME	SCIENTIFIC NAME	SIZE	RANGE	HABITAT	DIET
Russian tortoise	*Testudo horsfieldii*	6 to 10 in (15 to 26 cm)	Russia, Afghanistan, China		weeds, grasses
Gopher tortoise	*Gopherus polyphemus*	6.7 to 9.5 in (17 to 24 cm)	southeastern United States		herbivorous: grasses, leaves
Indian star tortoise	*Geochelone elegans*	5.9 to 15 in (15 to 38 cm)	southeastern Pakistan and India, Sri Lanka		primarily herbivorous: grasses, leaves, fruit, flowers; also insects, carrion, dung
Aldabra giant tortoise	*Dipsochelys dussumieri*	35.5 to 55 in (90 to 140 cm)	Seychelles		primarily herbivorous: grasses, leaves, woody plant stems, herbs, sedges
Red-footed tortoise	*Chelonoidis carbonaria*	up to 20 in (50.8 cm)	eastern Amazon Basin		fruit, flowers, dead and living foliage, soil, sand, pebbles, fungi, stems, carrion
South American yellow-footed tortoise	*Chelonoidis denticulata*	up to 32 in (82 cm)	Central America		omnivorous: leaves, vines, roots, bark, fruit, flowers; also fungi, insects, snails
African spurred tortoise	*Geochelone sulcata*	up to 32.6 in (83 cm)	South Sahara Africa		vegetarian: succulent plants
Asian forest tortoise	*Manouria emys*	19.7 to 23.6 in (50 to 60 cm)	southeastern Asia		herbivorous: grasses, vegetables, leaves, fruit
Forest hinge-back tortoise	*Kinixys erosa*	up to 14.7 in (37.5 cm)	central and western Africa		omnivorous: fungi, fruit, plant matter, invertebrates, carrion
Bell's hinge-back tortoise	*Kinixys belliana*	6 to 8.6 in (15 to 22 cm)	North and West Africa		omnivorous: leaves, grasses, sedges, fallen fruit, sugarcane, fungi; insects, snails, millipedes
Home's hinge-back tortoise	*Kinixys homeana*	up to 8.7 in (22.3 cm)	West Africa		omnivorous, eating both animal and plant food
Hermann's tortoise	*Testudo hermanni*	up to 10 in (20 cm)	Mediterranean Europe		mostly vegetarian: fruit, flowers, leaves; also slugs, snails, animal remains
Spur-thighed tortoise	*Testudo graeca*	about 10 in (20 cm)	Eastern Europe, North Africa		leaves, fruit; also carrion, mammal dung
Spiny softshell turtle	*Apalone spinifera*	5 to 19 in (12.7 to 48 cm)	central to eastern United States		macroinvertebrates, including aquatic insects, crayfish; also fish
Smooth softshell turtle	*Apalone mutica*	4.5 to 14 in (11.5 to 35.6 cm)	central United States		carnivorous, including amphibians, fish, snails, mollusks, arthropods, worms
Florida softshell turtle	*Apalone ferox*	5.9 to 29 in (15 to 73.6 cm)	southeastern United States		mostly carnivorous: snails, insects, crustaceans, fish, amphibians, small turtles
IGUANAS, CHAMELEONS, AND RELATIVES					
Agama lizard	*Agama agama*	7.9 to 9.8 in (20 to 25 cm)	sub-Saharan Africa		ants, grasshoppers, beetles, termites; also small mammals and reptiles, vegetation
Frilled lizard	*Chlamydosaurus kingii*	33 in (85 cm)	northern Australia, southern New Guinea		insectivores: mostly small invertebrates
Chinese water dragon	*Physignathus cocincinus*	up to 3 ft (90 cm)	India, China, East and Southeast Asia		plants, insects; some small fish or other vertebrates
Bearded dragon	*Pogona vitticeps*	13 to 24 in (33 to 61 cm)	eastern and central Australia		omnivorous: plant matter, insects, occasional small rodents or lizards
Common flying dragon	*Draco volans*	7.6 to 8.3 in (19.3 to 21.1 cm)	Philippine Islands		insectivorous: mostly ants and termites
Sailfin lizard	*Hydrosaurus amboinensis*	57 in (145 cm)	Indonesia, New Guinea		herbivorous: plant foods
Common chameleon	*Chamaeleo chamaeleon*	8 to 15 in (20.3 to 38.1 cm)	southern Europe, northern Africa		invertebrates, young birds, reptiles; some vegetation
Flap-necked chameleon	*Chamaeleo dilepis*	up to 15 in (38 cm)	southern and eastern Africa		insects
Jackson's chameleon	*Chamaeleo jacksonii*	6 to 14 in (15 to 35 cm)	East Africa		mainly insects and spiders
Namaqua chameleon	*Chamaeleo namaquensis*	5.5 to 6.2 in (14 to 16 cm)	southern Africa		locusts, crickets, beetles, small snakes, scorpions
Lesser chameleon	*Furcifer minor*	6 to 10 in (15.2 to 25.4 cm)	Madagascar		invertebrates
Parson's chameleon	*Calumma parsonii*	18.5 to 26.8 in (47 to 68 cm)	Madagascar		large insects and small vertebrates
Horned leaf chameleon	*Brookesia superciliaris*	3 to 4.7 in (8 to 12 cm)	Madagascar		insects
Helmeted iguana	*Corytophanes cristatus*	12 to 16 in (30 to 40 cm)	Central America		insects
Basilisk lizard	*Basiliscus vittatus*	about 23.6 in (60 cm)	Latin America		mostly insects; also fallen berries
Leopard lizard	*Gambelia sila*	up to 14 in (35.7 cm)	United States (California)		insects, including grasshoppers, beetles, bees, ants, wasps; also plant matter, lizards
Marine iguana	*Amblyrhynchus cristatus*	24 to 30 in (60 to 75 cm)	Galápagos		marine algae
Fiji banded iguana	*Brachylophus fasciatus*	up to 31 in (80 cm)	Fiji, Tonga		leaves, flowers, fruit; also insects
Land iguana	*Conolophus subcristatus*	3 to 4 ft (0.9 to 1.2 m)	Galápagos		largely vegetarian, especially fruit of prickly pear cactus
Black spiny tail iguana	*Ctenosaura similis*	3.3 to 4.1 ft (1 to 1.5 m)	Mexico, Panama, Central America		mainly herbivorous; also small animals, such as rodents, bats, frogs, insects, small birds
Rhinoceros iguana	*Cyclura cornuta*	2 to 4 ft (0.6 to 1.2 m)	Hispaniola		mainly herbivorous: leaves, fruits, flowers, seeds; sometimes animal matter
Grand Cayman iguana	*Cyclura lewisi*	16.3 to 20.3 in (41.5 to 51.6 cm)	Grand Cayman Island		mostly plant matter, including leaves and stems; also fruits, nuts, flowers
Lesser Antillean iguana	*Iguana delicatissima*	15 to 17 in (39 to 43 cm)	Caribbean		leaves, flowers, fruits
Desert iguana	*Dipsosaurus dorsalis*	up to 15 in (38 cm)	western United States, northwestern Mexico		mainly herbivorous: foliage and fruit of desert plants; also invertebrates
Chuckwalla	*Sauromalus obesus (ater)*	up to 16 in (40 cm)	western United States, northwestern Mexico		herbivorous: fruits, leaves, flowers
Fence lizard	*Sceloporus undulatus*	3.5 to 7.5 in (9 to 19 cm)	Mexico, United States		insects and other arthropods, including ants, weevils, beetles, spiders, centipedes; also snails

COMMON NAME	SCIENTIFIC NAME	SIZE	RANGE	HABITAT	DIET
Zebra tailed lizard	Callisaurus draconoides	6 to 9.2 in (15 to 23.4 cm)	southwestern U.S. and northern Mexico		insects, plant material, sloughed skin of other lizards; also eggs, insect larvae, carrion
Brown anole	Anolis sagrei	1.2 to 2.7 in (3.5 to 6.8 cm)	southern U.S., Mexico, Carribbean		insects, including moths, beetles, flies, grasshoppers; worms, snails, other invertebrates
Green anole	Anolis carolinensis	4 to 8 in (10.2 to 20.3 cm)	southeast U.S., Hawaii, Caribbean, Japan		arthropods, including beetles, flies, spiders; also mollusks, grains, seeds
Lava lizard	Microlophus albemarlensis	6.7 to 10 in (17 to 25 cm)	Galápagos		moths, flies, beetles, grasshoppers, ants, other insects; spiders, centipedes, other arthropods
Speckled worm lizard	Amphisbaena fuliginosa	12 to 18 in (30 to 45 cm)	northern South America		small vertebrates, insects
Red worm lizard	Amphisbaena alba	up to 30 in (75 cm)	South America		earthworms, beetles, ants, termites, spiders, crickets, larvae of various insects
European worm lizard	Blanus cinereus	4 to 8 in (10 to 20 cm)	Portugal, Spain		earthworms, small insects
Florida worm lizard	Rhineura floridana	10 to 14 in (25 to 35 cm)	southeastern United States		worms, spiders, termites
Two-legged worm lizard	Bipes biporus	6.5 to 9.5 in (17 to 24 cm)	Mexico (Baja)		worms, termites

GECKOS, SKINKS, AND MONITORS

COMMON NAME	SCIENTIFIC NAME	SIZE	RANGE	HABITAT	DIET
Leopard gecko	Eublepharis macularius	8 to 10 in (20 to 25 cm)	Middle East, northwest India		scorpions, beetles, spiders, grasshoppers
Common house gecko	Hemidactylus frenatus	4.7 to 6 in (12 to 15 cm)	tropical and subtropical regions worldwide		insects, spiders, smaller geckos
Kuhl's flying gecko	Ptychozoon kuhli	up to 4.2 in (10.8 cm)	Southeast Asia		mainly insects
Standing's day gecko	Phelsuma standingi	up to 12 in (30.5 cm)	Madagascar		insects
Striped day gecko	Phelsuma lineata	4 to 5.7 in (10 to 14.5 cm)	Madagascar, Mauritius		insects
Northern alligator lizard	Elgaria coerulea	about 10 in (25 cm)	western United States, southwestern Canada		insects, ticks, spiders, millipedes, snails
Southern alligator lizard	Elgaria multicarinata	2.8 to 7 in (7.3 to 17.8 cm)	western United States, Mexico		insects and other small creatures; scorpions, black widow spiders
Madrean alligator lizard	Elgaria kingii	up to 12.6 in (32 cm)	southwestern United States, northern Mexico		insects, spiders
Texas alligator lizard	Gerrhonotus liocephalus	up to 20 in (50.8 cm)	south Texas, eastern Mexico		arthropods, small rodents, snakes, other lizards
European glass lizard	Pseudopus apodus	up to 4.4 ft (1.3 m)	Greece, Eastern Europe, western Asia		slugs, snails, other invertebrates
Armadillo lizard	Cordylus cataphractus	3 to 4.1 in (7.5 to 10.5 cm)	west coast of South Africa		mainly insects, especially termites and beetles; millipedes; scorpions; plant material
Broadley's flat lizard	Platysaurus broadleyi	6 to 8 in (15 to 20 cm)	South Africa		insects, especially flies; also small berries
Rough-scaled plated lizard	Gerrhosaurus major	about 9 in (22.9 cm)	West Africa		fruit, flowers, invertebrates, small vertebrates, including smaller lizards
Yellow-throated plated lizard	Gerrhosaurus flavigularis	up to 18 in (45 cm)	sub-Saharan Africa		insects
Common wall lizard	Podarcis muralis	up to 9 in (23 cm)	Europe		insects such as flies and beetles; also spiders, earthworms, slugs, other invertebrates
Ibiza wall lizard	Podarcis pityusensis	6 to 8.5 in (15 to 21 cm)	Balearic Islands		primarily invertebrates, especially ants and beetles; also spiders; plant matter
Blotched blue-tongue lizard	Tiliqua nigrolutea	9.8 to 11.8 in (25 to 30 cm)	Australia		omnivorous: variety of plants and animals, especially snails and beetles
Spotted skink	Niveoscincus ocellatus	1.3 to 3 in (3.4 to 7.4 cm)	Tasmania		invertebrates, berries
Emerald skink	Lamprolepis smaragdina	3.2 to 4.2 in (8 to 10.7 cm)	Admiralty Islands, Marshall Islands, Indonesia		insects
Great Plains skink	Plestiodon obsoletus	3.9 to 5.5 in (10 to 14 cm)	western United States, northern Mexico		insects, spiders, small lizards
Otago skink	Oligosoma otagense	10 to 12 in (25 to 30 cm)	New Zealand		insects, fleshy fruit, smaller lizards
Short-tailed skink	Tiliqua rugosa	16 to 18 in (41 to 46 cm)	Australia		omnivorous: snails and plants
Common garden skink	Lampropholis guichenoti	up to 1.6 in (4 cm)	southern Australia		primarily insects
Sand skink	Neoseps reynoldsi	4 to 5 in (10 to 13 cm)	United States (Florida)		arthropods, including beetle larvae, termites, spiders, larval antlions; other invertebrates
Common tegu	Tupinambis teguixin	2 to 3 ft (0.6 to 0.9 m)	northern South America		insects and other invertebrates, birds, small mammals, other lizards, carrion
Argentine black tegu	Tupinambis merianae	3 to 4 ft (0.9 to 1.2 m)	Argentina, Bolivia, Brazil, Paraguay		wide range of animals and fruit
Jungle runner	Ameiva ameiva	4.7 to 7.1 in (12 to 18 cm)	United States (Florida), northern South America		insects, spiders, snails, other small invertebrates, small lizards
Whiptail lizard	genus Cnemidophorus	9.3 to 14.5 in (23.5 to 37 cm)	southwestern United States, northern Mexico		herbivorous: grasses, leaves
Desert night lizard	Xantusia vigilis	1.5 to 2.8 in (4 to 7 cm)	southwestern United States, Mexico		termites, ants, beetles, flies
Water monitor lizard	Dipsochelys dussumieri	35.5 to 55 in (90 to 140 cm)	Southeast Asia		carnivorous: small mammals, especially rats; fish; crocodiles; birds; frogs; snakes; tortoises
Earless monitor lizard	Lanthanotus borneensis	up to 1.6 ft (0.5 m)	Indonesia		in captivity: squid, fish, earthworms, liver, beaten eggs
Crocodile monitor lizard	Varanus salvadorii	up to 8 ft (2.4 m)	New Guinea		mainly birds; in captivity will eat mice, rats, chickens
Mexican beaded lizard	Heloderma horridum	29.5 to 35.4 in (75 to 90 cm)	Mexico		birds, eggs, small mammals, lizards, frogs, insects

COMMON NAME	SCIENTIFIC NAME	SIZE	RANGE	HABITAT	DIET
SNAKES					
False coral snake	Anilius scytale	about 27 in (70 cm)	Northern South America		other snakes, caecilians, amphisbaenids
Pygmy python	Antaresia perthensis	16.5 to 24.4 in (42 to 62 cm)	West Australia		small mammals, such as bats; also amphibians
Rosy boa	Charina trivirgata	16.9 to 44.1 in (43 to 112 cm)	southwestern United States, Mexico		birds, reptiles, small mammals
Emerald tree boa	Corallus caninus	5 to 6.5 ft (1.5 to 2 m)	northern South America		rodents, lizards, marsupials
Rainbow boa	Epicrates cenchria	3.3 to 6.5 ft (1 to 2 m)	South America		birds, lizards, small mammals
Kenyan sand boa	Gongylophis colubrinus	up to 30 in (77 cm)	northeast Africa		lizards and small rodents
Yellow anaconda	Eunectes notaeus	7.9 to 15 ft (2.40 to 4.60 m)	parts of South America		birds, bird eggs, small mammals, turtles, lizards; also fish, fish carrion, caimans
Carpet python	Morelia spilota	6.5 to 13 ft (2 to 4 m)	New Guinea, Australia		lizards, birds, small mammals
Green tree python	Morelia viridis	6 to 7.8 ft (1.8 to 2.4 m)	Australia, Indonesia, Papua New Guinea		small reptiles, invertebrates, mammals, birds
Burmese python	Python molurus	16 to 23 ft (5 to 7 m)	East Asia, Southeast Asia		primarily rodents and other mammals; also birds, amphibians, reptiles
Blood python	Python curtus, subspecies brongersmai	5 to 8 ft (1.5 to 2.5 m)	Singapore, Malay Peninsula		rodents
Reticulated python	Python reticulatus	20 to 33 ft (6 to 10 m)	Indonesia		birds and mammals
Round Island boa	Casarea dussumieri	3.25 to 5 ft (1 to 1.5 m)	Mauritius		lizards
Mexican burrowing python	Loxocemus bicolor	up to 5.2 ft. (1.6 m)	Central America		rodents, lizards
Caicos Islands dwarf boa	Tropidophis greenwayi	about 15 in (38 cm)	Caicos Island		lizards, frogs; sometimes invertebrates
Large shield-tailed snake	Pseudotyphlops philippinus	18 to 20 in (45 to 50 cm)	Sri Lanka		earthworms
Sunbeam snake	Xenopeltis unicolor	3.25 to 4.25 ft (1 to 1.3 m)	Southeast Asia		frogs, lizards, snakes, small mammals
Western slender blind snake	Leptotyphlops humilis	7 to 16 in (18 to 41 cm)	southwestern United States, Mexico		small invertebrates, especially ant broods, termites
Brahminy blind snake	Ramphotyphlops braminus	6 to 7 in (15 to 18 cm)	Middle East, North Africa		ants, termites and their eggs and larvae
File snake	Acrochordus arafurae	4.9 to 8.2 ft (1.5 to 2.5 m)	East Indonesia, New Guinea, North Australia		almost exclusively fish
Common kingsnake	Lampropeltis getula	3.2 to 60.2 in (8 to 153 cm)	East and Midwest United States		snakes, lizards, mice, birds
Rat snake	Elaphe obsoleta	42 to 72 in (106 to 183 cm)	Southern and Midwest United States		mainly mice and rats; also chipmunks, moles, other small rodents
Common garter snake	Thamnophis sirtalis	18.1 to 53.9 in (46 to 137 cm)	United States		worms, amphibians, slugs, snails, insects, leeches, crayfish, small fish, other snakes
Green vine snake	Oxybelis fulgidus	5 to 6.5 ft (1.5 to 2 m)	Central America, South America		birds, lizards
Dark green whipsnake	Coluber viridiflavus	up to 6.25 ft (1.9 m)	Western Europe		lizards, frogs, mammals, birds, other snakes
Blue racer	Coluber constrictor	35 to 75 in (90 to 190 cm)	southern Canada; United States		carnivorous: mainly insects, spiders, small frogs, small reptiles, young rodents, shrews
Red corn snake	Elaphe guttata	2 to 6 ft (0.6 to 1.8 m)	United States		young feed on lizards and tree frogs; adults eat larger prey such as mice, rats, birds, bats
Common slug snake	Pareas monticola	12 to 30 in (30 to 76 cm)	India, China		slugs, snails
Common bronzeback snake	Ophidiocephalus taeniatus	about 11 in (27 cm)	Australia		invertebrates: termites, cockroach nymphs, spiders, beetle and moth larvae
Ringneck snake	Diadophis punctatus	10 to 18.1 in (25.5 to 46 cm)	Canada, Mexico, United States		small salamanders, lizards, frogs; earthworms, juvenile snakes of other species
Northern water snake	Nerodia sipedon	24 to 55 in (61 to 140 cm)	southeastern Canada, Eastern United States		carnivorous: fish, crayfish, other snakes, turtles, birds, small mammals, large insects, leeches
Mangrove snake	Boiga dendrophila	up to 6.6 ft (2 m)	India		lizards, frogs, birds, small mammals
Boomslang	Dispholidus typus	3.9 to 6.6 ft (1.2 to 2.0 m)	Africa		lizards, especially chameleons; birds
Green whip snake	Hierophis viridiflavus	up to 59 in (150 cm)	Western Europe		mainly lizards; also rodents, other small mammals
Aesculapian snake	Elaphe longissima	up to 6.6 ft (2 m)	Europe		rodents, shrews, moles, birds, bird eggs
False water cobra	Hydrodynastes gigas	6 to 10 ft (2 to 3 m)	South America		fish, amphibians; also small animals
Western hognose snake	Heterodon nasicus	14.2 to 36.6 in (36 to 93 cm)	western United States, southern Canada		toads
Natal black snake	Macrelaps microlepidotus	35 to 47 in (90 to 120 cm)	South Africa		frogs, especially rain frogs; lizards; rodents, especially rats and mice; other snakes
Arafura file snake	Acrochordus arafurae	about 50 in (1.5 m)	East Indonesia, New Guinea, North Australia		almost exclusively fish
Schokari sand racer	Psammophis schokari	about 52 in (150 cm)	Southeast Asia, Middle East, North Africa		lizards, small birds, rodents, other snakes
Northern death adder	Acanthophis praelongus	up to 28 ft (70 m)	Australia, New Guinea and nearby islands		small mammals, lizards, birds
King cobra	Ophiophagus hannah	up to 18 ft (5.5 m)	Southeast Asia		cold-blooded animals, especially other snakes

COMMON NAME	SCIENTIFIC NAME	SIZE	RANGE	HABITAT	DIET
Taipan	*Oxyuranus scutellatus*	up to 11 ft (3.3 m)	South Papua New Guinea, Indonesia, Australia		rats, lizards, bandicoots and other small mammals
Red spitting cobra	*Naja pallida*	up to 5 ft (1.5 m)	North Africa		amphibians; also rodents, birds
Eastern coral snake	*Micrurus fulvius*	20 to 30 in (51 to 76 cm)	southern United States		small lizards, snakes
Black mamba	*Dendroaspis polylepis*	6.6 to 9.8 ft (2 to 3 m)	Africa		mostly small mammals, such as squirrels, dassies, and other rodents, hyraxes
Rennell Island sea krait	*Laticauda crockeri*	27 to 34 in (70 to 88 cm)	Solomon Islands		fish
Blue-lipped sea krait	*Laticauda laticaudata*	up to 3.5 ft (1.1 m)	Indian Ocean, Southeast Asia		eels
Banded sea krait	*Laticauda colubrina*	2.5 to 11.8 ft (0.7 to 3.5 m)	Indian Ocean, Southeast Asia		eels
Western brown snake	*Pseudonaja nuchalis*	up to 5.9 ft (1.8 m)	Australia		mice, other small mammals, reptiles
King brown snake	*Pseudechis australis*	up to 8.2 ft (2.5 m)	Australia, Indonesia, New Guinea		reptiles, especially lizards, snakes, other king browns; also birds, mammals, frogs
Yellow-bellied sea snake	*Pelamis platurus*	up to 44 in (113 cm)	Indian and Pacific Oceans, South China Sea		carnivorous: fish
Olive sea snake	*Aipysurus laevis*	up to 6.6 ft (2 m)	Australia, Southeast Asia, areas in Oceania		fish; also fish eggs, shrimp, crabs, mollusks
Turtle headed sea snake	*Emydocephalus annulatus*	up to 3 ft (0.9 m)	Australia, Southeast Asia, areas in Oceania		fish eggs
Broad-banded copperhead	*Agkistrodon contortrix laticinctus*	20 to 30 in (50 to 76 cm)	South and Midwest United States		small rodents, lizards, large insects like cicadas, ground birds, frogs, toads, other small snakes
Eastern diamondback rattlesnake	*Crotalus adamanteus*	33 to 72 in (83 to 182 cm)	South United States		primarily small mammals, from mice to rabbits; also birds
Sidewinder rattlesnake	*Crotalus cerastes*	about 30 in (76.2 cm)	southwestern United States, Mexico		carnivorous: lizards, burrowing rodents such as kangaroo rats and pocket mice, birds
Western diamond-back rattlesnake	*Crotalus atrox*	up to 5 ft (1.5 m)	southwestern United States, Mexico		small mammals, birds, lizards
Prairie rattlesnake	*Crotalus viridis*	35 to 44 in (89 to 114 cm)	Canada, U.S., Mexico		small mammals, ground-nesting birds, amphibians, reptiles, including other snakes
Copperhead	*Agkistrodon contortrix*	about 30 in (76.2 cm)	Mexico, United States		rodents, frogs, lizards, small snakes, amphibians, insects, especially cicadas
Bushmaster	*Lachesis muta*	6.6 to 11.8 ft (2 to 3.6 m)	northern South America		small rodents and other mammals

AMPHIBIANS

- ● ALERT
- ● IN TROUBLE
- ● STABLE
- ● DOMESTICATED
- ● UNDER STUDY
- ● NOT LISTED

COMMON NAME	SCIENTIFIC NAME	SIZE	RANGE	HABITAT	DIET
SALAMANDERS					
Northwestern salamander	*Ambystoma gracile*	5.5 to 8.7 in (14 to 22 cm)	western North America		soft-bodied invertebrates, including annelids, mollusks, amphipods, isopods, copepods
Spotted salamander	*Ambystoma maculatum*	5.9 to 9.8 in (1 to 25 cm)	eastern to midwestern United States		whatever small animals they can catch, including insects, crustaceans, tadpoles
Blue-spotted salamander	*Ambystoma laterale*	3.9 to 5.5 in (10 to 14 cm)	northeastern U.S. and southeastern Canada		carnivorous: invertebrates, including worms, insects, centipedes, snails, slugs, spiders
Reticulated flatwoods salamander	*Ambystoma bishopi*	3.5 to 5.1 in (9 to 13 cm)	southeastern United States		invertebrates
Flatwoods salamander	*Ambystoma cingulatum*	3.5 to 5.1 in (8.9 to 12.9 cm)	southeastern United States		zooplankton, earthworms, insects, other invertebrates
Mole salamander	*Ambystoma talpoideum*	3.2 to 4.7 in (8 to 12 cm)	southeastern United States		aquatic insects, tadpoles, earthworms, arthropods, other invertebrates
Jefferson's salamander	*Ambystoma jeffersonianum*	4.2 to 8.2 in (10.7 to 21 cm)	northeastern U.S. and southeastern Canada		insects and other invertebrates
Marbled salamander	*Ambystoma opacum*	3.5 to 4.2 in (9 to 10.7 cm)	eastern U.S.		carnivorous: small worms, insects, slugs, snails
Three-toed amphiuma	*Amphiuma tridactylum*	18 to 43 in (46 to 110 cm)	southern U.S.		crayfish, insects, worms, snails, small fish, small reptiles, other amphibians
Two-toed amphiuma	*Amphiuma means*	14.4 to 29.9 in (36.8 to 76 cm)	southeastern United States		salamanders, small frogs, crayfish, range of smaller invertebrates
One-toed amphiuma	*Amphiuma pholeter*	up to 12.9 in (33 cm)	southeastern United States		various invertebrates, such as worms, crustaceans, snails
Japanese giant salamander	*Andrias japonicus*	up to 4.5 ft (1.4 m)	Japan		fish, worms, crustaceans
Chinese giant salamander	*Andrias davidianus*	up to 35.4 in (90 cm)	China		aquatic invertebrates such as crayfish and crabs; fish, frogs
Pacific giant salamander	*Dicamptodon tenebrosus*	6.5 to 13.5 in (17 to 34 cm)	northwestern U.S. and southwestern Canada		invertebrates, including insect larvae and adults; mollusks; crayfish and other crustaceans

COMMON NAME	SCIENTIFIC NAME	SIZE	RANGE	HABITAT	DIET
Idaho giant salamander	*Dicamptodon aterrimus*	16.6 to 9.8 in (7 to 25 cm)	western U.S.		adults eat terrestrial invertebrates, small snakes, shrews, mice, other salamanders
California giant salamander	*Dicamptodon ensatus*	about 11.8 in (30 cm)	California		land snails and slugs; insects, including beetles, caddisfly larvae, moths, flies
Cope's giant salamander	*Dicamptodon copei*	up to 8.1 in (20.5 cm)	northwestern U.S.		opportunistic: invertebrates
Japanese clawed salamander	*Onychodactylus japonicus*	4.2 to 7.2 in (10.6 to 18.4 cm)	Japan		primarily insects and their larvae; also other invertebrates, such as spiders, millipedes, snails
Fischer's long-tailed clawed salamander	*Onychodactylus fischeri*	about 6.7 in (17 cm)	China, Korea and the Russian Far East		terrestrial insects, millipedes
Siberian salamander	*Salamandrella keyserlingii*	4.7 to 6.2 in (12 to 16 cm)	Russia, China		insects, small snails, earthworms; occasionally small fish
Western Chinese mountain salamander	*Batrachuperus pinchonii*	5 to 6 in (13 to 15 cm)	China		carnivorous: aquatic and terrestrial invertebrates, especially insects
Alpine stream salamander	*Batrachuperus tibetanus*	6.7 to 8.3 in (17 to 21.1 cm)	China		small crustaceans; aquatic and terrestrial insects
Longdong stream salamander	*Batrachuperus londongensis*	6.1 to 10.4 in (15.5 to 26.5 cm)	China		carnivorous: aquatic and terrestrial invertebrates, especially insects
Sonan's salamander	*Hynobius sonani*	3.9 to 4.7 in (10 to 2 cm)	Taiwan		invertebrates
Tokyo salamander	*Hynobius tokyoensis*	3.1 to 5.1 in (8 to 13 cm)	Tokyo, Japan		invertebrates
Oki salamander	*Hynobius okiensis*	4.7 to 5.2 in (12.1 to 13.3 cm)	Japan		invertebrates
Formosan salamander	*Hynobius formosanus*	about 3.9 in (10 cm)	Taiwan		sow bugs, earthworms, other terrestrial invertebrates
Red-backed salamander	*Plethodon cinereus*	2.5 to 5 in (6.5 to 12.5 cm)	northeastern U.S. and southeastern Canada		small terrestrial arthropods; sometimes snails, slugs, small earthworms
Appalachian salamander	*Plethodon jordani*	3.25 to 7.5 in (8.5 to 18.5 cm)	Appalachian Mountains		millipedes, beetles, insect larvae
Four-toed salamander	*Hemidactylium scutatum*	2 to 4 in (5 to 10.2 cm)	eastern U.S.		insects (beetles, flies, ants, bristletails) and their larvae, spiders, mites, snails, worms
Slimy salamander	*Plethodon glutinosus*	4.5 to 8 in (11.5 to 20 cm)	eastern to midwestern United States		ants, beetles, sowbugs, earthworms
Salvin's mushroom tongue salamander	*Bolitoglossa salvinii*	3.9 to 4.7 in (10 to 12 cm)	El Salvador, Guatemala		small invertebrates, such as insects
Blind cave salamander	*Proteus anguinus*	7.8 to 11.8 in (20 to 30 cm)	Bosnia, Croatia, Italy, Slovenia, France		insectivorous: small invertebrates, other arthropods; wide variety of insect larvae
Mudpuppy	*Necturus maculosus*	7.8 to 12.9 in (20 to 33 cm)	Midwestern U.S.		aquatic organisms, including crayfish, insect larvae, small fish, fish eggs, snails, amphibians
Neuse River waterdog	*Necturus lewisi*	6 to 9.1 in (15.2 to 23 cm)	eastern U.S.		crayfish, other crustaceans, insect larvae and nymphs, mollusks, plant remains, worms
Gulf Coast waterdog	*Necturus beyeri*	6.2 to 8.6 in (16 to 22 cm)	Gulf Coast of U.S.		crayfish, isopods, amphipods, mayflies, dragonflies, sphaeriid clams
Dwarf waterdog	*Necturus punctatus*	0.4 to 0.6 in (11.5 to 15.9 mm)	southeastern United States		mollusks, worms, crustaceans, spiders, centipedes, insects, other salamanders
Olympic torrent salamander	*Rhyacotriton olympicus*	up to 3.9 in (10 cm)	northeastern U.S.		aquatic and semi-aquatic invertebrates, including larval and adult beetles, flies, snails
Gold-striped salamander	*Chioglossa lusitanica*	up to 6.5 in (16.4 cm)	Portugal, Spain		invertebrates: spiders, flies, beetles

NEWTS

COMMON NAME	SCIENTIFIC NAME	SIZE	RANGE	HABITAT	DIET
Sword-tailed newt	*Cynops ensicauda*	4 to 7 in (10.3 to 17.9 cm)	Japan		aquatic and terrestrial invertebrates, including snails, slugs, tadpoles, newt eggs
California newt	*Taricha torosa*	5 to 8 in (12.5 to 20 cm)	California		invertebrates: earthworms, snails, slugs, sowbugs
Great crested newt	*Triturus cristatus*	4 to 5.5 in (10 to 14 cm)	Europe		aquatic invertebrates; some large prey, such as smooth newts, dragonflies
Spot-tailed warty newt	*Paramesotriton caudopunctatus*	4.8 to 6.1 in (12.2 to 15.4 cm)	China		insect larvae, arthropods, snails, frog eggs, earthworms
Kurdistan newt	*Neurergus microspilotus*	5.5 to 5.9 in (14 to 15 cm)	The Middle East		invertebrates
Fire-bellied newt	*Cynops cyanurus*	2.8 to 3.9 in (7.3 to 10 cm)	China		invertebrates

SIRENS

COMMON NAME	SCIENTIFIC NAME	SIZE	RANGE	HABITAT	DIET
Greater siren	*Siren lacertina*	20 to 35 in (50 to 90 cm)	southeastern United States		snails, insect larvae, small fish
Dwarf siren	*Pseudobranchus striatus*	4 to 9 in (10 to 22 cm)	southeastern United States		aquatic invertebrates

CAECILIANS

COMMON NAME	SCIENTIFIC NAME	SIZE	RANGE	HABITAT	DIET
Mexican caecilian	*Dermophis mexicanus*	4 to 23.5 in (10 to 60 cm)	Central America		invertebrates, including earthworms, termites, immature grasshoppers and crickets; lizards
Marbled caecilian	*Epicrionops marmoratus*	11.8 in (30 cm)	Ecuador		earthworms and soil arthropods
Banded caecilian	*Scolecomorphus vittatus*	5.5 to 14.8 in (14.1 to 37.6 cm)	United Republic of Tanzania		large, surface-active earthworms; soil arthropods
Cayenne caecilian	*Typhlonectes compressicauda*	12 to 23.5 in (30 to 60 cm)	northern South America		invertebrates

TOADS

COMMON NAME	SCIENTIFIC NAME	SIZE	RANGE	HABITAT	DIET
Costa Rican poison dart frog	*Atelopus varius*	1.06 to 1.9 in (27 to 48 cm)	Costa Rica, Panama		arthropods, including flies, wasps, ants, caterpillars, spiders
Cane toad	*Rhinella marina*	2 to 9 in (5 to 23 cm)	Central and South America		insects, especially ants, termites, beetles; other invertebrates; frogs, lizards, mice

COMMON NAME	SCIENTIFIC NAME	SIZE	RANGE	HABITAT	DIET
Natterjack toad	Epidalea calamita	1.9 to 2.7 in (5 to 7 cm)	Europe		moths, woodlice, other insects
Woodhouse's toad	Anaxyrus woodhousii	up to 5 in (12.7 cm)	southwestern U.S. and northern Mexico		small terrestrial arthropods
Canadian toad	Anaxyrus hemiophrys	1.5 to 3.3 in (3.7 to 8.3 cm)	northern U.S. and Canada		worms, beetles, ants
Puerto Rican crested toad	Peltophryne lemur	2.5 to 4.7 in (6.4 to 12 cm)	Puerto Rico, British Virgin Islands		worms, insect larvae, insects, other invertebrates
Golden toad	Incilius periglenes	1.5 to 2.2 in (3.9 to 5.6 cm)	Costa Rica		small invertebrates
Boreal toad	Anaxyrus boreas	2 to 5 in (5.1 to 2.7 cm)	Canada; Mexico; United States		variety of invertebrates, including worms, spiders, moths, beetles, ants
Great Plains toad	Anaxyrus cognatus	1.8 to 3.1 in (4.5 to 9 cm)	North and Central America		insectivorous: moths, flies, cutworms, beetles
Yosemite toad	Anaxyrus canorus	1.77 to 2.9 in (4.5 to 7.5 cm)	western U.S.		primarily insectivorous, including bees, ants, mosquitoes, spiders, centipedes, beetles
Wyoming toad	Anaxyrus baxteri	up to 2 in (5.1 cm)	United States		ants, beetles, other arthropods
Crested toad	Bufo divergens	1.1 to 2.1 in (2.8 to 5.5 cm)	Brunei, Indonesia, Malaysia		arthropods, especially ants and termites
Arroyo toad	Anaxyrus californicus	1.8 to 3.4 in (4.6 to 8.6 cm)	United States and Mexico		variety of invertebrates, mostly ants
Himalayan Toad	Bufo himalayanus	5.1 to 5.2 in (13 to 13.2 cm)	China, India, Nepal, Pakistan		grasshoppers, moths, ants, other invertebrates
Flat-backed toad	Amietophrynus maculatus	1.4 to 2.3 in (3.8 to 6 cm)	Africa		insects, especially ants, beetles
FROGS					
Green and black poison dart frog	Dendrobates auratus	1 to 2.25 in (2.5 to 5.7 cm)	Colombia, Nicaragua, Panama, Costa Rica, U.S.		small invertebrates, especially ants
Harlequin poison dart frog	Dendrobates histrionicus	1 to 1.5 in (2.5 to 3.8 cm)	Colombia		small invertebrates, including ants, termites, small beetles, other small arthropods
Dyeing poison frog	Dendrobates tinctorius	1.5 to 2.3 in (4 to 6 cm)	Brazil, French Guiana, Guyana, Suriname		insectivorous: ants, termites, other small insects, small spiders
Yellow-headed poison frog	Dendrobates leucomelas	1.2 to 2 in (3.1 to 5 cm)	Brazil, Colombia, Guyana, Venezuela		insectivorous: ants, termites, tiny beetles, crickets, other small insects, spiders
Striped poison dart frog	Phyllobates lugubris	0.8 to 0.9 in (2 to 2.3 cm)	Costa Rica, Nicaragua, Panama		ants, mites, beetles
Black-legged poison dart frog	Phyllobates bicolor	1.2 to 1.6 in (3.2 to 4.2 cm)	Colombia		ants, mites, beetles
Oriental fire-bellied toad	Bombina orientalis	1.25 to 2 in (3 to 5 cm)	China, Korea, Russia		terrestrial invertebrates: worms, mollusks, insects
Midwife toad	Alytes obstetricans	1.25 to 2 in (3 to 5 cm)	Europe		invertebrates
Painted frog	Discoglossus pictus	1.2 to 1.6 in (3.2 to 4.1 cm)	Algeria, Italy, Malta, Tunisia, France, Spain		invertebrates
Shovel-nosed frog	Hemisus marmoratus	0.8 to 1.9 in (2.2 to 4.9 cm)	Africa		ants and termites
Spotted snout-burrower	Hemisus guttatus	2 to 3 in (5 to 8 cm)	South Africa		termites and earthworms
Mountain chorus frog	Pseudacris brachyphona	1.02 to 1.34 in (2.6 to 3.4 cm)	United States		insects, including beetles, bugs, ants; spiders
Cuban tree frog	Osteopilus septentrionalis	2 to 5 in (5.1 to 2.7 cm)	Cuba and the Caribbean Islands		insectivorous: cockroaches and moths
Gray tree frog	Hyla versicolor	1.1 to 2 in (2.8 to 5 cm)	Canada, United States		insects and their larvae
Green tree frog	Hyla cinerea	1.3 to 2.5 in (3.2 to 6.4 cm)	United States, Puerto Rico		insectivorous: flies, mosquitoes, other small insects
Hourglass tree frog	Dendropsophus ebraccatus	1.1 to 1.4 in (2.8 to 3.7 cm)	Mexico, Central America, Colombia, Ecuador		probably small arthropods
Barking tree frog	Hyla gratiosa	2 to 2.8 in (5.1 to 7 cm)	United States		arboreal insects, crickets
Yucatán shovel-headed tree frog	Triprion petasatus	1.8 to 2.9 in (4.8 to 7.5 cm)	Belize, Guatemala, Honduras, Mexico		variety of small arthropods and small frogs
Pine Barrens tree frog	Hyla andersonii	1.1 to 1.8 in (3 to 4.7 cm)	United States		small invertebrates, including flies, crickets, small slugs, snails, beetles, butterflies, moths
Chinese tree frog	Hyla chinensis	0.9 to 1.2 in (2.5 to 3.3 cm)	China; Taiwan, Province of China		probably a variety of arthropods
Japanese tree frog	Hyla japonica	up to 1.7 in (4.5cm)	China, Japan, Korea, Mongolia, Russia		probably a variety of arthropods
Mountain tree frog	Hyla eximia	0.7 to 2.2 in (1.9 to 5.6 cm)	Mexico		insects, shrubs, dense grasses
Squirrel tree frog	Hyla squirella	0.9 to 1.4 in (2.3 to 3.7 cm)	United States and the Bahamas		insects, other small prey
Lemur leaf frog	Agalychnis lemur	up to 1.9 in (5 cm)	Colombia, Costa Rica, Panama		probably a variety of arthropods
Sardinian tree frog	Hyla sarda	1.5 in (3.8 cm)	France, Italy		probably a variety of arthropods
Lemon yellow tree frog	Hyla savignyi	1.1 to 1.8 in (3 to 4.7 cm)	western Asia and Arabian Peninsula		probably a variety of arthropods
Pacific chorus frog	Pseudacris regilla	1 to 1.89 in (2.5 to 4.8 cm)	Canada, United States, Mexico		probably a variety of arthropods
Mountain chorus frog	Pseudacris brachyphona	1.02 to 1.34 in (2.6 to 3.4 cm)	Appalachian Mountains		mostly insects, especially beetles, ants; also spiders, earthworms

COMMON NAME	SCIENTIFIC NAME	SIZE	RANGE	HABITAT	DIET
Brimley's chorus frog	Pseudacris brimleyi	up to 1.3 in (3.5 cm)	East Coast U.S.		probably a variety of arthropods
Spotted chorus frog	Pseudacris clarkii	1.2 in (3 cm)	southern U.S. and Mexico		probably a variety of arthropods
Strecker's chorus frog	Pseudacris streckeri	up to 1.8 in (4.6 cm)	southern U.S.		probably a variety of arthropods
Green and golden bell frog	Litoria aurea	up to 4.3 in (10.8 cm)	Australia and New Zealand		insects, other frogs
Booroolong frog	Litoria booroolongensis	1.7 in (4.5 cm)	Australia		probably a variety of arthropods
Yellow-spotted bell frog	Litoria castanea	up to 3.1 in (8 cm)	Australia		probably a variety of arthropods
Dainty green tree frog	Litoria gracilenta	1.7 in (4.5 cm)	Australia		probably a variety of arthropods
Leaf green tree frog	Litoria phyllochroa	1.5 in (4 cm)	Australia		probably a variety of arthropods
Marsupial frog	Assa darlingtoni	up to 0.8 in (2 cm)	Australia		arthropods
Horned marsupial frog	Gastrotheca cornuta	up to 3 in (7.7 cm)	Colombia, Costa Rica, Ecuador, Panama		probably a variety of arthropods
Cinnamon-bellied reed frog	Hyperolius cinnamomeoventris	up to 1.1 in (2.8 cm)	Africa		probably mostly insects
Delicate spiny reed frog	Afrixalus delicatus	up to 1 in (2.5 cm)	Africa		probably mostly insects
Knysna spiny reed frog	Afrixalus knysnae	1 in (2.5 cm)	South Africa		probably mostly insects
Brown New Zealand frog	Litoria ewingii	1.1 to 1.5 in (3 to 5 cm)	Australia and New Zealand		probably mostly insects
Hamilton's frog	Leiopelma hamiltoni	up to 1.9 in (4.9 cm)	New Zealand		probably mostly insects
Helmeted water toad	Caudiverbera caudiverbera	up to 12.8 in (32 cm)	Chile and Argentina		aquatic insect larvae, fish, frogs, small birds and mammals
Chacoan burrowing frog	Chacophrys pierottii	2.1 in (5.5 cm)	central South America		probably small arthropods
Monte Iberia eleuth frog	Eleutherodactylus iberia	0.3 in (1 cm)	Cuba		probably small arthropods
Mexican white-lipped frog	Leptodactylus fragilis	about 1.9 in (5 cm)	Central and South America		mostly arthropods
Mountain chicken frog	Leptodactylus fallax	up to 8.2 in (21 cm)	Dominica, Montserrat		probably small arthropods
Pepper frog	Leptodactylus labyrinthicus	up to 7.1 in (18 cm)	central South America		probably small arthropods
Moustached frog	Leptodactylus mystacinus	up to 2.6 in (6.7 cm)	South America		probably small arthropods
Emerald forest frog	Hylorina sylvatica	up to 2.5 in (6.2 cm)	Argentina, Chile		small arthropods
Lake Titicaca frog	Telmatobius culeus	up to 5.3 in (13.7 cm)	Bolivia, Peru		amphipods, snails, aquatic insects, tadpoles, fish
Asian horned frog	Megophrys montana	4.4 in (11.1 cm)	Indonesia		relatively large prey, including cockroaches, scorpions, snails
Long-nosed frog	Megophrys nasuta	up to 5 in (12.7 cm)	Southeast Asia		arachnids, nestling rodents, lizards, other frogs
Eastern narrow-mouthed toad	Gastrophryne carolinensis	up to 1.5 in (3.8 cm)	southeastern coast U.S.		small invertebrates, especially ants, beetles, termites
Ornate narrow-mouthed frog	Microhyla ornata	up to 1 in (2.5 cm)	southern Asia		small invertebrates
Malaysian painted frog	Kaloula pulchra	up to 3 in (7.5 cm)	southern Asia		ants and other small insects
Turtle frog	Myobatrachus gouldii	1.7 in (4.5 cm)	Australia		termites
Eastern banjo frog	Limnodynastes dumerilii	2 to 3.2 in (5.2 to 8.3 cm)	Australia		probably arthropods
Crucifix frog	Notaden bennettii	2.1 in (5.5 cm)	Australia		probably arthropods
Orange-bellied frog	Geocrinia vitellina	1 in (2.5 cm)	Australia		probably small arthropods
White-bellied frog	Geocrinia alba	1 in (2.5 cm)	Australia		probably small arthropods
Northern Corroboree frog	Pseudophryne pengilleyi	1 to 1.2 in (2.5 to 3 cm)	Australia		adults consume mainly ants
Southern Corroboree frog	Pseudophryne corroboree	1 to 1.1 in (2.5 to 3 cm)	Australia		mainly small invertebrates such as ants
Desert frog	Crinia deserticola	0.7 in (1.8 cm)	Australia		probably small arthropods
Sunset frog	Spicospina flammocaerulea	1.3 in (3.5 cm)	Australia		probably small arthropods
Marbled frog	Limnodynastes convexiusculus	2.1 in (5.5 cm)	Australia, Indonesia, Papua New Guinea		probably arthropods
Western bullfrog	Limnodynastes dorsalis	2.7 in (7 cm)	Australia		probably arthropods
Giant bullfrog	Limnodynastes interioris	3.54 in (9 cm)	Australia		probably arthropods
Spotted grass frog	Limnodynastes tasmaniensis	1.7 in (4.5 cm)	Australia		probably arthropods

COMMON NAME	SCIENTIFIC NAME	SIZE	RANGE	HABITAT	DIET
● Painted burrowing frog	*Scaphiophryne gottlebei*	up to 1.5 in (4 cm)	Madagascar		insects
● Large toadlet	*Pseudophryne major*	up to 1.5 in (4 cm)	Australia		probably small arthropods
● Eastern spadefoot toad	*Scaphiopus holbrookii*	1.75 to 2.25 in (4.3 to 5.7 cm)	eastern United States		worms and various arthropods
● Northern spadefoot toad	*Notaden melanoscaphus*	up to 1.9 in (4.9 cm)	Australia		small arthropods
● Common spadefoot toad	*Neobatrachus sudelli*	1.5 in (4 cm)	Australia		probably arthropods
● Common parsley frog	*Pelodytes punctatus*	1.6 in (4 cm)	France, Italy, Portugal, Spain		small invertebrates, including crickets and flies
● Surinam toad	*Pipa pipa*	up to 0.7 in (1.7 cm)	northern South America		worms, insects, crustaceans, small fish
● Pickerel frog	*Rana palustris*	1.7 to 2.9 in (4.5 to 7.5 cm)	Canada; United States		small insects and other invertebrates
● Green frog	*Rana clamitans*	2.9 to 4.9 in (7.5 to 12.5 cm)	eastern North America		insects and other invertebrates, including slugs, spiders, flies, snails, crayfish, moths
● Goliath frog	*Conraua goliath*	6.7 to 12.6 in (17 to 32 cm)	Africa		insects, crustaceans, fish, mollusks, small mammals, amphibians
● Northern red-legged frog	*Rana aurora*	1.7 to 8.3 in (4.4 to 8.4 cm)	Canada, United States		probably invertebrates
● European frog	*Rana temporaria*	2.4 to 3.7 in (6 to 9.5 cm)	Europe		insects and their larvae, snails, worms, wood lice, spiders
● Sahara frog	*Rana saharica*	up to 4.1 in (10.5 cm)	Africa		probably mainly invertebrates
● Amami tip-nosed frog	*Odorrana amamiensis*	up to 3.97 in (10.1 cm)	Japan		probably mainly invertebrates
● Columbian spotted frog	*Rana luteiventris*	4 in (10 cm)	Canada, United States		probably mainly invertebrates
● Crawfish frog	*Rana areolata*	up to 4.4 in (11.3 cm)	central United States		insects, small crayfish, reptiles, amphibians
● Northern leopard frog	*Rana pipiens*	2 to 4.37 in (5 to 11.1 cm)	Central and North America		terrestrial invertebrates: spiders, insects and their larvae, earthworms, slugs, snails
● Wood frog	*Rana sylvatica*	1.34 to 3 in (3.5 to 7.6 cm)	Canada, United States		insects and other small invertebrates: spiders, beetles, bugs, slugs, snails
● Mountain yellow-legged frog	*Rana muscosa*	1.5 to 3.5 in (4 to 8.9 cm)	western United States		aquatic and terrestrial invertebrates: beetles, ants, bees, wasps, flies, dragonflies
● Florida bog frog	*Rana okaloosae*	up to 1.8 in (4.8 cm)	southeast United States		probably mostly small invertebrates
● African bullfrog	*Pyxicephalus adspersus*	up to 9 in (23 cm)	Africa		vertebrates: mammals, birds, snakes, lizards, frogs
● Larut torrent frog	*Amolops larutensis*	up to 2.1 in (5.4 cm)	southern Asia		terrestrial and aquatic animals, especially insects
● Beautiful torrent frog	*Amolops formosus*	up to 3.3 in (8.5 cm)	Asia		unconfirmed
● Crowned or Victoria forest frog	*Astylosternus diadematus*	up to 2.7 in (7 cm)	Africa		small, forest-floor arthropods
● Japanese flying frog	*Rhacophorus arboreus*	up to 3.2 in (8.2 cm)	Japan		insects
● Javan gliding frog	*Rhacophorus reinwardtii*	up to 3.1 in (7.9 cm)	southern Asia		canopy insects
● Wallace's flying frog	*Rhacophorus nigropalmatus*	up to 4 in (10 cm)	southern Asia		mainly insects
● Golden mantella	*Mantella aurantiaca*	0.7 to 1 in (2 to 2.6 cm)	Madagascar		insectivorous, especially termites, fruit flies, ants
● Darwin's frog	*Rhinoderma darwinii*	up to 1.2 in (3.1 cm)	Argentina, Chile		mainly insects and other small invertebrates
● Mexican burrowing toad	*Rhinophrynus dorsalis*	1.9 to 2.7 in (5 to 7 cm)	Central America		termites
● Seychelle frog	*Sooglossus gardineri*	up to 0.4 in (11 mm)	Seychelles		small invertebrates
● Hairy frog	*Trichobatrachus robustus*	about 4.3 in (11 cm)	Africa		insects and other arthropods
● Tanzanian screeching frog	*Arthroleptis tanneri*	up to 2.2 in (5.5 cm)	United Republic of Tanzania		forest-floor arthropods, including small spiders
● Coastal tailed frog	*Ascaphus truei*	1 to 2 in (2.5 to 5 cm)	Canada, United States		terrestrial and aquatic insects, other invertebrates
● Rocky Mountain tailed frog	*Ascaphus montanus*	1.2 to 2 in (3 to 5 cm)	Canada, United States		terrestrial and aquatic insects
● Pumpkin toadlet	*Brachycephalus ephippium*	0.5 to 0.7 in (1.25 to 1.97 cm)	Brazil		small arthropods, especially springtails; also insect larvae, mites

FISH

COMMON NAME	SCIENTIFIC NAME	SIZE	RANGE	HABITAT	DIET
PRIMITIVE FISH					
Pacific hagfish	*Eptatretus stoutii*	25 in (63 cm)	Pacific Ocean off of Canada, Mexico, U.S.		dead or dying fish and mammals, marine invertebrates
Pouched lamprey	*Geotria australis*	24 in (62 cm)	Australia, New Zealnd, Chile, Argentina		blood and skin of other fish
Pacific lamprey	*Lampetra tridentata*	30 in (76 cm)	Pacific Coast of North America		blood and skin of other fish
Sea lamprey	*Petromyzon marinus*	47 in (120 cm)	North Atlantic Ocean		blood and skin of other fish
European river lamprey	*Lampetra fluviatilis*	20 in (50 cm)	North Atlantic Ocean; Med. and Adriatic Seas		blood and skin of other fish
Australian lungfish	*Neoceratodus forsteri*	67 in (170 cm)	Southeastern Queensland, Australia		frogs, fish, shrimp, snails, aquatic plants
South American lungfish	*Lepidosiren paradoxa*	49 in (125 cm)	Amazon River Basin in South America		fish, weeds, plants, shrimp, clams, snails, insects
West Indian Ocean coelacanth	*Latimeria chalumnae*	66 in (168 cm)	Western Indo-Pacific Ocean		fish and squid
Indonesian coelacanth	*Latimeria menadoensis*	55 in (140 cm)	Indonesia		cuttlefish, squid, lanternfish, cardinalfish, deepwater snapper fish
White sturgeon	*Acipenser transmontanus*	240 in (610 cm)	Western coast and rivers in U.S.; Canada		insects, small crustaceans and mollusks
European sturgeon	*Acipenser sturio*	236 in (600 cm)	Baltic and Black Seas, Eng. Channel, Europe		fish, crustaceans, mollusks
Beluga sturgeon	*Huso huso*	315 in (800 cm)	Adriatic, Azov, Black, and Caspian Seas		fish, crustaceans, mollusks
Atlantic sturgeon	*Acipenser sturio*	236 in (600 cm)	Baltic and Black Seas, Eng. Channel, Europe		crustaceans, small fish and worms
Chinese paddlefish	*Psephurus gladius*	118 in (300 cm)	Yangtze River, China		fish and crustaceans
Freshwater gar	*Xenentodon cancila*	16 in (40 cm)	Pakistan, India, Nepal, Sri Lanka, Myanmar, Thailand		crustaceans
Longnose butterflyfish	*Forcipiger longirostris*	9 in (22 cm)	Indo-Pacific Ocean		crustaceans
SHARKS					
Roughtail catshark	*Galeus arae*	14 in (36 cm)	southern U.S. and Central America		deepwater shrimp
Borneo catshark	*Apristurus platyrhynchus*	31 in (80 cm)	western Pacific Ocean		crustaceans, squid, small fish
Icelandic catshark	*Apristurus laurussonii*	27 in (68 cm)	Atlantic Ocean		crustaceans, squid, small fish
Striped catshark	*Poroderma africanum*	40 in (101 cm)	southeastern Atlantic and western Indian Oceans		crustaceans, squid, small fish
Blacktip reef shark	*Carcharhinus melanopterus*	79 in (200 cm)	Indian Ocean, Mediterranean Sea, Pacific Ocean		crustaceans and mollusks
Sandbar shark	*Carcharhinus plumbeus*	79 in (200 cm)	Indian, Atlantic, and Pacific Oceans		bony fish, rays, other small sharks
Bull shark	*Carcharhinus leucas*	157 in (400 cm)	Indian, Atlantic, and Pacific Oceans		bony fish, rays, other small sharks, crustaceans, sea turtles
Blacktail reef shark	*Carcharhinus amblyrhynchos*	89 in (225 cm)	Indian and Pacific Oceans		reef fish, squid, shrimp, octopuses
Spinner shark	*Carcharhinus brevipinna*	118 in (300 cm)	all oceans except polar; Med. and Black Seas		bony fish, small sharks, cuttlefish, squid, octopuses
Blacknose shark	*Carcharhinus acronotus*	79 in (200 cm)	Atlantic Ocean		small fish, including porcupine fish
Silvertip shark	*Carcharhinus albimarginatus*	118 in (300 cm)	Indian, Atlantic, and Pacific Oceans		bony fish, rays, cephalopods
Bignose shark	*Carcharhinus altimus*	118 in (300 cm)	all oceans except polar; Med. and Black Seas		bony fish, other sharks, stingrays, cuttlefish
Galápagos shark	*Carcharhinus galapagensis*	146 in (370 cm)	Indian, Atlantic, and Pacific Oceans		bottom fish, squid, octopuses
Blue shark	*Prionace glauca*	157 in (400 cm)	Indian, Atlantic, and Pacific Oceans		fish, small sharks, squid, crabs, seabirds
Bonnethead shark	*Sphyrna tiburo*	59 in (150 cm)	Atlantic and Pacific Oceans		crustaceans, octopuses, small fish
Smooth hammerhead	*Sphyrna zygaena*	197 in (500 cm)	**all oceans except polar; Med. and Black Seas**		small sharks, stingrays, bony fish, shrimp, crabs, cephalopods
Tope shark	*Galeorhinus galeus*	76 in (193 cm)	**all oceans except polar; Med. and Black Seas**		fish, crustaceans, worms
Galápagos bullhead shark	*Heterodontus quoyi*	42 in (107 cm)	Pacific Ocean near Galápagos Islands		shellfish and small invertebrates
Port Jackson shark	*Heterodontus portusjacksoni*	65 in (165 cm)	Indian and Pacific Oceans		sea urchins, sea stars, small fish, crabs
Sharpnose seven gill shark	*Heptranchias perlo*	54 in (137 cm)	all oceans except polar; Med. and Black Seas		small sharks, rays, bony fish, shrimp, crabs, lobsters, squid
Broadnose sevengill shark	*Notorynchus cepedianus*	118 in (300 cm)	Indian, Atlantic, and Pacific Oceans		other sharks, rays, dolphins, bony fish

COMMON NAME	SCIENTIFIC NAME	SIZE	RANGE	HABITAT	DIET
Sandbar shark	Carcharhinus plumbeus	98 in (250 cm)	all oceans except polar; Med. and Black Seas		bony fish, small sharks, rays, shrimp
Crocodile shark	Pseudocarcharias kamoharai	43 in (110 cm)	Indian, Atlantic, and Pacific Oceans		bony fish, squid, shrimp
Shortfin mako shark	Isurus oxyrinchus	157 in (400 cm)	all oceans except polar; Med. and Black Seas		bony fish, other sharks, cephalopods
Thresher shark	Alopias vulpinus	299 in (760 cm)	all oceans except polar; Med. and Black Seas		bony fish, squid, octopuses, crustaceans
Porbeagle shark	Lamna nasus	138 in (350 cm)	all oceans except Southern; Med and Black Seas		small fish, other sharks, squid
Arabian carpetshark	Chiloscyllium arabicum	31 in (78 cm)	western Indian Ocean		squid, crustaceans, eels
Zebra shark	Stegostoma fasciatum	139 in (354 cm)	Indian and Pacific Oceans		crustaceans and sea snakes
Whitespotted bambooshark	Chiloscyllium plagiosum	33 in (83 cm)	Indian and Pacific Oceans		bony fish and crustaceans
Longnose sawshark	Pristiophorus cirratus	54 in (137 cm)	eastern Indian and south-western Pacific Oceans		small fish and crustaceans
Longnose velvet dogfish	Centroscymnus crepidater	51 in (130 cm)	Atlantic, Indian, and Pacific Oceans		fish and cephalopods
Angular roughshark	Oxynotus centrina	59 in (150 cm)	Atlantic Ocean, Mediterranean and Black Seas		worms
Spined pygmy shark	Squaliolus laticaudus	9 in (22 cm)	Atlantic, Indian, and Pacific Oceans		squid and lanternfish
Bramble shark	Echinorhinus brucus	79 in (200 cm)	Atlantic, Indian, and Pacific Oceans		smaller sharks, bony fish, crabs
Prickly shark	Echinorhinus cookei	157 in (400 cm)	Indian and Pacific Oceans		small sharks, fish, squid
Atlantic angel shark	Squatina dumeril	59 in (150 cm)	Atlantic Ocean		fish and crustaceans
Pacific angel shark	Squatina californica	60 in (152 cm)	Pacific Ocean		fish and squid
Blackfin ghostshark	Hydrolagus lemures	35 in (88 cm)	Indian and Pacific Oceans		small fish
SKATES AND RAYS					
Long-tailed butterfly ray	Gymnura poecilura	98 in (250 cm)	Indian and Pacific Oceans		fish, mollusks, crustaceans
Japanese butterfly ray	Gymnura japonica	39 in (100 cm)	Pacific Ocean		fish
Spiny butterfly ray	Gymnura altavela	157 in (400 cm)	Atlantic Ocean, Mediterranean and Black Seas		fish, crustaceans, mollusks, plankton
Australian butterfly ray	Gymnura australis	29 in (73 cm)	Indian and Pacific Oceans		fish
Smooth butterfly ray	Gymnura micrura	54 in (137 cm)	Atlantic Ocean		fish and shrimp
Lesser devil ray	Mobula hypostoma	47 in (120 cm)	coasts of the western Atlantic Ocean		small fish and crustaceans
Deepwater stingray	Plesiobatis daviesi	106 in (270 cm)	Atlantic Ocean		fish, crabs, lobsters, eels, shrimp
Largetooth sawfish	Pristis microdon	276 in (700 cm)	Indian and Pacific Oceans		sea stars, clams, sea anemones, small fish
Ribbontail stingray	Taeniura lymma	14 in (35 cm)	Indian and Pacific Oceans		mollusks, shrimp, crabs
Ocellate river stingray	Potamotrygon motoro	20 in (50 cm)	Indian and Pacific Oceans		mollusks, crustaceans, fish
Porcupine river stingray	Potamotrygon histrix	16 in (40 cm)	Argentina, Brazil, Paraguay		invertebrates
Wedgenose skate	Dipturus whitleyi	67 in (170 cm)	Argentina, Brazil, Paraguay, Uruguay		crustaceans
Sydney skate	Dipturus australis	20 in (50 cm)	Indian and Pacific Oceans		crustaceans
Thornback ray	Raja clavata	41 in (105 cm)	southwest Pacific Ocean		crustaceans
California skate	Raja inornata	30 in (76 cm)	Atlantic Ocean, Mediterranean and Black Sea		worms and crustaceans
Longnose skate	Raja rhina	55 in (140 cm)	Pacific Ocean		worms and crustaceans
African ray	Raja africana	31 in (80 cm)	southwestern Mediterranean		crustaceans and bony fish
Spotted ray	Raja montagui	31 in (80 cm)	Atlantic Ocean, Mediterranean and Black Sea		crustaceans
Speckled ray	Raja polystigma	24 in (60 cm)	Mediterranean and Black Sea		crustaceans and bony fish
Big skate	Raja binoculata	8.1 ft (2.4 m)	northeastern and eastern central Pacific		crustaceans and bony fish
Mediterranean starry ray	Raja asterias	28 in (70 cm)	Mediterranean and Black Sea		crustaceans
Blonde ray	Raja brachyura	47 in (120 cm)	Atlantic Ocean, Mediterranean and Black seas		crustaceans
Atlantic guitarfish	Rhinobatos lentiginosus	30 in (75 cm)	Atlantic Ocean		mollusks and crustaceans
Marbled electric ray	Torpedo marmorata	39 in (100 cm)	Atlantic Ocean, Mediterranean and Black Seas		small fish
Undulate ray	Raja undulata	39 in (100 cm)	Atlantic Ocean, Mediterranean and Black Seas		crustaceans and worms

COMMON NAME	SCIENTIFIC NAME	SIZE	RANGE	HABITAT	DIET
EELS					
Abyssal cutthroat eel	*Meadia abyssalis*	29 in (73 cm)	Indo-Pacific Ocean		small fish and crustaceans
Grey cutthroat eel	*Synaphobranchus affinis*	63 in (160 cm)	Atlantic, Indian, and Pacific Oceans		invertebrates and fish
Brown garden eel	*Heteroconger longissimus*	20 in (51 cm)	eastern Atlantic Ocean		plankton
Taiwanese moray eel	*Gymnothorax taiwanensis*	21 in (52 cm)	Northwest Pacific: Taiwan		crustaceans and fish
Little conger eel	*Gnathophis habenatus*	17 in (43 cm)	Indo-Pacific Ocean		crustaceans and fish
Swollen-headed conger eel	*Bassanago bulbiceps*	20 in (50 cm)	Southwest Pacific Ocean		crustaceans and fish
White ribbon eel	*Pseudechidna brummeri*	3.4 ft (1 m)	Indo-Pacific Ocean		crustaceans and fish
Death-banded snake-eel	*Ophichthus frontalis*	34 in (86 cm)	Pacific Ocean		crustaceans and fish
European eel	*Anguilla anguilla*	3.2 ft (0.9 m)	Europe		invertebrates
Java spaghetti eel	*Moringua javanica*	47 in (120 cm)	Indo-Pacific		fish and crustaceans
Rusty spaghetti eel	*Moringua ferruginea*	55 in (140 cm)	Indo-Pacific		fish and crustaceans
Slender snipe eel	*Nemichthys scolopaceus*	51 in (130 cm)	Australia		crustaceans
Avocet snipe eel	*Avocettina infans*	29 in (74 cm)	Australia		crustaceans
Gulper eel	*Saccopharynx ampullaceus*	5.2 ft (1.6 m)	eastern Atlantic		fish
Clown knifefish	*Chitala chitala*	48 in (122 cm)	South Asia		aquatic insects, mollusks, fish
Glass knifefish	*Eigenmannia virescens*	14 in (36 cm)	South America		insects
Lesser spiny eel	*Macrognathus aculeatus*	15 in (38 cm)	Asia		small fish
Malabar spiny eel	*Macrognathus guentheri*	10 in (26 cm)	India		small fish
Asian swamp eel	*Monopterus albus*	39 in (100 cm)	South Asia and the U.S.		fish and crustaceans
Marbled swamp eel	*Synbranchus marmoratus*	59 in (150 cm)	Central and South America		fish and invertebrates
COD AND RELATIVES					
Pacific cod	*Gadus macrocephalus*	47 in (119 cm)	North Pacific Ocean		fish, octopuses, crustaceans
Offshore silver hake	*Merluccius albidus*	16 in (40 cm)	western central Atlantic Ocean		fish, crustaceans, squid
DEEP-SEA FISH					
Kroyer's deep-sea angler fish	*Ceratias holboelli*	30 in (77 cm)	Australia		fish and crustaceans
Soft leafvent angler	*Haplophryne mollis*	6 in (15 cm)	tropical and subtropical parts of all oceans		fish and crustaceans
Little dragonfish	*Eurypegasus draconis*	4 in (11 cm)	Australia, Oceania, parts of Asia and Africa		insects, worms, crustaceans
TROUT AND SALMON					
Pink salmon	*Oncorhynchus gorbuscha*	30 in (76 cm)	Pacific and Arctic Oceans		insects
Masu salmon	*Oncorhynchus masou masou*	31 in (79 cm)	northwestern Pacific Ocean		insects, fish, crustaceans
Coho salmon	*Oncorhynchus kisutch*	43 in (108 cm)	North Pacific		fish, jellyfish, squid
Chinook salmon	*Oncorhynchus tshawytscha*	59 in (150 cm)	Arctic, Northwest to Northeast Pacific		insects and crustaceans
Chum salmon	*Oncorhynchus keta*	39 in (100 cm)	North Pacific Ocean and Bering Sea		crustaceans, fish, squid
Brown trout	*Salmo trutta trutta*	55 in (140 cm)	Europe and Asia		insects, mollusks, crustaceans, and small fish
Bull trout	*Salvelinus confluentus*	41 in (103 cm)	Canada, United States		invertebrates and small fish
Golden trout	*Oncorhynchus aguabonita*	28 in (71 cm)	North America		insects and small crustaceans
Apache trout	*Oncorhynchus apache*	23 in (58 cm)	United States		insects
CATFISH, PIRANHAS, AND RELATIVES					
Black tetra	*Gymnocorymbus ternetzi*	3 in (8 cm)	South America		worms, crustaceans, plants
Glowlight tetra	*Hemigrammus erythrozonus*	1.5 in (4 cm)	South America: Essequibo River		worms, crustaceans, plants
African moon tetra	*Bathyaethiops caudomaculatus*	3 in (8 cm)	Africa		worms, crustaceans, plants
Copper tetra	*Hasemania melanura*	1.5 in (4 cm)	South America: Iguaçu River basin		worms, crustaceans, plants
Johnny darter	*Etheostoma nigrum*	3 in (7 cm)	North America		insects and larvae

COMMON NAME	SCIENTIFIC NAME	SIZE	RANGE	HABITAT	DIET
Gulf darter	Etheostoma swaini	3 in (8 cm)	North America		insects and larvae
Least darter	Etheostoma microperca	1.5 in (4 cm)	North America		larvae and microcrustaceans
Spotted hatchetfish	Gasteropelecus maculatus	2 in (5 cm)	Central and South America		crustaceans, larvae, insects
Marbled hatchetfish	Carnegiella strigata	1.5 in (4 cm)	South America		crustaceans and insects
Torrent sucker	Thoburnia rhothoeca	7 in (18 cm)	North America		plants and larvae
Desert sucker	Catostomus clarkii	13 in (33 cm)	North America		diatoms, detritus, invertebrates
Longnose sucker	Catostomus catostomus catostomus	25 in (63.5 cm)	North America		invertebrates
Mottled loach	Acanthocobitis botia	4 in (11 cm)	South Asia		invertebrates
Jonklaas's loach	Lepidocephalichthys jonklaasi	2 in (5 cm)	Sri Lanka		invertebrates
Almorha loach	Botia almorhae	6 in (15 cm)	India		invertebrates
Crucian carp	Carassius carassius	25 in (64 cm)	Europe		plankton and invertebrates
Bighead carp	Hypophthalmichthys nobilis	4.8 ft (1.5 m)	China		zooplankton
Hoven's carp	Leptobarbus hoevenii	39 in (100 cm)	Asia		plankton and invertebrates
Sailfin molly	Poecilia latipinna	6 in (15 cm)	North America		algae and plant material
Blackstripe topminnow	Fundulus notatus	3 in (8 cm)	Canada and midwestern United States		insects and larvae
Golden topminnow	Fundulus chrysotus	3.5 in (9 cm)	North America		insects and larvae
Mummichog	Fundulus heteroclitus heteroclitus	6 in (15 cm)	Western Atlantic		phytoplankton, crustaceans, larvae
Salt Creek pupfish	Cyprinodon salinus salinus	2.75 in (7 cm)	California		algae and small snails
Grass carp	Ctenopharyngodon idella	60 in (150 cm)	Asia		aquatic plants and insects
Green swordtail	Xiphophorus hellerii	5.5 in (14 cm)	North and Central America		insects, crustaceans, worms
Guppy	Poecilia reticulata	2 in (5 cm)	South America		zooplankton and insects
Foureyes	Anableps microlepis	13 in (33 cm)	Central and South America		insects
Slender walking catfish	Clarias nieuhofii	20 in (50 cm)	Southeast Asia		insects and crustaceans
Philippine catfish	Clarias batrachus	18.5 in (47 cm)	Asia		insects, fish, crustaceans
Striped eel catfish	Plotosus lineatus	13 in (33 cm)	Australia		crustaceans, mollusks, fish
African glass catfish	Pareutropius debauwi	4 in (11 cm)	Central Africa		crustaceans and insects
Giant river catfish	Sperata seenghala	60 in (150 cm)	Bangladesh, India, Nepal		fish
African catfish	Clarias gariepinus	67 in (170 cm)	Africa		insects, crustaceans, other invertebrates
PERCH AND RELATIVES					
Nile tilapia	Oreochromis niloticus niloticus	24 in (61 cm)	Indian and Pacific Oceans		phytoplankton and algae
Redbelly tilapia	Tilapia zillii	16 in (40 cm)	Africa and Eurasia		vegetation and invertebrates
Black drum	Pogonias cromis	67 in (170 cm)	Western Atlantic		crustaceans and fish
Freshwater drum	Aplodinotus grunniens	3.1 ft (0.9 m)	North and Central America		aquatic insects and fish
Striped snakehead	Channa striata	39 in (100 cm)	South Asia		snakes, frogs, insects, crustaceans
Barca snakehead	Channa barca	35 in (90 cm)	Australia		fish
Orange roughy slimehead	Hoplostethus atlanticus	30 in (75 cm)	Australia		fish and crustaceans
Mediterranean slimehead	Hoplostethus mediterraneus mediterraneus	17 in (42 cm)	Atlantic, Indian, and Pacific Oceans		fish and crustaceans
Panamic flashlight fish	Phthanophaneron harveyi	10 in (26 cm)	Pacific – eastern central		crustaceans
Splitfin flashlight fish	Anomalops katoptron	14 in (35.6 cm)	Pacific Ocean		zooplankton
White bass	Morone chrysops	18 in (45 cm)	Canada and United States		fish
Yellow bass	Morone mississippiensis	18 in (45 cm)	North America		fish
Bluespot mullet	Moolgarda seheli	24 in (61 cm)	Indo-Pacific		algae and diatoms
Starry flounder	Platichthys stellatus	36 in (91 cm)	North Pacific		crustaceans, worms, small fish

COMMON NAME	SCIENTIFIC NAME	SIZE	RANGE	HABITAT	DIET
European flounder	Platichthys flesus	24 in (60 cm)	Atlantic, Arctic Oceans; Med. and Black Seas		small fish and invertebrates
European plaice	Pleuronectes platessa	39 in (100 cm)	Europe		mollusks
Atlantic halibut	Hippoglossus hippoglossus	15.4 ft (4.7 m)	Atlantic Ocean		fish
Greenland halibut	Reinhardtius hippoglossoides	51 in (130 cm)	Circumglobal		crustaceans and fish
Common sole	Solea solea	28 in (70 cm)	Eastern Atlantic		worms, fish, crustaceans
Spotted rainbowfish	Glossolepis maculosus	2 in (5 cm)	Papua New Guinea		shrimp and worms
Red rainbowfish	Glossolepis incisus	6 in (15 cm)	Indonesia		insects and crustaceans
Atlantic silverside	Menidia menidia	6 in (15 cm)	Western Atlantic		shrimp, squid, worms
Panama silverside	Atherinella panamensis	4 in (11 cm)	Pacific Ocean		zooplankton and larvae
Common halfbeak	Hyporhamphus unifasciatus	12 in (30 cm)	Australia		algae and small animals
Ballyhoo halfbeak	Hemiramphus brasiliensis	22 in (55 cm)	Australia		seagrasses and small animals
Jumping halfbeak	Hemiramphus archipelagicus	13 in (33 cm)	Indo-Pacific		algae and small animals
Keeltail needlefish	Platybelone argalus argalus	20 in (50 cm)	Atlantic, Indian, and Pacific Oceans		small fish
Atlantic needlefish	Strongylura timucu	24 in (61 cm)	Western Atlantic		small fish
Ninespine stickleback	Pungitius pungitius	3.5 in (9 cm)	Europe and Asia		insects and larvae
Redmouth whalefish	Rondeletia loricata	4 in (11 cm)	Worldwide in tropical to temperate seas		crustaceans
TUNA, MARLIN, SWORDFISH, AND RELATIVES					
Albacore	Thunnus alalunga	55 in (140 cm)	All oceans except polar; Med. and Black Seas		crustaceans, fish, squid
Atlantic bluefin tuna	Thunnus thynnus	55 in (140 cm)	Atlantic Ocean; Mediterranean and Black Seas		crustaceans, fish, squid
Guachanche barracuda	Sphyraena guachancho	79 in (200 cm)	Australia		fish and squid
Atlantic blue marlin	Makaira nigricans	16.4 ft (5.0 m)	Atlantic, Pacific Oceans; Med. and Black Seas		fish
Indo-Pacific blue marlin	Makaira mazara	197 in (500 cm)	Indo-Pacific		squid, fish, crustaceans
Indo-Pacific sailfish	Istiophorus platypterus	137 in (348 cm)	All oceans except polar; Med. and Black Seas		fish and crustaceans
SCORPIONFISH AND SCULPINS					
Orange filefish	Aluterus schoepfii	24 in (60 cm)	Western Atlantic		algae and seagrass
Titan triggerfish	Balistoides viridescens	30 in (75 cm)	Indo-Pacific Ocean		crustaceans and mollusks
Ocean sunfish	Mola mola	131 in (333 cm)	Warm and temperate zones of all oceans		fish, jellyfish, zooplankton
Northern puffers	Sphoeroides maculatus	14 in (35.6 cm)	Western Atlantic		shellfish
White-spotted puffer	Arothron hispidus	20 in (50 cm)	Indo-Pacific Ocean		crustaceans, mollusks, worms
Leatherjackets	Oligoplites saurus	14 in (35.6 cm)	Western Atlantic Ocean		fish and crustaceans
Honeycomb cowfish	Acanthostracion polygonius	20 in (50 cm)	Western Atlantic Ocean		sponges and crustaceans
Scrawled cowfish	Acanthostracion quadricornis	22 in (55 cm)	Atlantic Ocean		sponges and crustaceans
Buffalo trunkfish	Lactophrys trigonus	22 in (55 cm)	Western Atlantic Ocean		crustaceans, mollusks, worms
Frillfin turkeyfish	Pterois mombasae	12 in (31 cm)	Indo-Pacific Ocean		fish and crustaceans
Blue rockfish	Sebastes mystinus	24 in (61 cm)	Eastern Pacific Ocean		plankton
Fringelip flathead	Sunagocia otaitensis	12 in (30 cm)	Indo-Pacific Ocean		fish and crustaceans
Dusky flathead	Platycephalus fuscus	47 in (120 cm)	Western Pacific Ocean		fish and crustaceans
European bullhead	Cottus gobio	7 in (18 cm)	Europe		crustaceans and insects
Alpine bullhead	Cottus poecilopus	6 in (15 cm)	Europe		algae, crustaceans, insects
Estuarine stonefish	Synanceia horrida	24 in (61 cm)	Indo-Pacific Ocean		crustaceans and small fish
Red Sea stonefish	Synanceia nana	5 in (13 cm)	Western Indian Ocean		crustaceans
REEF FISH AND SEAHORSES					
Belly pipefish	Hippichthys heptagonus	6 in (15 cm)	Indian and Pacific Oceans		fish

COMMON NAME	SCIENTIFIC NAME	SIZE	RANGE	HABITAT	DIET
● Freshwater pipefish	*Pseudophallus mindii*	6 in (15 cm)	Central and South America		fish
● Spotted seahorse	*Hippocampus kuda*	12 in (30 cm)	Indian and Oceans		zooplankton
● Short-snouted seahorse	*Hippocampus hippocampus*	6 in (15 cm)	Atlantic Ocean; Mediterranean and Black Seas		zooplankton
● Blue-and-yellow wrasse	*Anampses lennardi*	11 in (28 cm)	Indian Ocean		invertebrates
● Bluestreak cleaner wrasse	*Labroides dimidiatus*	5.5 in (14 cm)	Indian, Atlantic, and Pacific Oceans		crustaceans
● Day grouper	*Epinephelus striatus*	4 ft (1.2 m)	Atlantic Ocean		crustaceans and fish
● White grouper	*Epinephelus aeneus*	47 in (120 cm)	Atlantic Ocean		crustaceans and fish
● Banded archerfish	*Toxotes jaculatrix*	12 in (30 cm)	Asia and Oceania		insects and vegetation
● Spotted archerfish	*Toxotes chatareus*	16 in (40 cm)	Asia and Oceania		insects and vegetation
● Bluehead combtooth blenny	*Ecsenius lividanalis*	2 in (5 cm)	Western Pacific Ocean		algae and plant material
● Lined rockskipper	*Blenniella bilitonensis*	6 in (16 cm)	Western Pacific Ocean		algae
● Spotted surgeon fish	*Ctenochaetus strigosus*	5.5 in (14 cm)	Australia		detritus
● Giant gourami	*Osphronemus goramy*	28 in (70 cm)	Asia		plants, fish, frogs
● Snakeskin gourami	*Trichogaster pectoralis*	10 in (25 cm)	Asia		aquatic vegetation
● Common dragonet	*Callionymus lyra*	12 in (30 cm)	Eastern Atlantic Ocean		invertebrates, crustaceans, worms
● Blotchfin dragonet	*Callionymus filamentosus*	8 in (20 cm)	Indo-West Pacific Ocean		invertebrates, crustaceans, worms
● Puntang goby	*Exyrias puntang*	6 in (16 cm)	Western Pacific Ocean		crustaceans
● Dartfish	*Myxodagnus belone*	3 in (8 cm)	Western Central Atlantic Ocean		crustaceans
● Vermiculated spinefoot	*Siganus vermiculatus*	18 in (45 cm)	Australia		algae and plant material
● Foxface rabbitfish	*Siganus vulpinus*	10 in (25 cm)	Australia		algae and plant material
● John's snapper	*Lutjanus johnii*	38 in (97 cm)	Indo-West Pacific Ocean		fish and invertebrates
● Blacktail snapper	*Lutjanus fulvus*	16 in (40 cm)	Indo-Pacific Ocean		fish and shrimp
● Eastern kelpfish	*Chironemus marmoratus*	16 in (40 cm)	Southwest Pacific Ocean		invertebrates and fish
● Giant kelpfish	*Heterostichus rostratus*	24 in (61 cm)	Eastern Pacific Ocean		crustaceans and fish
● Mediterranean parrotfish	*Sparisoma cretense*	20 in (50 cm)	Atlantic Ocean; Mediterranean and Black Sea		invertebrates and algae
● Rivulated parrotfish	*Scarus rivulatus*	16 in (40 cm)	Indian and Pacific Oceans		algae
● Orange clownfish	*Amphiprion percula*	4 in (11 cm)	Western Pacific Ocean		zooplankton
● Clown anemonefish	*Amphiprion ocellaris*	4 in (11 cm)	Indo-Pacific Ocean		zooplankton and algae

INVERTEBRATES

- ● ALERT
- ● IN TROUBLE
- ● STABLE
- ● DOMESTICATED
- ● UNDER STUDY
- ● NOT LISTED

COMMON NAME	SCIENTIFIC NAME	SIZE	RANGE	HABITAT	DIET
SPONGES					
● Brown bowl sponge	*Cribrochalina vasculum*	8 to 18 in (20 to 45 cm)	Caribbean, Bahamas, south Florida		bacteria, tiny marine organisms
● Touch-me-not sponge	*Neofibularia nolitangere*	1 to 4 ft (30 to 120 cm)	Caribbean, Bahamas, Florida		bacteria, tiny marine organisms
● Yellow tube sponge	*Aplysina fistularis*	2 to 4 ft (30 to 60 cm)	Caribbean, Bahamas, Florida		bacteria, tiny marine organisms
● Black-ball sponge	*Ircinia strobilina*	1 to 2 ft (30 to 60 cm)	Caribbean, Bahamas, Florida		bacteria, tiny marine organisms
● Stinker sponge	*Ircinia felix*	6 to 12 in (15 to 30 cm)	Caribbean, Bahamas, Florida		bacteria, tiny marine organisms
● Dark volcano sponge	*Svenzea zeai*	1 to 3 ft (30 to 90 cm)	Caribbean and Florida		bacteria, tiny marine organisms

COMMON NAME	SCIENTIFIC NAME	SIZE	RANGE	HABITAT	DIET
Pink lumpy sponge	Monanchora unguifera	4 to 16 in (10 to 40 cm)	Caribbean, Bahamas, south Florida		bacteria, tiny marine organisms
Orange elephant ear sponge	Agelas clathrodes	2 to 6 ft (.6 to 1.8 m)	Caribbean, Bahamas, Florida		bacteria, tiny marine organisms
Row-pore rope sponge	Aplysina cauliformis	4 to 8 ft (1.2 to 2.5 m)	Caribbean, Bahamas, Florida		bacteria, tiny marine organisms
Red encrusting sponge	Monanchora barbadensis	4 to 10 in (10 to 25 cm)	Caribbean, Bahamas, Florida		bacteria, tiny marine organisms
Red boring sponge	Cliona delitrix	6 to 12 in (15 to 30 cm)	Caribbean, Bahamas, Florida		bacteria, tiny marine organisms
Yellow calcereous sponge	Clathrina canariensis	2 to 4 in (5 to 10 cm)	Caribbean, Bahamas, Florida		bacteria, tiny marine organisms
Orange icing encrusting sponge	Mycale laevis	4 to 18 in (10 to 45 cm)	Caribbean, Bahamas, Florida		bacteria, tiny marine organisms
Golf ball sponge	Cinachyrella australiensis	up to 3 in (8 cm)	Indo-West Pacific Ocean		bacteria, tiny marine organisms
Fan sponge	Phyllospongia lamellosa	up to 3 ft (1 m)	Indo-West Pacific Ocean		bacteria, tiny marine organisms
Glove sponge	Spongia officinalis	13.8 in (35 cm) in diameter	Mediterranean Sea		bacteria, tiny marine organisms
WORMS					
Racing stripe flatworm	Pseudoceros bifurcus	up to 2.25 in (6 cm)	west Pacific Ocean		tiny marine organisms
Leopard flatworm	Pseudobiceros pardalis	1 to 2 in (2.5 to 5 cm)	Caribbean, Bahamas, Florida		tiny marine organisms
Bearded fireworm	Hermodice carunculata	4 to 6 in (10 to 15 cm)	Caribbean, Bahamas, Florida		corals, anemones, small crustaceans
Star horseshoe worm	Pomatostegus stellatus	0.75 to 1.5 in (1.8 to 3.8 cm)	Caribbean, Bahamas, Florida		tiny marine organisms
Indian feather-duster worm	Sabellastarte spectabilis	up to 4 in (10 cm)	Indo-Pacific Ocean and Hawaii, U.S.		tiny marine particles
Pork tapeworm	Taenia solium	6.6 to 23 ft (2 to 7 m)	Worldwide	(in hosts)	food from human host
Sheep liver fluke	Fasciola hepatica	1 in (2.5 cm)	Europe, Mexico, Central America		sheep blood and liver
Dugesia flatworm	Dugesia sagitta	0.4 in (10 mm)	Corfu in Greece		tiny marine organisms
Freshwater planarian	Schmidtea mediterranea	up to 0.8 in (2 cm)	Europe		tiny marine organisms
Green earthworm	Allolobophora chlorotica	1.18 to 2.36 in (3 to 8 cm)	Europe		soil feeders
Black worm	Lumbriculus variegatus	3.94 in (10 cm)	Europe and North America		microorganisms and organic material
Sludge worm	Tubifex tubifex	7.9 in (20 cm)	worldwide		bacteria and sediments
Grindal worm	Enchytraeus buchholzi	0.5 to 1.5 in (12 to 38 mm)	many areas worldwide		anything organic
Kinabalu giant red leech	Pheretima darnleiensis	27.5 in (70 cm)	Southeast Asia		worms, such as the Kinabalu giant earthworm
Japanese mountain leech	Haemadipsa zeylanica	up to 2.4 in (6 cm)	Japan		blood
CORALS					
Branching fire coral	Millepora alcicornis	1 to 18 in (2.5 to 45 cm)	Caribbean, Bahamas, Florida		algae that reside within the coral's tissue, small organisms, plankton
Venus sea fan	Gorgonia flabellum	2 to 3.5 ft (60 to 100 cm)	Caribbean and Bahamas		algae and small particles
Corky sea finger	Briareum asbestinum	0.5 to 2 ft (15 to 60 cm)	Caribbean, Bahamas, Florida		algae and small particles
Colorful sea rod	Diodogorgia nodulifera	4 to 12 in (10 to 30 cm)	Caribbean, Bahamas, Florida		algae and small particles
Feathery black coral	Antipathes pennacea	1 to 5 ft (.3 to 1.5 m)	Caribbean and Bahamas		algae and small particles
Ten-ray star coral	Madracis decactis	1 to 6 in (2.5 to 15 cm)	Caribbean, Bahamas, Florida		algae and small particles
Grooved brain coral	Diploria labyrinthiformis	1 to 4 ft (30 to 120 cm)	Caribbean, Bahamas, Florida		algae and small particles
Knobby brain coral	Diploria clivosa	6 in to 4 ft (15 to 120 cm)	Caribbean, Bahamas, Florida		algae and small particles
Thin leaf lettuce coral	Agaricia tenuifolia	4 to 12 ft (1 to 3.5 m)	northwest Caribbean		algae and small particles
Smooth flower coral	Eusmilia fastiginia	polyps: .75 to 1.25 in (2 to 3 cm)	Caribbean, Bahamas, Florida		algae and small particles
Common razor coral	Fungia scutaria	4 to 7 in (10 to 18 cm)	Indo-Pacific Ocean, Hawaii in U.S., Red Sea		algae and small particles
Common mushroom coral	Fungia fungites	11.8 in (30 cm)	Indo-Pacific Ocean, Australia, Red Sea		algae and small particles
Elkhorn coral	Acropora palmata	2.5 ft (0.75 m)	southern Florida to northern Venezuela		algae that live in their tissues
Fire coral	Millepora alcicornis	2.5 ft (0.75 m)	Caribbean Sea		small particles
ANEMONES AND JELLYFISH					
Sun anemone	Stichodactyla helianthus	disc: 4 to 6 in (10 to 15 cm)	Caribbean and Bahamas		fish, shrimp, isopods, amphipods, plankton

COMMON NAME	SCIENTIFIC NAME	SIZE	RANGE	HABITAT	DIET
Warty sea anemone	Bunodosoma cavernata	1 to 3 in (2.5 to 7.6 cm)	Caribbean, Bahamas, Florida, Gulf of Mexico		fish, shrimp, isopods, amphipods, plankton
Elegant anemone	Actinoporus elegans	7 to 9 in (18 to 23 cm)	Caribbean		fish, shrimp, isopods, amphipods, plankton
Leathery sea anemone	Heteractis crispa	up to 20 in (50 cm)	Indo-Pacific, Australia, Polynesia, Red Sea		fish, shrimp, isopods, amphipods, plankton
Hermit crab anemone	Calliactis polypus	up to 3 in (7.6 cm)	Indo-Pacific, Hawaii, Red Sea		fish, shrimp, isopods, amphipods, plankton
Orange ball corallimorph	Pseudocorynactis caribbeorum	1 to 2 in (2.5 to 5 cm)	Caribbean and Bahamas		small fish and particles
Christmas tree hydroid	Pennaria disticha	3 to 5 in (7.6 to 13 cm)	Caribbean, Bahamas, Florida, Hawaii		plankton
Upside-down jelly	Cassiopea frondosa	4 to 5 in (10 to 13 cm)	Caribbean, Bahamas, Florida		zooplankton, algae, aquatic crustaceans and other marine invertebrates
Sea thimble jellyfish	Linuche unguiculata	0.5 to 0.75 in (1.25 to 2 cm)	Circumtropical		aquatic crustaceans and other marine invertebrates, zooplankton, algae
Sponge zoanthid	Parazoanthus parasiticus	0.25 in (0.7 cm)	Caribbean, Bahamas, Florida, Bermuda		algae, aquatic crustaceans and other marine invertebrates, zooplankton
Red-spot comb jelly	Eurhamphaea vexilligera	1 to 2 in (2.5 to 5 cm)	Pacific, Caribbean, Gulf of Mex., Fla., Bermuda		zooplankton: mollusk and fish larvae, copepods, amphipods, krill
Stinging bush hydroid	Macrorhynchia robusta	4 to 8 in (10 to 20 cm)	Caribbean, Bahamas, Florida		zooplankton: mollusk and fish larvae, copepods, amphipods, krill
Spotted Jelly	Mastigias pupua	24 in (61 cm)	Pacific and Indian Oceans, China Sea		zooplankton
Lion's mane jellyfish	Cyanea capillata	11 to 70 in (30 to 180 cm)	Arctic, north Atlantic, north Pacific Oceans		mainly fish
Box jellyfish, or sea wasp	Chironex fleckeri	9.84 ft (3 m)	Australia, New Guinea to Phillipines, Asia		fish and aquatic crustaceans
SNAILS AND SLUGS					
Black slug	Arion ater	1 to 6 in (2.5 to 15 cm)	England and Pacific Northwest		fungi, plants, worms, insects, decaying vegetation, feces
Moon snail	Euspira lewisii	4 in (10 cm)	Pacific Ocean coast, Vancouver Island to Mexico		clams, mussels, mollusks
Painted elysia	Thuridilla picta	0.5 to 1 in (1 to 2.5 cm)	Caribbean, Bahamas, Florida		algae
Spotted sea hare	Aplysia dactylomela	3 to 8 in (7.6 to 20 cm)	Circumtropical		algae
Lettuce sea slug	Elysia crispata	1 to 2 in (2 to 5 cm)	Caribbean, Bahamas, Florida		algae
Purple-spotted sea goddess	Hypselodoris marci	0.5 to 1 in (1.2 to 2.5 cm)	Bay Islands (Honduras), Belize, Venezuela		algae
Fried-egg nudibranch	Phyllidia varicosa	2 to 3 in (5 to 7.6 cm)	Indo-Pacific, Hawaii, Red Sea		sponges
Tiger cowry	Cypraea tigris	3 to 5 in (7.6 to 12 cm)	Indo-Pacific, Hawaii, Red Sea		soft corals, sponges, anemones
Queen conch	Strombus gigas	6 to 9 in (15 to 23 cm)	Caribbean, Bahamas, South Florida		algae and detritus
West Indian top snail	Cittarium pica	2 to 4 in (5 to 10 cm)	Caribbean, Bahamas, Florida		algae; sometimes detritus
Edible snail	Helix pomatia	1.50 to 1.97 in (3.8 to 5.0 cm)	Europe, Asia, the Americas		leaves, fruit, flowers, sap or other plant fluids
CLAMS, OYSTERS, MUSSELS, AND SCALLOPS					
Antillean fileclam	Lima pellucida	.75 to 1 in (1.8 to 2.5 cm)	Caribbean, Bahamas, Florida		microscopic marine plants and animals
Atlantic thorny oyster	Spondylus americanus	3 to 5 in (8 to 13 cm)	Caribbean, Bahamas, Florida		microscopic marine plants and animals
Frond oyster	Dendostrea frons	1.5 to 2.5 in (4 to 6 cm)	Caribbean, Bahamas, Florida		microscopic marine plants and animals
Giant clam	Tridacna gigas	up to 50 in (130 cm)	Indo-Pacific Ocean and Great Barrier Reef		microscopic marine plants and animals
Smooth giant clam	Tridacna derasa	up to 20 in (50 cm)	Indo-West Pacific Ocean and Australia		dissolved organic compounds from the water; zooxanthellae algae in its tissues
Fluted giant clam	Tridacna squamosa	up to 16 in (40 cm)	Indo-Pacific Ocean		dissolved organic compounds from the water; zooxanthellae algae in its tissues
Fuzzy chiton	Acanthopleura granulata	3 in (7.6 cm)	Caribbean, Bahamas, Florida		microscopic marine plants
California mussel	Mytilus californicus	8 in (20 cm)	California in U.S.		microscopic marine plants
Freshwater pearl mussel	Margaritifera margaritifera	4.53 in (11.5 cm)	Norway to Spain and Great Britian		fungal spores, bacteria, tiny phytoplankton and zooplankton, other filterable particles
Zebra mussel	Dreissena polymorpha	0.79 in (2 cm)	Great Lakes and many North American rivers		bacteria, blue-green algae, small green algae, protozoans
Atlantic sea scallop	Placopecten magellanicus	5.9 in (15 cm)	western Atlantic Ocean		microscopic plants, bacteria, organic particles
OCTOPUSES AND RELATIVES					
Common octopus	Octopus vulgaris	1 to 3 ft (30 to 90 cm)	Caribbean, Bahamas, Florida		gastropods and bivalves
Caribbean reef octopus	Octopus briareus	1 to 2 ft (30 to 60 cm)	Caribbean, Bahamas, Florida		crabs and shrimp
Chambered nautilus	Nautilus pompilius	8 in (20 cm)	Indo-Pacific Ocean		crabs and fish
Broadclub cuttlefish	Sepia latimanus	6 to 20 in. (15 to 50 cm)	Indo-Pacific Ocean and Great Barrier Reef		crabs and fish

COMMON NAME	SCIENTIFIC NAME	SIZE	RANGE	HABITAT	DIET
European squid	*Loligo vulgaris*	5.9 to 9.8 in (15 to 25 cm)	Europe and the Mediterranean Sea		small fish
Greater blue-ringed octopus	*Hapalochlaena lunulata*	1.96 to 2.755 in (5 to 7 cm)	Indo-Pacific and Indian Oceans		fish, crabs, mollusks, other small marine animals
ECHINODERMS					
Cookie-dough sea cucumber	*Isostichopus badionotus*	0.06 to 6.56 ft (.02 to 2 m)	Pacific coast South Am., and Galápagos Islands		detritus or sediments
Pin-cushion sea star	*Culcita novaeguineae*	7 to 10 in (18 to 25 cm)	Indo-Pacific, Hawaii, Polynesia		detritus; small invertebrates, including stony corals
Comet star	*Ophidiaster guildingi*	2 to 4 in (5 to 10 cm)	Caribbean Sea and Florida Keys		detritus; small invertebrates, including stony corals
Crown-of-thorns	*Acanthaster planci*	8 to 24 in (20 to 60 cm)	Indo-Pacific, Hawaii, Red Sea, Polynesia, East Pacific		cnidarians and other marine invertebrates; algae
Beautiful feather star	*Cenometra bella*	arms up to 6 in (15 cm)	West Pacific		detritus; small invertebrates, including stony corals
Sponge brittle star	*Ophiothrix suensonii*	2 to 3 in (5 to 8 cm)	Caribbean, Bahamas, Florida, Bermuda		detritus; small invertebrates, including stony corals
Pebble collector urchin	*Pseudoboletia indiana*	4 to 5 in (10 to 13 cm)	Indo-Pacific Ocean and Hawaii		small nutritive matter in the sand
Red heart urchin	*Meoma ventricosa*	4 to 6 in (10 to 15 cm)	Caribbean, Bahamas, Florida		small nutritive matter in the sand
Donkey dung sea cucumber	*Holothuria mexicana*	10 to 14 in (25 to 35 cm)	Caribbean, Bahamas, Florida Keys		algae, tiny aquatic organisms, detritus
Difficult sea cucumber	*Holothuria difficilis*	up to 5 in (13 cm)	Indo-Pacific Ocean and Hawaii		algae, tiny aquatic organisms, detritus
Giant sea cucumber	*Thelenota anax*	20 to 40 in (50 to 100 cm)	Indo-Pacific Ocean		algae, tiny aquatic organisms, detritus
Leopard sea cucumber	*Bohadschia argus*	10 to 50 in (25 to 50 cm)	Indo-Pacific Ocean		plankton and decaying organic matter
CRABS, SHRIMP, AND LOBSTERS					
American lobster	*Homarus americanus*	3.61 ft (1.1 m)	Atlantic coast of North America		fish, carrion, mollusks, crustaceans, algae, macroalgae
Red-banded lobster	*Justitia longimanus*	5 to 8 in (12 to 20 cm)	Caribbean, Florida, Bermuda, Indo-Pacific, Hawaii		fish, carrion, mollusks, crustaceans, algae, macroalgae
Red reef lobster	*Enoplometopus occidentalis*	up to 5 in (12 cm)	Indo-Pacific Ocean and Hawaii		algae, small fish, small invertebrates
Red snapping shrimp	*Alpheus spp.*	1 to 2 in (2.5 to 5 cm)	Caribbean, Bahamas, Florida		algae, small fish, small invertebrates
Magnificent anemone shrimp	*Ancylomenes magnificus*	up to 1 in (2.5 cm)	West Pacific		detritus and small invertebrates
Glass anemone shrimp	*Periclimenes brevicarpalis*	0.8 to 1.5 in (2 to 4 cm)	Indo-Pacific, Australia, Red Sea		detritus and small invertebrates
Spotted cleaner shrimp	*Periclimenes yucatanicus*	0.75 to 1 in (1.8 to 2.5 cm)	Caribbean, Bahamas, South Florida		detritus and small inverts
Banded coral shrimp	*Stenopus hispidus*	2.4 in (6.2 cm)	Indo-Pacific Ocean		marine worms, aquatic crustaceans, and other marine invertebrates, zooplankton
Hawaiian swimming crab	*Charybdis hawaiensis*	up to 3 in (7.6 cm)	Central Pacific Ocean and Polynesia		fish, mollusks, marine worms, aquatic crustaceans, other marine invertebrates, leaves
Blue-eyed rock crab	*Percnon affine*	up to 3 in (7.6 cm)	Pacific Ocean and Hawaii		fish, mollusks, marine worms, aquatic crustaceans, other marine invertebrates, leaves
Atlantic blue crab	*Callinectes sapidus*	4.7 to 6.7 in (12 to 17 cm)	Atlantic Ocean; Asia and Europe		fish, mollusks, marine worms, aquatic crustaceans, other marine invertebrates, leaves
Japanese spider crab	*Macrocheira kaempferi*	9.8 ft (3 m)	Japanese islands of Konshu and Kyushu		fish, carrion, aquatic crustaceans, and other marine invertebrates, algae
Poll's stellate barnacle	*Chthamalus stellatus*	0.55 in (1.4 cm)	British Isles		plankton and detritus
Acorn barnacle	*Semibalanus balanoides*	up to 0.5 in (1.3 cm)	Pacific and Atlantic coasts		filter particles of food
Giant freshwater crayfish	*Astacopsis gouldi*	15.8 in (40 cm)	Australia and Tasmania		decaying wood
SPIDERS, SCORPIONS, TICKS, AND MITES					
Fishing spider	*Dolomedes triton*	0.4 to 1.0 in. (9 to 26 mm)	Texas to the Atlantic Coast		insect larvae, tadpoles, small fish
Sydney funnel-web spider	*Atrax robustus*	1 to 1.3 in (25 to 35 mm)	Sydney, Australia		beetles, cockroaches, insect larvae, land snails, millipedes; also frogs, other small vertebrates
Large Carolina wolf spider	*Hogna carolinensis*	.7 to 1.3 in (18 to 35 mm)	United States		grasshoppers, crickets, other similar agricultural pests
Yellow garden spider	*Argiope aurantia*	.25 to 1.4 in (5 to 28 mm)	southern Canada to Costa Rica		insects, such as aphids, flies, grasshoppers, Hymenoptera
Pinktoe tarantula	*Avicularia avicularia*	4.5 in (11 cm)	northern South America		crickets, cockroaches, flying insects
American dog tick	*Dermacentor variabilis*	0.25 in (6.35 mm)	North America		blood from host
Brazilian wandering spider	*Phoneutria fera*	4 to 5 in (10 to 12.7 cm)	Central and South America		insects, small lizards, pinkie mice
Asian forest scorpion	*Heterometrus longimanus*	3.5 to 5 in (8.9 to 12.7 cm)	Southeast Asia		insects and other arthropods
Brown recluse spider	*Loxosceles reclusa*	0.5 in (12.7 mm)	Midwestern United States		insects
Feather-legged orb weaver	*Uloborus glomosus*	0.06 to 2.75 in (2 to 30 mm)	Eastern North America		insects
Goliath bird-eating tarantula	*Theraphosa blondi*	12 in (30 cm)	South America		insects and other invertebrates; also a wide variety of vertebrates

COMMON NAME	SCIENTIFIC NAME	SIZE	RANGE	HABITAT	DIET
Hobo spider	*Tegenaria agrestis*	2 in (5 cm)	Europe and North America		insects
Honey bee mite	*Acarapis woodi*	0.007 in (.02 cm)	in tracheae of bees		live off host
Northern black widow spider	*Latrodectus variolus*	.25 to .50 in (.6 to 1.3 cm)	northern Florida to southeastern Canada		insects
Deathstalker scorpion	*Leiurus quinquestriatus*	1.2 to 3.0 in (30 to 77 mm)	North Africa and the Middle East		insects and other invertebrates

CENTIPEDES AND MILLIPEDES

COMMON NAME	SCIENTIFIC NAME	SIZE	RANGE	HABITAT	DIET
Australian house centipede	*Allothereua maculata*	0.8 to 1.0 in (20 to 25 mm)	southern Australia		insects and other arthropods
Mediterranean banded centipede	*Scolopendra cingulata*	4 to 6 in (10 to 15 cm)	Southern Europe and the Mediterranean		insects and other small animals
Stone centipede	*Lithobius forficatus*	0.7 to 1.3 in (18 to 30 mm)	Europe		insects, spiders, and other small invertebrates, including centipedes
Amazonian giant centipede	*Scolopendra gigantea*	12 in (30 cm)	Northern South America		small invertebrates, such as crickets, worms, snails, roaches; also lizards, toads, mice
European pill millipede	*Glomeris marginata*	0.2 to 0.7 in (7 to 20 mm)	Britain		organic matter
Bristly millipede	*Polyxenus fasciculatus*	0.08 in (2 mm)	Britain		leaves and dead plant matter
Flat-backed millipede	*Polydesmus angustus*	0.55 to 0.98 in (14 to 25 mm)	northwest Europe and parts of North America		roots, dead leaves, other bits of decayed plant matter; also strawberries, other fruit
Yellow-spotted millipede	*Harpaphe haydeniana*	1.6 to 2 in (4 to 5 cm)	Pacific coast of North America		humus and leaf litter
Black millipede	*Tachypodoiulus niger*	0.59 to 1.53 (15 to 39mm)	Europe		encrusting algae, detritus; sometimes raspberries, other fruit

INSECTS

COMMON NAME	SCIENTIFIC NAME	SIZE	RANGE	HABITAT	DIET
Tree lobster	*Dryococelus australis*	5.9 in (15 cm)	Lord Howe Island in Australia		various plants
Southern two-striped walking stick	*Anisomorpha buprestoides*	1.61 to 2.64 in (41 to 67 mm)	southern North America		various plants
Pacific dampwood termite	*Zootermopsis angusticollis*	0.04 in (1 mm)	Pacific coast of North America		damp wood
South Asian tar baby termite	*Globitermes sulphureus*	.06 in (1.5 mm)	central and southern Vietnam		wood
Common earwig	*Forficula auricularia*	0.5 in (13 mm)	throughout Europe		insects, detritus, fruit, plant matter
Silverfish	*Lepisma saccharina*	0.31 to 0.75 in (7.9 to 19.1 mm)	worldwide		glue, wallpaper paste, bookbindings, paper, photographs, starch in clothing, cotton, linen
True katydid	*Pterophylla camellifolia*	1.75 to 2.12 in (45 to 55 mm)	Eastern U.S. west to Texas and northeast to Ontario		leaves of oaks and most other deciduous trees and shrubs
Desert locust	*Schistocerca gregaria*	2.36 to 3.54 in (60 to 90 mm)	Africa, the Middle East, Asia		various plants
Migratory locust	*Locusta migratoria*	1.37 to 2.16 in (35 to 55 mm)	Africa, Asia, Australia and New Zealand, Europe		various plants
Australian plague locust	*Chortoicetes terminifera*	0.787 to 1.77 in (20 to 45 mm)	Australia		crops and other plants
Differential grasshopper	*Melanoplus differentialis*	0.10 to 1.96 in (28 to 50 mm)	Central America and central North America		corn, cotton, deciduous fruit crops
Eastern lubber grasshopper	*Romalea guttata*	3 in (76 mm)	southeastern United States		various plants

BEETLES

COMMON NAME	SCIENTIFIC NAME	SIZE	RANGE	HABITAT	DIET
Mountain pine beetle	*Dendroctonus ponderosae*	0.19 in (5 mm)	North America from Mexico to British Columbia		various plants
American burying beetle	*Nicrophorus americanus*	0.98 to 1.77 in (25 to 45 mm)	United States		carcasses of dead animals
Bombadier beetle	*Brachinus crepitans*	0.25 to 0.3 in (6.5 to 9.5 mm)	central and southern Europe and North Africa		flowers, leaves, other insects
Colorado potato beetle	*Leptinotarsa decemlineata*	2 to 4.3 in (5.5 to 11 cm)	South Texas and Mexico		potatoes and related plants
Ladybug	*Coccinella septempunctata*	height: 0.2 to 0.3 in (7 to 8 mm)	western Europe, and North America		insects
Rhinoceros beetle	*Dynastinae*	5.9 in (15 cm)	Africa and Mediterranean		rotten wood, plant sap, fruit, nectar
Long-horned beetle	*Anoplophora glabripennis*	0.79 to 1.38 in (20 to 35 mm)	China, Korea, United States		wood, bark, or stems; sap or other plant fluids
Cowboy beetle	*Chondropyga dorsalis*	0.7 to 0.9 in (20 to 25 mm)	southeastern Australia		nectar-bearing shrubs and trees
Red flour beetle	*Tribolium castaneum*	0.09 to 0.17 in (2.3 to 4.4 mm)	worldwide		grain products, such as flour, cereals, pasta, biscuits, beans, nuts
Cowpea beetle	*Callosobruchus chinensis*	0.03 to 0.8 in (1 to 22 mm)	cosmopolitan areas and tropics of the world		beans or grains
Bark beetle	*Scolytinae*	0.19 in (5 mm)	worldwide		tree bark
Mealworm	*Tenebrio molitor*	0.5 to 0.7 in (13 to 18 mm)	temperate regions worldwide		organic material
Lightning bug	*Photuris pennsylvanica*	0.75 in (2 cm)	North America		insects and other invertebrates

COMMON NAME	SCIENTIFIC NAME	SIZE	RANGE	HABITAT	DIET
BUGS					
Bedbug	Cimex lectularius	0.20 to 0.37 in (5 to 9.5 mm)	All continents except Antarctica		primarily parasitic on humans
Kissing bug	Triatoma infestans	0.20 to 1.38 in (5 to 35 mm)	South and Central America		animal and human blood
Masked hunter assassin bug	Reduvius personatus	.6 to .8 in (17 to 22 mm)	North America		small arthropods, such as woodlice, lacewings, earwigs, bedbugs
Southern green stinkbug	Nezara viridula	.5 to .6 in (14 to 17 mm)	North America		wide variety of crop plants
Jewel bug	Chrysocoris stolli	.2 to .8 in (5 to 20 mm)	Worldwide		various plants
Hawthorn shield bug	Acanthosoma haemorrhoidale	.67 in (17 mm)	Europe		fruit of the hawthorn tree
Beet leafhopper	Circulifer tenellus	0.6 in (15 mm)	North, Central, and South America, and Europe		various plants
Glassy-winged sharpshooter	Homalodisca vitripennis	0.5 in (12 mm)	North America		various plants
Annual cicada	Tibicen llinnei	1 to 2 in (2.5 to 5 cm)	North America		various plants
Dogday cicada	Tibicen canicularis	1 to 1.2 in (27 to 33 mm)	North America		pines and allied conifers
Common water strider	Gerris remigis	.1 to .6 in (3 to 16 mm)	worldwide		small living or dead insects on the surface of water
Water measurer	Hydrometra stagnorum	0.5 in (13 mm)	Europe		mosquito larvae and water fleas
Giant water bug	Belostomatidae	0.5 to 3 in (13 to 75 mm)	worldwide		aquatic arthropods, snails, small fish, amphibians
American burying beetle	Nicrophorus americanus	1 to 1.8 in (25 to 45 mm)	Oklahoma and Block Island in Rhode Island		carrion
FLIES					
Botfly	Cuterebra lepivora	.5 in (12.7 mm)	west coast of the United States		parasitic on rabbits
Gnat	Anisopodidae	0.16 to 0.31 in (4 to 8 mm)	Worldwide		various plants
Midge	Chironomidae	0.039 to 0.39 in (1 to 10 mm)	Worldwide		small invertebrates
Housefly	Muscidae	0.16-0.28 (4 to 7 mm)	Worldwide		various types of plant and animal discharges
Common green bottle fly	Lucilia sericata	0.23 to 0.35 (6 to 9 mm)	Worldwide		various types of plant and animal discharges
Screwworm fly	Cochliomyia macellaria	0.3 to 0.4 in (8 to 10 mm)	North, Central and South America		flesh of living organisms
Emperor dragonfly	Anax imperator	3.07 in (78 mm)	North America, Europe, and parts of Asia		insects and small fish
Green darner	Anax junius	2.67 to 3.30 in (6.8 to 8.4 cm)	North America		flying insects, including butterflies and other dragonflies
Common hawker	Aeshna juncea	2.9 in (74 mm)	Eurasia and North America		small invertebrates
Southern yellowjack	Notogomphus praetorius	4.92 in (125 mm)	South America		small invertebrates
Two-striped skimmer	Orthetrum caffrum	1.57 in (40 mm)	Africa		small invertebrates
Common bluetail damselfly	Ischnura heterosticta	1.3 in (34 mm)	Australia		small invertebrates
Mosquito	Anopheles stephensi	0.6 in (16 mm)	Worldwide		animal and human blood
Southern house mosquito	Culex quinquefasciatus	0.6 in (16 mm)	India		animal and human blood
Giant forest damselfly	Megaloprepus caerulatus	7.5 in (19 cm)	Central and South America		orb-weaver spiders
Basking malachite damselfly	Chlorolestes apricans	1.7 to 1.8 in (43 to 45 mm)	South Africa		insects
BUTTERFLIES AND MOTHS					
White-barred emperor butterfly	Charaxes brutus	2.3 to 2.9 in (60 to 75 mm)	South Africa		fermenting fruit and tree sap
Common buckeye butterfly	Junonia coenia	1.57 to 2.36 in (4 to 6 cm)	North America		leaves and nectar
Common castor butterfly	Ariadne merione	1.1 to 1.3 in (30 to 35 mm)	Southeastern Asia		castor bean plant
Karner blue butterfly	Lycaeides melissa samuelis	0.4 to 0.6 in (1.2 to 1.6 cm)	Northwestern United States and Canada		leaves and nectar
Passion butterfly	Agraulis vanillae,	2.0 to 2.5 in (5.08 to 6.35 cm)	southern United States and Central America		maypops and other passion-vine species
Numata longwing butterfly	Heliconius numata	2 in (5 cm)	South America		red or orange flowers; larvae and eggs found on low-growing vines of Passiflora
Australian painted lady butterfly	Vanessa kershawi	1.6 to 1.8 in (43 to 47 mm)	Australia		flower nectar
Small white butterfly	Pieris rapae	1.7 to 2.1 in (4.5 to 5.5 cm)	Europe and northwest Africa		leaves and nectar
Spicebush swallowtail	Papilio troilus	3.15 to 4.53 in (8.0 to 11.5 cm)	North America		nectar, especially honeysuckle, clover, thistle flowers
Mallow skipper	Carcharodus alceae	1 to 1.3 in (26 to 34 mm)	Europe, northern Africa, Central Asia		nectar from herbaceous plants

COMMON NAME	SCIENTIFIC NAME	SIZE	RANGE	HABITAT	DIET
Atlas moth	*Attacus atlas*	9.8 to 11.8 in (25 to 30 cm)	Southeast Asia and Malay Islands		adults do not eat
Bogong moth	*Agrotis infusa*	1.7 in (45 mm)	Southern Australia		plant-eaters, including beets, barley, flax, alfalfa, wheat
Peppered moth	*Biston betularia*	1.7 to 2.4 in (45 to 62 mm)	most of the British Isles		deciduous trees and shrubs
Gypsy moth	*Lymantria dispar*	1.4 in (38 mm)	Europe, Asia, North America		various trees, especially red oaks, cherries, willows, hickories, pines
Corn earworm	*Helicoverpa zea*	1.2 to 1.7 in (32 to 45 mm)	North Am., except north-ern Canada and Alaska		crops and nectar
BEES AND WASPS					
Eastern carpenter bee	*Xylocopa virginica*	0.7 to 0.9 in (19 to 23 mm)	Eastern and east-central U.S., and southern Canada		nectar from flowers
Southern yellow jacket	*Vespula squamosa*	0.5 to 0.75 in (12 to 19 mm)	Eastern U.S. through Mexico to Honduras		nectar and other fluids
Bald-faced hornet	*Dolichovespula maculata*	0.75 in (2 cm)	North America and southern Canada		nectar, tree sap, fruit pulp
Cuckoo bee	*Bombus vestalis*	0.6 to 0.9 in (15 to 24 mm)	Europe, Africa, Asia		flowers
Spider-hunting wasp	*Heterodotonyx bicolor*	0.4 in (10 mm)	Central and South America; East Asia		spiders
Saxon wasp	*Dolichovespula saxonica*	0.4 to 0.6 in (11 to 17 mm)	Europe: mainly Britain and Scotland		nectar and pollen
Alfalfa leafcutter bee	*Megachile rotundata*	2.36 to 7.48 in (6 to 19 cm)	Asia, Europe, North America, Africa		nectar and pollen
Orchard mason bee	*Osmia lignaria*	0.4 to 1.7 in (11 to 14 mm)	Canada and New England states in the U.S.		flowers of trees, especially cherry, pear, apple; also quince, laburnum, blueberry
Eastern cicada killer wasp	*Sphecius speciosus*	0.6 to 2 in (1.5 to 5 cm)	East of the Rocky Mountains and south to Mexico		nectar from flowers
Organ-pipe mud dauber	*Trypoxylon politum*	1 in (2.5 cm)	Maine to Florida and Kansas and Texas in the U.S.		spiders
Black-and-yellow mud dauber	*Sceliphron caementarium*	0.9 to 1.1 in (24 to 28 mm)	North America		nectar
Stingless honey bee	*Meliponula ferruginea*	0.8 in (2.1 mm)	Australia, Africa, South-east Asia, Americas		nectar and honey
ANTS					
Common fire ant	*Myrmica rubra*	0.78 to 0.23 in (2 to 6 mm)	northeastern United States and Canada		small animals
Argentine ant	*Linepithema humile*	0.11 in (3 mm)	Americas, South Africa, Japan, Australia, Europe		plants, dead animals, rotting fruit
Pavement ant	*Tetramorium caespitum*	0.13 in (3.25 mm)	eastern and southern United States		plant and animal fluids, carrion, arthropods, seeds, grains, nuts, fruit, flowers, nectar, pollen
Northern wood ant	*Formica aquilonia*	0.2 to 0.47 in (5 to 12 mm)	Scottish Highlands		honeydew, other invertebrates, some vertebrates
Meat ant	*Iridomyrmex purpureus*	0.39 in (10 mm)	Australia		carrion, tree sap, honeydew
Inchman bull ant	*Myrmecia forficata*	0.59 to 0.98 in (15 to 25mm)	Australia		invertebrates and other small animals
Jack jumper ant	*Myrmecia pilosula*	0.39 to 0.47 in (10 to 12 mm)	Australia		carrion
Fungus-growing ant	*Mycocepurus smithii*	0.12 in (3 mm)	Central and South America		fungi
Bullet ant	*Paraponera clavata*	0.70 to 1.18 in (18 to 30 mm)	Nicaragua to Paraguay		nectar and small anthropods
Mexican leafcutter ant	*Atta mexicana*	1.2 in (30 mm)	Central and South America; southern U.S.		vegetation, such as leaves, flowers, grasses
Ghose ant	*Tapinoma melanocephalum*	0.59 in (1.5 mm)	Tropical areas worldwide		sweets (fruits), grease, living or dead insects
Red harvester ant	*Pogonomyrmex barbatus*	.25 in to .5 in (6.3 to 12.7 mm)	Parts of the United States into Mexico		mostly seeds; also dead insects

GLOSSARY

Adaptation *noun* a change in the body or behavior of a species, often over many generations, making it better able to survive.

Amphibian *noun* cold-blooded animal with a backbone that has moist skin and no scales.

Aquatic *adjective* living all or most of the time in water.

Arthropod *noun* animal whose body and legs are divided into segments. The bodies of arthropods have a hard covering called an exoskeleton.

Bioluminescence *noun* light emitted by living organisms through chemical reactions in their bodies.

Boreal forest *noun* a belt of coniferous, or cone-bearing, trees that stretches across northern Asia, Europe, and North America. The region experiences long, snowy winters and short, cool summers.

Breed *verb* to reproduce by giving birth to live young or laying eggs.

Burrow *noun* hole or tunnel in the ground dug by an animal. *Verb* to dig a hole or tunnel in the ground.

Camouflage *noun* an organism's ability to disguise its appearance, often by using its coloring or body shape to blend in with its surroundings.

Canopy *noun* the highest level of a forest, formed by the tops of the tallest trees.

Carnivore *noun* organism that eats meat.

Circumpolar *adjective* located near or inhabiting one of Earth's polar regions.

Classification *noun* grouping based on physical and genetic characteristics.

Climate *noun* average weather conditions of an area over an extended period of time.

Colony *noun* a group of the same kind of organism living or growing together.

Crustacean *noun* organism that lives mostly in water and has a hard shell and a body divided into segments.

Desert *noun* an area of land that receives less than ten inches (25 cm) of precipitation a year.

DNA *noun* (deoxyribonucleic acid) chemical code that contains information about an organism's body.

Domestication *noun* the process of taming and breeding an animal for human use. Domestic animals include pets, such as cats; work animals, such as oxen; and sport animals, such as horses.

Dorsal fin *noun* fin on the back of an aquatic animal that helps the animal keep its balance as it moves.

Echolocation *noun* a sensory system in some animals in which sounds are emitted and their echoes interpreted to determine the direction and distance of objects. Bats and dolphins use echolocation to navigate and find food.

Ecosystem *noun* community and interactions of living and nonliving things in an area.

Embryo *noun* unborn offspring produced after a male and female mate.

Endangered *adjective* relating to an animal or plant that is found in such small numbers that it is at risk of becoming extinct, or no longer existing.

Extinct *adjective* no longer existing.

Fermentation *noun* the breaking down of larger chemical compounds by natural or artificial processes.

Food chain *noun* series of organisms dependent on one another for food. In a food chain, one organism is a source of food for another organism, which in turn is a source of food for another.

Freshwater *adjective* containing water with little or no salt.

Gastropod *noun* mollusk that has a head with eyes and feelers. A gastropod has a muscle under its body that it uses to move.

Genus *noun* a grouping of organisms that have many shared characteristics but cannot produce offspring together. Tigers and lions belong to the same genus, *Panthera*.

Gills *noun* organs present in the bodies of some water-dwelling animals that help the organisms breathe. Gills absorb, or take in, oxygen from the water and send it to an organism's bloodstream.

RED-EYED TREE FROG

Grassland *noun* a large, flat area of land that is covered with grasses and has few trees.

Habitat *noun* a place in nature where an organism lives throughout the year or for shorter periods of time.

Hatchling *noun* a very young animal that has recently hatched from its egg.

Herbivore *noun* organism that eats mainly plants.

Hibernation *noun* the process of reducing activity almost to sleeping to conserve food and energy, usually in winter.

Incubate *verb* to keep eggs or very young organisms warm so they can hatch or grow.

Indo-Pacific *noun* a region consisting of the tropical waters of the Indian Ocean, the western and central Pacific Ocean, and the seas connecting the two in the general area of Indonesia.

Insectivore *noun* organism that mostly eats insects.

Invertebrate *noun* an organism without a backbone. Invertebrates can include,

ARCTIC FOX

but are not limited to, insects, arachnids, crustaceans, and mollusks.

Krill *noun* a small marine crustacean, similar to shrimp.

Larva *noun* an animal in the early stage of development that looks different than how it will look in the adult stage.

Lateral line *noun* a sensory organ found on the side of fish that detects movement and pressure changes in water.

Life cycle *noun* process of changes undertaken by an organism or group of organisms over the course of their existence. Birth, growth, and death usually characterize the life cycle of animals.

Mammal *noun* warm-blooded animal with hair that gives birth to live offspring and produces milk to feed its young.

Marine *adjective* living in or near the sea.

Marsupial *noun* mammal that gives birth to young that are not fully developed. A marsupial usually carries its young—which can move independently—in a pouch for protection.

Metabolism *noun* chemical reactions that take place in cells and allow organisms to grow and function.

Metamorphosis *noun* complete change in form and structure from one part of

the life cycle to the next, such as caterpillar to pupa, and pupa to butterfly.

Migration *noun* process in which a community of organisms leaves a habitat for part of the year or part of their lives, and moves to other habitats that are more hospitable.

Mimicry *noun* an organism's ability to mimic, or copy, another organism's appearance or behavior.

Mollusk *noun* animal with a soft body that usually lives inside a hard shell. Most mollusks live in water.

Molt *verb* to shed an outer covering, such as feathers or skin, so that it can be replaced by a new one.

Nocturnal *adjective* active at night.

Omnivore *noun* organism that eats a variety of organisms, including plants, animals, and fungi.

Osteoderm *noun* lump of bone in the skin of reptiles that provides protection from predators.

GLOSSARY

Oviparous *adjective* reproducing by laying eggs.

Photophore *noun* light-emitting organ present in some bioluminescent organisms.

Placenta *noun* an organ present in the body of a pregnant mammal that nourishes and maintains the embryo as it develops.

Plankton *noun* microscopic plant or animal organisms that float in salt water or fresh water.

Pollution *noun* introduction of harmful materials into the environment.

Population *noun* a group of the same kind of organism living in the same environment.

Predator *noun* animal that hunts other animals for food.

Prehensile *adjective* able to seize, grasp, or hold by wrapping around an object.

Prey *noun* animal that is hunted and eaten by other animals.

Primate *noun* a type of mammal that is intelligent and has forward-facing eyes. Most primates have opposable thumbs.

Proboscis *noun* long, tube-shaped part of an animal's body used for feeding.

Rain forest *noun* a dense forest in which at least 160 inches (406 cm) of rain falls each year.

BEE

Reproduce to create offspring, by sexual or asexual means.

Reptile *noun* cold-blooded animal that breathes air, has a backbone, and usually has scales.

Ruminant *noun* hoofed animal with a four-chambered stomach.

Scavenger *noun* organism that eats dead or rotting flesh.

Species *noun* a group of similar organisms that can reproduce with one another.

Temperate *adjective* characterized by a warm summer and a cool winter. Most temperate regions are located between the tropics and the polar regions.

Terrestrial *adjective* living all or most of the time on land.

Tundra *noun* a cold, treeless area of the Arctic region with permafrost, a layer of soil that remains frozen throughout the year.

Venom *noun* poison fluid made in the bodies of some organisms and secreted for hunting and protection.

Vertebrate *noun* an organism with a backbone. Vertebrates can include mammals, fish, reptiles, amphibians, and birds.

AMERICAN BULLFROG

FIND OUT MORE

WEBSITES

Association of Zoos
and Aquariums
Aza.org/kids-and-families

Defenders of Wildlife
KidsPlanet.org

National Geographic Kids
Kids.NationalGeographic.com

National Geographic Society
NationalGeographic.com

BOOKS

*125 True Stories of
Amazing Animals*
National Geographic Society
2012

Animal Tracks and Signs
National Geographic Society
2008

First Big Book of Animals
National Geographic Society
2010

Great Migrations
National Geographic Society
2010

National Geographic Kids
Readers Series

Nat Geo Wild Animal Atlas
National Geographic Society
2010

Oceans
National Geographic Society
2010

PLACES TO VISIT

United States
National Aquarium
www.Aqua.org

Smithsonian National
Zoological Park
www.NationalZoo.si.edu/
Audiences/Kids

San Diego Zoo
www.sandiegozoo.org

Alaska SeaLife Center
www.alaskasealife.org

Sea World
www.SeaWorldParks.com

Columbus Zoo and
Aquarium
www.colszoo.org

Canada
Toronto Zoo
www.Torontozoo.com

Australia
Australia Zoo
www.australiazoo.com.au

England
Zoological Society
of London
www.zsl.org

Singapore
Singapore Zoo
www.zoo.com.sg

South Africa
National Zoological
Gardens of South Africa
www.nzg.ac.za

 DVDs

African Cats
Disney Nature 2011

Arctic Tale
National Geographic Society
2007

Born to Be Wild
Warner Brothers 2011

Chimpanzee
Disney Nature 2012

Great Migrations
National Geographic Society
2010

The Last Lions
National Geographic Society
2011

March of the Penguins
National Geographic Society
2005

*National Geographic:
The Wildlife Collection*
National Geographic Society
2006

INDEX

Illustrations are indicated by **boldface.** If illustrations are included within a page span, the entire span is **boldface.**

STINGRAY

BISON CALF

BUG

BLACK BEAR

LADYBUG

FISH

CANADA GOOSE GOSLING

ACKNUWLEDGMENTS

Thanks go to my friends, family, and colleagues for their advice and support, especially: Rob Currier, Susan Doyle, Susan Hradil, Jackie Jeffers, Naomi Kirschenbaum, Ted Mashima, Leppy McCarthy, Jody Rein, Jennie Rice, Michael Walsh, and Hank Wietsmaj.

Special thanks go to project editor Priyanka Lamichhane for asking me to do this book, and to everyone at National Geographic who gathered the beautiful photographs, excellent maps, fun facts, and exciting field reports—and put it all together.

To the many individuals who study, help, celebrate, protect, and educate others about animals, thank you. Your efforts have contributed to this book in countless ways!

The publisher would like to thank National Geographic Explorers-in-Residence Sylvia Earle and Dereck and Beverly Joubert, Emerging Explorers Adrian Seymour, Emma Stokes, and Zoltan Takacs, Fellow Zeb Hogan, grantees Brady Barr, Lisa Dabek, Nicole Duplaix, Robert Jackson, and Rory Wilson, and photographers Jim Brandenburg, David Doubilet, John Eastcott, Mark Moffett, Yva Momatiuk, Darlyne Murawski, and Flip Nicklin for generously contributing their stories for this book. And a special thank you to photographer Matt Propert for traveling to find and photograph hundreds of animals featured in this book.

Sources for Conservation Map: IUCN and UNEP-WCMC (2012); The World Database on Protected Areas (WDPA) Cambridge, UK: UNEP-WCMC. Available at www.protectedplanet.net. June 2012 Monthly Release.

303

ATLANTIC PUFFIN

Published by the National Geographic Society
John M. Fahey, *Chairman of the Board and Chief Executive Officer*
Timothy T. Kelly, *President*
Declan Moore, *Executive Vice President; President, Publishing and Digital Media*
Melina Gerosa Bellows, *Executive Vice President; Chief Creative Officer, Books, Kids, and Family*

Prepared by the Book Division
Hector Sierra, *Senior Vice President and General Manager*
Nancy Laties Feresten, *Senior Vice President, Kids Publishing and Media*
Jonathan Halling, *Design Director, Books and Children's Publishing*
Jay Sumner, *Director of Photography, Children's Publishing*
Jennifer Emmett, *Vice President, Editorial Director, Children's Books*
Eva Absher-Schantz, *Design Director, Kids Publishing and Media*
Carl Mehler, *Director of Maps*
R. Gary Colbert, *Production Director*
Jennifer A. Thornton, *Director of Managing Editorial*

Staff for This Book
Priyanka Lamichhane, *Project Editor*
Eva Absher-Schantz, *Art Director*
Lori Epstein, *Senior Illustrations Editor*
Angela Terry, *Project Design Company, Designer*
Jennifer Agresta, Julie C. Beer, *Researchers*
Jeff Maurtizen, Matt Propert, *Photographers*
Kate Olesin, *Associate Editor*
Kathryn Robbins, *Associate Designer*
Hillary Moloney, *Illustrations Assistant*
Sven M. Dolling and Michael McNey, *Map Research and Production*
Becky Baines, Ashlee Brown, Nancy Honovich, *Contributing Writers*
Grace Hill, *Associate Managing Editor*
Joan Gossett, *Production Editor*
Suzanne Fonda, *Release Editor*
Michaela Berkon, Riley Kirkpatrick, Carly Larkin, *Editorial Interns*
Lewis R. Bassford, *Production Manager*
Susan Borke, *Legal and Business Affairs*

Manufacturing and Quality Management
Phillip L. Schlosser, *Senior Vice President*
Chris Brown, *Vice President, Book Manufacturing*
George Bounelis, *Vice President, Production Services*
Nicole Elliott, *Manager*
Rachel Faulise, *Manager*
Robert L. Barr, *Manager*

The National Geographic Society supported the *National Geographic Animal Encyclopedia* with a research and development grant to enhance the book's editorial budget and process. The grant financed photography in wild areas, zoos, and aquariums throughout the world, created video to enhance the digital version of the book, and gathered thousands of animal facts on hundreds of animal species. National Geographic is committed to be a leading source of unparalleled nonfiction animal content for children.

The National Geographic Society is one of the world's largest nonprofit scientific and educational organizations. Founded in 1888 to "increase and diffuse geographic knowledge," the Society's mission is to inspire people to care about the planet. It reaches more than 400 million people worldwide each month through its official journal, *National Geographic*, and other magazines; National Geographic Channel; television documentaries; music; radio; films; books; DVDs; maps; exhibitions; live events; school publishing programs; interactive media; and merchandise. National Geographic has funded more than 10,000 scientific research, conservation and exploration projects and supports an education program promoting geographic literacy.

For more information, please visit www.national-geographic.com, call 1-800-NGS LINE (647-5463), or write to the following address:
National Geographic Society
1145 17th Street N.W.
Washington, D.C. 20036-4688 U.S.A.

Visit us online at www.nationalgeographic.com/books

For librarians and teachers:
www.ngchildrensbooks.org

More for kids from National Geographic:
kids.nationalgeographic.com

For information about special discounts for bulk purchases, please contact National Geographic Books Special Sales: ngspecsales@ngs.org

For rights or permissions inquiries, please contact National Geographic Books Subsidiary Rights: ngbookrights@ngs.org

Hardcover ISBN: 978-1-4263-1022-5
Library edition ISBN: 978-1-4263-1023-2

Printed in the USA
12/RRDW-LPH/1